T3-BNI-849

Library of
Davidson College

OXFORD HISTORICAL MONOGRAPHS

Editors

M. G. BROCK   BARBARA HARVEY

H. M. MAYR-HARTING   H. G. PITT

K. V. THOMAS   A. F. THOMPSON

PHILO-SEMITISM AND THE READMISSION OF THE JEWS TO ENGLAND 1603–1655

DAVID S. KATZ

CLARENDON PRESS · OXFORD
1982

Oxford University Press, Walton Street, Oxford OX2 6DP

London Glasgow New York Toronto
Delhi Bombay Calcutta Madras Karachi
Kuala Lumpur Singapore Hong Kong Tokyo
Nairobi Dar es Salaam Cape Town
Melbourne Auckland
and associates in
Beirut Berlin Ibadan Mexico City Nicosia

Published in the United States by
Oxford University Press, New York

942.06
K19p

© David S. Katz 1982

All rights reserved. No part of this publication may be reproduced,
stored in a retrieval system, or transmitted, in any form or by any means,
electronic, mechanical, photocopying, recording, or otherwise, without
the prior permission of Oxford University Press

British Library Cataloguing in Publications Data
Katz, David S.
Philo-semitism and the readmission of the
Jews to England 1603–1655. — (Oxford
historical monographs)
1. Jews in Great Britain—History
2. Great Britain—Politics and government—
1603–1714
I. Title
941.06   DA375
ISBN 0–19–821885–0

82-8113

Typeset by Phoenix Photosetting, Chatham
Printed in Great Britain
at the University Press, Oxford
by Eric Buckley
Printer to the University

To
Sarah Koch

ACKNOWLEDGEMENTS

This work is based on my 1978 Oxford D.Phil. thesis, which was supervised by Professor Hugh Trevor-Roper, now Lord Dacre. One is constantly amazed and excited by his ability to sense the direction of the historical trail even at the very beginning of the chase. Only those fortunate enough to have been his students can appreciate fully the depth of his learning and the breadth of his insight.

Chimen Abramsky, the Goldsmid Professor of Hebrew and Jewish Studies at University College, London, was of immense assistance throughout the writing of this work, ceaselessly providing a stream of references from his encyclopaedic knowledge of Jewish history and literature.

Dr Blair Worden showed interest in this study from its inception, and his encouragement and careful reading of the text is deeply appreciated.

Keith Thomas, C. S. L. Davies, and Penry Williams read earlier versions of this text: their comments and criticism proved to be very useful. Others who helped in various ways include: Robin Briggs, Molly Burke, John Creasey, Simon Cuttler, Jonathan Israel, Raphael Loewe, Stephen Macfarlane, Edgar Samuel, John Stoye, Joan Thirsk, David Vaisey, and David Wasserstein.

The first half of the research for this book was supported by Columbia University's Kellett Fellowship to Oxford. I should especially like to thank J. M. W. Bean, professor of history at Columbia, for his help and interest during my time there, as well as Stephen Koss and Sheila Biddle.

The latter part of research was financed by the National and Memorial Foundations for Jewish Culture. Their generous grants enabled me to complete this work.

Finally, I would like to thank the staffs of the various libraries cited in the bibliography, but especially the librarians of the Upper Reading Room of the Bodleian Library in Oxford.

Tel Aviv

CONTENTS

INTRODUCTION

One usually thinks of the modern era of Anglo-Jewish history as beginning with the Whitehall Conference. On 14 November 1655, four members of Oliver Cromwell's Council of State selected twenty-eight delegates to a committee which was to begin meeting three weeks later near the Council chambers in Whitehall. They were summoned, wrote Henry Jessey, a Baptist minister who was one of those chosen, 'to consider of Proposals in behalf of the JEWES, by Rabbi Manasses Ben Israel, an Agent come to London in behalf of many of them, to live and Trade here, and desiring to have free use of their Synagogues.' The force of pamphlets, petitions, and public opinion had wrested the question of Jewish readmission from the hands of theologians, millenarians, and outlandish theorisers of all persuasions, and placed it before the Protectorate of Oliver Cromwell.[1]

At first glance, it appears very odd that the English government should decide to convene a special conference to discuss the fate of the Jews. In theory, all Jews had been expelled from England on 18 July 1290 by an act of Edward I in his Council. Writs were issued to the sheriffs of each county ordering them to ensure that all Jews had left the realm by 1 November, the feast of All Saints. Any Jews remaining were to be punished by death.[2] Nevertheless, the *Domus Conversorum* established in 1232 for converts from Judaism was never completely empty, and

[1] *Cal. S. P. Dom., 1655–6*, p. 20; [H. Jessey], *A Narrative Of the late Proceeds at White-Hall* (London, 1656), pp. 1–2.

[2] H. G. Richardson, *The English Jewry under Angevin Kings* (London, 1960), pp. 213–33; G. H. Leonard, 'Expulsion of the Jews', *Trs. Roy. Hist. Soc.*, 2nd ser., v (1891), 103–46; B. L. Abrahams, 'The Expulsion of the Jews', *Jew. Qly. Rev.*, vii (1895), 75–100, 236–58, 428–58; P. Elman, 'Economic Causes of the Expulsion of the Jews', *Econ. Hist. Rev.*, vii (1937), 145–54.

quite a number of references to individual Jews appear in the
records throughout the period when England was supposedly
without a Jewish population.[3]

In any case, the number of Jews and converts from Judaism
in England was minute in comparison with the great Continental Jewish communities which flourished throughout the Middle Ages despite periodic expulsions from one area or another.
Before the beginning of the sixteenth century, however, many
Jews began to feel that their situation was becoming increas-
ingly desperate. 'I think that the afflictions visited on the Jews
in all the Christian kingdoms between the years 5250–55
[1490–95],' wrote a rabbi from Rhodes, 'are the messianic birth
pangs.'[4] Ferdinand and Isabella expelled the Jews from Spain
in 1492, and the king of Portugal exiled or forcibly baptized
them five years later. The Iberian Jews had threaded their way
up to the highest levels of power in Spain and Portugal, and
occupied eminent positions in government, scholarship, the
army, and even in the Church. Some of these Jews chose to
remain in the Peninsula after the expulsion by accepting the
Catholic religion; these were called *conversos*, or 'New Christians'. Others became *marranos*—the word means 'swine' in
Spanish—practising Judaism secretly while pretending to be
devout Catholics to the outside world. The Inquisition never
had any authority over Jews; its task was to root out backsliding
apostasy only among those who had already accepted the
Catholic faith. The rest of the Jews bowed to the edicts of 1492
and 1497 and left for Turkey, Palestine, or Italy.[5] Some of these
Sephardic Jews joined the Ashkenazic communities in France,
Germany, and eastern Europe.[6]

A very small proportion of these Jews eventually settled in
England, and when they did they were highly secretive. The
great Sephardic crypto-Jews of England—men like Antonio
Ferdinando Carvajal and Antonio Rodrigues Robles—were

[3] See M. Adler, *Jews of Medieval England* (London, 1939), pp. 307–39.
[4] G. Scholem, *Sabbatai Ṣevi* (London, 1973), p. 18n.
[5] C. Roth, *A History of the Marranos* (Philadelphia, 1941), *passim*.
[6] The adjective 'Sephardic' derives from the Hebrew *Sfarad* (Obad. 20) and is used
loosely to refer to the Jews of Spain, the Mediterranean, and the middle east. 'Ashkenazic' Jews (from the Hebrew *'Ashkenaz*, Gen. 10:3) are generally those from western
or eastern Europe. The two communities differ in details of liturgy and Hebrew
pronunciation.

Spanish or Portuguese subjects and Roman Catholics in the eyes of the law, as well as of nearly everyone in London who was acquainted with them and their little colony in the City. Only about thirty-five Jewish men, mostly heads of families, were living in England by the Restoration, and this figure includes the small population increases of 1656–8 when English relations with Spain deteriorated.[7] The English Jews worshipped at the Spanish Embassy until after the Whitehall Conference. They were normally buried with Roman Catholics even after 1655: of the individuals known to have been resident in England before 1659, only about one-third are buried in the Jewish cemetery at Mile End.[8] If we accept John Bossy's criterion for membership in the English Catholic community as 'habitual, though in view of physical difficulties not necessarily very frequent, resort to the service of a priest and, from at least the later seventeenth century, a degree of continuous congregational participation', then Anglo-Jewry in the half-century before readmission must be included among the most devoted Papists.[9]

The uniqueness of the Jewish case everywhere in Europe should be stressed at the outset. Catholics in England might well be regarded as political traitors as well as religious obscurantists: as John Selden explained, 'the papists where ere they live have another King att Rome, all other Religions are subject to the present state & have no prince else where.'[10] Sectarians in the seventeenth century, even Unitarians and Ranters, were Englishmen who had come to conclusions about the proper organization of religious life which were regarded as erroneous or even dangerous by the ecclesiastical authorities. Nevertheless, devotion to one of the respectable shades of Protestant belief would render the ex-Catholic or reformed sectarian acceptable to both Church and State.

The Jews were less fortunate however, victims of a pattern of medieval diabolization. For it is the demonological, supernatural element in the early modern attitude to the Jews which

---

[7] Brit. Lib., Addit. MS 29,868, fos. 15–16: da Costa lists of Jews in London, *c.* 1660.

[8] 'The Burial Register of the Spanish and Portuguese Jews, London 1657–1735', ed. R. D. Barnett, *Misc. Jew. Hist. Soc. Eng.*, vi (1962), 1–72.

[9] J. Bossy, *The English Catholic Community* (London, 1975), pp. 183–4.

[10] *Table Talk of John Selden*, ed. F. Pollock (London, 1927), p. 98.

renders it quite different from other forms of opposition to religious minorities and outcasts. 'Ye are of *your* father the devil,' John admonished the Jews, 'and the lusts of your father ye will do.'[11] Luther himself declared that a 'Jew is as full of idolatry and sorcery as nine cows have hair on their backs, that is: without number and without end.'[12] The Jews were thought to have some cosmic connection with the Antichrist. They were believed to carry a particular smell (*Foetor Judaicus*), to poison Christians, desecrate hosts, murder Christian children and use their blood for ritual purposes. Among the earliest instances of the ritual murder accusation in Europe were the cases of William of Norwich (1144) and Little St. Hugh of Lincoln (1255), whose memories were kept alive through the centuries in popular song and story, only to reappear once again in Willam Prynne's *Demurrer* to Jewish readmission which was so influential before the final session of the Whitehall Conference.

The fine points of Jewish demonology were hammered out on the Continent where Jews still formed an obtrusive and noticeable part of society. Eventually, as Joshua Trachtenberg wrote in his study of the problem, the 'mythical Jew, outlined by early Christian theology and ultimately puffed out to impossible proportions, supplanted the real Jew in the medieval mind, until that real Jew to all intents and purposes ceased to exist. The only Jew whom the medieval Christian recognized was a figment of the imagination.'[13] Although the most compelling evidence of this persistent pattern of thought comes from the Continent, one need only quote the stock references from Marlowe and Shakespeare to demonstrate that the demonic aspect of the Jew had not only survived the three centuries when England was apparently free from Jews, but even incorporated European elements from abroad. For one of the oddest features of this debate was that the lack of Jews in England should have made possible a positive view of them, despite the negative foreign, and indeed medieval English stereotypes which were available for adoption.

The argument here is essentially divided into two parts. In

[11] John 8:44.

[12] Quoted in J. Trachtenberg, *The Devil and the Jews* (Philadelphia, 1961), p. ix.

[13] Ibid., p. 216. Generally, see ibid., *passim*; N. Cohn, *Europe's Inner Demons* (London, 1975), *cap.* i; H. R. Trevor-Roper, *The European Witch-Craze of the 16th and 17th Centuries* (Pelican edn., Harmondsworth, 1969), pp. 32–9.

the first three chapters, we examine the speculative issues that awakened the minds of Englishmen to the very existence of contemporary Jewry as opposed to ancient Israelites. Most important among these were the controversy over the validity of the Mosaic law and the practices of the Judaizers, the glorification of Hebrew and the search for a universal language, and the scandalous activities of the popular millenarians who thrust the Jews into a prominent eschatological role. The search for the lost ten tribes of Israel provided the bridge to concrete action on behalf of readmission, for it was this debate that turned the attention of Rabbi Menasseh ben Israel to England. In the second part the active campaign for the resettlement of the Jews is studied. Once a movement for readmission was under way, its proponents were able to draw on the concurrent controversy over the merits of religious toleration which often seemed to countenance acceptance of the Jews as well. The final chapter deals with the concluding phase of the campaign for readmission from the Barebones Parliament to the Whitehall Conference of December 1655.

The Whitehall Conference took place at the juncture of a number of important intellectual movements. The more speculative concerns with the Mosaic law, the supernatural qualities of Hebrew, millenarianism, and the lost ten tribes reached the peak of their persuasiveness and intensity about the time of the Conference, when it appeared as if the supporting evidence in each of these spheres pointed irresistibly towards the necessity and desirability of readmitting the Jews to England. Afterwards, each of these issues followed its own dynamic unrelated to the Jews and readmission. But by December 1655, as we shall see, the constant discussion of the role of the Jews with their distinctive religion and culture had thrust the issue of contemporary Jewry into the centre of the stage, where it would be taken up and carried to the Whitehall Conference, when all of these elements would be debated and a final decision reached.

The intent here is to look at readmission from the point of view of the English and English history. This study will therefore not include a full discussion of the history of the secret Jews in England during the first half of the seventeenth century; serviceable if somewhat antique works already exist in this field.[14] What has been completely neglected in previous works is an examination of the debates, scandals, and controversies that awakened an awareness of the very existence of contemporary Jews in Englishmen already inoculated with an admiration for biblical Israelites. The belief that the Jews were destined to play a major role in English life and history is, in the words of Dr Christopher Hill, 'one of the few interpretations of the Civil War that has not yet been taken up by a modern historian.'[15] The underlying reasons for the renewed English concern with the Jews in the seventeenth century, three hundred years after their expulsion, have never been explained adequately, nor have the sources and controversies that stimulated and prolonged this interest been traced with precision. The Whitehall Conference was merely the most public manifestation of a much larger philo-semitic movement in English religious and intellectual life which becomes visible at least from the beginning of the reign of James I.

A similar pattern might be traced in other parts of Europe. Professor H. J. Schoeps, Dr J. Van Den Berg, and Professor Michael Roberts have studied the influence and importance of noted European philo-semites such as Paul Felgenhauer, Isaac la Peyrère, Johann Peter Spaeth, Jean de Labadie, Pierre Jurieu, Johannes Bureus, Sigfrid Aron Forsius, and Jon Olofsson. But English philo-semitism operated within its own insular environment, receiving some influences from the Continent, and adapting them to peculiar, fluctuating political and social circumstances.[16]

---

[14] A basic, continuous course of reading might include: L. Wolf, 'Jews in Tudor England', *Essays in Jewish History*, ed. C. Roth (London, 1934), pp. 73–90; idem, 'Jews in Elizabethan England', *Trs. Jew. Hist. Soc. Eng.*, xi (1928), 1–91; E. R. Samuel, 'Portuguese Jews in Jacobean London', *Trs. Jew. Hist. Soc. Eng.*, xviii (1958), 171–230; L. Wolf, 'Crypto-Jews Under the Commonwealth', *Trs. Jew. Hist. Soc. Eng.*, i (1895), 55–88; idem, 'The Jewry of the Restoration', *Trs. Jew. Hist. Soc. Eng.*, v (1908), 5–33. This series is corrected by C. Roth, 'The Middle Period of Anglo-Jewish History (1290–1655) Reconsidered', *Trs. Jew Hist. Soc. Eng.*, xix (1960), 1–12.

[15] C. Hill, *Change and Continuity in Seventeeth-Century England* (London, 1974), p. 58; almost identically in his *Antichrist in Seventeenth-Century England* (London, 1971), pp. 114–15.

[16] H. J. Schoeps, *Philosemitismus im Barock* (Tübingen, 1952), idem, 'Philo-semitism in the Baroque Period', *Jew. Qly. Rev.*, n.s., xlvii (1956–7), 139–44; idem, *Barocke Juden Christen Judenchristen* (Bern and München, 1965); J. Van Den Berg, 'Eschatological Expectations Concerning the Conversion of the Jews in the Netherlands during the Seventeenth Century', *Puritans, the Millennium and the Future of Israel*, ed. P. Toon

This is primarily a study in intellectual history rather than a political narrative or an analysis of economic factors. Nevertheless, English philo-semitism was often convoluted and complex, and its proponents frequently assimilated a variety of motives. This phenomenon is amply illustrated by Major-General Edward Whalley's confession to John Thurloe, while the Whitehall Conference was still in session, that he could not 'conceive the reason, why so great varietye of opinion should bee amongst such men, as I heare are called to consult about them. It seemes to me, that there are both politique and divine reasons; which strongly make for theyre admission into a cohabitation and civill commerce with us. Doubtlesse to say no more, they will bring in much wealth into this commonwealth'.[17] Well-informed men like Whalley combined arguments into an alloy for use towards Jewish readmission. But it should be remembered that to be in favour of readmitting Jewish capital was quite another matter from pressing for readmitting the Jewish people. The argument that the readmission of the Jews would help English economic life to prosper was not the product of emergent philo-semitism. This was a straightforward, often reluctant, appreciation of Jewish commercial skill which became influential only after Englishmen had obtained some first-hand experience of Jews. Economic motives for encouraging resettlement therefore became widespread only after 1660, when the Jews of London had revealed themselves and demonstrated the potency of their international business connections.

In any case, the application of economic criteria to the question of the readmission of the Jews, more often than not, tended to produce a negative conclusion. As we shall see, this was especially apparent during the Whitehall Conference, when the merchants brought pressure to bear against readmission, and the divines themselves were reduced to putting the economic case for resettlement merely to counterbalance the commercial objections of the businessmen.

It was during the early seventeenth century that a positive, philo-semitic view of contemporary Jewry developed in England.

(Cambridge and London, 1970), pp. 137–53; M. Roberts, *Gustavus Adolphus* (London, 1953), i.517–26.

[17] *State Papers of John Thurloe*, ed. T. Birch (London, 1742), iv. 308.

Anyone familiar with the sermon and pamphlet literature, and even the highly biblical wash over the language of the period, has already noticed the frequency with which the Jews intruded into discussions of all varieties. As we shall see, an analysis of the Jews and their historical role is crucial to the understanding of sabbatarianism, millenarianism, and the history of linguistics, let alone the reasons behind the calling of the Whitehall Conference. By examining the debates and scandals of English philo-semitism, we can trace the complex changes in religious and intellectual life which permitted Rabbi Menasseh ben Israel, the Jewish advocate of readmission, to write that 'today the English nation is no longer our ancient enemy, but has changed the Papistical religion and become excellently affected to our nation, as an oppressed people whereof it has good hope.'[18]

[18] Encyclical letter of Menasseh ben Israel to world Jewry, 2 Sept. 5415 = 1655, in Venetian archives: repr. *Trs. Jew. Hist. Soc. Eng.*, xi (1928), 116, 136.

1

JEWS AND JUDAIZERS

Sir James Whitelocke recalled in adulthood that his widowed
mother 'did bring up all her children in as good sort as any
gentleman in England wulde do, as in singing, dancing, playing
on the lute and other instruments, the Latin, Greek, Hebrew,
and Frenche tongues, and to write fair'. Whitelocke may well
have been guilty of ante-dating his interest in 'all the lefthand
tongs' which he certainly pursued as an undergraduate at
Oxford. Nevertheless, his testimony does highlight the interest
in Hebrew studies which blossomed in England during the late
sixteenth and early seventeenth centuries as a consequence of
the emphasis that Reformation theologians placed on the reading and understanding of the text which recorded the word of
God.[1] The validity of the Old Testament commandments for
Christians was an issue of critical importance during the
Reformation, for upon it hinged the nature of their approach to
Scripture, and the authority of biblical law. Even the distinction between moral, ceremonial, and judicial law did not free
Reformation theologians from the difficult necessity of
rationalizing the rejection of divine injunction.[2] The events
recounted in the Old Testament were at the very least instructive examples of God acting in history, if not illustrations which
foreshadowed the future glory of the fully reformed Christian
faith. The significance of the actual Old Testament text was
therefore raised to new heights in England after the Reforma-

---

[1] *Liber Famelicus of Sir James Whitelocke*, ed. J. Bruce (Camden Soc., lxx, 1858), p. 6.
[2] See P. D. L. Avis, 'Moses and the Magistrate: a Study in the rise of Protestant
Legalism', *Jnl. Eccl. Hist.*, xxvi (1975), 149–72.

tion, and the importance of the Hebrew language itself became apparent. This revitalized branch of scholarly study inevitably led Englishmen to contemporary Jews as the guardians of the Hebraic tradition, although imprisoned in a brand of Mosaic legalism which no Christian could accept in its entirety. The growth and development of Hebrew and Old Testament studies must be the point of departure when tracing the rise of the Judaizers and of English philo-semitism in general.

English scholars of the Old Testament language were a rare breed in the sixteenth century, although their numbers were increasing.[3] Henry VIII needed to employ both Christian and Jewish theologians and canonists to explain away the inconvenient text in Deuteronomy, for by 1529–30 his divorce was a subject of international debate, and thus his campaign to discredit levirate marriage accelerated the pace of the introduction of Hebraic studies to England.[4] Students at St. John's College, Cambridge, were forbidden after 1530 to carry on their conversations in Hall in any language but Latin, Greek, or Hebrew, although the third option was probably chosen rather infrequently.[5] A serious study of the Old Testament text could be pursued at a comparatively high level a decade later after the establishment in 1540 of the Regius chairs in Hebrew at Oxford and Cambridge.[6] The first Regius professor of Hebrew at Cambridge was Thomas Wakefield; his brother Robert was the first Hebrew Reader at Oxford. The Oxford Wakefeld had published his *Oratio de laudibus & utilitate trium linguarum* in 1524, and thus he inaugurated Hebrew printing in England even before Henry's divorce proceedings provided an additional impetus for Hebrew studies.[7] A fair number of Hebrew grammars, in Latin, were available to the translators who worked on

[3] See A. C. Partridge, *English Biblical Translation* (London, 1973), pp. 33–138.

[4] J. J. Scarisbrick, *Henry VIII* (London, 1968), pp. 256–7; C. Roth, *The Jews in the Renaissance* (New York, 1959), *cap.* vii.

[5] R. Loewe, 'Jewish Scholarship in England' in *Three Centuries of Anglo-Jewish History*, ed. V. D. Lipman (London, 1961), pp. 125–48.

[6] E. I. J. Rosenthal, 'Edward Lively: Cambridge Hebraist' in *Essays . . . Presented to S. A. Cook*, ed. D. W. Thomas (London, 1950), pp. 95–112.

[7] C. Roth, 'The Origins of Hebrew Typography in England', *Jnl. Jew. Biblio.*, i (1938), 1–8; idem, 'The Marrano Typography in England', *Trans. Biblio. Soc.* (1960), 118–28; idem, 'Edward Pococke and the First Hebrew Printing in Oxford', *Bodl. Lib. Rec.*, ii (1948), 215–20. Pococke corresponded with Selden in 1652 on the problems of obtaining Hebrew type: see Bodl., MS. Selden supra 109, fos. 349, 392.

the Authorized Version; the first Hebrew grammar in English was produced by John Udall and published in Leiden in 1593.[8] By the beginning of the seventeenth century, not only were Hebrew Bibles, grammars and lexicons circulating in England from across the Channel, but also separate editions of the rabbinical commentaries, codes of law, kabbalistic analyses, and Midrashic and Talmudic texts.[9]

Much of this material was certainly of very little value. Anthony Wood reported as late as 1691 that 'Roger Altham became Hebrew professor . . . but doth not read because he is no Hebritian. Yet being a Ch. Ch. [Christ Church] man he was admitted'.[10] Still, it was during this period that English scholars of the Bible began to show at least a familiarity with rabbinic scholarship and medieval Jewish literature.[11] Foreign-born Jewish converts to Christianity contributed to this influx of Jewish learning. The most important of these was Philip Ferdinand, a Polish Jew who matriculated at Cambridge in 1596. He had already passed through Catholicism to Protestantism, and so was permitted to teach Hebrew at both Universities.[12] John Immanuel Tremellius, another convert from Judaism, held the office of King's Hebrew Reader at Cambridge.[13]

Other Jews or recent converts to Christianity occasionally surfaced at Oxford or Cambridge. In 1607, Sir Thomas Bodley sought 'to gette the helpe of the Iewe, for the Hebrewe catalogue.'[14] Perhaps he was referring to Jacob Wolfgang, probably the first registered Jewish reader at the Bodleian

---

[8] I. Udall, *The Key Of The Holy Tongve* (Leiden, 1593), also reprinted 1650; cf. L. and R. Fuks, 'The Hebrew Production of the Plantin-Raphelengius Presses in Leyden, 1585–1615', *Stud. Rosenthaliana*, iv (1970), 1–24.

[9] See I. Baroway, 'Toward Understanding Tudor-Jacobean Hebrew Studies', *Jew. Soc. Stud.*, xviii (1956), 3–24; C. Roth, *A History of the Jews in England* (3rd edn., Oxford, 1964), pp. 145–6.

[10] *The Life and Times of Anthony Wood*, ed. A. Clark (Oxford, 1891–1900), iii. 375.

[11] See H. F. Fletcher, *Milton's Semitic Studies* (Chicago, 1926), esp. pp. 3–12, 27–31, 42–9, 54–60, 88–93; and his *Milton's Rabbinical Readings* (Urbana, 1930), pp. 46–78.

[12] S. Stein, 'Phillipus Ferdinandus Polonus A Sixteenth-Century Hebraist in England', *Essays in honour of . . . J. H. Hertz*, ed. I. Epstein (London, 1944), pp. 397–412.

[13] C. Roth, 'Jews in Oxford after 1290', *Oxoniensia*, xv (1950), 64–8; *Dict. Nat. Biog.*

[14] *Letters of Sir Thomas Bodley to Thomas James*, ed. G. W. Wheeler (Oxford, 1926), p. 173. For more on Bodley's Hebraic connections see C. Roth, 'Sir Thomas Bodley—Hebraist', *Bodl. Lib. Rec.*, vii (1966), 242–51; L. Fuks, 'Het Hebreeuwse Brievenboek van Johannes Drusius Jr.', *Stud. Rosenthaliana*, iii (1969), 1–52.

Library, who matriculated in 1608 after renouncing his faith
and accepting baptism. John Ley, a Cheshire divine, remembered Wolfgang as a teacher who 'had but little learning, either
in divinity or humanity, and so little acquaintance with the
Latin tongue, that hee could not (without much difficulty)
dictate two lines in that language with congruity.'[15] Also at
Oxford was Jacob (or Joseph) Barnet,

a Jew both by nation and superstition, who read Hebrew to divers young
Students, [who] had cunningly pretended and held forth that he embraced
and believed JESUS to be the true Messias. . . . he deceived many of the learned
Doctors, especially Dr. Lake, Warden of New College . . . But the very day
before he was to be baptized [in St. Mary's Church] this dissembling Jew ran
away. Dr. Lake being informed thereof, sent some on horseback, others on
foot to pursue him, who overtaking him, brought him back, tho' against his
will, to Oxford, where, on his own accord, he professed that he was returned
to his old Judaism, which he had forsworn.

Dr William Twisse, who had been scheduled to speak at Barnet's baptism, quickly prepared a new sermon on the treachery
of the Jews.[16] The Privy Council had Barnet hustled out of the
realm on 16 November 1613.[17]

What is clearly needed is a biographical register of Tudor
and Stuart Hebraists and an assessment of their work.[18] It
remains certain nevertheless that a wealth of Jewish scholarship and a fair number of Jewish scholars were available in
England to the translators of the Authorized Version in 1611.[19]
Although no Jews participated in this effort, the result plainly
indicates the influence of rabbinic thought and interpretation.[20] The demand for a new translation 'out of the original
tongues' rather than from the Latin Vulgate was the product of
an increased awareness that the Word of God was written in
Hebrew, and that a profound understanding required familiarity with the original text. As Reuchlin himself put it at the
beginning of his famous struggle, 'The language of the Hebrews

[15] J. Ley, *Sunday A Sabbath* (London, 1641), pp. 56–7; Roth, 'Oxford', p. 65.

[16] A. Wood, *The History and Antiquities of the University of Oxford*, ed. J. Gutch (Oxford,
1792–6), ii. 316; idem, *Life*, i. 422.

[17] *Acts of the Privy Council, 1613–14*, pp. 272–3.

[18] Meanwhile, see the list of Christian Hebraists (1100–1890) compiled by Mr R. J.
Loewe, *Ency. Jud.* (Jerusalem, 1971–2), viii. 9–71. About 150 Englishmen are included
in this roster.

[19] D. Daiches, *The King James Version* (Chicago, 1941), *passim*.

[20] E. I. J. Rosenthal, 'Rashi and the English Bible', *Bull. J. Ryl. Lib.* xxiv (1940),
138–67.

is simple, uncorrupted, holy, terse and vigorous; God confers in it direct with men, and men with angels, without interpreters, face to face, as one friend converses with another.'[21]

Yet this increased emphasis on biblical studies and translation from the Hebrew involved other problems as well, for if priestly mediators were abolished, then God was left speaking directly to his elect, either through his written word or through his prophets. 'Every man, nay, every boy and wench, that could read English', complained Hobbes, 'thought they spoke with God Almighty, and understood what he said, when by a certain number of chapters a day they had read the Scriptures once or twice over . . . this licence of interpreting the Scripture was the cause of so many several sects, as having lain hid till the beginning of the late King's reign, did then appear to the disturbance of the commonwealth.'[22] Bibles were relatively cheap as book prices went, and some were available even in pocket editions.[23] Arise Evans, the Welsh tailor–preacher, explained his own spiritual path.[24] 'Afore I looked upon the Scripture as a history of things that passed in other Countreys pertaining to other persons, but now I looked upon it as a mysterie to be opened at this time belonging also to us'.[25]

It was during the sixteenth and seventeenth centuries that the Old Testament regained a place of honour beside the newer partner which was thought to have superseded it. The central text in the Hebrew Bible is the Ten Commandments, to which was accorded special respect even by those who argued that the Mosaic law had been fulfilled and abrogated by the coming of Christ. Nine of the commandments could be incorporated into existing codes of behaviour without much difficulty: murder, theft, and adultery were sins in any man's law. But the fourth commandment proved more difficult to assimilate:

Remember the sabbath day, to keep it holy. Six days shalt thou labour, and do all thy work: But the seventh day *is* the sabbath of the LORD thy God: *in it* thou shalt not do any work, thou, nor thy son, nor thy daughter, thy manservant, nor thy maidservant, nor thy cattle, nor thy stranger that *is* within thy gates: For *in* six days the LORD made heaven and earth, the sea, and

[21] Quoted in H. Graetz, *History of the Jews* (London, 1892), iv. 463.
[22] T. Hobbes, *Behemoth*, ed. F. Tönnies (London, 1889), pp. 21–2.
[23] C. Hill, *The World Turned Upside Down* (New York, 1973), p. 75.
[24] For more on Arise Evans, see below, pp. 121–4.
[25] A. Evans, *An Eccho* (London, 1652), p. 17.

all that in them *is*, and rested the seventh day: wherefore the LORD blessed the sabbath day, and hallowed it.[26]

As John Ley the Cheshire divine put it, not 'all the Commandements of the Decalogue, besides that of the *Sabbath* (which for number have the oddes of nine to one) have suffered more or worse, under the strife of tongues, or conflict of pens, then it hath done.'[27] The chief reason why the Sabbath became 'as a Ball, betwixt two Rackets' was that some early modern Englishmen, called Sabbatarians, observed more strictly the commandment to rest once each week. They believed that the Sabbath derived from Creation, and thus antedates the Fall which necessitated the codification of God's rules in the Mosaic law. Their Lord's Day commemorated the second creation in the Resurrection, and therefore its observance derived from divine order rather than mere ecclesiastical custom. Such ideas had been present in English thought at least since the Lollards, but it was not until the later sixteenth century that they came to wield persuasive force.[28]

Strict Sabbatarianism was not a doctrine associated with the earliest Reformers, except perhaps Andreas Karlstadt.[29] 'If anywhere the day is made holy for the mere day's sake,' Luther advised, 'then I order you to work on it, to ride on it, to feast on it, to do anything to remove this reproach from Christian liberty.'[30] Tyndale protested that 'we be lords over the Saboth; and may yet change it into the Monday, or any other day, as we see need . . . Neither needed we any holy day at all, if the people might be taught without it.'[31] By the 1580s, however, Reformed theologians on the Continent were talking about the Sabbath as a perpetual, moral obligation rather than as a 'type' fulfilled by the coming of Christ. These sentiments are found in the works

---

[26] Exodus 20:8–11.

[27] Ley, *Sunday*, sig. c3^{r-v}.

[28] On English Sabbatarianism generally, see C. Hill, *Society and Puritanism* (2nd edn., New York, 1967), *cap.* 5; P. Collinson, 'The Beginnings of English Sabbatarianism', *Stud. Ch. Hist.*, i (1964), 207–21; R. Cox, *The Literature of the Sabbath Question* (Edinburgh, 1865).

[29] G. Rupp, 'Andrew Karlstadt and Reformation Puritanism', *Jnl. Theo. Stud.*, n.s., x (1959), 318–19.

[30] Quoted in Hill, *Society*, p. 210.

[31] W. Tyndale, *An Answer to Sir Thomas More's Dialogue*, ed. H. Walter (Parker Soc., xxxviii, 1850), pp. 97–8.

of Bullinger, John Hooper, Bucer, Peter Martyr, and Theodore Beza, among others.[32]

Yet these Continental Sabbatarians realized quite early the difficulties inherent in a literal observance of the fourth commandment. Calvin argued that one day was as good as the next; servants ought to be allowed time to rest, but the Church could designate this period as less or more frequent than one day in seven.

Thus vanish all the dreams of false prophets who in past ages have infected the people with a Jewish notion; affirming that nothing but the ceremonial part of this commandment, which according to them is the appointment of the seventh day, has been abrogated, but that the moral part of it, that is the observance of one day in seven, still remains.[33]

The commandment, after all, clearly stated that 'the seventh day *is* the sabbath of the LORD'; the argument for transferring the Sabbath from Saturday to Sunday rested on very weak scriptural ground. 'For, goe through the whole Commandement;' asked John Dod and Robert Cleaver, 'what one word in all of it hath any note of ceremony? what reason sauours of any speciall thing to the Iewes, that the Commandement should bee tied onely to them?'[34] Despite protests that such views confounded 'our Sunday with the Jewes' Sabaoth . . . which doctrine is superstitious,' Saturday-Sabbatarianism developed as a religious philosophy in its own right.[35]

Peter Heylyn wrote in his *History of the Sabbath* that when Sabbatarian theologians began to document their case, 'No passage of Gods Booke [was] unransacked, where there was mention of a *Sabbath*, whether the *Legall Sabbath*, charged the *Iewes*, or the *spirituall Sabbath* of the Soule, from sinne; which was not fitted and applyed to the present purpose.' The most extreme in this group 'endeavoured to bring backe againe the *Iewish Sabbath*, as that which is expressly mentioned in the *fourth Commandement*; and abrogate the Lords day for altogether, as having no foundation in it, nor warrant by it.' These were the men who 'trenched too neere upon the *Rabbins*, in binding men

[32] Collinson, 'Sabbatarianism', pp. 210–12.

[33] Quoted in M. M. Knappen, *Tudor Puritanism* (2nd edn., Chicago, 1970), p. 446.

[34] J. Dod and R. Cleaver, *A Plaine and Familiar Exposition of the Ten Commandements* (6th edn., London, 1615), p. 126.

[35] Quoted in Collinson, 'Sabbatarianism', p. 209.

to nice & scrupulous observances; which neither we, nor our Forefathers, were ever able to endure.' Heylyn's *History* cited numerous cases throughout the ages when men 'began to *Iudaize* a little; in the imposing of so strict a rest upon this day'.[36]

We shall look at the chief Judaizer of seventeenth-century England in a moment, but first it is necessary to follow the history of the term itself. To accuse someone of 'Judaizing' or of practising Judaism was a condemnation which had broader applications than simply to Saturday-Sabbatarians.[37] As early as 1585 a certain John Smith of Cambridge was cited before the University for advocating a Jewish observance of the Lord's Day.[38] Thomas Fuller explained that the Book of Sports was issued in 1617 'to suppresse the dangerous endeavour of such, who now began in their Pulpits, to *broach* the *dregs* of *Judaism*, and force *Christians* to *drink them*.'[39] After the Declaration had been issued, James asked parish ministers to report to him the names of 'all such kind of people as are said to encline to a kind of Judaisme by neither eatinge meate themselves nor sufferinge others to dress it upon the Lord's day.'[40] Two years later he ordered the chancellor, vice-chancellor, and heads of colleges in Cambridge to investigate and reform 'any fanciful conceit savouring of Judaism.'[41]

The term itself began to lose its specific meaning. As early as 1572, Whitgift told Cartwright, 'you *Judaizare*, "play the Jew."' Cartwright had argued that 'we have the same laws to direct us in the service of God' that the Jews had; Whitgift could certainly make a case that his 'assertion . . . tendeth to Judaism.'[42] Yet within seventy years, that accusation could already be applied to a wider variety of offences. Sir Robert Berkeley argued in Hampden's ship money case that

I would be loth to irritate any differing from me with provoking or odious terms, but I cannot more fully express myself (and so I desire it may be taken

---

[36] P. Heylyn, *The History of the Sabbath* (London, 1636), ii. 114, 188, 252–3, 259.

[37] See J. Friedman, 'Michael Servetus: the Case for a Jewish Christianity', *Sixteenth Cent. Jnl.*, iv (1973), 87–110.

[38] J. Strype, *Annals of the Reformation* (Oxford, 1824), iii. 495.

[39] T. Fuller, *The Church-History of Britain* (London, 1656), x. 76.

[40] J. Tait, 'The Declaration of Sports for Lancashire (1617)', *Eng. Hist. Rev.*, xxxii (1917), 565.

[41] M. H. Curtis, *Oxford and Cambridge in Transition* (Oxford, 1959), p. 172.

[42] *The Works of John Whitgift*, ed. J. Ayre (Parker Soc., 1851–3), i. 271.

as an expression, and not as a comparison) than in saying, that it is a dangerous tenet, a kind of judaizing opinion, to hold that the weal public must be exposed to peril of utter ruin and subversion, rather than such a charge as this, which may secure the commonwealth, may be imposed by the King upon the subject, without common consent in Parliament.[43]

The 204 members of Parliament who opposed Strafford in 1641 were called 'The Anabaptists, Jews, and Brownists of the House of Commons'.[44] When London Common Council removed the Cheapside Cross, Sir Humphrey Mildmay wrote in his diary sarcastically that it was taken down 'by the Jews'.[45]

Although a Jewish colony certainly did exist in London, it is only on extremely rare occasions that individual Jews ever surface in the records. Richard Bruern, Regius professor of Hebrew at Oxford after 1548, was denounced as a Jew, but also as a Roman Catholic, a homosexual, and an adulterer.[46] When William Cotton, bishop of Exeter, reports in 1600 that 'There was lately a passover intended, but by a sudden search prevented,' we need to know how broad his interpretation of Judaism actually was before we confirm that a Jewish colony existed in south-west England.[47] Actual experience of Judaism and practising Jews was completely lacking. Even a man like the Scottish minister John Weemse, who advocated the readmission of the Jews to England, insisted that 'the Iewes have a loathsome and stinking smell, and . . . a stinking breath.'[48] The revival of Old Testament and Hebrew studies at least familiarized Englishmen with the rudiments of Judaism, and the appearance of Jews, even though converts. At the same time, the growth of Saturday-Sabbatarianism and Judaizing doctrines prompted men like Christopher Dow to worry that 'men

[43] J. P. Kenyon, *The Stuart Constitution* (Cambridge, 1969), p. 112.
[44] *Cal. S. P. Dom.*, *1640–1*, p. 560. Similarly, after the Restoration Henry Townshend noted the name of 'Miles Corbett called the Jew' in his *Diary*, ed. J. W. Willis Bund (Worcestershire Hist. Soc., xxxi, 1915–20), i. 87. Similarly, Anon., *The Second Part of Saint George for England* (n.p., [1659]), brdsht. Lambert was called a Jew in Anon., *A Pack of Hell-hounds* (n.p., n.d.), brdsht.
[45] P. L. Ralph, *Sir Humphrey Mildmay* (New Brunswick, 1947), p. 164. Cf. J. Harris, *The Pvritanes Impvritie* (London, 1641), pp. 4–5 for use of word 'Synagogue' for puritan church.
[46] J. Fines, '"Judaising" in the Period of the English Reformation—The Case of Richard Bruern', *Trs. Jew. Hist. Soc. Eng.*, xxi (1968), 323–6.
[47] Hist. MSS Comm., ix, *Salisbury MSS*, x, pp. 450–1.
[48] J. Weemse, *A Treatise of the Fovre Degenerate Sonnes* (London, 1636), p. 330.

may not be deceived with shewes, and mistake *Iudaisme* for *Christianity*.'[49]

II

'Now of the Broakers of Judaisme,' wrote Thomas Fuller, '*John Thraske* was a principall.'[50] Many early seventeenth-century Englishmen were misleadingly labelled as Judaizers, but Traske certainly deserved this designation. Yet despite the fact that Traske caused a major scandal which interested the king and 'caus'd many of his Auditors to weep, and even to roar in such Manner, that the Inhabitants in many Parts of *London* were often disturb'd in the Night by his Converts,'[51] virtually no secondary work exists which explores his sect in any detail.[52] The Traskites and the official reaction to their Judaizing opinions provided the first public forum for a debate on the literal interpretation of the Mosaic law and the nature of Christian–Jewish relations in over three hundred years.

John Traske was born in Somerset about 1585. Someone of that name, the youngest son of Lionell Traske, was baptized on 15 October 1585 at East Coker, Somerset and married on 23 November 1606 in the same parish.[53] These local records are corroborated by the statement which Traske the Judaizer gave later before marrying Dorothy Coome in 1617, when he was said to be a widower of 'thirty-two years or thereabouts'.[54] John Falconer, an English Jesuit who later wrote a description of Traske's life and beliefs, says that Traske was a school-master at a gentleman's house in Somerset before he began his outrageous career.[55] He afterwards applied for ordination to James

---

[49] C. Dow, *A Discourse of the Sabbath* (2nd ed., London, 1636), p. 1.

[50] Fuller, *History*, x. 76.

[51] [Anon.], *The History of King = Killers* (London, 1719), p. 35.

[52] The only secondary sources that discuss the Traskites at any length are: a lecture given by H. E. I. Phillips in 1938 and repr. as 'An Early Stuart Judaising Sect', *Trs. Jew. Hist. Soc. Eng.*, xv (1946), 63–72; and B. R. White, 'John Traske (1585–1636) and London Puritanism', *Trs. Cong. Hist. Soc.*, xx (1968), 223–33.

[53] W. B. Trask, *The Traske Family in England* (Boston, 1900), pp. 3–5; idem, *Capt. William Traske and Some of his Descendants* (Boston, 1904); both repr. from *New Eng. Hist. and Geneol. Reg.*, liv–lvii (1900–3).

[54] Guildhall Lib., MS 10,091/6, f.26ʳ: Traske marries Dorothy Coome, 12 Feb. 1616–17; repr. in *Allegations for Marriage Licenses issued by the Bishop of London 1611 to 1828*, ed. G. J. Armytage (Pubs. Harleian Soc., xxvi, 1887), p. 49.

[55] D. B. [J. Falconer], *A Briefe Refutation Of Iohn Traskes Ivdaical And Novel Fancyes* (n.p., 1618), p. 9.

Montague, bishop of Bath and Wells, but was rejected by Dr
Samuel Ward, the bishop's chaplain, for insufficiency; Fuller
affirms that Traske eventually was ordained.[56] Traske published two sermons about this time, in 1615, which gave little
indication of the Judaizing views for which he was to become
famous, although he was imprisoned in Newgate at the end of
that year 'for goinge upp and downe as a wandering minister'.[57]

By 1616, one had to be wary about associating with Traske.
This, presumably, was the period of Traske's 'aboad with
Maister Drake in Deuonshire' when he gave public lectures and
left his chamber open 'to all comers, day and night for priuate
instruction'.[58] John Bodley (Sir Thomas's nephew) left £400 in
his will to Exeter for the maintenance of a preacher to speak on
the Sabbath. John Hazard was nominated, and the adminis-
trators of the fund wrote to William Cotton, the bishop of
Exeter, to ask if he had any objections to Hazard. Cotton (the
man who discovered a 'passover' at Exeter at the turn of the
century) interviewed Hazard on 5 April 1616 and told him,
'You have preached false doctrine . . . And beside (sayth he)
you have been a companion with Trasque.' 'My lord,' Hazard
replied, 'ytt is not so, for I can bringe good testimony that I
have twise publickly in two severall sermons att Lyme confuted
the erroneous fancyes of Trasque . . . the whole towne of Lyme
can wittnes the same.' George Abbott, the archbishop of Canterbury, was eventually called upon to make the final decision:
Hazard got the lectureship in spite of his alleged connection
with Traske, although he left a year later for unknown
reasons.[59]

Traske arrived in London again about the beginning of 1617,
remarried, and soon gained a reputation for powerful preaching. 'His owne and his disciples prayers are commonly
roaringes.' Falconer reported, 'and such loud out-cries as may
be heard in distant roomes and houses, voluntarily framed
and filled for the most part with frequent imprecations, that

[56] Fuller, *History*, x. 76.
[57] J. Traske, *A Pearle For A Prince* (London, 1615); *Middlesex Sessions Records*, ed. W. Le
Hardy (n.s., London, 1935–7), iii.107.
[58] [Falconer], *Refvtation*, pp. 7–11.
[59] Hist. MSS Comm., lxxiii, *Exeter*, pp. 94–6.

God would confound the aduersaries and persecutors of his
little flocke'.[60]

Even at this early date, before he began his Judaizing, Traske
differed from other preachers in several theological
peculiarities. He argued that only the converted could convert
others, and that the elect could recognize another's election as
well as his own. Traske ranked his followers into three distinct
estates: that of Nature, that of Repentance, and that of Grace.
These estates were successive; to recover men out of the state of
Nature, he preached Repentance. 'The great Bait in his preaching was,' a contemporary explained, 'that his Repentance, or
penitential Course was not to be continu'd to the End of their
Lives, but only till that third Estate was obtain'd; . . . and that
once gain'd, they . . . should have no more Sorrow, but all Joy.'
It was on this basis that he taught that a true minister of Christ
could not teach any error, and that to doubt his teaching was a sin.
Falconer was told that Traske could determine whether a particular person would be damned or saved by examining his face.[61]

At this point, Traske was not yet a Judaizer, only another
popular preacher. It was not until he enlisted a certain tailor
named Hamlet Jackson among his disciples that Traske was
pushed towards Judaizing practices. Jackson had studied the
plain text of scripture on his own, and came to believe that the
portions of the New Testament that dealt with the Mosaic law
did not entirely abrogate their provisions. He discussed his
views with Traske, who at first tried to dissuade him, but
eventually became convinced by Jackson's argument.[62]
'Behold here Gods righteous dealing,' noted a friend in a letter
to Traske's wife in 1634, 'Mr. *Trask* draweth *Hamlet Iackson* from
the Church, accusing it of falshood both in doctrin and government; and *Hamlet Iackson* draweth Mr *Trask* to points of
Judaism, as to the observation of Laws touching Meat, Drink,
Apparel, Resting, Working, Building, and many other matters.'[63]

At first, Traske, Jackson and their followers were content to

[60] [Falconer], *Refutation*, pp. 7–11.
[61] *King = Killers*, p. 35; [Falconer], *Refutation*, pp. 7, 13.
[62] *King = Killers*, p. 36.
[63] E. Pagitt, *Heresiography* (6th edn., London, 1661), p. 165: letter by 'T.S.' to
Traske's wife, 26 Dec. 1634.

mix Jewish and Christian traditions, and continued to observe the Lord's Day, although they refrained from kindling fires or dressing meat on Sunday.[64] Advice on the application and understanding of biblical and rabbinic law was certainly available in England, but it is unclear whether Traske and Jackson were equipped with the tools to conduct a proper inquiry. One critic alleged that Traske 'learned and studied the *Hebrew* and *Greek*, and got a smattering thereof, that by *Indexes* he could do some little matter'.[65] 'This Runagate *Iackson*', it was said, 'cannot write true English, nor read it truly, but as he learnt lately by a habit of reading.'[66]

The Traskites apparently grew in number nevertheless, and their leader decided to evangelize on a larger scale. As one contemporary reports, 'he made choice of four Men of those of his third Estate, on whom he in a Pontifical manner laid his Hands, and sent them abroad to preach; he pretending to give the Holy Ghost by the Imposition of his Hands, and they to cure Diseases, by anointing with Oil'.[67] Jackson was one of those men, sent into the country to preach the Judaizing doctrine. As he was travelling 'on a *Saturday*, which he then thought to be the right Sabbath, tho' he did not yet observe it, as he said himself; . . . fancy'd he saw . . . a shining Light about him, which struck him with Amazement. Hereupon he concluded, that the Light of the Law was more fully discover'd to him, than to any since the Apostles.'[68] Jackson was now convinced of the necessity of keeping the Saturday Sabbath according to the full Mosaic law, and once again persuaded his master Traske, who reconverted his disciples to this Judaizing doctrine.[69]

The most scandalous offence of the Traskites was now that they kept the Saturday Sabbath and ignored the Lord's Day as an ordinary day of work. Traske's wife taught children to read, but she 'would teach them only five dayes in the week: for upon Saturday she would not teach them, because she esteemed that the Sabbath day; and upon Sunday (which is the Christian

[64] *King = Killers*, p. 36.

[65] E. Norice, *The New Gospel, not the True Gospel* (London, 1638), sig. B2: letter by 'T.S.'.

[66] Pagitt, *Heresiography*, p. 167: 'T.S.' letter.

[67] *King = Killers*, p. 36.

[68] Ibid., pp. 37, 39.

[69] Ibid., pp. 36–7; Norice, *Gospel*, sigs. B2^{r-v}: 'T.S.' letter.

Sabbath) I suppose she durst not.'[70] The group does not appear
to have been completely in agreement over doctrine, however,
according to contemporary testimony. 'You and others sinned
by separating from the Church,' a critic wrote to Mrs Traske,
'and were you not punished by separating one from another?
while there were many that observed the same lawes, yet
differing among themselves about *walking with God*, would not
communicate one with another? Did you not Excommunicate
one another in your mind? witness you and Mr. *Hebden*, and
others also.'[71]

The name of this 'Mr. Hebden' is one of the few that survives
of the Jacobean Traskite group. Certainly this is Returne Hebdon, Falconer's 'poore seduced Gentleman, better skilled in
Hebrew then [Traske] and equally conuersant in Scripture'.
The introduction to a posthumous edition of Hebdon's 'meditations' reveals him to be 'a Gentlemans Sonne of *Fashion*, in the
Town of *Holmeshurst*, in the Country of *Sussex*' who left 'both
Father and Mother, and meanes . . . for the Commandement of
Gods sake, by his desiring to rest on the seventh day'.[72] Few
other names have survived: a certain Christopher Sands
appears frequently; he was said to have converted 'one Mr.
Wright, a Minister, and his Wife' as well as Mary Chester, who
became well known in the 1630s with Theophilus Brabourne, a
later Judaizer. Jackson the Judaizing tailor converted his own
wife and a William Hilliard, as well as Christopher Sands; he
'somewhat shook one *Thomas Whitaker*'.[73] Edward Norice mentions 'one Mr. *Gr.*' as another Traskite; Falconer refers to a
'Comfit-maker' who understood Latin, and a perfumer as
well.[74] Later, while in prison, Traske appears to have converted
Edward and Nicholas Rookwood of Euston, Suffolk, father and
son, two gentlemen who had been imprisoned for debt.[75] In
short, the Traskites in the reign of James I could boast of
relatively few leaders, and have left very few first-hand records.

---

[70] Pagitt, *Heresiography*, p. 209: anon. letter 'Concerning Mrs. *Trask*'.

[71] Ibid., p. 167: 'T.S.' letter.

[72] [Falconer], *Refutation*, p. 11; R. Hebdon, *A Guide To the Godly* (n.p., 1648), sig. A2.

[73] *King = Killers*, pp. 37, 40–1; Pagitt, *Heresiography*, p. 192: 'Life . . . of . . . *Trask*',
which Pagitt claims was written in 1635.

[74] Norice, *Gospel*, p. 2; [Falconer], *Refutation*, pp. 11, 76.

[75] *The Œconomy of the Fleete*, ed. A. Jessopp (Camden Soc., n.s., xxv, 1879), pp. 49,
129–30, 187.

Despite their Judaizing, they were decidedly a Christian sect, at least during this period; Traske's argument was that many of the Old Testament Mosaic laws applied to Christians as well as Jews. This is why Norice objected that the Traskites were Jews, 'yea Iews, and worse than Iewes, their congregations not true, but pretended Christian assemblies'.[76] Another contemporary admitted that some of the Traskites may not be so certain, 'but yet in a doubting manner, think they may be Jewes, for ought they know to the contrary; and therefore conclude, that seeing they do doubt, it is safest for them to keep Sabbaths, and to live as do the Jews'.[77]

By the beginning of 1618, about a year after Traske first arrived in London, the Judaizing sect could no longer be ignored. Traske and some of his followers were soon in prison. On 14 February 1618, John Chamberlain wrote to Sir Dudley Carleton about

one Trash or Thrash who was first a puritan, then a separatist, and now is become a Jewish Christian, observing the Sabath on Saterday, abstaining from swines-flesh and all things commaunded in the law. You will not thincke what a number of foolish followers he hath in this towne and some other parts, and yet he hath not ben long of this opinion. He and divers of them are in prison, but continue obstinat, whereby a man may see there can arise no such absurd opinion but shall find followers and disciples.[78]

James himself followed the case: 'Theyr opinions made his Majestie exceeding merrie on Sunday at dinner,' it was reported, '& were almost the sole subject of his discourse. Amongst other things which they foolishly maintein, they hould it absolutely unlawful to eat . . . blacke puddings.'[79] The Old Testament dietary laws, of course, prohibit the eating of blood in any form, as well as swine's flesh.

Traske was kept in prison until June 'with no other allowance then bread and water, whilest in the interim Popists priests were there suffred to feast and banquet, and that indeed was his fare, but of swine's flesh he might have eaten his fill every day, for so it was ordred.'[80] William Hudson thought that

[76] Norice, *Gospel*, p. 2.
[77] Pagitt, *Heresiography*, p. 178: 'T.S.' letter.
[78] *The Letters of John Chamberlain*, ed. N. E. McClure (Philadelphia, 1939), ii. 65; similarly, *Cal. S. P. Dom.*, *1611–18*, p. 521.
[79] *Chamberlain*, ii. 140n.; similarly, *Cal. S. P. Dom.*, *1611–18*, p. 524.
[80] Hist. MSS Comm., lviii, *Bath MSS*, ii. 67–8: T. Lorkin to ——, 23 June 1618.

this punishment demonstrated the wisdom and creativity of Star Chamber.[81] £11 6s. were stolen from Traske's trunk by the warden of the Fleet and his servants, yet when finally sentenced he nevertheless offered 'to make good for that half a yeer together they had kept him in prison.'[82]

Traske was sentenced in Star Chamber on 19 June 1618 to be kept close prisoner in the Fleet for the rest of his life so as to prevent him from infecting others; he was also fined £1,000 and expelled from the ministry. Traske was guilty of 'haueing a fantasticall opynion of himselfe with ambicion to bee the Father of a Jewish faccion', and of having written two 'scandalous' letters to the king, the second of which 'vseth the vncivill terme of Thow and Thee to the Kinges most excellent Maiestie'. Traske was 'to bee whipped from the prison of the Fleete to the Pallace of Westminster with a paper on his head . . . then to bee sett on the Pillory and to haue one of his eares nayled to the Pillory, and after hee hath stood there some convenient tyme, to bee burnte in the forehead with the lettre J: in token that hee broached Jewish opynions'. Finally, Traske was to 'bee whipped from the Fleete into Cheepeside . . . sett in the Pillory and haue his other Eare nayled thervnto'.[83] Thomas Lorkin reported twelve days later that 'the sentence against the Jew hath been put in execution'.[84]

Traske's sentencing provoked comment from high places, which shows that he was regarded as more than an insignificant crank. Lancelot Andrewes delivered a speech in Star Chamber 'against the two Ivdaicall opinions of Mr. Traske', one of the three occasions in which he took part in Star Chamber cases. 'It is a good work to make a Jew a Christian:' he admonished, 'but to make Christian men Jews, hath ever been holden a foul act, and severely to be punished'. As far as Andrewes was concerned, Traske was 'a very christened Jew, a Maran, the worst sort of Jews that is.'[85] Lord Chancellor Bacon was concerned as

[81] W. Hudson, 'A Treatise of the Court of Star Chamber', *Collectanea Juridica*, ii. 225: undated, but classified as a pre-1635 tract.

[82] *Œconomy of the Fleete*, p. 47; Hist. MSS Comm., lviii, *Bath MSS*, ii. 67–8.

[83] Bodl. Lib., Addit. MSS C 303, fos. 38ᵛ–45ʳ: repr. in *Trs. Bap. Hist. Soc.*, v (1916–7), 8–11. For an eyewitness report of the sentencing see J. Ussher, *Works*, ed. C. R. Elrington and J. M. Todd (Dublin, 1847–64), xvi. 359.

[84] *The Court and Times of James the First*, ed. R. F. Williams (London, 1848), ii. 77.

[85] *Miscellaneous Works of Lancelot Andrewes*, ed. J. Bliss (Library of Anglo-Catholic

well: notes for his speech to the Judges in Star Chamber on 26 June 1618 show that he expressed the view that 'New opinions spread very dangerous, the late Traske a dangerous person. Prentices learn the Hebrew tongue.'[86] James himself talked about Traske in his *Meditation Vpon The Lords Prayer* published in 1619, a book which D. H. Willson thought was 'startling proof of decline in his mental powers'.[87] 'Holde fast therefore your profession,' the king warned,

trust not to that priuate spirit or holy ghost which our *Puritanes* glory in; for then a little fierie zeale will make thee turne *Separatist*, and then proceed stil on from *Brownist* to some one Sect or other of *Anabaptist*, and from one of these to another, then to become a Iudaized *Traskite*, and in the ende a profane *Familist*.[88]

The chief Judaizer, meanwhile, settled himself in the Fleet for what appeared to be a long prison sentence. Falconer reports that the Traskites in prison practised the 'Iewish manner of keeping Easter' and attempted to conduct a Passover *seder* ritual. Traske's fellow-prisoners observed him and his disciples 'eate contrary to their custome at other times, white vnleauened loaues, and seeming in his speeches to allow of the obseruance of that festiuity, albeit of the manner he be somthing doubtfull, as peraduenture, whether it must be with a Phascall Lambe eaten.'[89]

Traske himself later discussed his relations with, as he put it then, the 'holy and tender mother, the Church of England', and sought to explain his spiritual history since his arrest and imprisonment. The 'first thing I vnderstood,' he recalled, 'was my Mothers great Authoritie; this was I throughly setled in (about six moneths) ere I came to see my foule failings, in

---

[86] Notes by Sir Julius Caesar, *The Letters and The Life of Francis Bacon*, ed. J. Spedding (London, 1872), vi. 315. The connection between Bacon and the Jews has not yet been fully appreciated: cf. F. Yates, 'Science, Salvation, and the Cabala', *N.Y. Rev. Books*, 27 May 1976, pp. 27–9.

[87] D. H. Willson, *King James VI and I* (London, 1956), p. 401.

[88] [James I], *A Meditation Vpon The Lords Prayer* (London, 1619), p. 18.

[89] [Falconer], *Refvtation*, pp. 17–8, 58–9. Falconer (p. 10) also says that Traske wrote a long letter to Edmund Howes while in prison, in a vain attempt to win a comprehensive entry in Stow's chronicle: Traske was dealt with in twelve lines: I. Stow and E. Howes, *Annales* (London, 1631), p. 1029.

those points of *Iudaisme*, at what time I set my selfe more
seriously to seeke the Lord'.[90] Traske indeed appeared to have
changed his views by 1 December 1619, after nearly a year in
prison, when Bacon wrote to Buckingham that

This day also Traske in open court made a retraction of his wicked opinions in
writing. The form was as good as may be; . . . it is a rare thing for a Sectary,
that hath once suffered smart and shame, to turn so unfeignedly, as he seemed
to do.[91]

Traske was soon free, promising 'that as I haue been stout for
Moses, and *Christ* together: so I may bee as resolute for Christ
alone', and once released from prison, he avoided all further overt
connection with Judaizing doctrines, and published a short work
in 1620 entitled *A Treatise of Libertie From Iudaisme*.[92]

Traske continued to preach after his release; three years later he
claimed to be a preacher at Tillingham in Essex.[93] At some point
between the end of his imprisonment in 1620, and 1627, he was
suspended from the ministry 'yet freed from that by his Maiesties
pardon under the great seale, and if hee want a Curates Lycense
for ye Last place he was in, hee was alsoe ready to take it out, and
onely hindered by the Incumbent who retayned him with him not
as his curate but as his friend.'[94] Fuller said that Traske travelled
around the country, 'as unsetled in judgment, as place' and
presumably it was on one of these tours that he heard the retired
Judaizer speak. When 'his Auditors have *forgotten* the matter,' he
relates, 'they will *remember* the *loudness* of his stentorious voice,
which indeed had more strength, than any thing else he delivered.'[95]

Traske was in trouble yet again by summer 1627, seven years
after his release from prison, in an incident which reveals his
continuing popularity. Joshua Purcas, 'a violent Puritan', was
hanged in London at the end of July for rape. Traske testified that
he had spoken to Purcas in Newgate on the request of his relatives
and by permission of the chaplain, but that he was 'utterly
unacquainted with the prisoner till that day' and had tried to
persuade him to confess to the crime, for 'att the tyme of his death

[90] J. Traske, *A Treatise of Libertie From Iudaisme* (London, 1620), sigs. A3–4; p. 41.
[91] *Bacon*, ed. Spedding, vii. 67.
[92] Traske, *Libertie*, sigs. A3–4, p. 41.
[93] Idem, *The Power of Preaching* (London, 1623), title page.
[94] *Cal. S. P. Dom, 1627–8*, p. 278: text repr. White, 'Traske', p. 230.
[95] Fuller, *History*, x. 77.

he denied it stoutly.' Traske preached at the hanging, and then was invited to speak at the funeral, but he was obliged to refuse because he had already agreed to preach at a christening at St. Sepulchre's. Some of Purcas's friends had attended under the false impression that Traske was going to speak about him. Meanwhile, when the curate preached at the funeral, the entire congregation walked out. Bishop Montaigne of London wrote to Laud that he had refused permission for Traske—'you know him well'—to speak at the funeral anyway. Traske, in Montaigne's view, was 'an unworthy person, and a Jew.' The record of Traske's examination, endorsed by Laud, shows that while he claimed to have given up Saturday-Sabbatarianism, he admitted that his wife still observed the Jewish Sabbath 'notwithstanding all the reasons he can gyve her to the contrary'. His testimony in Purcas's case does not appear to have been completely convincing, for two years later Traske is found writing to Laud, complaining that he refuses to 'permit the writer the exercise of his function, or prescribe him some other way to walk in without offence'. Traske emphasized that, as far as Laud was concerned, he was 'a man unseen, unheard, unknown, and never spoken with to this day.'[96]

The fate of the other prominent Traskites is rather more difficult to trace, but we can still get an idea of what happened to the first important Judaizers of seventeenth-century England. As Traske himself said, his wife was extremely tenacious of her Judaizing opinions. A letter which Laud endorsed on 31 August 1639 reported that Traske's wife 'hath laien in ye new prison wch is dissolved, & hath beene in ye gate-house: in both [each?] prisons 11 yeares.' Throughout this period she would

receiue no gifts from any, thinking it a curse to beg or borrow; I could never heare yt she had any more yn 40s yearely in annuety, paid her . . . & being committed refused to bedde wth her husband (although both in one prison) . . . she hath not eaten any flesh these 7 yeares, neither (for ye most) drunke any thing but water, she will not go out of doores to take ye aire, saying yt is not for her[97]

Traske's wife remained a prisoner at least until early 1645,

[96] Cal. S. P. Dom., 1627–8, pp. 278, 281, 289; 1628–9, p. 576: for partial texts see White, 'Traske', pp. 230–1.
[97] Cal. S. P. Dom., 1639, pp. 466–7: text repr. Bap. Qly., xxiv (1971–2), 18–9: 'T.S.' letter.

when she began to follow the advice of fellow-prisoner Paul
Best, the author of the first Socinian work in English, and
changed her diet. She soon fell sick and prevailed upon the
gaoler 'that he should not bury her in any Church (which she
needed not much to have feared) nor in any Church-yard, but
in the Fields.'[98]

Another prominent Traskite spent the remainder of his life in
prison. Returne Hebdon, the gentleman's son from Sussex,
died about 1625 after eight years in prison, according to a friend
of Traske's wife, 'in which time he gave himselfe to continuall
study, in fasting and prayer'. He left a book of 'meditations' for
Dorothy Traske, which was published in 1648.[99]

Hamlet Jackson, the tailor who taught Judaizing doctrines to
Traske, was lodged in the new prison in Maiden Lane where
Traske's wife was originally incarcerated, although 'he
doubted not but that the Doors of the same would all fly open
and give him free Passage, when he should think fit; but having
put the same to the Tryal, he found by Experience that his
Faith fail'd him.'[100] Once released, he seems to have given up
Judaizing observations in favour of outright conversion to
Judaism in Amsterdam. The Jewish community there told
Jackson and Christopher Sands, another Traskite who travelled with him, that they would have to be circumcised before
being accepted into the congregation. 'Whereupon Mr. *Christopher Sands* was content only to be a National Saint, or Saint of
the Gentiles, by observing the seven precepts [of Noah]: but
Jackson would not be so content; he would be circumcised, and
so made a Jewish Proselyte.' The Dutch Jews did not approve
of Traskite Saturday-Sabbatarianism either, and told Jackson,
Sands, 'and others', that 'unless they were also circumcised,
their observation thereof was groundless.'[101]

These Dutch Jews had very close links with the small group
of Jewish merchants living and trading in London in the first
half of the seventeenth century. These contacts are exceedingly
difficult to penetrate, but it is clear that the Jewish community

---

[98] Pagitt, *Heresiography*, p. 210; *King = Killers*, p. 40. For Best see H. J. McLachlan,
Socinianism in Seventeenth-Century England (Oxford, 1951), *cap.* ix and *Dict. Nat. Biog.* Best
was imprisoned in early 1645 (McLachlan, p. 151).

[99] Hebdon, *Guide*, sigs. A2^{r-v}.

[100] *King=Killers*, p. 40.

[101] Pagitt, *Heresiography*, p. 168: 'T.S.' letter; similarly, *King=Killers*, p. 40.

in Amsterdam followed English affairs with great interest, and saw London as a useful neutral port for dealings with Spain and as a conduit for both goods and refugees. If contemporary reports are correct in their claim that a number of Traskites did go to Amsterdam to make contact with the Jewish community there, then we may have discovered the first tentative links between religious radicals in England and the influential Jewish community in Holland, links which would become very important when Dutch rabbi Menasseh ben Israel would be invited to present his case to the Council of State.

Unfortunately, the evidence for these early connections appears to be rather inconclusive. If Hamlet Jackson did become a convert to Judaism, then some mention of these events should appear in the records of Dutch Jewry. The *Livro De Bet Haim Do Kahal Kados De Bet Yahacob*, the burial register of the Jewish community in Amsterdam, does make mention of a certain 'Abraham Ger ingres' six times; his wife Sarah was buried on 9 March 1625.[102] 'Abraham' and 'Sarah' are the traditional names taken by converts to Judaism, and the word 'Ger' in Hebrew means 'convert'. However, a reference to an 'Abraham Ger' occurs in the tax records for 1615 and 1616, before Traske even arrived in London. This man was poor; so was the 'Abraham Ger ingres' who was given this national designation between 1623 and 1625. We may be dealing with two different 'Abraham Gers' here, but it is difficult to be certain because the burial of neither man appears in the records. In short, it cannot be confirmed from the burial register that Hamlet Jackson joined the Jewish community in Amsterdam. Abraham Ger was not the only convert recorded: there are references to Eliau Ger, Jacob Ger, Judique Gerina, and two different Sarah Gers in addition to Abraham's wife.[103]

The elaborately carved tombstones of the *Beth Haim*, the Jewish cemetery, at the little town of Ouderkerk outside Amsterdam often provide important biographical information. Unfortunately, the ground there is so soft that most of the flat

---

[102] Ed. W. C. Pieterse (Assen, 1970), pp. 108, 112 (twice), 126 (twice), 137. Also a simple reference to an 'ingres judeu' for 9 Aug. 1623, who is presumably Abraham Ger as well.

[103] Ibid., pp. 25, 145 (Abraham Ger); 161 (Eliau Ger); 116 (Jacob Ger); 116, 138 (Sarah Israel Gera); 122 (Sarah Ger); 117, 139 (Judique Gerina).

gravestones have sunk into the earth. Until 1916, the Dutch
Jews buried their dead so close to one another that there was no
room to walk; today the seventeenth-century part of the cemetery is simply a hilly field dotted with a few gravestones. These
were the stones which David Henriques de Castro restored in
the late nineteenth century: the graves of famous men like
Menasseh ben Israel, Samuel Palache the Jewish pirate, and
Michael De Espinoza, the philosopher's father. The Jewish
community in Amsterdam is in the process of uncovering,
mapping, and registering the gravestones at Ouderkerk, and
Sarah Ger's monument may yet provide a definitive answer to
some murky questions regarding Christian–Jewish relations in
England during the first half of the seventeenth century.[104]

This search for the Dutch Traskites has taken us rather far
away from Traske himself. By 1634, an observer could write
that some Traskites 'are returned to the Church, some to
prophaneness, others fallen to flat Judaism.' In his view, Traskism was a faith which 'only two or three women do now
uphold.'[105] Nevertheless, the Traskites and their Judaizing
views were thought to remain a viable force in English spiritual
life throughout this period. For example, on 16 February 1621,
Thomas Shepherd 'was censured to be cast out of the House as
an unworthy member and so he was.' Shepherd had made a
violent speech against Sabbath-breaking, criticizing Puritans
and JPs. 'The punishment of Shepherd,' Professor Notestein
explained, 'was a parliamentary gesture against the opinions of
the Sabbatarians, particularly the Traskites whose doctrines
had caused recent excitement and were to influence the amend-
ing of this very bill against which Shepherd spoke.'[106] It was on
this occasion that Pym delivered his maiden speech. On 24
May 1621, the archbishop of Canterbury spoke for the House of
Lords in criticizing Coke's bill for the Sabbath. Pym noted in
his diary that there was no objection to the body of the bill, 'but
only to the word Sabboth in the Tytle. The reasons wereof were
declared by the Arch Bishopp, First the aptnes of divers to

[104] Cf. L. A. Vega, *The Beth Haim of Ouderkerk aan de Amstel* (Assen/Amsterdam, 1975);
D. Henriques de Castro, *Keur Van Grafsteenen op de Nederl.-Portug.Israël. Begraafplaats*
(Leiden, 1883).

[105] Pagitt, *Heresiography*, p. 168: 'T.S.' letter.

[106] W. Notestein, *et al.*, *Commons Debates 1621* (New Haven, 1935), ii. 96n.

Enclyne to Judaisme as the newe sect of the Thraskites and other oppinionists concerninge the terrene Kingdome of the Jewes. That therefore their desire was that it might be called the Lords daie.'[107] When the Commissioners for Ecclesiastical Causes came to list the sects that ought to be suppressed in 1636, they included the Traskites.[108] James Harrington corresponded with Charles I about the Sabbath in 1647 and approved of 'Bishop Andrews' speech in the Star Chamber at the censure of Mr. Traske'; Harrington would later propose that the Jews be settled in Ireland.[109] Moses Wall defended himself even in 1650 against those who would criticize his translation of Menasseh ben Israel's work by affirming that he was far 'from the wilde opinions of Mr. *Thrask*.'[110]

The later life of Traske himself is rather more obscure than his long-lasting popular reputation: he is alternatively said to have 'relapsed, not into the same, but other Opinions, rather humerous, than hurtfull,' given 'into the Errors of the *Antinomians*,' or 'turned himselfe to the Iacobites, or Semi-Separatists.'[111] Traske's name came up in a court case in 1634 when Sir Richard Strode of Cattistock, Dorset, was charged with seizing his kinsman's aisle in the parish church. High Commission claimed that Strode, who appears in numerous other litigation during this period,

a few years last past did entertaine the said Thraske into his house, where he . . . did pronounce prayers . . . and expounded a chapter or text of Scripture to the said Sir Richard Stroud and his family. And besides . . . Stroud carried him . . . abroad with him into the Country to preach in other places. And . . . Sir Richard became a Suitor unto the late Lord Bp of Canterbury and other his Maties Commissioners ecclesiastical for Mr. Thraskes restitution and dismission out of the Commission Court[112]

Strode may have been connected by marriage with Traske's earlier employer in Devonshire.[113]

[107] Ibid., iv. 377–8.
[108] *Cal. S. P. Dom.*, *1635–6*, p. 242.
[109] *Cal. S. P. Dom.*, *1645–7*, p. 549; J. Harrington, *The Common-Wealth of Oceana* (London, 1656), sig. B2: see below, p. 240.
[110] M. W[all], 'The answer to the Letter [of Sir Edward Spencer]', in Menasseh ben Israel, *The Hope of Israel* (London, 1652), p. 59.
[111] Fuller, *History*, x. 77; *King=Killers*, p. 38; Norice, *Gospel*, sig. B2ᵛ: 'T.S.' letter.
[112] *Cal. S. P. Dom.*, *1634–5*, p. 121: text repr. White, 'Traske', p. 232.
[113] See *Diary of Walter Yonge*, ed. G. Roberts (Camden Soc., xli, 1848), intro.; White, 'Traske', p. 231.

Traske ended his life as a Baptist. Henry Jessey took the place of John Lathrop as pastor of an Independent congregation in London from the summer of 1637. Lathrop and the members of his flock were continually harassed and eventually imprisoned for a time, and Jessey was involved with the group during this difficult period. On 20 February 1635–6, the Court of High Commission ordered John Wragg to seek out sectaries, including 'Thraskists'. The so-called Jessey Records of this congregation include the following note of a persecution that took place in 1636:

Iohn Trash was taken by Rag at Mr Digbeys & not Yelding to Rags general warrant was had to ye L. Mayor . . . & was comitted to ye Poultrey Counter for ten days & then was released upon Bail, wanted his health & was shortly after translated.[114]

Traske died while visiting followers, or at least friends,

from whose house some of that societie carried him to his grave in *Lambeth* Church-yard, where they cast him in, with the heeles that way that the heads of other men lie, contrary to all men, and least the Minister should come to bury him, according to the order, they ranne all away, and there left him to bee covered by others: some beholding their carriages thought them to be drunk[115]

The entry of the early Baptists into the life story of the most important Judaizer is of immense significance, and unfortunately there is insufficient space to do more than discuss this briefly here. Henry Jessey, the pastor of Traske's Baptist church until 1663 and a powerful advocate of Jewish readmission, was the author of the most reliable eyewitness narrative of the Whitehall Conference in which the formal resettlement of the Jews in England was debated. He was also a Saturday-Sabbatarian: he 'kept his opinion much to himself', wrote Jessey's biographer in 1671, 'and then afterwards (when he had communicated it to others) he observed the day in his own Chamber, with onely 4 or 5 more of the same mind [including Traske?] and on the first day of the week he preached, and met

---

[114] *Cal. S. P. Dom.*, *1635–6*, p. 242; C. Burrage, *The Early English Dissenters* (Cambridge, 1912), i. 313–25; [B. Stinton], 'A Repository of Divers Historical Matters relating to the English Antipedobaptists' (*c.* 1712), Regent's Park College, Oxford, MS, p. 7: repr. ibid., ii. 300; membership list of Jacob-Jessey Church, 1616–78 in *Trs. Bap. Hist. Soc.*, i (1908–9), 250–6.

[115] Norice, *Gospel*, sig. B2ᵛ: 'T.S.' letter; similarly, *King=Killers*, p. 38; and Fuller, *History*, x. 77.

publickly and privately as before.'[116] A certain Samuel Herring petitioned the Barebones Parliament for Jewish toleration; he was a member of the Baptist church in Swan Alley where Jessey was an over-seer.[117] Jessey corresponded with Rabbi Menasseh ben Israel, and received an autographed Latin copy of his *Hope of Israel*.[118] Jessey knew Paul Isaiah alias Eleazar Bargishai, the professional Jewish convert who appears so frequently in the records of the Baptist congregation under Saturday-Sabbatarian Peter Chamberlen. Jessey wrote a letter in 1653 to John More of that congregation on behalf of Peter Samuel alias Abraham bar Samuel, a Jewish rapist and beggar who travelled with Paul Isaiah.[119] Jessey organized a collection for the Jews of Jerusalem when the flow of alms from eastern Europe was disrupted in 1657.[120] The name of Henry Jessey appears again and again when examining the pattern of sectarian involvement with Jews and Judaizers in seventeenth-century England.

A similar pattern of involvement could be delineated for Thomas Tillam, another Baptist clergyman, from the 'False Jew' case at Hexham in 1653—when a Scottish Roman Catholic was passed off as a Jew wishing to be baptized—through Chamberlen's church, to his organization of an emigration scheme after the Restoration whereby as many as two hundred Saturday-Sabbatarian families were evacuated to the Rhineland.[121] The mysterious 'T.S.' who provides a good

[116] [Anon.], *The Life and Death of Mr. Henry Jessey* (n.p., 1671), p. 87. Other general accounts of Jessey and his church include: B. R. White, 'Henry Jessey in the Great Rebellion', *Reformation, Conformity and Dissent*, ed. R. B. Knox (London, 1977, pp. 132–53, esp. pp. 147–8; M. Tolmie, *The Triumph of the Saints* (Cambridge, 1977).

[117] *Original Letters and Papers of State Addressed to Oliver Cromwell*, ed. J. Nickolls (London, 1743), p. 100; G. F. Nuttall, *Visible Saints* (Oxford, 1957), p. 145.

[118] P. Felgenhawer, *Bonum Nuncium Israeli* (Amsterdam, 1655), p. 106; Jessey's copy of *Spes Israelis* is now Dr Williams's Lib., 3008 D 22.

[119] Bodl., MS Rawl. D 828: records of Baptist church at Lothbury Square, London, 1652–4: partially repr., *Trs. Bap. Hist. Soc.*, ii (1910–11), 132–60; cf. W. S. Samuel, 'The Strayings of Paul Isaiah in England, 1651–1656', *Trs. Jew. Hist. Soc. Eng.*, xiv (1940), 77–87; see below, p. 223.

[120] [Anon.], *Jessey*, p. 69; [H. Jessey], *An Information, Concerning The Present State Of The Jewish Nation* (London, 1658); cf. C. Roth, 'The Jews of Jerusalem in the Seventeenth Century An English Account', *Misc. Jew. Hist. Soc. Eng.*, ii (1935), 99–104.

[121] R. Howell, *Newcastle Upon Tyne and the Puritan Revolution* (Oxford, 1967), pp. 250–1, 262; E. A. Payne, 'Thomas Tillam', *Bap. Qly.*, xvii (1957–8), 61–6; J. W. Thirtle, 'A Sabbatarian Pioneer—Dr. Peter Chamberlen', *Trs. Bap. Hist. Soc.*, ii (1910–11), 9–30, 110–17; idem, 'Dr. Peter Chamberlen', *Trs. Bap. Hist. Soc.*, iii (1912–13), 176–89; W.

deal of information about Traske in a variety of different con-
texts, also reported on the activities of Baptists.[122] Rice Boye, a
member of the Jacob-Jessey church, may have published
another book by Traske after his death which has not survived.[123] Saturday-Sabbatarian Peter Chamberlen was called a
Jew in 1680; W. T. Whitley the Baptist historian believed that
Thomas Tillam actually was one.[124] The line was often extremely
difficult to draw.

III

Traske was merely the first of a long line of seventeenth-century
Judaizers and Saturday-Sabbatarians, and his example stayed
in the public mind. Followers of Traske's teaching were said
still to exist in 1715.[125] Even today, the Seventh-Day Baptists
claim him as one of their earliest antecedents.[126] The pedigree
of the Judaizing doctrine is therefore extremely interesting.
Probably the most notorious of Traske's successors was
Theophilus Brabourne, 'an obscure and ignorant School-
master' according to Hamon L'Estrange, who asserted 'the
perpetual and indispensable morality of the *Sabbath* of the
fourth Commandement.'[127] Brabourne was a native of Norwich, born in 1590 to a Puritan hosier. He worked in his father's
business for a time, but seems to have been ordained before
1628. At the end of that year he published a long *Discourse upon
the Sabbath Day* which sought to prove 'That the seaventh day
Sabbath is now still in force.' Brabourne's Saturday-
Sabbatarianism got him into trouble even before the release of
his first tract, and he explained that 'by reason of some troubles
raised up against both my selfe, and this my booke, I was

T. Whitley, 'Militant Baptists', *Trs. Bap. Hist. Soc.*, i (1908–9), 148–55; B. S. Capp, *The Fifth Monarchy Men* (London, 1972), pp. 244–5, 266. See also G. Fox, *An Answer To Thomas Tillams Book* (London, 1659) for a Quaker point of view.

[122] *Cal. S. P. Dom., 1639*, pp. 466–7: text repr. *Bap. Qly.*, xxiv (1971–2), 18–19.

[123] Norice, *Gospel*, p. 4.

[124] Bodl., MS Tanner 160, f.71ʳ: Chamberlen to Sancroft, 21 July 1680: 'I understand that I have lately been traduced to yᵉ Grace as a Jew.'; W. T. Whitley, *A History of British Baptists* (London, 1923), p. 81.

[125] [Anon.], *Dissenters and Schismaticks Expos'd* (London, 1715), p. 86.

[126] See e.g. J. L. Gamble and C. H. Greene, 'The Sabbath in the British Isles', *Seventh Day Baptists in Europe and America* (Plainfield, NJ, 1910), p. 40.

[127] [H. L'Estrange], *The Reign of King Charles* (London, 1655), p. 128.

enforced to absent my selfe, & there to dispose my work, where
I could not be present at the presse'.[128]

It was Brabourne's conviction that the fourth commandment was still in force including all of the scriptural rigours,
and that it applied to Saturday instead of to Sunday. Despite
this Judaizing interpretation, his work is signed with the
prayer, 'Thine in Christ Iesus'; Brabourne is most definitely a
Christian. To those who would say, 'this were to bringe into the
Church Iudaizme againe, and that strict rigorous observation
of the Sabbath which they used', Brabourne answered,
'Iudaizme is when obedience is yielded to a Law Ceremoniall,
but he that keepes the Sabbath day, doth it in obedience to a
Law Morall'.[129]

Unlike Traske, Brabourne was most anxious to avoid the
creation of a sectarian following. '*Let no rente be from our Church in
practise*,' he pleaded. 'How were it to be lamented . . . to see a
fewe keepe Saturday for Sabbath, and a multitude to keepe
Sunday Sabbath, what a confusion, and what an hart-burning
may it breede'. Until the time of reformation, he advised, the
best and safest procedure would be to keep Sunday 'according
to all the ordinances of the Sabbath, on the seaventh day'.[130]

In spite of the provocative nature of Brabourne's first book,
official reprisals did not begin until he published an expanded
version of his earlier work in 1632; by 1634 he was in the
Gatehouse. Brabourne freely admitted his Saturday-
Sabbatarianism before Archbishop Laud and High Commission, which pronounced him 'a Jew, a heretic and schismatic,
and adjudged him worthy to be severely punished.' Brabourne
was degraded from the ministry, excommunicated, fined
£1,000, forced to pay court expenses, and ordered to make a
public submission before his release from prison could be secured.[131]

Brabourne returned to Norwich in 1635, and probably
resumed his ministry for a time, but gave up preaching when he
received some property on the death of a brother, although one

---

[128] *Dict. Nat. Biog.*, s.v., 'Brabourne'; T. Brabourne, *A Discourse upon the Sabbath Day*
(n.p., 1628), title page, p. *4.

[129] Ibid., p. 222.

[130] Ibid., pp. 228, 238.

[131] *Cal. S. P. Dom., 1634–5*, pp. 122, 126–7, 533, 549.

critic alleged that he was simply 'weary of preaching to the walls'.[132] The relative freedom of the Commonwealth press provided him with an opportunity to spread his Saturday-Sabbatarian doctrines once again, and the fierce pamphlet war he carried on with John Collinges, another Norwich minister, indicates that his views could still provoke violent opposition.[133] After the Restoration he wrote several pamphlets dealing with liberty of conscience, while continuing to uphold the royal supremacy in religious affairs. His final tract was published on 18 March 1661, and this is the last that we hear of him.[134]

Theophilus Brabourne was most certainly not a Traskite. He was barely a Judaizer, and achieved almost a kind of respectability as a Sabbatarian supporter of a national church. Especially in later life, the strict interpretation of the fourth commandment was only one of his many concerns; he was especially worried about arbitrary suspension from the sacrament as well.[135] But the distinction between the doctrines of Traske and Brabourne seemed very fine to contemporaries: as far as they were concerned '*Theophilus Brabron* was another Teacher of this *Jewish* Doctrine.'[136] Peter Heylyn wrote that in the reign of King James, Traske followed the Jewish Sabbath 'and therewithall tooke up another *Iewish* Doctrine, about Meates and Drinkes: as in the time of our dread Soveraigne now being, *Theophilus Braborne*, grounding himselfe on the so much applauded Doctrine of the *moralitie* of the *Sabbath*; maintained, that the *Iewish Sabbath* ought to be observed'. Heylyn went on to describe their punishments, and Brabourne's recantation, of which he was satisfied, as if the two men were contemporaries. 'Of these,' he explained, 'I have here spoke together, because the ground of their Opinions, so farre as it concerned the

---

[132] *Dict. Nat. Biog.*; J. Collinges, *A New Lesson For the Indoctus Doctor* (London, 1654), p. 13.

[133] Ibid., and other pamphlets issued as follows: J. Collinges, *Responsoria ad Erratica Piscatoris* (London, 1653); idem, *Indoctus Doctor Edoctus* (London, 1654) idem, *Responsoria Bipartita* (London, 1654); T. Brabourne, *A Reply to Mr. Collings* (London, 1654); idem, *The Second Vindication* (London, 1654). See also Ley, *Sunday*, pp. 8–10, 14, 24, 29, 32, 79, 123, 148–56 and T. Shepard, *Theses Sabbaticae* (London, 1649), ii. 5, 26, 30; iii. 4 for replies to Brabourne's theories.

[134] T. Brabourne, *Of the Lawfulness of the Oath of Allegiance* (London, 1661).

[135] See e.g. Brabourne, *Reply, passim*.

[136] *King=Killers*, p. 38. John Ley called Brabourne a Jew: *Sunday*, p. 158.

Sabbath, were the very same; they onely making the conclusions, which of necessitie must follow from the former premisses'.[137]

Edward Norice was very worried by what seemed to be a resurgence of Traskism, and published two works after the founder's death which condemned his opinions and his morals. He railed against Traske's 'ingemniated adulteries' and 'tongue fornications', and his love of 'frollike, especially with that sexe, in which hee most delighted, towards whom hee used such familiarity, with his embracings . . . as they that were modest, utterly abhorred his private society'.[138] Norice believed that there had been a direct connection between Traske and Brabourne:

Whereas M[r]. *Iohn Trask* some certaine yeares since was justly censured in a High Court of this Land, for *Iudaisme*, and the dependant errours, it is so that not long after, he fell (the cause of himselfe remaining) into contrary extremities, of Evangelicall pretense, under the specious shewes and names of *Christ*, of *Faith*, of the *Gospell*, of *Ioy*, and such like alluring titles; thereunder hiding, and secretly venting many pernicious errours, to the endangering of none of the worse people, and of late is growne to a great extremitie herein.[139]

Yet by the time that Norice wrote, the sect had disappeared. Speaking of the men that Traske sent out into the country to preach his word, an observer wrote that 'three of which Apostolicall men are dead, the fourth is yet alive, but hath renounced those fooleries.' It was one of these men 'which Mr. Doctor *Gouge* helped to reduce unto the truth.'[140]

'Mary Chester, Jewess, prisoner in the Bridewell', was released from prison by High Commission at the end of 1635 or the beginning of 1636, having recanted of her errors 'in holding certain Judaical tenets touching the Sabbath and distinction of meats.' She had petitioned the court for release on 12 November 1635, and was referred to Gouge a week later, 'who took no small Pains to reduce and settle her in the right Mysteries of Faith.'[141]

Mary Chester had been converted to Traske's views by Christopher Sands, one of the Traskites who fled to the Jewish

[137] Heylyn, *History*, pp. 259–60.
[138] Norice, *Gospel*, sig. B[v], p. 3.
[139] E. Norice, *A Treatise Maintaining that Temporall Blessings are to bee sought* (London, 1636), p. 157.
[140] Norice, *Gospel*, sig. B2[r–v]: 'T.S.' letter.
[141] *Cal. S. P. Dom., 1635–6*, pp. 111, 122, 132.

community in Amsterdam. Mrs Wright, another Traskite, was
converted by Mary Chester, and later 'declar'd', that the said
Mary was as absolute against CHRIST as *Sands* himself, which was
verified by many Speeches of hers after her Apprehension'. She
remained in prison a number of years, and when she appeared
to Gouge to have given up her former errors, she was released.
Mary Chester wrote a letter to Sands before she left Bridewell
which described her conversion. 'I have had much trouble
concerning your worldly Estate,' she wrote, 'in regard of your
poor Wife and Children'. Mary advised Sands 'not to hid nor
conceal any thing from those before whom you are to come,
considering they are in God's stead in that Place.' She was still
her friend, she said, 'desiring your good as much as my own.'[142]

Some of these details are impossible to understand: perhaps
Sands's family had been left behind in England, but his life in
Amsterdam is wholly unknown after his first meeting with the
Jewish community there. At any rate, it was reported that
within a year after she had been set free, Mary Chester resumed
her former 'Judaical and Absurd' views. An account of her later
life does not exist.[143] Yet it is not wholly unreasonable to
surmise that Norice was speaking of Mary Chester when he
reported the link between the views of Traske and those of
Brabourne. She was the only one of the founders who was still
an active Judaizer, and Brabourne confessed that his principles
had been adopted from '*Sabbatarian Dogmatists*'.[144] It is possible
that Chester had some connection with Brabourne even before
she left prison and more likely afterwards. 'The Seed of the
Woman,' Mary quoted in prison, 'shall bruise the Serpent's
Head.'[145]

IV

Contemporaries were uncertain as to how one might define the
religious beliefs of men like Traske and Brabourne. Alexander
Harris, the warden of the Fleet during Traske's imprisonment
there, was not sure whether he was 'a Jewdaiser or halfe
Jewe'.[146] For despite Traske's confused devotion to the Mosaic

---

[142] *King=Killers*, pp. 41–3.

[143] Ibid., pp. 43–4.

[144] F. White, *A Treatise Of The Sabbath-Day* (3rd edn., London, 1636), sig. A3.

[145] *King=Killers*, p. 41.

[146] *Œconomy of the Fleete*, p. 47. During the interregnum, he would be likened to the
Ranters: [Anon.], *The Arraignment and Tryall . . . of the Ranters* (n.p., 1650), p. 5.

law he never wavered in his faith in Jesus Christ. Even Edward
Norice, one of Traske's most bitter critics, affirmed that Traske
believed that 'Christ Iesus is the King, Priest, and Prophet of
his Church'.[147] Traske's adventures are well-documented and
it is readily apparent that he is a Christian Judaizer rather than
a genuine Jew either by birth or religion. This is by no means
clear when dealing with the numerous isolated examples of
Jews and Judaizers that occasionally appear in the records. In
any case, the distinction between a Judaizer and a Jew was
altogether too fine for most Englishmen before the Civil War
and the beginnings of political agitation for Jewish readmission. The fact that the settled Sephardic Jewish community in
London was so secretive meant that a major part of the knowledge which most Englishmen could obtain of Judaism derived
from the controversial practices of the Judaizers and the few
Jews who suddenly appeared in the public eye.

Most of these elusive Jews and Judaizers have left very few
traces. John Foxe baptized a Spanish Jew in the parish church
of All Hallows in Lombard Street in 1578.[148] Samuel Palache, a
distinguished member of the Jewish community in Amsterdam
and envoy of the Sultan of Morocco to the States-General, was
arrested at Plymouth in 1614 on a charge of piracy against
Spanish shipping. Despite the efforts of the Spanish ambassador to have him punished, Palache was released by the
English authorities and returned to the Netherlands.[149] An
Irish fanatic named Grey murdered his son in December 1621
with the idea of procuring the restoration of the Jews by shed-
ding innocent blood.[150] A Jew named Paul Jacob was converted
by the bishop of Londonderry and then petitioned James I for a
small allowance, on the grounds that as 'the scepter is departed
from Judah . . . you onely are the true King of the Jews' and
therefore he deserved support as James's child and subject; he

---

[147] Norice, *Gospel*, p. 46.

[148] J. Foxe, *A Sermon preached at the Christening of a certaine Iew* (London, 1578). A
photograph of his *Domus Conversorum* receipt, the Latin text, and an English trans.
appear in M. Adler, *Jews of Medieval England* (London, 1939), p. 375 and plate.

[149] *Acts of the Privy Council, 1613–4*, pp. 636, 665–7, 671; *1615–16*, pp. 28, 74–5,
308–10; *Letters of John Chamberlain*, ed. McClure, i. 559–60 and similarly *Cal. S. P. Dom.,
1611–18*, p. 260; L. Abrahams, 'Two Jews Before the Privy Council in 1614–15', *Jew.
Qly. Rev.*, xiv (1901–2), 354–8; D. Abulafia-Corcos, 'Samuel Pallache and his London
Trial' (Hebrew), *Zion*, xxv (1960), 122–33.

[150] *Cal. S. P. Dom., 1619–23*, pp. 319–20.

Davidson College Library

tried a similar ploy again after the Restoration.[151] Jas.
Whitehall was imprisoned towards the end of James's reign for
preaching Judaism, and continued his Judaizing even within
his cell at Dublin Castle.[152] Sixpence was paid out at Ipswich in
1572 'for whippinge of an Jewishe man'.[153] The first coffee-
house in England was opened by 'Jacob a Jew' at Oxford in
1650: he appears to have been driven out of business when
another man described as a Jew, Cirques Jobson, opened
another one across the High Street four years later.[154] A pension of £40 per annum was awarded to 'a Jew at Cambridge' in
1625 'so long as he shall remain in his Majesty's dominions.'[155]

Other examples of Jews and Judaizers come from the provinces as well.[156] A certain Widow Constable at Brentford was
said to have bid 'Religion quite adieu, Turn'd from a Nonconformist to a Jew.'[157] Thomas Edwards, the great heresy hunter,
was reliably informed that a group of sectaries from Colchester
'went up to *London* to speak with a *Iew*' who discussed with them
their theory that an earthquake would strike England within
the month.[158] A contemporary jingle ran that 'If one affirm he
learned it of a Jew, The silly people think it must be true.'[159]
Anne Curtyn was committed to the New Prison at Clerkenwell
'for being a professed Jew and causing children to be circum-
sided'; despite the protests of the Assembly of Divines, the
secular courts released her in 1649 on the grounds that her
offense was 'merely ecclesiasticall'.[160] William Birchley had it
from Exeter in 1651 that 'divers of the Inhabitants there do
openly professe the *Jewish Opinion*, and keep *Saturday Sabbath*,

---

[151] *Cal. S. P. Dom., 1623–5*, p. 517: text repr. Adler, *Jews*, p. 376; *Cal. S. P. Dom., 1660–1*. p. 171.

[152] *Cal. S. P. Dom., 1623–5*, p. 435.

[153] Hist. MSS Comm., viii, *App. to the 9th Rep.*, i. 249b.

[154] *Life . . . of Anthony Wood*, i. 168–9; ii. 212–13. Cf. B. Lillywhite, *London Coffee Houses* (London, 1963), pp. 17, 281–2.

[155] *Cal. S. P. Dom., 1625–6*, p. 98.

[156] But note that the MS printed in W. A. Gunnell, *Sketches of Hull Celebrities* (Hull, 1876), pp. 9, 183–8, 200–4, is of doubtful authenticity.

[157] J. Taylor, *A Swarme of Sectaries* (n.p., 1641), p. 7.

[158] T. Edwards, *Gangraena* (2nd edn., London, 1646), p. 121.

[159] K. Thomas, *Religion and the Decline of Magic* (Penguin edn., Harmondsworth, 1973), p. 350.

[160] *Middlesex County Records*, ed. J. C. Jeaffreson (Middlesex County Rec. Soc., 1886–92), iii. 186–7.

Davidson College Library

performing their servile works on the Lords day, without any punishment or sequestration'.[161] One news-sheet reported a meeting of Jews in Hackney at the beginning of June 1655. They were said to be commemorating their Sabbath, all 'very clean and neat in the corner of a Garden by an house, all of them with their faces towards the East; Their Minister formost, and the rest all behind him.'[162]

The open Jews and Judaizers of this period are interesting in their own right, but they are important here in that they provided the major medium for the transmission of a (usually garbled) account of Jewish beliefs. The very appearance of a Jew at the occasional public conversion went some way towards dispelling the notion, reinforced by church sculpture and portraits, that all Jews had horns. The shrines of 'Little' St. Hugh of Lincoln and St. William of Norwich were destroyed during the Reformation, and although their memories continued to be passed on in popular ballads, official discouragement of saints and miracles helped to weaken these potent rallying-points against Jews.[163] The honoured Christian Hebraists of seventeenth-century England such as Edward Pococke and John Lightfoot certainly advanced Hebrew scholarship, and provided the scholarly background for those who wanted it, but the Judaizers and, as we shall see, notorious millenarians, polemical language theorists, and religious tolerationists pushed the Jewish question into a prominent position in the political arena.

When Brabourne transmitted Judaizing ideas through the interregnum, the worst he suffered was insults in the pamphlets of fellow-preacher John Collinges; under Charles he had been imprisoned. Mary Chester, one of Brabourne's fellow-prisoners, was a Traskite. The Saturday-Sabbatarian churches of the interregnum, at Mill Yard (and later at Bell Lane) in London, at Natton in Gloucestershire, at Burton-on-Trent (Derbyshire), at Leominster in Herefordshire, at Hexham in Northumberland, and at Dorchester and Colchester, are all

---

[161] W. Birchley, *The Christian Moderator* (2nd edn., London, 1652), p. 21.

[162] *Perfect Proceedings of State-Affaires*, 297 (31 May–7 June 1655), p. 4714; similarly, *The Weekly Intelligencer* (5–12 June 1655), p. 19.

[163] Cf. J. Parkes, 'Jewish–Christian Relations in England' in *Three Centuries*, ed. Lipman, p. 152.

connected through Jessey, Tillam, Chamberlen, and the Jews and Judaizers who clustered around them.[164]

Before John Traske appeared in London in 1617, Jews—as opposed to ancient Israelites—hardly came up in discussion. The debate over his beliefs and activities provided virtually the first public forum in over three centuries for a discussion on the literal interpretation of the Mosaic law and the nature of contemporary Christian–Jewish relations. Jacobean England seemed to be an inhospitable place for Judaizing ideas to take root; both Church and State fought bitterly against them. Yet by the time that Menasseh ben Israel was invited to England forty years later as the ambassador of the Jewish nation, the situation had improved radically. Traske's spiritual descendants had come of age: Rabbi Menasseh ben Israel became the hero of English society as the role that the Jews were expected to play in seventeenth-century England became a vital contemporary issue.

Hobbes was worried that too much Sabbatarian discussion would 'put such thoughts into the heads of vulgar people as will confer little to their good life. For when they see one of the ten commandments to be *jus humanum* merely (as it must be, if the church can alter it) they will hope also that the other nine may be so too. For every man hitherto did believe that the ten commandments were the moral, that is an eternal, law.'[165] Yet at the same time, men like Traske and his disciples, and the many who followed his career, began to see that the Old Testament recorded the voice of the Lord speaking directly to Englishmen as well as to Jews, and their thoughts inevitably turned to that 'anciently beloved people of God, the seed of *Abraham, Isaac* and *Jacob*'.[166]

[164] Gamble and Greene, 'Sabbath', pp. 21–115; W. T. Whitley, 'Seventh Day Baptists in England', *Bap. Qly.*, xii (1946–8), 252–8; E. A. Payne, 'More about the Sabbatarian Baptists', *Bap. Qly.*, xiv (1951–2), 161–6; see above, p. 33 n. 121.

[165] Quoted in Hill, *Society*, p. 180.

[166] M. Cary, *The Little Horns Doom* (London, 1651), p. 161.

2

BABEL REVERS'D:

The Search for a Universal Language and the Glorification of Hebrew

Englishmen were beginning to discover by the seventeenth century that Latin was no longer the international language that it once had been. When Richard Flecknoe the Papist poet travelled across Europe, he reported that '*Latine* and *English* (to tell you true) they only served me to stop holes with'. Flecknoe discovered that 'the *English* Language out of our Dominions [was] like our *English* money . . . none will take it of your hands.' Latin, even in conversation with clerics, only 'serves to *interlard* other Languages, than to make an intire meal of discourse'.[1] With the decline of Latin, mankind was as unfortunate as it had been immediately after the Confusion at Babel, when 'the Lord did there confound the language of all the earth'. The goal, as John Webster put it, was to find a 'potent means . . . to have repaired the ruines of *Babell*'.[2] This quest, at first glance far removed from the efforts of Menasseh ben Israel and the Whitehall Conference, was nevertheless to prove enormously influential in the readmission of the Jews to England.

Various schemes were offered throughout the seventeenth century for a universal language which would restore the linguistic unity that mankind had enjoyed before Babel. The first reports of the Chinese character were just beginning to be digested in Europe, and early linguistic planners hoped to

---

[1] R. Fleckno, *A Relation Of ten Years Travells* (London, 1656), p. 105.
[2] Gen. 11:9; J. Webster, *Academiarum Examen* (London, 1654), p. 25.

provide a system of English hieroglyphs or numerical codes' which could facilitate international communication in the same way. When these schemes proved to be impractical, the planners turned towards the idea of reorganizing communication completely to provide a language which would be not only universal, but also 'philosophical', that is, a perfect mirror of reality. The seventeenth-century obsession with 'things' rather than 'words', a cast of thought which produced not only the stark plainness of the Puritan prose style, but also the extreme Nominalist philosophy of a man like Hobbes, reached its high point with John Wilkins's *Essay Towards a Real Character, And a Philosophical Language*, published in 1668. Wilkins, one of the founders of the Royal Society, the Cromwellian warden of Wadham and later the bishop of Chester, hoped that he could persuade scholars across Europe to adopt his plan, which might not only replace Latin as an international means of communication, but would also go one step further and eliminate the ambiguity which necessarily derives from imprecise words, with great benefit to both science and philosophy.

The evolution of these universal language schemes has long been of interest to philologists and scholars of English literature, intent on seeking the origins of the distinctive English prose style of the mid-seventeenth century. Concentrating on origins, they have become embroiled in debating whether Francis Bacon or Jan Amos Comenius the Czech reformer deserves to be called the father of the philosophical language. Yet for seventeenth-century Englishmen, the linguistic state of mankind before Babel was more than a convenient explanatory myth. They hoped to recover all aspects of the original language, not only its universality. The language of mankind before Babel, the very tongue that Adam spoke in the Garden of Eden before the Fall, was endowed with divine and supernatural qualities. Words and things were perfectly congruent in the Garden. 'In the beginning was the Word, and the Word was with God, and the Word was God': all things were created when God spoke.[3] By the mid-seventeenth century, after much discussion, most Englishmen agreed that God spoke Hebrew.

This glorification of Hebrew in the era of the Whitehall

---

[3] John 1:1.

Conference was to be of momentous importance towards the readmission of the Jews to England. For ordinary Bible-readers, Hebrew was the language of the Old Testament which recorded the word of God. For men who thought more deeply about the nature of speech, Hebrew provided a model for a reformed language because it was a remnant of the Adamic tongue in which words perfectly represented things. Whether or not Comenius deserves to be known as the father of artificial languages, he and his followers in England were certainly at the forefront of the language planners, and were also devotees of Christian kabbalah. The supernatural qualities of the Hebrew language, the search for the original *lingua humana*, and the development of a philosophical language were linked in their minds. And it was this group, especially Samuel Hartlib and John Dury, which engineered the mission of Menasseh ben Israel to England. Philo-Hebraism, not only philo-semitism, was at its height at the time of the Whitehall Conference, and the advocates of Jewish readmission were able to take advantage of these sentiments to promote their cause.

I

'After the fall of *Adam*,' wrote John Wilkins, 'there were two general curses inflicted on Mankinde: The one upon their *labours*; the other upon their *language*.' This second curse seemed to promise an easier solution than the first, for as Wilkins believed, 'the confusion at *Babel* might this way have been remedied, if every one could have expressed his own meaning by the same kinde of Character.'[4] Latin had lost its position as virtually the sole written European language of scholarship by the beginning of the seventeenth century. Wilkins and others argued that all branches of learning and inquiry would benefit from a kind of international sign-language, a system whereby scholars throughout the world could read their own tongue from a single set of characters.

This conception of a 'real character' of 'radical' or 'primitive' basic words, in large measure derived from the first detailed reports of the Chinese language which were beginning to reach

---

[4] I. W[ilkins], *Mercury* (London, 1641), pp. 105–6.

the Western world. The earliest account was that of the Augustinian friar Juan Gonzalez de Mendoza, which was translated into English by Robert Parke and published in 1588. More influential were the journals of Matteo Ricci, the Italian missionary who founded the Jesuit mission in Peking. Nichola Trigault published Ricci's manuscript at the beginning of the seventeenth century, which provided the best account of Chinese until the work of his fellow Jesuit Athanasius Kircher over fifty years later.[5]

Seventeenth-century English language reformers usually credited Francis Bacon with their initial inspiration, and the influence of the Chinese model is apparent even in his early speculations. We understand, he wrote, 'that it is the use of China and the kingdoms of the high Levant to write in Characters Real, which express neither letters nor words in gross, but Things or Notions'. The advantage of this system was that 'countries and provinces, which understand not one another's language, can nevertheless read one another's writings'. Such a means of international communication would be of immediate and obvious advantage, although Bacon did recognize that it would entail 'a vast multitude of characters; as many, I suppose, as radical words.'[6]

In spite of these daunting difficulties, English language projectors soon began to formulate schemes of new-model ideograms towards a 'real character', always giving due credit to 'our great Advancer of Learning'.[7] A fair number of universal writing and language systems began to circulate among the learned of England and France: some inventors tinkered with Arabic numerals, others with alchemical symbols or signs of the zodiac. Nevertheless, it was not until Francis Lodwick pub-

[5] J. Gonzalez de Mendoza, *Historia Delas Cosas . . . Del gran Reyno dela China* (Roma, 1585); idem, *The Historie of the great and mightie kingdome of China . . . Translated . . . by R. Parke* (London, 1588), also ed. G. T. Staunton (Hakluyt Soc., 1st ser., xiv–xv, 1853); *China in the Sixteenth Century: the journals of Matthew Ricci*, trans. L. J. Gallagher (New York, 1953), being the compilation by Trigault. For the relationship between Chinese and the universal language see W. W. Appleton, *A Cycle of Cathay* (New York, 1951), cap. ii; and P. Cornelius, *Languages in Seventeenth- and Early Eighteenth-Century Imaginary Voyages* (Geneva, 1965), *caps*. ii and iv; and H. N. Davies, 'Bishop Godwin's "Lunatique Language"', *Jnl. Warb. Ctld, Inst.*, xxx (1967), 296–316.

[6] F. Bacon, *Works*, ed. J. Spedding, *et al.* (London, 1857–9), iii. 399–401.

[7] H. Edmundson, *Lingua Linguarum The Naturall Language* (London, 1655), sig. f3ʳ.

lished his *Common Writing* in 1647 that details were spelled out.[8] Lodwick was the English-born son of Protestant refugees from the Continent, a London merchant who later became a fellow of the Royal Society. Lodwick was brought up in the Dutch parish of Austin Friars, London, and his linguistic ideas were no doubt stimulated by the polyglot atmosphere there, as well as by the fact that he had a French mother and a Dutch father.[9] This earliest effort towards a 'real character' was followed by another one from Lodwick himself in 1652, which was modified and improved by Cave Beck, George Dalgarno, and Sir Thomas Urquhart.[10]

Despite all good intentions, however, these early efforts seemed to bear out Bacon's warning: they were cumbersome, idiosyncratic rather than universal, and very difficult to learn, let alone to practise. Cave Beck, for example, claimed that dexterity with his universal character could be 'Attained in two Hours space, Observing the Grammatical Directions.' Yet his bulky list of radical words and numerical codes gives the lie to this promise: he even institutes two separate universal words for 'a bee' and 'a humming bee'.[11] Such deficiencies were noticed by contemporaries. Elias Ashmole thought at first that a universal character would not only 'much sweeten the *Curse* of *Babels* Confusion' but would also save the time and expense of translation. Ashmole believed that such a system was within man's reach, and that the language planners might 'draw some helps from the *Egyptian Hieroglyphicks, Symbols, Musical Notes, Stenography, Algebra*, &c.' There were also signs for the planets, metals, minerals, weights, and so on, 'all which have the power of *Letters*, and run currant in the *Vnderstanding of every Language*'. Yet despite this optimism, Ashmole accepted that the main problem with such inventions would be the failure to guard that

[8] F. Lodowyck, *A Common Writing* (n.p., '1646'), repr. below.

[9] F. Lodwick, *Works*, ed. V. Salmon (London, 1972), pp. 3–7.

[10] F. Lodowyck, *The Ground Work* (n.p., 1652), repr. above; C. Beck, *The Universal Character* (London, 1657); G. Dalgarno, *Ars Signorum* (London, 1661); T. Urquhart, *The Discovery of A most exquisite Jewel* (London, 1652); idem, *Logopandecteision* (London, 1653). Urquhart's linguistic plans were often more satirical than serious: cf. his *Works* (Edinburgh, 1834). See J. R. Knowlson, 'The Idea of Gesture as a Universal Language in the XVIIth and XVIIIth Centuries', *Jnl. Hist. Ideas*, xxvi (1965), 495–508; and the checklist in idem, *Universal language schemes* (Toronto and Buffalo, 1975), pp. 224–32.

[11] Beck, *Character*, title page, sig. D7v.

'the useful *radical words*, if numbred, would not swell beyond our *Memories* fathom'.[12] Robert Boyle began with high hopes as well. 'If the design of *the Real Character* take effect,' he wrote to Samuel Hartlib, 'it will in good part make amends to mankind for what their pride lost them at the tower of *Babel*.' A fortnight later, however, after having read Lodwick's first pamphlet, he was worried that its dictionary did not 'over-swell and disease it of a tympany'. His fears were not entirely suppressed, he wrote, 'lest that this way of saving the labour of learning a language should prove like a new device, I have lately seen, to perform all the operations of arithmetic by the help of an instrument, where I found it much more difficult to learn the uses of the instrument, than the rules of the art.'[13]

For the universal or real character was meant to be only a tool towards the general amelioration of the linguistic diversity of mankind. The point of the system, explained Joseph Waite, was to have 'Tongues in Brief; *Babel* revers'd'. A secondary advantage of the universal character, Nathaniel Smart pointed out, was 'that divers Languages no longer may, Upon our trading such Embargoes lay'.[14] Without a common language, thought Oxford preacher William Whately, mankind would be like 'the builders of *Babel* in an heape as it were'.[15] These were glorious hopes which were disappointed by the early language reformers.

At some point, the projectors came to see that what they were really working on was a sort of glorified shorthand which almost created more problems than it solved. Early efforts in 'brachygraphy' (shorthand), cryptography and in the development of an international language were still confusingly lumped together. John Wilkins, who would later produce the most comprehensive plan for a universal language, also published the first English textbook on cryptography on the eve of the Civil War.[16] George Dalgarno initially thought of his *ars*

[12] [E. Ashmole], *Fasciculus Chemicus* (London, 1650), sigs. A7^{r-v}.

[13] T. Birch, *Life of . . . Boyle* (London, 1744), pp. 73, 76: 19 Mar. and 8 Apr. 1647.

[14] In Beck, *Character*, sigs. A5^v, A6^r.

[15] W. Whately, *Prototypes* (London, 1640), p. 79.

[16] W[ilkins], *Mercvry, passim*; E. Sams and J. Moore, 'Cryptanalysis and historical research', *Times Lit. Supp.*, 4 Mar. 1977, p. 253.

signorum as a type of shorthand.[17] Timothe Bright promised that his *Characterie*, the first English system of shorthand, would be 'shorte, swifte, *and secrete*'.[18] This conceptual confusion inhibited efforts towards a universal language in the initial stages, and it was not until after the Restoration that these various disciplines were clearly differentiated.

Nevertheless, language planners were beginning to realize by the 1640s that they were on the wrong track. The Chinese language did enable speakers of different dialects to communicate with one another, even if they could not engage in conversation, and an English system of ideograms might be useful in the same way. When actual attempts at the formulation of such a character failed, the projectors, instead of losing hope, became much more ambitious. To return to the linguistic state of mankind before Babel was surely desirable, but might it not be even more profitable to return to that happy condition of language before the Fall itself, when there was a one-to-one relationship between words and things, when language perfectly expressed man's thoughts? This shift in emphasis from a universal but flawed language to a universal 'philosophical' language became most obvious during the years immediately before the Civil War, and it is for this reason that some scholars have emphasized the influence of Comenius, and have linked this change with his visit to England in 1641–2. In any case, the arguments of recent secondary works have tended to shift rather too quickly from humble men like Cave Beck the linguist–vicar and George Dalgarno the Oxford school-master to Leibniz, Herder, the symbolic logicians and the logical positivists. Surely it is a distortion to begin with modern linguistic philosophy and work backwards, or even to start with the *Philosophischen Schriften* and look for parallels in earlier writings.

In mid-seventeenth century England, the essential points of reference could be found in Scripture, and if we are to understand the quest for the universal philosophical language in the terms of the projectors themselves, we need to come back to the

---

[17] R. Plot, *The Natural History of Oxford-Shire* (Oxford, 1677), p. 282.
[18] T. Bright, *Characterie* (London, 1588), title-p.; see also W. J. Carlton, *Timothe Bright* (London, 1911), pp. 77–108; and P. Friedrich, *Timothe Brights Characterie entwicklungsgeschichtlich und kritisch betrachtet* (Leipzig, 1914).

essential verses in Genesis which were cited in nearly all early
modern linguistic works:

And out of the ground the LORD God formed every beast of the field, and every
fowl of the air; and brought *them* unto Adam to see what he would call them:
and whatsoever Adam called every living creature, that *was* the name thereof.
And Adam gave names to all cattle, and to the fowl of the air, and to every
beast of the field[19]

For early modern Englishmen, the tags which Adam gave to
God's creatures were not mere arbitrary sounds. 'He came into
the World a Philosopher,' explained churchman Robert South,
'which sufficiently appeared by his writing the Nature of things
upon their Names: he could view Essences in themselves, and
read Forms without the comment of their respective Properties'.[20] According to Joshua Sylvester the poet and translator,
Adam was given 'power (as Master) to impose Fit sense-full
Names'.[21]

Most scholars believed that the names which Adam gave to
the creatures expressed in some way their essential natures, so
that naming was equivalent to knowing. This model condition
prevailed until the expulsion from the Garden of Eden, when
man began worldly life with a curse both upon his labours and
upon his language. It would be 'too-too happy!' lamented
Sylvester, 'had that fall of thine Not cancell'd so the Character
divine.' John Donne believed that 'names are to instruct us,
and express natures and essences. This *Adam* was able to do.'[22]
Theophilus Gale, formerly of Magdalen College, Oxford, noted
that we can no longer 'give *names* exactly suited to the natures of
things, as *Adam* before them did.'[23] Sir Kenelm Digby, one of
the founders of the Royal Society, and Thomas White, his
Catholic friend, thought that Adam could not have understood
God's prohibition against the Tree of Knowledge nor could he
have tended the Garden of Eden had he not understood the
essential qualities of plants. 'Lastly,' explain Digby and White,
'since 'tis expressely said of the Beast and Birds, that, by only

---

[19] Gen. 2: 19–20.
[20] R. South, *A Sermon Preached At . . . St. Paul, Novemb. 9. 1662* (London, 1663), p. 11.
[21] J. Sylvester, *Du Bartas His Diuine Weekes* (London, 1641), p. 57.
[22] Ibid.; J. Donne, *Essays in Divinity*, ed. E. M. Simpson (Oxford, 1952), p. 23: written
about 1615; first pub. 1651.
[23] T. Gale, *The Covrt Of The Gentiles* (Oxford, 1669–77), ii. 7.

seeing them, he throughly saw into their nature, . . . 'tis most certain that the names were fitted to the nature of things, and consequently, were impos'd upon the knowledge of them'.[24]

These were all commonplace views throughout the seventeenth century and were held by Francis Bacon as well, at the very outset of the universal language discussion. The 'first acts which man performed in Paradise,' he had written, 'consisted of the two summary parts of knowledge; the view of creatures, and the imposition of names.' Bacon praised 'that pure and uncorrupted natural knowledge whereby Adam gave names to the creatures according to their propriety'.[25] Milton would make exactly the same point. His Adam talks of how he 'nam'd them, as they pass'd, and understood Thir Nature, with such knowledge God endu'd My sudden apprehension'. 'Moreover', he wrote less poetically, 'he could not have given names to the animals in that extempore way, without very great intelligence'.[26]

The significance of the episode in Genesis formed a part of the Webster–Ward educational debate as well. 'I cannot but conceive,' John Webster argued, 'that *Adam* did understand both their internal and external signatures, and that the imposition of their names was adaequately agreeing with their natures: otherwise it could not univocally and truely be said to be their names'. For there was an exact correspondence between words and things before the Fall, and if Adam's names did 'not exactly agree in all things, then there is a difference and disparity between them, and in that incongruity lies error and falshood'. This was an impossible assumption, and such an assertion had wide implications. As Webster explained, if

there is not absolute congruency betwixt the notion and and the thing, the intellect and the thing understood, and so it is no longer verity, but a ly, and falsity. And therefore if *Adam* did not truly see into, and understand their intrinsecall natures, then had his intellect false notions of them, and so he

---

[24] K. Digby and T. White, *Peripateticall Institutions* (London, 1656), p. 375.

[25] Bacon, *Works*, iii. 296; iv. 20.

[26] J. Milton, *Complete Poems and Major Prose*, ed. M. Y. Hughes (New York, 1957), pp. 371 (*Par. Lost* viii. 352–4); *Complete Prose Works of John Milton*, ed. D. M. Wolfe, *et al.* (New Haven, 1953–   ), vi. 324 (*Chr. Doc.*, bk. i, *cap.* vii); cf. ii. 602. (*Tetrachordon*). See also S. E. Fish, *Surprised By Sin* (Berkeley and London, 1971), pp. 107–30.

imposed lying names upon them, and then the text would be false too, which avers that what he called them was their names.[27]

When Seth Ward made his anonymous critique of Webster's examination, he denounced his discussion of the language of Adam as 'passing the bounds of sence and reason'. The Adamic language which Webster described would be a 'naturall Language, and would afford that which the *Cabalists* and *Rosycrucians* have vainely sought for in the Hebrew'.[28] This mystical point of view may not have been much to Ward's liking, but it was shared by most of the language projectors. The 'dictates of right reason and Art,' Dalgarno claimed, 'certainly have not been followed in the primary Institution of any language unless it be of the Hebrew alone'.[29] The implication here is that there is an intrinsic connection if not an identity between the perfect language which Adam and Eve spoke in the Garden of Eden and modern-day Hebrew. Yet in spite of the fact that Hebrew is the language of the Old Testament, this assertion was a source of continuing scholarly controversy across early modern Europe and helped to determine attitudes towards the Jews and their holy language.

II

Languages, explained Milton, 'both that first one which Adam spoke in Eden, and those varied ones also possibly derived from the first, which the builders of the tower of Babel suddenly received, are without doubt divinely given.'[30] Milton's careful study of both Christian and Jewish sources left him unsure whether some vestiges of the builders' language had survived the Confusion. The principal problem was that the Bible makes no mention of the Hebrew language at all. The closest approach to an identification is Isaiah's reference to 'the language of Canaan'.[31] But it did seem self-evident to Milton that

---

[27] Webster, *Academiarum*, pp. 29–30.

[28] [S. Ward and J. Wilkins], *Vindiciae Academiarum* (Oxford, 1654), p. 22. For a fuller discussion of the Webster–Ward–Wilkins debate and repr. of the principal pamphlets, see A. G. Debus, *Science and Education in the Seventeenth Century* (London and New York, 1970).

[29] G. Dalgarno, *Didascalocophus* (Oxford, 1680), p. 113.

[30] J. Milton, *Works*, ed. F. A. Patterson, *et al.* (New York, 1931–40), xi. 220–1 (*Art of Logic*, bk. i, *cap.* xxiv).

[31] Isaiah 19:18.

until that great Confusion mankind enjoyed linguistic unity in the Adamic vernacular. These were hardly controversial viewpoints: Milton's bare statement expressed the few notions of language and the results of Babel which were untainted by doubt in early modern Europe.

The nature of language before Babel, and the relationship between this Adamic speech and contemporary dialects, was a great intellectual problem during the half-century before Jewish resettlement. If, as many scholars maintained, Adam spoke the same Hebrew tongue as modern Jews, then they became the guardians of the Word by which God created the universe. This supernatural, divine glorification of the Hebrew language provided a much more dynamic and powerful motivating force than the simple revival of Semitic studies in early modern England. The outcome of this discussion would in large measure help to determine the English attitude towards the Jews and the millennial role they would be expected to play.

Most scholars found it difficult to believe, as John Webb the architect put it, 'that the language spoke by our first Parents, admitted any whatever alteration either in the Form or Dialect and pronunciation thereof, before the *Confusion of Tongues* at *Babel*'. This original language, he said, was called '*Lingua humana*, the *Humane Tongue*.'[32] Until the sixteenth century, most Western thinkers assumed that this first language was Hebrew. This was the belief of Isidore of Seville in the seventh century, and of Dante seven hundred years later.[33] Among the most frequently cited classical sources in these discussions was Plato's *Cratylus*, which is concerned with the nature and origin of languages, but provides little help towards the identification of the *lingua humana*. Socrates believed that 'words should as far as possible resemble things . . . if we could always, or almost always, use likenesses which are perfectly appropriate, this

---

[32] J. Webb, *An Historical Essay* (London, 1669), pp. 16–17.
[33] W. S. Allen, 'Ancient Ideas on the Origin and Development of Language', *Trans. Philol. Soc.*, *1948*, 35–60. The classic work on this subject is A. Borst, *Der Turmbau von Babel* (Stuttgart, 1957–63), iii/1. See also L. Courturat and L. Leau, *Histoire de la langue universelle* (Paris, 1903) and L. Formigari, *Linguistica ed empirismo nel Seicento inglese* (Bari, 1970). For the medieval Nominalists, Hobbes, and a discussion of the quest for a 'universal grammar' see G. A. Padley, *Grammatical Theory in Western Europe 1500–1700* (Cambridge, 1976), pp. 141–3, 154–209.

would be the most perfect state of language'.[34] These were the
goals of the philosophical language planners, but they were also
interested in further details concerning the perfect state of
language in the Garden of Eden. Saint Augustine helped to
establish this, with his assertion that 'the language that, not
without good reason, is believed to have served previously as the
common speech of all mankind was thereafter called Hebrew'.[35]

Yet the rival testimony that most captured the imagination
of early modern Europeans was provided by Herodotus in his
famous story of Psammetichus, king of Egypt, who 'took two
newborn children of common men and gave them to a shepherd
to bring up among his flocks. He gave charge that none should
speak any word in their hearing.' Psammetichus wanted 'to
hear what speech would first break from the children'. They
said nothing for two years, but 'one day as he opened the door
and entered both the children ran to him stretching out their
hands and calling "Bekos."' The king made enquiries and
discovered that 'Bekos' was the Phrygian word signifying
bread. 'Reasoning from this fact,' Herodotus concludes, 'the
Egyptians confessed that the Phrygians were older than they.'[36]

The experiment of Psammetichus was for most early modern
English scholars important but not conclusive empirical evidence, in part because it seemed to disprove the Hebraic origin
of language. Samuel Purchas the great cataloguer of religions
thought that the children's utterance was simply 'the voice that
they had heard of their nurses the Goats'. Purchas cited a
similar experiment with thirty children, in which the aim was
to discover which 'Religion whereto they should addict themselues. But neither could they euer speake', let alone follow a
particular rite.[37] Joshua Sylvester expressed the same point in
verse:

> Fools which perceiv'd not, that the bleating flocks
> W^{ch} powl'd the neighbour Mountains motly locks
> Had taught this tearm, and that no tearms of *Rome*,
> *Greece, Egypt, England, France, Troy, Jewry*, come,
> Come born with us: but every Countries tongue
> Is learnt by much use, and frequenting long.[38]

[34] *The Dialogues of Plato*, trans. B. Jowett (3rd edn., Oxford, 1892), i. 382–3.
[35] Augustine, *The City of God*, xvi. 11 (ed. Sanford and Green, v. 61, 63).
[36] Herodotus, ii. 2 (ed. Godley, i. 275, 277).
[37] S. Purchas, *Pvrchas his Pilgrimage* (2nd edn., London, 1614), p. 46.
[38] Sylvester, *Du Bartas*, p. 122.

An English report of the 'conferences of the French virtuosi' included a note that 'Women have such a facility of speaking, that if two Children especially of different sexes were bred up together, 'tis likely the female would speak first . . . Which was the reason of the miscarriage of the King of *Egypts* trial, which he made only with Boys.'[39] Still, despite these doubts, this text from Herodotus made a great impression on the language planners. Nathaniel Smart, in his introductory poem to Cave Beck's scheme for a universal character, even said that the children's words were prophetic, as if to say 'to retrive again One common speech should be thy work O *Beck*'.[40]

Nevertheless, there was one very important piece of evidence which softened the impact of this story from Herodotus, and with which all scholars eventually had to come to terms. All of the proper names in Genesis have a particular meaning in Hebrew well suited to that individual. This simple fact in itself often provided convincing proof that Hebrew was the Adamic language. As Sylvester explained:

> *Adam* (meaneth) made of clay: his wife
> *Eva* (translated signifieth life:
> *Cain* first begot, *Abel*, as vain, and *Seth*
> Put in his place; and he that, underneath
> The generall Deluge, saw the World distrest,
> In true interpretation, foundeth Rest.

On the basis of this evidence, Sylvester concluded that 'Gods ancient vvill vvas first enrowled by an *Hebrew* quill'.[41]

But this standard method of verification could be applied in more imaginative ways. The most extreme and influential among the dissenters from the Hebraic orthodoxy was Johannes Goropius Becanus, the Netherlandish physician and linguist. Goropius Becanus found Dutch equivalents for all of the proper names in Genesis, with the aim of establishing his own mother tongue as the *lingua humana*.[42] The novel and unscriptural hypothesis that Adam spoke Dutch in Paradise provoked

---

[39] G. Havers and J. Davies, *Another Collection Of Philosophical Conferences* (London, 1665), p. 215.

[40] Beck, *Character*, sig. A5ᵛ.

[41] Sylvester, *Du Bartas*, p. 122.

[42] J. Goropius Becanus, *Origines Antwerpianae* (Antwerp, 1569), esp. pp. 539–51; A. Williams, *The Common Expositor* (Chapel Hill, 1948), p. 229.

great scholarly mirth across Europe, and in England as well.
Samuel Purchas was merciless:

Goropius by a few Dutch Etymologies grew into conceit, and would haue the
world beleeue him that Dutch was the first language; which if it were, we
English should raigne with them as a Colonie of that Dutch Citie, a streame
from that fountaine, by commerce and conquests since manifoldly mixed. But
his euidence is too weake, his authoritie too new.[43]

Nevertheless, Goropius Becanus did find some supporters, or
at least some sympathizers. His fellow-countryman, Abraham
Mylius, although a proponent of the Hebraic origin of language, saw much truth in his theories, and provided several
additional arguments.[44] The work of Goropius Becanus was
carried forward in the next generation by Adrian van Schriek
(Schriekius) who not only posited Dutch as the *lingua humana*,
but also sought to prove that Celtic derived from Hebrew, a
point which was developed by Samuel Bochart and Pierre
Borel.[45]

The Dutch challenge to Hebrew for the honour of being the
Adamic vernacular was introduced into England by Richard
Rowlands, the eccentric Roman Catholic student of Anglo-
Saxon from Christ Church, Oxford. Rowlands was London-
born, a cooper's son, but when he found himself barred by
religion from taking his degree, he emigrated to the Low Countries, whence his grandfather had come, and adopted the original family name of Verstegan. Richard Verstegan became a
printer in Antwerp, corresponded with Sir Robert Cotton, and
even managed to procure an interview with Philip II in 1595.[46]
Verstegan was very sympathetic to this new theory, and began
to make enquiries. 'In conference one day with *Abraham Ortelius*
(who had bin acquainted with *Becanus*)', he recounted,

I asked him yf hee thought that *Becanus* himself beeing so learned as hee was,
did in deed belieue this language to bee the first of all languages of the world,
to wit, that which was spoke by *Adam*: he told mee that hee verely thought

---

    [43] Purchas, *Pilgrimage*, p. 46.
    [44] G. J. Metcalf, 'Abraham Mylius on Historical Linguistics', *Proc. Mod. Lang. Assoc.*,
lxviii (1953), 535–54.
    [45] G. Dottin, *La Langue Gauloise* (Paris, 1920), pp. 6–7; V. Tourneur, *Esquisse d'une
histoire des études celtiques* (Liège, 1905), pp. 191, 195, 197; G. Bonfante, 'Ideas on the
Kinship of the European Languages from 1200 to 1800', *Jnl. Wrld. Hist.*, i (1953–4),
678–99, esp. pp. 685ff.
    [46] *Dict. Nat. Biog.*, *s.v.* 'Rowlands'.

Becanus did so belieue: and added further, that many learned men might peraduenture laugh at that which hee had written, but that none would bee able to confute it

Whereby, Verstegan concluded, 'I gessed that *Ortelius* did much enclyne vnto *Becanus*'. That Abraham Oertel, the great sixteenth-century Flemish geographer whose atlas was a standard work, should be sympathetic to the idea that Dutch had been spoken in the Garden of Eden, was a powerful recommendation. Verstegan himself rehearsed the etymologies of Goropius Becanus, and concluded that the Dutch language 'is able to yeild as fit and proper significations for these moste ancient names, as the very Hebrew it self'. If it was not absolutely clear that Dutch was the Adamic language, then surely 'it cannot bee denied to bee one of the moste ancientest of the world.'[47]

Verstegan's work alone lacked the ability to establish the antiquity of Dutch. Most Englishmen, like Samuel Butler, found it difficult to believe that when Eve was in the Garden 'the Devil tempted her By a *high Dutch* Interpreter'.[48] In any case, other languages besides Dutch had supporters who put them forward as rivals to Hebrew. In Spain, John Huarte argued that the 'frantike persons speaking of Latine, without that he euer learned the same in his health time' implied not only 'the consonance which the Latin toong holds with the reasonable soule' but quite possibly the identity or at least equivalence with the language Adam used to name the animals.[49] The French royal physician Jourdain Guibelet devoted a long work simply to the refutation of Huarte's book 'où il remet ceste vieille dispute sur le bureau, si les langues sont de l'inuention des hommes, ou de l'institution de la nature'. Guibelet thought that Huarte's claim for Latin was nonsense, but did not agree with those who thought that if Psammetichus

---

[47] R. Verstegan, *A Restitution of Decayed Intelligence* (Antwerp, 1605), sigs. + +^{r-v}; pp. 190–3: a second edn. appeared at London 35 years after his death, in 1655.

[48] S. Butler, *Hudibras*, ed. J. Wilders (Oxford, 1967), p. 6. See also, for example, Ben Jonson's *Alchemist* (II. i. 84–6):

> Surley: 'Did ADAM write, sir, in high-*Dutch*?'
> Epicure Mammon: 'He did: Which proues it was the primitiue tongue.'

(*Ben Jonson*, ed. C. H. Herford and Evelyn and Percy Simpson [Oxford, 1925–52], v. 317; x. 71).

[49] J. Huarte, *Examen de Jngenios* (London, 1594), pp. 46–7.

had performed his experiment properly, each child would have spoke Hebrew. 'L'esprit de l'homme au commencement de la vie est cõme vne carte blanche,' he wrote; human beings brought up in such a manner would be 'sans doute en fins de temps muets, comme poissons, & plus stupides qu'vn rocher . . . & sans cognoissance d'aucune langue, Phrygienne ou autre, quelques fables que l'on ait apporté au contraire.'[50]

Among these 'fables' were further claims for other languages, as a great debate concerning the identity of the *lingua humana* raged on the Continent. Guillaume Postel, the famous sixteenth-century French linguist and translator, rejected the story from Herodotus, and claimed Hebrew as the original language, despite some doubts. Conrad Gesner the Swiss naturalist defended Hebrew as well, as did most scholars in sixteenth-century Europe. Other great figures of early linguistics did not agree. Wolfgang Lazius collected evidence that the French, Spanish, and Italians once spoke German dialects in the remote past. Athanasius Kircher, the German Jesuit scholar, not only conducted research into the Chinese language, but also sought to prove that German is a dialect of Hebrew spoken by Ashkenaz the son of Gomer, the ancestor of the Teutonic race. Nicholas Serarius reported that Samaritan was in fact older than Hebrew, and was fiercely attacked by Kircher and by Brian Walton, the editor of the Polyglot Bible. Perhaps most importantly, the works of Scaliger were being disseminated and digested by Edward Brerewood and others, along with his classification of the European languages into eleven unrelated 'mother tongues'.[51]

But the most bizarre theory was an English contribution, and came from the architect John Webb, the pupil, relation, and executor of Inigo Jones. Webb was the man whom Christopher Wren defeated for the post of Surveyor of Works after the Restoration. 'When then it is reputed ridiculous to hear that *Adam* spoke *Dutch* in Paradice', Webb thought, it might be

[50] J. Guibelet, *Examen De L'Examen Des Esprits* (Paris, 1631), pp. 386–92.

[51] Borst, *Babel*, iii/1; M. T. Hodgen, *Early Anthropology in the Sixteenth and Seventeenth Centuries* (Philadelphia, 1964), *cap.* viii; D. C. Allen, 'Some Theories of the Growth and Origin of Language in Milton's Age', *Philol. Qly.*, xxviii (1949), 5–16; Lodwick, *Works*, *cap.* iii; Bonfante, 'Ideas', 678–99; Knowlson, *Universal language, cap.* i; Cornelius, *Languages, cap.* i; Williams, *Expositor, cap.* xi; D. Abercrombie, 'Forgotten Phoneticians', *Trans. Philol. Soc., 1948*, 1–34.

worthwhile to consider the argument that 'the Language of the Empire of CHINA, is, the PRIMITIVE Tongue, which was common to the whole World before the Flood'. This novel concept could be proved by the fact that the Chinese 'were primitively planted in CHINA, if not by *Noah* himself, by some of the Issue of *Sem*, before the remove of *Nimrod* to *Shinaar*, and the *Confusion* of *Tongues* at *Babel*'. The Chinese language could not have changed because their country had never been conquered 'as could prejudice, but rather dilate their language'. The Chinese had always been isolated from commercial and cultural contacts, lest their language and customs become corrupted. The Hebrew names in the Old Testament were simply translations from the Chinese. Adam quite clearly spoke Chinese in the Garden because language 'was not a studied or artificial speech, nor taught our *First Parents* by Art and by degrees as their Generations have been, but concreated with them'. Despite Webb's unique beliefs on the origin of language, he joined in the common hope that a '*Real Character*' might be found so that 'we might no longer complain of the unhappy consequences that succeeded the *Confusion at Babel*, nor *China* glory that she alone shall evermore triumph in the full fruition of those abundant felicities that attended mankind, whilst one common language was spoken throughout the World.'[52]

At the other extreme from Webb and his Chinese theory of the origin of language were those few who believed that all languages had been lost at the Tower of Babel. Hobbes held to this view, stating that 'every man was stricken for his rebellion, with an oblivion of his former language.' It was only afterwards, when mankind dispersed to all parts of the world, 'that the diversity of Tongues that now is, proceeded by degrees from them, in such manner, as need (the mother of all inventions) taught them; and in tract of time grew every where more copious.'[53] A contemporary in France agreed, saying that otherwise 'if God had then infus'd an actual knowledg and

---

[52] Webb, *Essay*, pp. 42–4, 146, 187–8; S. Ch'en, 'John Webb: A Forgotten Page in the Early History of Sinology in Europe', *Chinese Social and Political Science Rev.*, xix (1935), 295–330.

[53] T. Hobbes, *Leviathan*, ed. C. B. Macpherson (Harmondsworth, 1968), p. 101 (*cap.* iv).

habit of several Languages in all those Workmen, this had not
been a punishment but a reward of their arrogance, and in
some sort parallel to that famous gift of Tongues by the Holy
Ghost at *Pentecost*.'[54]

Samuel Purchas had made a similar point fifty years earlier,
in his hope that atheists could have seen the Apostles use the
gift of tongues. Then they would not claim that 'all man could
not be of one; because of this diuersitie of Languages.' Instead,
'they might then haue seene the like power in a contrarie effect
to this of Babylon. Mans sinne caused this, Gods mercie that:
the one came from Babylon, the other from Hierusalem'.[55]
School-master Henry Edmundson coupled these two ideas as
well, lamenting that the gift of tongues, 'the greatest Blessings
to men', was no longer given, so that every book, and especially
the Bible, 'hath a double Lock or seal, by the obscurity of the
matter and the obscurity of the language.'[56] In spite of these
varied dissenting claims, and the protests of men like John
Webb, who believed that 'the *Hebrews* have no surer foundation
to erect their Language upon, than only a bare Tradition of
their own', most early modern Englishmen, and the majority of
scholars across Europe, believed that Adam and Eve spoke
Hebrew in the Garden of Eden, and that this language was
substantially the same as the one used by modern-day Jews.[57]

III

'The common and more receiued opinion is,' wrote Samuel
Purchas in the middle of James I's reign, 'that the Hebrew was
the first, confirmed also by vniuersalitie, antiquitie, and consent of the Christian Fathers and learned men'.[58] Among these
Fathers Purchas cited Augustine, whose testimony on a wide
variety of controversial questions relating to the origin and
dispersion of early man would prove so influential in the seventeenth century. Augustine believed that 'the language originally used by men was the one later called Hebrew from the
name of Heber, in whose family it stayed unchanged when the

---

[54] Havers and Davies, *Conferences*, p. 214.
[55] Purchas, *Pilgrimage*, p. 45.
[56] Edmundson, *Lingua*, sig. f3ᵛ.
[57] Webb, *Essay*, p. 42.
[58] Purchas, *Pilgrimage*, p. 46.

diversity of languages began.' Heber, or Eber as he is called in
the Authorized Version, was the great-grandson of Noah's son
Shem. Augustine cited the 'well-founded tradition' even in his
own time, that 'the Hebrews were given his name, being called,
as it were, *Heberaei*.' Eber's son was named Peleg, 'which means
"Division," namely, because he was born to him at the time
when the earth was divided among different languages'.[59] Purchas tinkered with Augustine's analysis, but maintained the
belief that 'the puritie of Religion and Language remained in
Hebers posteritie.' As a result, the 'Nation and Language of
Israel borrow their name (Hebrew) of him.'[60]

One finds echoes of these ideas throughout the linguistic
writings of the seventeenth century. This was the viewpoint of
Pedro Mexia, the popular Spanish encyclopaedist whose works
were translated into English as well as other European languages. The Hebrews, he thought, took their name from Heber,
and 'neuer loste their firste and aunciente tongue.' Mexia
quoted Augustine here for support. In a greatly expanded
encyclopaedia, published in England almost fifty years later,
Mexia wrote that Hebrew 'was the first vsuall tongue among
men; before the confusion of Tongues'. It was in Hebrew that
'God spake first to his Prophets; as the like our blessed Lord
and Sauiour did, when he was conuersant among men.'[61]

Nicholas Gibbens, Cambridge-educated preacher, published a detailed commentary on the first fourteen chapters of
Genesis, during the last year of Elizabeth's reign. Gibbens used
Jewish sources freely, and his citations indicate that he was
familiar with the rabbinical Bibles published during the sixteenth century. What 'language it was yᵗ men spake,' he asked,
'before this confusion of tōgues?' Gibbens refused to credit the
story from Herodotus, and proceeded to argue that 'the Hebrue
was the originall and mother of all.' Syriac and Chaldee
(Aramaic) could be thought of as mere dialects of Hebrew,
whose influence was felt closest to Palestine: 'the languages
which are farthest disagreeing, are (for the most part) farthest
scattered.' The proper names of Genesis could only be Hebrew

---

[59] Augustine, *The City of God*, xvi. 3, 11 (ed. Sanford & Green, v. 21, 61, 63); Gen. 10.
[60] Purchas, *Pilgrimage*, p. 46.
[61] P. Mexia, *The Foreste or Collection of Histories* (London, 1571), p. 106ʳ; idem, *Times Store-Hovse* (London, 1619), p. 701.

words, and it is inconceivable that Moses translated these
names into the Holy Tongue.[62]

Even Richard Verstegan, writing about the same time as
Gibbens, repeated some of these ideas, despite his devotion to
the Dutch theories of Goropius Becanus. All of mankind took
part in the building of the Tower, he thought, 'except *Heber* and
his family' who gave that name to 'his posteritie, who there-
vpon were called *Hebrewes*.'[63] Joshua Sylvester agreed, expres-
sing the same point more poetically: Hebrew, he said,

> (*Adams* language) pure persisted since,
> Till th'yron Age of that cloud climbing Prince;
> Resounding onely, through all mortall tents,
> The peer-lesse accents of rich eloquence;
> But then (as partiall) it it self retir'd
> To *Hebers* house, whether, of the conspir'd
> Rebels, he were not; but in sober quiet,
> Dwelt far from *Shinar*, and their furious ryot:[64]

Others expressed their doubts. Sir Thomas Browne discus-
sed the issue in his 'enquiries into vulgar and common errors'.
He wished, he said, that children committed unto the school of
Nature would speak Hebrew 'not only for the easie attainment
of that useful tongue, but to determine the true and primitive
Hebrew.' But he remained uncertain whether modern-day
Hebrew could be the 'unconfounded language of Babel' which
had been preserved by the children of Heber. Nevertheless,
Browne did believe that 'probability stands fairest' for this
theory, rather than that 'the language of Phaenicia and
Canaan' was the original tongue.[65] Brian Walton, the editor of
the Polyglot Bible, expressed a similar point of view.[66] Richard
Flecknoe the poet was not quite sure either. He wondered
whether all languages 'derived from the *Hebrew* or no (as tis
most probable)'.[67]

The compilers of the few Hebrew grammars in English were

[62] N. Gibbens, *Qvestions And Dispvtations Concerning The Holy Scriptvre* (London, 1602),
p. 429.
[63] Verstegan, *Restitution*, p. 7.
[64] Sylvester, *Du Bartas*, p. 23.
[65] T. Browne, *Pseudodoxia Epidemica* (London, 1646) in *Works*, ed. G. Keynes (London, 1964), ii. 393.
[66] Cornelius, *Languages*, p. 10.
[67] R. Fleckno, *Miscellania* (London, 1653), p. 109.

less equivocal in their support for the ultimate antiquity of Hebrew. That of William Robertson, of the University of Edinburgh, was one of the most popular, and the second section was reprinted for general use as late as the nineteenth century. One could read the 'Oracles of God' in Hebrew, which included 'the very first, Primitive, and Originall Words of his own Spirit'. Robertson's grammar was prefaced by a declaration from some of the most influential London ministers and preachers, who encouraged the 'attaining of this Sacred and Original Language'. Among the group which signed this statement was Joseph Caryl, one of the few members of the Whitehall Conference who supported unconditional readmission of the Jews. Another of the ministers who signed this statement, Thomas Sympson of Tottenham High-Crosse, expressed his feelings in rather a stronger fashion: 'O Tongue of Tongues! of Languages the *first* . . . Nay, *once* the *only* Language! none beside Was spoken in the world, till *Babels* pride.' Hebrew, the footnote in Robertson's edition explains somewhat superfluously, was spoken, 'as the Learned observe, by *Adam* in Paradise.'[68]

These same sentiments were expressed in another Hebrew grammar published by John Davis the following year, immediately after the Whitehall Conference. Hebrew, he wrote, 'is the Language of *God's Word*, the Language of *Canaan*'. Grammarian Edward Leigh believed that Hebrew was 'the most ancient and holy Tongue; for Antiquity it is the Tongue of *Adam*, for sanctity the Tongue of God.' It was in Hebrew that 'God spake to the Prophets and Patriarcks, in this Tongue the Angels spake to men, in this Tongue the Prophets wrote the Old Testament'. This statement appeared in all editions of his *Critica Sacra*, both before the Civil War and after the Restoration.[69]

Theophilus Gale, fellow at Oxford during the Commonwealth and nonconformist tutor afterwards, attempted the same sort of explanation as a part of a much grander project. It was Gale's life-work to prove that all languages, philosophy,

---

[68] W. Robertson, *Gate . . . To the Holy Tongue* (London, 1654–5), sigs. a1^{r-v} (1st Gate); a5^{r-v} (2nd Gate). See also G. F. Black, 'The Beginnings of the Study of Hebrew in Scotland', *Studies in Jewish Bibliography*, ed. L. Ginzberg, *et al.* (New York, 1929), pp. 463–80.

[69] J. Davis, *A Short Introduction To The Hebrew Tongue* (London, 1656), sig. A4^{v}; E. Leigh, *Critica Sacra* (3rd Heb. edn., London, 1662), sig. A2^{r}. First edn. of Leigh's book published in 1641.

and learning derived from the Hebrews and their scriptures.
His goal was a sort of reformed Platonism, but of course Plato
was 'reported to have lived fourteen years with the *Jews* in
Egypt; and, we need no way dout, derived the choisest of his
contemplations . . . from the Jewish Church'. The name of the
Hebrew language derived from Heber, and continued in purity
from the Garden through the Confusion, until the Babylonian
Captivity; all languages, including Greek, derived from the
Hebrew. That the ultimate source of all languages was 'the
Hebrew, or *Jewish* Tongue,' he insisted, 'is an *Assertion* generally
owned, and maintained by the most learned *Philologists* of this
Age, and that not without the consent of some of the *Ancients*,
and learned *Heathens*.' Gale quoted Plato's *Cratylus*, the standard Jewish commentaries in the sixteenth-century rabbinical
Bibles, and even pointed to some kabbalistic theories. For
further information, he advised, one only had to look in 'the six
dayes volume of the Book, VVhere *God*, and mighty *Nature* doth
appear, VVrot in an *Vniversal Character*'. Hebrew in the Garden
of Eden was perfectly expressive of meaning: 'So *pure*, and of so
Vniversal sense, God thought it best for *Innocence*.'[70]

The same trends were readily noticeable in France, and
Englishmen were kept informed of intellectual developments
there. One of the earliest proposals for a common writing, in
fact, originated in France in the form of a prospectus sent by
Marin Mersenne to his friend Descartes in November 1629.
Descartes expressed his opinion on the plan at the end of the
month, saying that 'des Vallees', the author of the prospectus
which has now disappeared, claimed to have discovered the
mother tongue from which all other languages are descended.
Charles Sorel the historiographer claimed that those who put
forward such claims always denied that they were referring to
Hebrew, because they wanted others to believe that their language was extraordinarily secret and mysterious.[71] Leibniz,
commenting fifty years later on Descartes's letter, thought that
such an artificial language 'sera d'un secours merveilleux et
pour se servir de ce que nous sçavons, et pour voir ce qui nous

[70] Gale, *Gentiles*, i. sigs. *3^{r-v}, **3^{r-v}, ***^{v}; pp. 51, 53–4, 59; iii. 117–18.
[71] In M. Mersenne, *Correspondance*, ed. P. Tannery, *et al.* (Paris, 1945–   ), ii. 323–9;
Knowlson, *Universal language*, pp. 44–50, 65–70. Cf. N. Chomsky, *Cartesian Linguistics*
(New York, 1966).

manque, et pour inventer les moyens d'y arriver, mais sur tout pour exterminer les controverses dans les matieres qui dependent du raisonnement. Car alors raisonner et calculer sera la même chose.'[72] Leibniz, of course, was rather hopeful here about universal languages, and pointed in the direction of his own mathematical inclinations, which would be taken up with great vigour by later linguistic philosophers. Some of Leibniz's contemporaries in France expressed other views of the Adamic vernacular. One of the 'virtuosi' announced that Hebrew, Latin, and Greek were all perfect 'Mother-Languages'. Another argued that 'all the Language of *Adam*, who gave names suitable to the nature of every thing [was] lost except the name of God (for that reason so much esteemed by the Jews)'. All of these deliberations were transmitted to England, where scholars compared their own thoughts with the Continental developments.[73]

Yet although the majority of learned opinion sided with those who believed that Adam and Eve spoke Hebrew in the Garden of Eden, scholars who actually set out to prove this theory were driven back on the sort of etymologies which they ridiculed in the works of Goropius Becanus. William Robertson the Scottish grammarian proved the antiquity of Hebrew by reciting that the 'name of the first man was *Adam*, which signifieth, *earthly man*, So, the name of his wife, the first woman, was *Chavah*, which signifieth, *living*', Goropius Becanus was able to find Low German equivalents for these scriptural names, despite Robertson's claim that these names 'are acknowledged to signifie thus, in the Hebrew onely, and not in any other Language.'[74] As Edward Leigh exulted, 'How many proper Names in the Scripture are derived from the Hebrew! And how significant are their Etymologies!'[75]

Certainly by the middle of the seventeenth century, Hebrew was the unopposed ancient mother of languages for most English thinkers. The Hebrew language was glorified as the *lingua humana*, the language spoken by Adam and Eve in the Garden of

---

[72] G. W. Leibniz, *Opuscules et fragments inédits*, ed. L. Couturat (Paris, 1903), pp. 27–8.

[73] Havers and Davies, *Conferences*, pp. 304–5. For more on the French view of Hebrew, see D. P. Walker, *The Ancient Theology* (London, 1972), pp. 99–101.

[74] Robertson, *Gate*, sigs. A5ᵛ–A6ʳ (2nd Gate).

[75] Leigh, *Critica*, sig. A2ʳ.

Eden, by mankind until the Confusion at the Tower of Babel, and by the Jews, the descendants of Heber who, although they took on other vernaculars, still preserved the sacred tongue and the crown of its literature, the Hebrew Old Testament. William Robertson wrote that the 'usefulnesse' of Hebrew

> is infinitely to be valued above any thing which is attainable by the Latine; because in these the Oracles of God are delivered to us, in their Originall Purity; and in them, those very words, which were the words of him, who spoke by them as never man spoke, . . . the very first, Primitive, and Originall Words of his own Spirit, in the Old and New Testament, which no language in the World besides these can boast of.

Far more extravagantly, Robertson boasted that the 'Learned are verily perswaded, that, without doubt, there shall be a Language spoken in heaven, for ever: and that there shall be one Language: and also, that *this* shall be that very Language.' The four and twenty elders and the four beasts of Revelation, after all, said 'Amen; Allelujah', which are Hebrew words.[76] Edward Leigh agreed that Hebrew, 'as is thought, shall the Saints speak in Heaven.'[77] If 'we Shall speak this Language to Eternity,' asked Thomas Sympson, London preacher, 'If so; what paines, what cost should not be given, To learn on earth, what we shal speak in heaven?'[78]

Hebrew became a very fashionable learned language, and took its rightful place among Latin and Greek, those languages which, as Richard Flecknoe put it, 'subsist, as it were, upon the stock of their Ancestors.' Flecknoe even complained of 'the *Scripture* style amongst the common *Rabble*, who are our *Rabbies* now, and . . . cant it in the *Hebrew* phrase.'[79] Respect for the Hebrew was especially prevalent among sectarian preachers. The seventeenth-century biographer of John Cotton, the famous New England pioneer, recounted with pride that when Cotton was examined for a fellowship at Emmanuel College, Cambridge, the examiner set a particularly difficult translation from Isaiah, but 'though a . . . resolution thereof might have put a good Hebrician to a stand, yet such was his dexterity, as made those difficult words facil, and

---

[76] Robertson, *Gate*, sigs. A4^r (1st Gate); A6^r (2nd Gate).
[77] Leigh, *Critica*, sig. A2^r.
[78] In Robertson, *Gate*, sig. A5^r (2nd Gate).
[79] Fleckno, *Miscellania*, pp. 77, 80.

rendred him a prompt Respondent.'[80] Richard Corbett, the poet
of Christ Church, makes his 'Distracted Puritane' lament that

> In the holy tongue of Chanaan
> I plac'd my cheifest pleasure:
> Till I prickt my foote
> With an Hebrew roote,
> That I bledd beyond all measure.[81]

The aim of the Hebrew grammars directed to the popular
market was to open up some of this Hebrew learning to the
general Bible reader. William Robertson thought that the principal impediment to Hebrew study was the overabundance of
Latin grammars of Hebrew, and the difficulty in finding an
English textbook. With the proper tools, he thought, even the
'Female sexe' could learn Hebrew. Still, the lack of qualified
teachers was a problem: 'the studie of the Hebrew,' Robertson
wrote, was

counted not long ago, the highest and the rarest piece of knowledge, and
which indeed, Very few amongst the greatest of scholars were much
acquainted with: for till of late, *Loqui latine, intelligere graeca*, and but *legere
haebraica*, was thought to be great learning: so that he was esteemed a scholar,
who if he could speak Latine, and understand Greek, could but read Hebrew:
yea many great Scholars and most of the ancient Fathers did greatly resent it,
as a great imperfection of their Age, that they scarce did so much as know the
very *Hebrew* letters of the Alphabet (for that was not the appointed time for
revealing that part of knowledge:)[82]

Grammarian John Davis expressed the same point, defending
himself against those who objected to a Hebrew grammar with
English instead of Latin instruction: this, he said, was 'a very
great injurie to the publick (to wit) of endeavouring the *mono-
polizing* that *commoditie*, which should be *every mans money*.' The
chief purpose of Davis's work, like that of Robertson, was to
produce a grammar that would be 'usefull for *English* as Latin
Scholars'.[83]

Some observers thought that this fascination with Hebrew
was getting out of hand. The introduction to the Bay Psalm

---

[80] J. Norton, *Abel being Dead yet speaketh . . . Life . . . Of . . . John Cotton* (London, 1658),
p. 10

[81] *The Poems of Richard Corbett*, ed. J. A. W. Bennett and H. R. Trevor-Roper (Oxford,
1955), pp. 56–9.

[82] Robertson, *Gate*, title page, sigs. 8^r–A^r (2nd Gate).

[83] Davis, *Introduction*, sigs. A4^v–A5^r.

Book praised the English Bibles which 'used the Idioms of our
owne tongue in stead of Hebraismes, lest they might seeme
english barbarisms.'[84] Samuel Butler's Hudibras was well
equipped with

> *Hebrew* Roots, although th' are found
> To flourish most in barren ground,
> He had such plenty, as suffic'd
> To make some think him circumcis'd
> And truly so perhaps, he was
> 'Tis many a Pious Christians case.[85]

John Webster thought that 'while men trust to their skill in the
understanding of the original tongues, they become utterly
ignorant of the true original tongue, . . . which no man can
understand or speak, but he that is . . . taught the language of
the holy Ghost'.[86] Thomas Hobbes was rather more emphatic
about the subject. 'A minister,' he wrote, 'ought not to think
that his skill in the Latin, Greek, or Hebrew tongues, if he have
any, gives him a privilege to impose upon all his fellow subjects
his own sense, or what he pretends to be his sense, of every
obscure place of Scripture'. And later on:

As for the Latin, Greek, and Hebrew tongues, it was once . . . very profitable,
or rather necessary; but now that is done, and we have the Scripture in
English, and preaching in English, I see no great need of Latin, Greek, and
Hebrew. I should think myself better qualified by understanding well the
languages of our neighbours, French, Dutch, and Spanish.[87]

But, as Hobbes no doubt understood, the utility of Hebrew
was more than simply linguistic. Augustine, whose writings, as
we have seen, were so influential among early modern linguistic
thinkers, here too set the stage for further discussion. 'This
Hebrew tongue,' he wrote, 'is the exclusive possession of the
people of Israel, among whom the city of God has passed its
pilgrimage as well as among the saints, while it has been less
perfectly represented by its mysteries among all men.'[88] Pedro
Mexia brought up the same point, saying that Hebrew was
'particular to the Iewes, and the mysteries and prophecies (as

---

[84] *The VVhole Booke of Psalmes* ([Cambridge, Mass.], 1640), sig. **3ʳ.
[85] Butler, *Hudibras*, p. 3.
[86] Webster, *Academiarum*, p. 8.
[87] T. Hobbes, *Behemoth*, ed. F. Tönnies (London, 1889), pp. 53, 90.
[88] Augustine, *The City of God*, xvi. 3 (ed. Sanford and Green, v. 21).

also the coming of Christ) being concealed therein: it was very requisite, that such mysteries should bee written in a tong more common then the Hebrue'.[89] It was these 'mysteries' that contemporaries hoped to uncover, and some thought that even the English language might hold open a door to them. For these early modern cultural historians lacked any modern notion of cultural or linguistic change; any deviation was thought of as decay. Cultural similarities could only derive from imitation, with an inevitable decline from the quality of the original.[90] All of mankind, with each culture and language, ultimately had its roots in the Garden of Eden, and when a man like Isaac la Peyrère, the French philosopher of marrano background whose *Men Before Adam* was banned and burnt everywhere, proposed a second Creation, he was immediately arrested and vilified in print by writers as diverse as Rabbi Menasseh ben Israel and the Pope.[91]

If, therefore, all languages are merely degeneration from the Hebrew in some way, then one might find answers to mystical questions close to home. As Augustine concluded, from 'the sons of Noah . . . seventy-two nations and the same number of languages came into existence on earth, and by their increase filled even the islands. Moreover, the nations increased much more in number than the languages did.'[92] Nicholas Gibbens, who had read Augustine, also believed that every nation at Babel forgot their native language and 'afterwards they inuented to themselues other words and sounds to expresse their minds; diuers, after their diuers wits and dispositions'. They also kept 'so much as they remembered of their primitie tongue: By this meanes it came to passe, that no language but hath some remainder of the Hebrue.' Even English 'hath many words which are common with the Hebrue, and seeme to be deriued from the same.'[93] Sir Thomas Browne, inquiring into vulgar and common errors, nevertheless thought it reasonable

[89] Mexia, *Store-Hovse*, p. 701.
[90] See Hodgen, *Anthropology*, caps. vi–vii.
[91] H. J. Schoeps, *Philosemitismus im Barock* (Tübingen, 1952), pp. 3–18, 81–7; R. H. Popkin, 'Menasseh ben Israel and Isaac La Peyrère', *Stud. Rosenthaliana*, viii (1974), 59–63; I. Robinson, 'Isaac de la Peyrère and the Recall of the Jews', *Jew. Soc. Stud.*, xl (1978), 117–30.
[92] Augustine, *The City of God*, xvi. 6 (ed. Sanford and Green, v. 39).
[93] Gibbens, *Qvestions*, p. 442.

that 'at the confusion of tongues, there was no constitution of a
new speech in every family: but a variation and permutation of
the old; out of one common language raising several Dialects:
the primitive tongue remaining still intire.' This would explain
how Abraham of the family of Heber could manage to communicate with men from other nations.[94]

The Hebrew language, in other words, was not completely
remote from the English frame of reference. There was some
connection between English and the sacred language, even if
only through what Margaret Hodgen has called 'documentary
magic'.[95] For it was this magical element which was important
for early modern Englishmen, especially the language planners
and linguistic theorists. Sir Thomas Urquhart, for example,
criticized those who did not believe that some elements of
Hebrew remained in all languages, saying that they were mistaken

not so much for that they had not perused the interpretation of the Rabbies on
that text, declaring the misunderstandings whereunto the builders were
involved by diversity of speech, to have proceeded from nothing else, but their
various and discrepant pronunciation of one and the same Language, as that
they deemed Languages to be of an invention so sublime, that naturally the
wit of man was not able to reach their composure.[96]

Urquhart was right: seventeenth-century linguistic thinkers
and planners did peruse the interpretation of the rabbis,
because at the very same time that Englishmen were talking
about the mystical qualities of the Adamic vernacular and the
purity of language in the Garden of Eden, Jewish kabbalistic
mystics were working out these problems with great care.
Englishmen pointed the way to this kabbalistic Hebraic lore,
but few, if any, could comprehend even the outlines of this
esoteric discipline. Joshua Sylvester, for example, expressed
the feelings of the period. Of language in the Garden he
laments:

> What shall I more say? Then, all spake the speech
> Of God himself: th' old sacred *Idiom* rich,
> Rich perfect language, where's no point, nor signe,
> But hides some rare deep mystery divine;

[94] Browne, *Pseudodoxia*, p. 394.
[95] Hodgen, *Anthropology*, p. 308.
[96] Urquhart, *Logopandecteision*, p. 8.

But since that pride, each people hath a-part
A bastard gibberish, harsh and over-thwart;
Which dayly chang'd, and loosing light, wel-neer
Nothing retains of that first language cleer.

For Sylvester, and for most seventeenth-century English language theorists, the very words of Hebrew were divinely
significant. Hebrew had 'no word but weighs, whose Elements
Flow with hid sense, thy points with Sacraments.'[97] The universal language planners hoped to return to linguistic innocence,
and hoped that the Jewish kabbalists could show them the way.

IV

Schemes for a universal language and debates concerning the
identity of the *lingua humana* continued side by side throughout
the seventeenth century. Once English projectors had come to
the conclusion that Adam spoke Hebrew in the perfect state of
language which they were now attempting to duplicate, they
were of necessity driven to Jewish interpretations of language.
The Hebrew language has had a supernatural element for Jews
throughout the Christian era, and the mystical interpretation
of language formed a central part of Jewish mysticism (the
kabbalah) by the mid-seventeenth century. English language
reformers were thus fascinated by the reports they received of
the Jewish approach to a problem that was comparatively new
for Christians, but which the Jews had been studying for over
1,500 years. The kabbalistic conception of language is very
complex, but the outlines of the Jewish discussion need to be
summarized in order to understand what attracted the attention of early modern English linguistic philosophers.

Mystical Jewish notions of language can be found as early as
the second century AD. 'When I was studying under R. Akiba,'
the Talmud quotes Rabbi Meir,

I used to put vitriol into my ink and he told me nothing [against it], but when I
subsequently came to R. Ishmael the latter said to me, 'My son, what is your
occupation?' I told him, 'I am a scribe', and he said to me, 'Be meticulous in
your work, for your occupation is a sacred one; should you perchance omit or
add one single letter you would thereby destroy all the universe'.[98]

[97] Sylvester, *Du Bartas*, pp. 121–2.
[98] Erubin 13a: in *The Babylonian Talmud*, ed. I. Epstein (London, 1935–1952), Seder
Mo'ed, iii. 81.

This is the classic statement of the notion of a divine language, in which ordinary words have a significance much greater than their literal meanings. Virtually all we know of kabbalah comes from the research of Professor Gershom Scholem, who has pointed to divine names and their component letters as one of the 'most important kinds of symbolism used by the Kabbalists to communicate their ideas.' As Professor Scholem explains:

From the very beginnings of Kabbalistic doctrine these two manners of speaking appear side by side. The secret world of the godhead is a world of language, a world of divine names that unfold in accordance with a law of their own. The elements of the divine language appear as the letters of the Holy Scriptures. Letters and names are not only conventional means of communication. They are far more. Each one of them represents a concentration of energy and expresses a wealth of meaning which cannot be translated, or not fully at least, into human language.[99]

The true significance of the Torah (the Pentateuch) was defined according to several principles.[100] First of all, the Torah was, in the words of one commentator, 'like an explication of, and a commentary on, the Name of God', if not the Name of God itself.[101] Secondly, the Torah was thought of as a living organism, *binyan 'elohy*, a divine construction, in which 'to omit so much as one letter or point from the Torah is like removing some part of a perfect edifice.'[102] Therefore, the Name of God breaks down into different parts of an organic being in the Torah. Thirdly, the Torah was thought to possess infinite meanings according to what Professor Scholem calls 'the unlimited mystical plasticity of the divine word'.[103] The scripture had many meanings at many different levels and according to the capacity of the reader. The kabbalists were influenced by the Christian four-fold method of scriptural interpretation, and developed their own equivalent categories: the literal (*peshat*), the allegorical (*remez*), the hermeneutical (*derash*), and the mys-

---

[99] G. Scholem, *On the Kabbalah and Its Symbolism* (New York, 1969), p. 36.

[100] For what follows see ibid., 'The Meaning of the Torah in Jewish Mysticism', pp. 32–86; idem, *Major Trends in Jewish Mysticism* (Jerusalem, 1941), pp. 202–282; idem, *Sabbatai Ṣevi* (London, 1973), pp. 1–102; idem, *Kabbalah* (Jerusalem, 1974), pp. 87–203.

[101] Joseph Gikatilla, *Sha'arey 'Orah* (13th cent.) quoted in Scholem, *Kabbalah*, p. 171 and idem, *Symbolism*, p. 42.

[102] Azriel of Gerona, *Perush 'Aggadoth* (13th cent.) quoted in Scholem, *Symbolism*, p. 45.

[103] Ibid., p. 76.

then by the persecutions during the Swedish–Russian war (1655–6). 'In fact,' Professor Scholem explains, 'Lurianic kabbalism was the one well-articulated and generally accepted form of Jewish theology at the time.'[108]

These kabbalistic ideas, then, were Jewish commonplaces; but to what extent did they percolate down to Christian interpreters whose works might have influenced the language planners of seventeenth-century England? There is insufficient space here to recite the entire history of Christian kabbalah, but its main features can be delineated.[109] Jewish converts played an important role, but the father of Christian kabbalah is certainly the Florentine Giovanni Pico della Mirandola. Pico had a large body of kabbalistic literature translated into Latin for him by a Jewish convert known as Flavius Mithridates. Pico believed that Christian doctrines such as the Trinity and Reincarnation could be proven through the use of kabbalah, and his works were enormously influential in the Christian world. Pico was followed in kabbalistic study by Johannes Reuchlin, the famous Hebraist, and Guillaume Postel of France, who helped to integrate kabbalah with contemporary Christian intellectual developments. Another well-known exponent of this mystical lore was Jacob Boehme.[110]

But the major breakthrough in Christian kabbalah did not come until Christian Knorr von Rosenroth published his *Kabbala Denudata* in 1677. Knorr was the son of a Silesian Protestant minister, and became interested in the writings of Boehme during his travels through Europe. Knorr eventually settled in the Bavarian city of Sulzbach, where from 1668 until his death in 1689 he was a close adviser of the mystically-minded Prince Christian August. Knorr's book was the major non-Jewish source on kabbalah until the beginning of this century, and included not only parts of the *Zohar* but major segments of the Lurianic kabbalah as well. The book also contained writings by

---

[108] Scholem, *Sabbatai Ṣevi*, p. 25.

[109] See esp. idem, *Kabbalah*, pp. 196–201; J. L. Blau, *The Christian Interpretation of the Cabala in the Renaissance* (New York, 1944); F. Secret, *Les Kabbalistes Chrétiens de la Renaissance* (Paris, 1964).

[110] See esp. A. Koyré, *La Philosophie de Jacob Boehme* (Paris, 1929); S. Hutin, *Les Disciples Anglais de Jacob Boehme aux XVIIe et XVIIIe siècles* (Paris, 1960); M. L. Bailey, *Milton and Jakob Boehme* (New York, 1914); D. Hirst, *Hidden Riches* (London, 1964), *cap.* iii.

Henry More and the Netherlandish mystic Franciscus Mercurius Van Helmont, and was the first satisfactory treatment of kabbalah published in any language other than Hebrew.[111]

The *Kabbala Denudata*, of course, was not available to the principal English language planners of the seventeenth century. Later on, when Knorr's work became a standard text, many intellectuals, not only linguistic speculators, made a systematic inquiry into the Lurianic doctrines. Leibniz, for example, one of the most influential seventeenth-century philosophers of language, was so impressed by Knorr's book that he visited him in 1687 and discussed kabbalistic subjects.[112]

But the new Jewish ideas were in the air, and second- and third-hand reports began to move down the grapevine of Christian kabbalah. One can see an awareness of this branch of mystical knowledge among the language planners most clearly in the reply of Seth Ward and John Wilkins to John Webster's examination of academies. When Webster argued that languages were not necessary to theology, Ward and Wilkins objected sarcastically that:

Tongues, nay Letters, have taught a way of Mysticall Theology, as mysticall as need to be, and not unworthy to be compared to his which followes; 'tis pitty he had not heard of the mysteries of the *Gnosticks*, nor the *Ziruph Gematry* and *Notariacon* of the *Cabalists*, that one might have gained his favour to the Greek, the other to the Hebrew Tongue, to the advancement of *Marcus* and *Colarbasus*, and the sparing of *Behemen* & *De Fluctibus*.[113]

John Wilkins, the English language planner whose scheme for a philosophical as well as a universal language was the most highly refined, certainly knew of these kabbalistic tools. *Gematria* is a means of explaining a word by computing its numerical value, perhaps through *ṣairuf*, the transposition of letters; *notarikon* involves the interpretation of each letter in a word as an abbreviation for entire sentences. These means of interpretation were useful in understanding the divine speech according to the *sod* or mystical meaning, with the ultimate objective of *tiqqun* or restoration of the Adamic state or, even better, of the cosmic position before the breaking of the vessels. This is what

---

[111] Scholem, *Kabbalah*, pp. 416–19.
[112] Ibid.
[113] [Ward and Wilkins], *Vindiciae*, p. '5' = 13.

John Wilkins meant when he wrote that 'if you will beleeve the Jews, the Holy spirit hath purposely involved in the words of Scripture, every secret that belongs to any Art or Science, under such Cabalisms as these.' More importantly, he thought, 'if a man were but expert in unfolding of them, it were easie for him to get as much knowledge as *Adam* had in his innocencie, or human nature is capable of.'[114]

V

'The end then of learning,' wrote Milton to Samuel Hartlib in 1644, 'is to repair the ruins of our first parents by regaining to know God aright, and out of that knowledge to love him, to imitate him, to be like him'.[115] The image of Adam before the Fall was a popular and powerful one for Puritan projectors. Charles Webster has cogently demonstrated the strength of this image in the fields of education, science, and even agriculture. As Webster reminds us, to the Puritans of the seventeenth century, 'the Garden of Eden and the New Jerusalem were more than a poorly-authenticated record of man's ancestry, or a confused fantasy about the future. To the author of *Paradise Lost*, the Garden of Eden represented an ideal state of affairs which had an indisputable historical basis.'[116] This utopian image was very important for both Jews and Christians in the seventeenth century: the state of language before Adam's Fall was the distant goal of the language planners.

This element in their thinking has been relatively neglected in the most recent discussions of the universal language and real character in England. The earlier standard view had emphasized the Baconian origins of the language schemes. During the past twenty years, however, scholars have been weighing the claims of Comenius and Cyprian Kinner the Silesian educational theorist put forward by Benjamin DeMott.[117]

[114] W[ilkins], *Mercury*, p. '83' = 101.

[115] Milton, *Complete Prose Works*, ii. 366–7 (*Of Education*).

[116] C. Webster, *The Great Instauration* (London, 1975), p. 16.

[117] B. DeMott, 'Comenius and the Real Character in England', *Proc. Mod. Lang. Assoc.*, lxx (1955), 1068–81; idem, 'The Sources and Development of John Wilkins' Philosophical Language', *Jnl. Eng. and Germ. Philol.*, lvii (1958), 1–13. O. Funke defends his earlier book, *Zum Weltsprachenproblem in England im 17. Jahrhundert* (Heidelberg, 1929), in 'On the Sources of John Wilkins' Philosophical Language (1668)', *Eng. Stud.*, xl (1959), 208–14.

Comenius was certainly interested in the idea of a philosophical language, and expressed his theories in his *Via Lucis*, the manuscript of which was left with Samuel Hartlib and Wilkins when the Czech mystic returned to the Continent in 1642. Nevertheless, the concept of a language in which words and things would be immediately congruent was at least a dozen years older, as we have seen, and can be found in the writings of Descartes and Mersenne. Kinner's famous letter of 27 June 1647 similarly discusses what he calls *voculas technicas*; Kinner was also interested in the idea of using symbols instead of letters. Yet despite all of the evidence which linguistic historians have collected concerning the influence of the Comenius circle, Vivian Salmon, one of the most recent writers, has chosen to stress the Baconian scientific origins of the linguistic projects, almost as if mysticism and science were mutually exclusive realms of thought.[118]

Instead of attempting to assign the credit for the development of the philosophical languages to one or two men, a far more productive line of research involves the study of the ideas which enabled men like Descartes, Mersenne, and Comenius to put their theories forward and to find general acceptance among their followers. Frances Yates and Paolo Rossi have done this to some extent by showing how 'these efforts come straight out of the memory tradition with its search for signs and symbols to use as memory images.' They stress that the universal languages were also to be used as aids to memory, and that the real characters originated with the magic images of occult tradition and in the art of Ramon Lull. 'The seventeenth-century universal language enthusiasts,' Dr Yates writes, 'are translating into rational terms efforts such as those of Giordano Bruno to found universal memory systems on magic images which he thought of as directly in contact with reality.'[119]

---

[118] Kinner's letter in Hartlib MSS: see DeMott, 'Sources'; V. Salmon, 'Language Planning in Seventeenth-Century England; Its Context and Aims', *In Memory of J. R. Firth*, ed. C. E. Bazell, *et al.* (London, 1966), pp. 370–97.

[119] F. A. Yates, *The Art of Memory* (London, 1966), pp. 378–89, esp. p. 378; P. Rossi, *Clavis Universalis Arti Mnemoniche e Logica Combinatoria de Lullo a Leibniz* (Milano–Napoli, 1960), *cap.* vii; cf. B. DeMott, 'Science versus Mnemonics/ Notes on John Ray and on John Wilkins' *Essay . . .*', *Isis*, xlviii (1957), 3–12.

The other important sub-structure of the language planners which has hardly been mentioned in the secondary literature is the utopian ideal of the return to Adamic purity and innocence, and the kabbalistic aids towards this end. English scholars of the seventeenth century were very nearly in complete agreement that the perfect language which Adam and Eve spoke in the Garden of Eden was Hebrew; the kabbalists, as John Donne put it, who 'are the Anatomists of words, and have a Theologicall Alchimy to draw soveraigne tinctures and spirits from plain and grosse literall matter, observe in every variety some great mystick signification'.[120] This, as we shall see, was exactly what the seventeenth-century English language planners hoped to accomplish.

Comenius was certainly thinking along these lines, even if his claim to be the father of the philosophical language can be disputed. Comenius held to the standard beliefs that language first began with Adam in Paradise and that Moses was the first author. 'For the Universal Light,' he wrote, 'there are four requisites: Universal Books; Universal Schools; a Universal College; a Universal Language.' These would be the means towards Universal Wisdom. All of these components were present even in the unreformed world to some extent except for the Universal Language which, he said:

is alone wanting; though of old, in the state of man's innocence, it was not wanting. If we had continued steadfastly in that state, we should have had no need of any other books, any other school, any other Collegiate Society. But since we have gone astray and fallen into countless errors and are still wandering afar, and have to make our way back, we need an universal reassembling or re-collecting and must have the instruments or means for thus gathering ourselves together.

In other words, Comenius was delineating his own fourfold method of *tiqqun*. Comenius did not think that Latin would make a suitable universal language because it was riddled with all of the same faults which plagued any language that developed haphazardly, and because it was too difficult and strange for uncivilized peoples. Comenius wanted a philosophical language which would be 'a universal antidote to confusion of thought' with precisely the same number of names

---

[120] Donne, *Essays*, p. 48.

as there were things in the world. Symbolic characters, such as those used by the Chinese, would hardly be sufficient towards this end, especially when one considered 'those monstrous six thousand characters of the Chinese'. These were all points which the Czech reformer put forward for consideration, leaving the details of language construction to his followers.[121]

The passage in Genesis where Adam names the animals provided crucial evidence for Comenius as it had for so many others before. Comenius thought that this indicated divine approval for the formation of a new language, leaving mankind 'free to adjust our concepts of things to the forms of things themselves . . . to fit language to the more exact expression of more exact concepts'. At the end of days all languages would be gathered together and undergo 'conversion' [like the Jews?]. 'so that with one speech and with one accord all men may serve him.' Those 'most ingenious Frenchmen, Mersenne and le Maire' believe that they have already laid the foundations of this: 'they claim with confidence that they can converse not only with the inhabitants of every part of the world, but with the denizens, if there are any, of the moon not less.'[122]

But Comenius was much more vague about the future: with regard to the universal language, he wrote, 'there must be no attempt to establish it till Pansophia has been made complete at least in the correct definition of the kind, the ideas and the qualities of things' lest yet another inadequate language come into the world to increase the confusion it was meant to alleviate. In the meantime, Comenius advised men to 'cultivate their own native languages' and to use Hebrew and Greek 'in the first rank' and Latin for learned discourse. 'When an Universal Language has been achieved and accepted in the use of all peoples,' he hoped,

When this is seen the children of Israel now scattered to the four corners of the earth shall gather themselves together again; and beginning to look forth they will seek both Jehovah, their God, and David, their King (Hos. iii.), and they themselves will be brought back with a great returning. The most sacred promises of this sort, concerning the last general and solemn restoration of the Jews, are to be found in every part of the Scriptures.

[121] J. A. Comenius, *The Way of Light*, trans. E. T. Campagnac (Liverpool and London, 1938), pp. 137–8, 183, 186–7.
[122] Ibid., pp. 188–91.

When the plan for a Universal Light became a reality, the Jews would 'be roused to zeal by the very multitude of the nations which will be converted—so that the circle of God's loving kindness may end with those with whom it began.'[123]

Whether or not Comenius deserves to be remembered as the originator of the idea of the philosophical language, he was extraordinarily influential among English language planners. George Dalgarno was the first projector to present a detailed scheme which was meant not only to return to the state of language before Babel, but also to that before the Fall. He later described his system as 'a Synopsis of a Philosophical Grammar and Lexicon; thereby shewing a way to remedy the difficulties and absurdities which all languages are clogg'd with ever since the confusion'. In Dalgarno's view, any reform of language should involve 'cutting off all Redundancy, rectifying all Anomoly, taking away all Ambiguity and Aequivocation, contracting the Primitives to a few number, and even those not to be of a meer arbitrary, but a rational Institution'.[124] For post-Adamic language was most certainly not a rational institution, but rather a hodge-podge of confused and often contradictory verbal symbols that frequently impeded the communication of ideas. Dalgarno's solution essentially was a compromise between the old notion of a 'real character' to stand for existing words, and the newer idea of inventing a language based on things. Dalgarno ordered all knowledge into a series of lists and tables and assigned each component a particular symbol. 'Thus having formed *Tables* both of *Integrals* and *Particles*, to be expressed by single *Characters*,' explained Robert Plot the Oxfordshire historian, Dalgarno 'perceived at length that he . . . discovered a *real Character* equally applicable to all *Languages*'. More importantly, Dalgarno had made an effort to eliminate ambiguity and unnecessary shades of meaning. Dalgarno's scheme, Plot thought, might go some way towards a restoration of that happy time when '*Adam* gave names to the *Creatures* according to their *Natures*'.[125]

---

[123] Ibid., pp. 192, 199, 219–20, 225.
[124] Dalgarno, *Didascalocophus*, sig. F2^r. For more on Dalgarno, see M. M. C. McIntosh, 'The Phonetic and Linguistic Theory of The Royal Society School' (Oxford Univ. B. Litt. thesis 1956), appendix; and *Works* (Edinburgh, 1834).
[125] Plot, *History*, pp. 282–3.

But it was John Wilkins' still-born plan for a philosophical
language which was the most extensive, and if nothing else
inspired Peter Mark Roget to produce his famous *Thesaurus* in
the nineteenth century. Wilkins was a member of the Comenius
circle at Duke's Place in 1641–2, and a friend of Theodore
Haak, a Palatine refugee and disciple of Comenius, who
worked with Robert Hooke and Francis Lodwick to improve
Wilkins's *Essay* after it was published.[126]

Wilkins published *Mercvry*, the first English textbook on cryptography, in 1641, shortly after the ideas of Comenius had
begun to make some impact in England. Wilkins knew something at least of talmudic fable, and told the famous story of the
lion of Elay whose roaring shook the walls of Rome.[127] Wilkins
was also familiar with *sairuf*, '*albam*, '*atbash*, and *notarikon*, some
of the standard variants of *gematria*. ''Tis observed by the
Rabbies,' he wrote, 'that many grand mysteries are this way
implied in the words of Scripture.' Wilkins also rehearsed the
famous proof of the Trinity from Christian kabbalah, used first
by Peter Lombard in the twelfth century and repeated
throughout the Middle Ages until Calvin and others began to
reject it, that the second word of the Hebrew version of Genesis is
an acronym for father, son, and Holy Spirit. As we have already
seen, Wilkins thought that the Jewish kabbalah might help
mankind 'to get as much knowledge as *Adam* had in his
innocencie, or human nature is capable of.'[128] Similarly, the
critique by Wilkins and Seth Ward of Webster's examination of
academies included discussion of

the Combinatorian Jews (*viz.* the Author of *Jezirah* and others) and from them
J. Picus: Schalichius Lully, and others, have made Symbols of the Letters of the
Alphabet, so that א signifies with them *God*: ב the *Angelicall Nature* &c.

Their alchemical critique of Webster's understanding of symbols and the naming of the animals by Adam is also conducted

[126] Cf. B. J. Shapiro, *John Wilkins* (Berkeley and Los Angeles, 1969); H. R. Trevor-
Roper, 'Three Foreigners: The Philosophers of the Puritan Revolution', *Religion the
Reformation and Social Change* (London, 1967), pp. 237–93.

[127] W[ilkins], *Mercury*, p. 19. The story was from Buxtorf, and also appeared in R.
Burton, *The Anatomy of Melancholy*, ed. H. Jackson (Everyman edn., London, 1972), iii.
362.

[128] W[ilkins], *Mercvry*, pp. 68–71, 78–9, 82–3, '81–2'=99–100. For more on the proof
of the Trinity, see J. Donne, *Sermons*, ed. E. M. Simpson and G. R. Potter (Berkeley and
Los Angeles, 1953–62), x. 329ff.

with reference to the '*Ensoph*' and other kabbalistic terminology.[129]

These concerns are continued in Wilkins's famous *Essay Towards a Real Character* published fourteen years later. Wilkins summarizes all of the linguistic disputes of the century: the origin of language, the beginnings of writing, change and decay in language, the number of mother tongues, and so on, quoting the major authors from Scaliger to '*Rabbi Judah Chiug* of *Fez* in *Afric*', the eleventh-century grammarian. The *Essay* was a very thorough work, and even John Webb thought it 'a fair overture'. Wilkins entertained some doubts concerning the purity of biblical Hebrew. He wondered whether Hebrew was Isaiah's 'language of Canaan'. Wilkins reasoned that the language 'is exceedingly defective in many other words required to humane discourse' so that it was reasonable to suppose that it is 'not to be the same which was con-created with our first Parents, and spoken by *Adam* in *Paradise*.'[130]

At first glance, this criticism of Hebrew might seem strange in Wilkins's *Essay*, the high-water mark of English linguistic planning in the seventeenth century. Wilkins certainly believed that the Hebrew letters were a divine gift, and he pointed out that ''tis most generally agreed, that *Adam* (though not immediately after his Creation, yet) . . . did invent the ancient *Hebrew* Character'.[131] Wilkins understood that had he taken a much firmer stand on the purity and antiquity of Hebrew, in which words and things were exactly congruent according to the authority of Genesis, then there would have been no need to labour on a philosophical language, complete with complex tables which classified existing knowledge in order to provide an important tool for new discoveries. John Webb, the champion of the Chinese origin of language, faced a similar problem. Hebrew was the model for the universal philosophical language, but Chinese provided the prototype for a universal character. Webb fused the two ideas together and promoted Chinese not only as the exemplar of language before Babel but

---

[129] [Ward and Wilkins], *Vindiciae*, pp. 19, 22.

[130] J. Wilkins, *An Essay Towards a Real Character, And a Philosophical Language* (London, 1668), pp. 5, 19; Webb, *Essay*, p. 187.

[131] Wilkins, *Essay*, p. 11. The question of the origin of writing and the antiquity of Hebrew letters was also very controversial: see e.g. S. Purchas, *Pvrchas His Pilgrimes* (Glasgow, 1905), i. 485–505: first edition published in 1625.

before the Fall as well. Yet he still hoped for a revitalized system
of 'real characters' and never suggested that all mankind
should learn the Chinese system of writing. Adam may have
given the animals Hebrew or even Chinese names, but even the
perfect Adamic language was deemed unsuitable for fallen
man. A new way would have to be found to linguistic purity; the
gates to the Garden of Eden were barred forever.

The conceptual paradox of working towards a philosophical
language while already possessing one which was supposed to
be perfect while plainly was not, was thus a thorny problem for
the language planners. In 1641, Wilkins thought that in framing a universal language, 'the *Hebrew* is the best patterne,
because that language consists of fewest Radicalls.' By 1668,
Wilkins had discussed his linguistic plans with others, the
influence of Comenius had become more widespread, and the
Hebrew model was abandoned as an inadequate idea. Speaking of Seth Ward, Wilkins wrote then that

It was from this suggestion of his, that I first had any distinct apprehension of
the proper course to be observed, in such an undertaking; having in a Treatise
I had published some years before, proposed the *Hebrew* Tongue as consisting
of fewest Radicals, to be the fittest ground work for such a design.

In 1653, Ward and Wilkins objected to the doubts which
Webster threw on the originality of the Hebrew canon; by 1668,
Wilkins agreed with him. The plans for a genuine philosophical
language had come a long way during the interregnum, and the
inadequacy of Hebrew as a successful model had to be admitted.[132]

Other language planners besides Wilkins toyed with the idea
of using Hebrew as the model for a universal language. John
Eliot, the famous apostle to the Indians in New England, wrote
to Boyle with this suggestion. Eliot's revelations concerning the
Lost Ten Tribes of Israel, as we shall see in Chapter Four, were
instrumental in sparking the agitation which ultimately led to
the return of the Jews to England.[133] William Bedell, bishop of
Kilmore in Ireland and a supporter of Comenius and Dury,
also made an attempt at a universal language, but was prevented from publishing it by the Irish rebellion. Bedell was an

---

[132] W[ilkins], *Mercvry*, p. 109; idem, *Essay*, sig. B2ʳ, pp. 5, 19; Webster, *Academiarum*,
p. 6; [Ward and Wilkins], *Vindiciae*, p. 5.

[133] J. Stoughton, *Ecclesiastical History of England* (London, 1867–74), ii. 248–9.

Hebraist and even 'found opportunity of converse with some of the learneder sort of the Jews' when living in Italy. It is very possible that his Hebrew learning was reflected in his artificial language.[134] Even the young Isaac Newton, in the reformed spelling he developed for his rationalized language, utilized the Hebrew letters ע, ה, and ש, to indicate 'ng', 'gh' and 'sh', respectively. In what was probably an imaginary letter to a friend, Newton signed himself 'ispeשali ... Yoʳ veri luviע frend I.N.'[135]

Leibniz had been interested in the idea of a universal language at least from the age of eighteen, when he devised a scheme of using either fractions or prime numbers so that classifying could be accomplished arithmetically. Two years later he published his work, *Arte Combinatoria*, a treatise which showed the influence of Lull and Athanasius Kircher, the German Jesuit scholar and popularizer of Lullist ideas. Leibniz knew of the work of Dalgarno and Wilkins, but hoped to find a system of mathematical calculation which could lead to an infallibility of thinking. Much of this early symbolic logic may seem far away from Adam and Eve and Hebrew in Paradise but, as we have seen, Leibniz was interested in kabbalah and visited Knorr in Sulzbach. Leibniz thought that a language in which words perfectly expressed things would be a 'natural language' such as that described by Plato, the language of Adam, in which he named the animals, and that which all mankind spoke until the Confusion at Babel. Leibniz was sympathetic to the Dutch theories of Goropius Becanus, but when asked if Adam spoke Hebrew, Leibniz replied that the only question was whether Hebrew is nearer than other languages to the common root, which is completely unknown. Leibniz was well in the Hebraic tradition of seventeenth-century language planning.[136]

---

[134] G. Burnet, *The Life of William Bedell* (London, 1692), p. 79; *A True Relation of the Life . . . of . . . Bedell*, ed. T. W. Jones (Camden Soc., n.s., iv, 1872), pp. 3, 6, 9. Bedell was also chaplain to Sir Henry Wotton in Venice from 1607 to 1610, where he studied Hebrew with the famous Rabbi Leone da Modena: Burnet, *Life*, pp. 16–17. See also C. Roth, 'Leone da Modena and his English Correspondents', *Trs. Jew. Hist. Soc. Eng.*, xvii (1951–2), 39–43.

[135] I. Newton, MS notebook, c. 1660–2, in Pierpont Morgan Lib., NY: extracts in R. W. V. Elliott, 'Isaac Newton as Phonetician', *Mod. Lang. Rev.*, lii (1957), 1–18.

[136] L. Couturat, *La logique de Leibniz* (Paris, 1901), pp. 33–118, 541–52, 554–61, esp. p. 77; D. P. Walker, 'Leibniz and Language', *Jnl. Warb. Ctld. Inst.*, xxxv (1972),

VI

'There is scarce any subject that hath been more throughly scanned and debated amongst Learned men,' wrote John Wilkins, 'than the *Original* of *Languages* and *Letters*.'[137] Yet despite this intense study, there was very little that could be thought to be indisputable fact among seventeenth-century linguistic scholars. Detailed schemes for artificial improved languages developed nevertheless even without an agreed theoretical underpinning, first in France, then in England, until the peak was reached with Wilkins's philosophical tables. Ultimately, of course, all of these careful constructions proved to be inadequate. By 1726, Jonathan Swift could satirize the whole concept with his description of the School of Languages in Laputa:

> since Words are only Names for *Things*, it would be more convenient for all Men to carry about them, such *Things* as were necessary to express the particular Business they are to discourse on . . . if a Man's Business be very great, and of various Kinds, he must be obliged to carry a greater Bundle of *Things* upon his Back . . . when they met in the Streets [they] would lay down their Loads, open their Sacks, and hold Conversation for an Hour together; then put up their Implements, help each other to resume their Burthens, and take their Leave.

One great advantage of this scheme, Swift pointed out, was that 'it would serve as an universal Language to be understood in all civilized Nations, whose Goods and Utensils are generally of the same kind'.[138] Present-day scholars have not resolved whether Bacon or Comenius was the true inventor of the concept of the universal language but, it is important to note, both of them warned their readers against trying to put their speculations into practice.[139]

The important point here is that the Hebraic factor runs

294–307: see p. 301 for Leibniz support of Goropius; M. V. David, *Le Débat sur les écritures et l'hiéroglyphe aux XVIIe et XVIIIe siècles* (Paris, 1965), pp. 59–71; J. Cohen, 'On The Project of a Universal Character', *Mind*, lxiii (1954), 49–63; H. Aarsleff, 'Leibniz on Locke on Language', *Amer. Philos. Qly.*, i (1964), 165–88; Yates, *Memory*, pp. 379–88. Leibniz was very interested in Chinese as well, esp. the theory of Dutch orientalist Jacob Gohl (Golius) that Chinese had been invented to be a 'real character': D. F. Lach, 'Leibniz and China', *Jnl. Hist. Ideas*, vi (1945), 436–55, esp. p. 437; idem, 'The Chinese Studies of Andreas Müller', *Jnl. Or. Soc.*, lx (1940), 564–75; D. P. Walker, *The Ancient Theology* (London, 1972), *cap.* vi.

[137] Wilkins, *Essay*, p. 2.

[138] J. Swift, *Gulliver's Travels*, ed. H. Davis (Oxford, 1965), pp. 185–6: Part III, *cap.* 5.

[139] Bacon, *Works*, iii. 399–401; Comenius, *Light*, pp. 219–20.

through the entire history of artificial languages, from Francis Bacon to Lazarus Ludwig Zamenhof, the Jewish oculist from Warsaw who invented Esperanto at the end of the nineteenth century. Hebrew may have been the *lingua humana*, but it was also an artificial language, revived by Eliezer Ben-Yehuda in the 1880s as the Zionist vernacular. Throughout the seventeenth century, the bulk of English scholarly opinion confirmed that 'it be commonly thought the *Hebrew* Language was the common Language of the *Canaanites*'.[140] The preoccupation of the seventeenth-century language planners with restoring the linguistic harmony of the Garden of Eden and returning to the clear glass of Adam's Hebrew was of a more highly developed intensity. Kabbalistic ideas and terminology had begun to filter into English circles at least through second-hand sources by the seventeenth century, and only the Jews could decipher this branch of esoteric knowledge.

Gibbon complained that the great Cambridge Hebraist John Lightfoot, 'by constant reading of the rabbis, became almost a rabbi himself'.[141] To some extent this criticism might apply to the entire Comenius circle, advocates of what Charles Webster has called 'extreme philo-semitism, resulting in intense curiosity about Jewish law, language and the mystical philosophy of the Cabbala.' This movement, he says, 'was ultimately influential in persuading Oliver Cromwell to readmit the Jews into England in 1656.'[142] As we shall see, it was John Dury who sparked the active political campaign for readmission with a letter to Menasseh ben Israel at Amsterdam. The search for a universal language helped to intensify their interest in the Jews, and no doubt was an important topic of conversation when Menasseh was called to London. It was this mystical aspect of Hebrew, quite aside from the mere recognition of the Jewish tongue as the language of Scripture, which evoked their admiration.

On a more general scholarly level, the virtual agreement in England that Adam and Eve spoke Hebrew in the Garden of Eden, when words perfectly signified things, helped to put Jews

---

[140] M. Hale, *The Primitive Origination of Mankind* (London, 1677), p. 163. Hale also thought that Webb's Chinese theory was 'but a novel Conceit.' (ibid.).

[141] *Dict. Nat. Biog.*, *s.v.*, 'Lightfoot'.

[142] C. Webster, *Samuel Hartlib and the Advancement of Learning* (Cambridge, 1970), p. 39.

in a favourable light as guardians of that sacred heritage. On a
popular level, the continuous glorification of Hebrew, not only
as a sacred language like Greek, but as a unique divinely
infused, supernatural method of communication, helped to
turn men's minds towards Jews and to erode the medieval
conception of the obscurantist, Pharisaic Jew. Hebrew's star
continued to shine until well after the Restoration when the
Aristotelian dream of John Wilkins was finally delivered to the
Royal Society that had commissioned it. At the time of the
Whitehall Conference in December 1655, Hebrew was king,
the divine language of Canaan in England's New Jerusalem.

3

THE CALLING OF THE JEWS

When Andrew Marvell made his overtures 'To His Coy Mistress', he expressed his 'vegetable love' in an idiom of the time:

> I would
> Love you ten years before the Flood:
> And you should, if you please, refuse
> Till the Conversion of the Jews.

To speak of Noah's Flood and the conversion of the Jews in the same breath was not to indulge in difficult literary metaphor: these two events were linked in the minds of contemporaries. Zachary Crofton summarized the chronology in the context of a fierce pamphlet war with John Rogers, the Fifth Monarchy Man who had published an account of the divine scheme. 'There is argument for it, it is analogical', wrote Crofton, 'It was in 1656, the flood came on the old world, and lasted fourty daies: Ergo in that year 1656, fire must come on this world and last fourty years'. On this Day of Judgement, 'the Jews will sure be suddenly called, and Antichrist ruined'.[1] As Rogers and other Englishmen turned during the middle 1650s towards the End of Days and the means necessary to hasten the Second Coming, many began to agree with Abraham Cowley the poet that 'There wants, methinks, but the *Conversion* of . . . the *Jews*, for the accomplishing of the *Kingdom of Christ*.'[2] The belief that the end of the world was imminent, and that the Jews were

---

[1] Z. Crofton, *Bethshemesh Clouded* (London, 1653), pp. 3–4.
[2] A. Cowley, *Poems* (London, 1656), sig. B2ᵛ.

destined to play a major role in this final drama, was widespread in England during this period, and helped to mould public opinion regarding readmission.

We have already seen how the scattered open Jews and flamboyant Judaizers helped to awaken Englishmen to contemporary Jewry, and how the debate over the universal language and the glorification of Hebrew helped to put Jews in a favourable light with both the learned scholars of the Comenius circle and more humble readers of the Old Testament. But more pervasive was the attention paid to Jews in the writings of the millenarians in the first half of the seventeenth century. Nevertheless, despite the fact that concern with the Jews is apparent in all of the major millenarian works, and analysis of their fate was indeed an essential component of the millenarian interpretation of history, detailed exposition of the place of the Jews in this schema has been lacking in secondary works.

Historians have traced the origin of millenarianism from the Reformation, as some men began to doubt Augustine's assurance that the prophecies and histories of scripture were primarily allegorical. The vague promises of the Old and New Testaments came to acquire a more literal immediacy, and the prominence of the Jews in these narratives was striking. Luther himself came to believe that the Papacy could be identified with the Fourth Monarchy of Daniel and the Beast of Revelation.[3] The attitudes of English millenarians towards the Jews also developed during this period, but when historians have discussed the importance of Jews to this divine plan they have jumped rather too quickly from the calling of the Jews to the summoning of Menasseh ben Israel from Amsterdam. The approach to the Jewish question evolved over this period of time, and this can be demonstrated not only from the writings of the great millenarian theorists, but also from the more popular works that appeared in the half-century before the Whitehall Conference.

I

Saint Paul had promised that 'all Israel shall be saved' once 'the fulness of the Gentiles be come in.'[4] This prediction was

---

[3] E. L. Tuveson, *Millennium and Utopia* (Berkeley and Los Angeles, 1949), pp. 17, 24–9; B. S. Capp, *The Fifth Monarchy Men* (London, 1972), *cap.* 1.

[4] Romans 11: 25–6.

recognized in England even at the beginning of the Puritan challenge to English orthodoxy. Ralph Durden, a Cambridge-educated minister, claimed as early as 1586 that he would lead the Jews and the Christian faithful to Jerusalem, where he would found the kingdom which would rule for a thousand years. His identification of the Tudor monarchy with the Beast was more problematic, and this lack of discretion landed him in prison when he predicted its ultimate downfall.[5] Andrew Willett published a work entirely devoted to the calling of the Jews, although he rejected the idea that the entire nation would be converted suddenly.[6] But this Elizabethan interest in the ultimate fate of the Jews merely foreshadowed later more spectacular developments.

The importance of the Jews to the millenarian plan is apparent in the works of the high priests of English seventeenth-century millenarianism, Brightman, Alsted, and Mede.[7] Thomas Brightman (1562–1607), minister of Hawnes, Bedfordshire, under Elizabeth, produced a brand of millenarian doctrine that was the product of an earlier, more hopeful generation. Brightman argued that the millennium had begun about 1300, had been steadily increasing in glory, and would soon reach perfection with the fall of Rome. According to Brightman's interpretation, the promises of the book of Revelation were being fulfilled progressively. Determined proselytizing could therefore bring about 'the full restoring of the Iewish Nation, out of the dust of destruction, and their calling to the faith in Christ'. Brightman noted that 'many large and pleasant Prophesies do ayme at the calling of the Iewes'. Careful reading of Scripture revealed that the first step would be the fall of Rome, then the conversion of the Jews, and finally the destruction of the Turkish Empire. The Turks would be defeated by the conversion of the Jews. Jews would abandon their legal idolatry, and their Church would reign upon the earth for a thousand years. 'The Jewes were alwayes wont to finde the Gentiles most hatefull and spightfull against them in former

[5] J. Strype, *Annals of the Reformation* (Oxford, 1824), II. i. 693–4; ii. 479–87; Capp, *Fifth Monarchy*, p. 29.

[6] See M. Vereté, 'The Restoration of the Jews in English Protestant Thought 1790–1840', *Middle Eastern Studies*, viii (1972), 15, 45.

[7] Generally, see now P. Christianson, *Reformers and Babylon* (Toronto, 1978); and K. R. Firth, *The Apocalyptic Tradition in Reformation Britain* (Oxford, 1979).

Ages', Brightman lamented, 'as who laboured by all meanes possible to annoy and to mischiefe them; but now the case shall be quite altered, the Jewes shall have no cause to feare any harme or wrong at the hands of the Gentiles'. Brightman's translator in the next generation was not content to leave philo-semitism for the End of Days, and called upon Englishmen to patch up their quarrel with the Jews while there was still time.[8]

Like many others after him, Brightman attempted to prophesy the precise moment of Christ's victory. The key text was in the book of Daniel:

And from the time *that* the daily *sacrifice* shall be taken away, and the abomination that maketh desolate set up, *there shall be* a thousand two hundred and ninety days. Blessed *is* he that waiteth, and cometh to the thousand three hundred and five and thirty days.[9]

Brightman thought that the daily sacrifice was finally removed with 'the last open overthrow of all the legall worship, which came to passe in the dayes of *Iulian*, about the year 360'. The children of Israel were punished for their transgressions parallel to the number of days which the spies of Moses spent in surveying the land of Canaan, 'each day for a year.' According to this logic, if 1,290 years were added to the figure 360, it seemed certain that the reappearance of Christ would occur in 1650, followed by the institution of a new Jerusalem forty-five years later. 'And then, indeed, shall all the Saints be blessed,' Brightman predicted, 'who shall have a glorious resurrection, and be raised out of the dust of destruction, . . . when the Saints shall see new *Ierusalem* comming down from Heaven, themselves inrolled citizens thereof, dogs excluded, and whatsoever is unclean'. Brightman therefore predicted, half a century before the anticipated Day of Judgement, that the Jews would be converted to Christianity by 1650. Brightman's works were among the most respected and influential of millenarian writings, and were reissued in England after the onset of the Civil War. His translator then emphasized the role of the Protestants

---

[8] T. Brightman, *The Revelation of St. Iohn Illustrated* (4th edn., London, 1644), sig. A2ᵛ; pp. 850, 874, 894, 898, 1076–7; cf. P. Toon, 'The Latter-Day Glory' in his *Puritans, the Millennium and the Future of Israel* (Cambridge and London, 1970), pp. 26–32; Capp, *Fifth Monarchy*, pp. 28–9.

[9] Dan. 12: 11–12.

in the calling of the Jews to Christ, and surely Brightman's confident predictions of their conversion before 1650 helped to agitate his English disciples to work as the servants of fate.[10]

The eschatology of Joseph Mede (1586–1668) was of a much more radical and violent nature. Mede, a fellow of Christ's College, Cambridge, was the English exponent of the views popularized on the Continent by Johann Heinrich Alsted (1588–1638), professor at Herborn in Hesse-Nassau. Mede taught that the millennium was wholly future, but would be established imminently by a cataclysmic series of events. Mede's God would deal with the Jews according to His own inscrutable, divine plan, and the efforts of mankind to hasten their conversion were completely worthless. Mede clarified this point in a letter of 1629 which was meant as a reply to a question posed to him by William Twisse:

For my part, I incline to think that no such thing will provoke them; but that they shall be called by *Vision* and *Voice from Heaven*, as S. *Paul* was . . . They will never believe that Christ reigns at the right hand of God, until they see him. It must be an invincible evidence which must convert them after so many hundred years settled obstinacy. But this I speak of the body of the Nation; there may be some *Praeludia* of some particulars converted upon other motives, as a forerunner of the great and main Conversion.[11]

Mede thought that the Jews would become 'the most Zealous and fervent of the Nations' once they were converted to Christianity; Twisse disagreed.[12] Mede, the champion of apocalyptic millenarianism, thus ironically advocated a passive attitude towards the Jews.

Brightman, Alsted, and Mede were among the most influential of the academic millenarians. Brightman died when Mede was only twenty-one, but the writings of all three of these men achieved their greatest prominence at the same time as a result of the relative freedom of the press in England during the 1640s. The impact on contemporary religious and social thought of the liberty to publish a wide variety of radical and

[10] Num. 14: 34; Brightman, *Revelation*, sig. A2ᵛ, pp. 967–8.

[11] J. Mede, *Works* (London, 1677), p. 761; cf. B. S. Capp, '*Godly Rule* and English Millenarianism', *Past and Present*, lii (1971), 114–15; idem, *Fifth Monarchy*, pp. 28–9; R. G. Clouse, 'The Rebirth of Millenarianism', *Future of Israel*, ed. Toon, pp. 42–65.

[12] J. Mede, *Remaines On some Passages in The Revelation* (London, 1650), p. 39; idem, *Works*, pp. 764–5.

even subversive opinions cannot be overestimated. Among the
numerous heterodox and bizarre pamphlets which issued during the Civil War and Commonwealth period were analyses of
the role of the Jews in bringing about the Second Coming, as
well as outright pleas for their readmission. Many of the lesser
millenarian writers and radicals acknowledged their debt to
Brightman, Alsted, and Mede, but even failing this they can
rightly be regarded as their intellectual children, if only from
the chronological point of view.

Nevertheless, one can certainly find evidence of this brand of
millenarianism even during the relatively placid days of James
I. The earliest seventeenth-century discussion of the calling of
the Jews, in fact, contains the germs of most of the major issues.
Thomas Draxe published such an account as early as 1608,
specifically devoted to the calling of the Jews. Draxe explained
that their conversion would take place only after the fall of
Rome had purified Christianity and rendered it acceptable to
Jews throughout the world. The Jews would accept Jesus *en
masse*, although some stragglers might continue to reject him in
the face of overwhelming theological evidence. The Gospel
would be suddenly revived, even in those places where the New
Testament was already known. Draxe believed that 'there
shalbe some reasonable distance of time betweene the burning
of Rome and the end of the worlde, in which it is more conson-
ant to truth that the Iewes shalbe called'. Their conversion
would be 'the last generall signe & fore-runner of Christs
second comming'.[13]

Another important element of the millenarian plan for the
Jews was the notion of their restoration to Zion, and Draxe
comments on this as well. He denied that the Jews were ever
promised that they would be restored to the Holy Land, and
pointed out that practically 'neither haue they any possibility of
meanes to compasse it.'[14] Yet despite Draxe's scepticism at this
early stage in the seventeenth-century philo-semitic agitation,
the proto-Zionism of the millenarians emerges as a pervasive
strand in the debate over readmission.

In any case, it was far easier to predict the ultimate conver-

[13] T. Draxe, *The Worldes Resvrrection* (London, 1608), pp. 51, 88–91, 94.
[14] Ibid., p. 89.

sion and spiritual rehabilitation of the Jews than to work on their behalf during the more restricted years before the Civil War. Draxe contented himself with the advice that Christian princes should compel the Jews to hear the Gospel and should restrict Jewish usury. Christian subjects might provide an admirable example, for if they conducted themselves with piety 'doubtlesly in many places many more Iewes then now are, would be moued and drawne to embrace the Gospell.'[15]

Thomas Draxe, however, was hardly a leading light of Jacobean intellectual life. Declarations of support for the Jews from high places needed to be offered with care before the outbreak of the Civil War. Serjeant Sir Henry Finch, a renowned lawyer and the author of a highly respected treatise on the common law, anonymously published a book in 1621 entitled *The Worlds Great Restavration. Or The Calling of the Iewes*. Finch proclaimed to world Jewry that

Out of all the places of thy dispersion, East, West, North, and South, his purpose is to bring thee home againe, & to marry thee to himselfe by faith for euermore. In stead that thou wast desolate and forsaken, and sattest as a widdow, thou shalt flourish as in the dayes of thy youth. Nay, aboue and beyond thy youth.

William Gouge, the famous Puritan preacher in Blackfriars, contributed a signed epistle to the Christian reader. 'I haue bin moued to publish this Treatise,' he explained, 'and to commend it to thy reading. And this is all that I haue done. The worke it selfe is the worke of one who hath diued deeper into that mysterie then I can doe. His great vnderstanding of the Hebrew tongue hath bin a great helpe to him therein.'[16]

'This work was written not by a religious maniac,' Dr Hill reminds us, and 'the government was clearly alarmed.'[17] By 18 April 1621, Finch was in the Fleet. John Chamberlain wrote that Finch was incarcerated 'for setting out a booke on the conversion of the Jewes, wherein he discovers himself to hold many foolish and fantasticall (yf not impious) opinions.'[18] Gouge was punished as well, even though the book 'was only

[15] Ibid., p. 94.

[16] [H. Finch], *The Calling Of The Ievves* (London, 1621), f. 4^r, sig. A2, p. 1.

[17] C. Hill, *Society and Puritanism* (2nd edn., New York, 1967), p. 203.

[18] *Letters of John Chamberlain*, ed. N. E. McClure (Philadelphia, 1939), ii. 363: C. to Carleton, 18 Apr. 1621: similarly, *Cal. S. P. Dom.*, *1619–23*, p. 248.

published by him, and the true Author acknowledged: yet for publishing it, was he committed nine weekes to prison.' Thomas Gouge explained that

King James imagined that the *Serjeant* had in that book declared, that the *Jewes* should have a Regiment above all other kingdomes, thereupon was beyond all patience impatient. And *B. Neal* and others putting him on especially against the Publisher of the Book, made him so fierce as he would admit no Apology.[19]

Thomas Fuller jested that Finch 'so enlarged the future amplitude of the Jewish State that thereby he occasioned a confining to himself.'[20] Both Finch and Gouge were kept in prison until their recantations were approved.

Gouge was being modest about his Hebrew learning. While still an undergraduate at King's College, Cambridge, Gouge studied Hebrew with a Jew, probably a convert, 'who was entertained into sundry Colleges to teach the *Hebrew tongue*'. After the Jew had left Cambridge, Gouge was approached by the other students there who 'intreated him to instruct them in the grounds of *Hebrew*, which accordingly he did, whereby he became very expert therein.'[21] Gouge's private views on the calling of the Jews were, as we shall see, expressed more fully in a fast sermon delivered at the height of the Civil War. Finch himself does not appear to have been particularly learned in Hebrew, but a man in his position could not have failed to appreciate the harsh treatment of John Traske, whose case had come to prominence only a few years before.

The Finch–Gouge scandal provoked sharp rebuke, but it was relatively short-lived. Laud, then dean of Gloucester, preached a birthday sermon before the king on 19 June 1621 against the 'errour of the Iewes' which Finch promoted in his 'vanitie'.[22] John Chamberlain sent a copy of Laud's work to Sir Dudley Carleton 'because yt somwhat touches the ydle conceit of Sergeant Finches booke of the calling of the Jews.'[23] Finch was sixty-three years old when the controversy began, and

---

[19] W. Gouge, *Commentary on . . . Hebrewes* (London, 1655), sigs. b^v–b2^r.

[20] T. Fuller, *A Pisgah-Sight of Palestine* (London, 1650), p. 194.

[21] Gouge, *Commentary*, sig. b2^r.

[22] W. Laud, *A Sermon Preached Before His Maiesty* (London, 1621), pp. 24–8, esp. p. 24: repr. *Works*, ed. W. Scott and J. Bliss (Libr. of Anglo-Catholic Theology, lvii–lxv, 1847–1860), i. 1–29.

[23] *Letters of . . . Chamberlain*, ed. McClure, ii. 391: Ch. to C., 21 July 1621: similarly, *Cal. S. P. Dom., 1619–23*, p. 277.

although he was eventually reinstated in his office, by 1623 his son John was granted probation for one year from arrest for the debts of his father which he had agreed to pay. Finch died in October 1625.[24]

The issues which Finch and Gouge raised remained controversial. Joseph Mede was impressed by Finch's book: 'God forgive me,' he wrote, 'if it be a sin, but I have thought so many a day'. Mede published his famous *Clavis Apocalyptica* six years after he read *The Calling Of The Iewes*.[25] Nearly three decades after the event, Thomas Fuller was still outraged by what he saw as Finch's 'expressions (indiscreetly uttered, or uncharitably construed) importing, that all Christian Princes should surrender their power as homagers to the temporall supreme Empire of the Jewish nation.'[26] Although no doubt many men agreed with Sir Henry Finch and William Gouge that the calling of the Jews to Christ was integrally related to the Redemption, these views were hardly expressed in public between Finch's death and the beginning of disturbances in the 1640s. Gouge was content to learn the lessons of Finch and Traske and to wait until the victory of the saints before discussing the subject again in full.

By the time that the Long Parliament began to sit, the conversion of the Jews became a subject of controversy once again. One anonymous author devoted a pamphlet to debunking the notion that the Jews could ever return to Palestine in triumph. The writer accepted the validity of the prophecy itself, that the Jews would one day be gathered from out of the countries in which they now lived, 'from the foure Winds, as well they of the tenne Tribes of Israell'. Graves would open, and the Lord would bring them back to the land of their forefathers according to the prophecies of Ezekiel and Zechariah. Belief was strained, the writer explained, not by the gloriousness of the prophecy, but by the idea that it should be

---

[24] *Dict. Nat. Biog.*, s.v. 'Finch'; cf. F. Kobler, 'Sir Henry Finch (1558–1625) and the first English advocates of the Restoration of the Jews to Palestine', *Trs. Jew. Hist. Soc. Eng.*, xvi (1952), 101–20; W. R. Prest, 'The Art of Law and the Law of God: Sir Henry Finch (1558–1625)' in *Puritans and Revolutionaries*, ed. D. Pennington and K. Thomas (Oxford, 1978), pp. 94–117.

[25] See W. H. G. Armytage, *Heavens Below: Utopian Experiments in England* (London, 1961), p. 14.

[26] Fuller, *Pisgah-Sight*, p. 194.

'here in this poluted world fulfilled on a latter off spring of Iewes
remaining, or as the Millinaries would have it of a comming of
Christ'. He rejected the notion that the Church of the Jews
would reign over the world for a thousand years with the aid of
their resurrected brethren and called upon the godly to provide
adequate and convincing scriptural evidence or to desist from
promulgating this fantasy.[27]

Despite these protests, the scholarly works of millenarian
academics such as Brightman, Alsted, and Mede amply
demonstrated that abundant evidence could be found in the
Bible to prove that the calling of the Jews, even to their ancient
homeland of Canaan, was imminent. The most vociferous disputes during this speculative period before the political movement for readmission began in earnest were concerned rather
more with the chronology of redemption than the truth of the
prophetical interpretations. John Archer, pastor of the English
church at Arnhem, was typical of this pattern of thought. He
rejected the most popular date for the projected millennium,
which was 1666, since the number of the Beast in the book of
Revelation '*is* Six hundred threescore *and* six.'[28] But whereas
Brightman and others added Daniel's other figure of 1290 to
the imagined date of the reign of Julian the Apostate (360 AD),
and claimed that 1650 would see the beginning of the Redemption, Archer thought it might be more correct to date Julian's
reign as 366 AD, thus moving up the date 'in which the Israelites
are to be delivered' to 1656.[29] Stanley Gower preached one of
the semi-official fast sermons to Parliament in July 1644 and
advocated 1650 as the date for the end of the 'Turkish tyranny'
and the conversion of the Jews. This would be 'a returne so
strange, a delivery so great,' he wrote, 'that it is resembled to a
resurrection from the grave.'[30] Mary Cary, the Fifth Monarchist,
agreed with Archer's chronology and wrote that the Jews will
be converted 'very suddenly, and very admirably.' This would

[27] I.E., *The Land Of Promise* (London, 1641), pp. 18–19, 23, 35.
[28] Rev. 13: 18; on eschatological chronology generally see C. Hill, *Antichrist in
Seventeenth-Century England* (London, 1971), pp. 111–15; K. Thomas, *Religion and the
Decline of Magic* (Penguin edn., Harmondsworth, 1973), pp. 166–71; P. G. Rogers, *The
Fifth Monarchy Men* (London, 1966), *cap.* 1.
[29] I. Archer, *The Personall Reigne of Christ* (London, 1642), p. 48.
[30] S. Gower, *Things Now-a-doing* (London, 1644), sigs. A2^v–A3.

be accomplished 'before any work is visibly begun, and before those ordinary preparations to such a worke, that do use to precede the same work in others, at other times, when others have been begotten and borne to Christ'. She insisted that the entire Jewish nation would be converted and 'brought forth in one day'.[31] Ralph Josselin the Essex minister believed that 'wee may expect a preparation to the Jewes conversion' in 1654 or 1655.[32] Henry Jessey expected the *conversion of the* JEWS probably before 1658'.[33] John Tillinghast, the Independent minister, thought that 'the beginning of the *Jews delivery*, is likely to be, either in the year it selfe, or thereabouts of our Lord . . . 1656.' He was sure that 'wee are fallen into that age in which the Jews shall be converted.' Tillinghast also thought that Brightman and Archer were 'godly judicious men.'[34]

Much of this material was collected and compared with Jewish sources by Nathaniel Homes, one of Menasseh ben Israel's English correspondents, who concluded that 'we can expect no more *then*, in the said 1655 yeer, but the call of the *Jewes*, who from that time shall strive with the *Turke*, and all enemies of the *Jewes* conversion five and forty yeers, *Dan.* 12. afore their settlement, before which *Call* I expect the fall of the *Roman Antichrist.*' Homes quoted similar views from the works of Peter Martyr, Alsted, Mede, and Twisse for support.[35] He was still hopeful of their conversion in 1665.[36] John Evelyn recorded that William Oughtred the famous mathematician thought that Christ would appear to convert the Jews in 1656.[37] An anonymous author in 1647 rejected all these views. 'We are sufficiently informed in the Scriptures,' he claimed, 'and next to them from others, that the day of Doome is even now at hand, and that the second coming of Christ is each day and houre to be expected'.[38]

---

[31] M. Cary, *The Little Horns Doom* (London, 1651), pp. 145, 164–5, 205–9.

[32] *The Diary of Ralph Josselin*, ed. A. Macfarlane (London, 1976), p. 228: 2 Jan. 1650–1.

[33] In Cary, *Doom*, sig. A5.

[34] J. Tillinghast, *Generation Work* (London, 1653), pp. 54, 64.

[35] N. Homes, *The Resurrection Revealed* (London, 1654), pp. 30, 427, 562.

[36] N. Homes, 'A brief Chronology concerning the Jews', in *Two Journeys to Jerusalem*, ed. R. B. (London, 1719), pp. 118–23: dated in text, Dec. 1665.

[37] *The Diary of John Evelyn*, ed. E. S. de Beer (Oxford, 1955), iii. 157–8: 28 Aug. 1655.

[38] [Anon.], *Doomes-Day* (London, 1647), p. 6.

Despite these minor disagreements about the precise date of
the Second Coming and the conversion of the Jews, most
millenarians were in agreement that the Jews would be called
to Christ before the Redemption and the fall of Rome. They
thus excluded Roman Catholicism from any kind of evangeliz-
ing function among the Jews, and expressed sympathy and
understanding for the rejection by Jews, in countries under the
Roman rite, of Christianity in general. The intensifying debate
over the role of the Jews in the Second Coming, coupled with
the notorious scandals of Traske's Judaizing and Finch's millennial dreams, helped to promote speculation about modern
Jews and to publicize the contemporary state of world Jewry.
Most Englishmen, if they thought about Jews at all, saw them
as an ancient people who provided a 'type' fulfilled by Christ's
mission on earth. The millenarian preoccupation with the calling of contemporary Jewry to Christ naturally precipitated an
awareness of the state of the Jews who were to be called. Jews
formed an ever obtrusive presence on the Continent, but English memories needed to be jogged before they would consider
the fate of world Jewry. As we shall see, it was this aspect of
seventeenth-century English religious thought which was
among the most influential in securing the readmission of the
Jews to England.

These points were expressed very forcefully by Robert
Maton, a minister who published a short book on the subject in
the same year that saw the beginning of the Civil War. The aim
of his work was put succinctly in a dedicatory poem: he hoped
that the book would show Englishmen

> the wonders of Gods mighty hand,
> When Jews come backe unto the holy Land.
> That they, (if possible) by faith may shun
> That dayes great Wrath, before that day's begun.
> For wit, nor wealth, nor Warlike force shall hold
> That chosen people from their promis'd Fold.

Maton was convinced that the Jews would be redeemed from
captivity in the Diaspora, and would recover Palestine once
again. He argued that the simple unadorned conversion of the
Jews to Christianity would not be sufficiently miraculous to
merit the wonderous signs and portents which would accom-

pany them to their salvation. The prophets must have meant 'the Jewes inhabiting againe of their owne land, and the bringing of all other Nations into subjection to them; then it is evident, that Christs comming at this time, shall be to accomplish this thing to *Israel*'. Maton advised Christians to be on guard that they do not 'contemne or revile the Jewes, a fault too common in the Christian world', presumably because the Jewes would one day become their rulers.[39]

These were the subjects to which William Gouge returned in 1645 when his earlier courage was finally vindicated as he preached one of the semi-official fast sermons to Parliament, on 24 September. As Keith Thomas explains, the leaders of the Long Parliament 'used Fast Day sermons as a means of rallying members and signalling changes in the party line.'[40] While it would be rash to attribute Gouge's views on the calling of the Jews to each member of Parliament, it must be stressed that this sermon was no ordinary exposition of a particular text, but was rather more in the nature of an official statement on the role of the Jews in the Second Coming. Gouge's sermon included a careful analysis of Paul's promise concerning the calling of the Jews. He dealt with all of the possible objections to this prophecy in turn, and disposed of each one. Gouge insisted that 'there is a time to come, when not only two or three, or a few *Jews* here and there thorowout the Christian Church (as have been in all ages thereof) but the whole Nation shall be called.' When this glorious work would be accomplished, 'their calling shall be as a resurrection from the dead'. The conversion of the Jews to Christ was at hand, but before that miraculous moment the English could expect a radical improvement in their fortunes. The English, just like the chosen people of ancient times, might expect a similar mercy before the Second Coming. For the Jews were blessed before the First Coming with a return from captivity, a second temple, and a restoration of the Law. 'This may further be exemplified', Gouge concluded, 'by Gods doing better for us here in *England* then at our beginnings.'[41]

Gouge's sermon before the Long Parliament illustrates both

[39] R. Maton, *Israels Redemption* (London, 1642), p. *vs.* title-p.; pp. 5, 50, 68–9.
[40] Thomas, *Magic*, p. 174; cf. H. R. Trevor-Roper, *Religion the Reformation and Social Change* (London, 1967), *cap.* vi.
[41] W. Gouge, *The Progresse of Divine Providence* (London, 1645), pp. 29–33.

of the functions of fast sermons which Mr Thomas emphasizes. Inasmuch as the sermon was almost an official document, Gouge was careful to dissociate himself from the Judaizing heresies of Traske and Brabourne. 'Some, whom we may well stile *Jewish Christians*, so farre manifest their folly', he confided, that they 'actually conform themselves to that servile pedagogy.' Not only did they observe the Jewish dietary laws, but they also kept the Saturday Sabbath in contravention to Christian practice. 'Too near to these doe they come.' he admonished, 'who though they do not tie themselves to the very same rites and ordinances, whereto the Jews were bound, yet treat too near upon their heels, and too apishly imitate them'. These Jewish Christians only encouraged genuine Jews to persist in their Mosaical ceremonies 'when they see such as professe themselves Christians, come so near there unto.'[42]

William Gouge, and the ecclesiastical establishment which stood behind his sermon and printed it, thus demonstrated that it was possible to await the calling of the Jews to Christ without falling into the Judaizing extremes of Traske and Brabourne. Those millenarians who came after him were often less circumspect. Gouge's sermon was a scholarly and Hebraic analysis of Ezekiel 26: 11. The 'Doomes-Day' pamphlet of 1647, on the other hand, was an hysterical report that 'the Jews, according to certaine and credible information, are at this time assembling themselves together into one body from out of all countreys, wherinto they have been driven with a resolution to regaine the holy land once more out of the hand of *Ottaman*'. They were said to be under the leadership of one '*Josias Catzius*, and according to Letters from beyond the Seas, they are numerous, and shew themselves in great bodies in Illyria, Bethinia and Cappadocia.'[43] No doubt reports like this one strained the credibility of the millenarian case. As one critic complained, 'that all the Jewes and Israelites now remaining, should be all converted to the faith of Christ, and become a great nation and kingdome, this is a thing not onely beyond all probability in reason, but also besides all grounds of Scripture.'[44]

---

[42] Ibid., pp. 22–4.

[43] *Doomes-Day*, p. 2.

[44] [Anon.], *The Great Day at the Dore* (London, 1648), p. 19. When Ralph Josselin read

One of the most interesting aspects of philo-semitic millenarianism during the Civil War and interregnum, aside from the more flamboyant antics of some of its exponents, was the extent to which it was believed that England was chosen to lead the Jews to salvation. John Eachard, for example, a Suffolk minister, confessed that he was 'perswaded that the *Jewes* shall receive their Christs Nativitie day from *England*, and from our blossoming Thorne, rather than from any other Church in Christendome.'[45] As we have already seen, many Englishmen were sympathetic, even gratified, that the Jews rejected Christianity as interpreted by 'that great Whore, the city of *Rome*'.[46] Most millenarians agreed with John Sadler when he exclaimed that 'the *Iewes*, and Their Returne. It is so Cleare; and so full in the Scriptures'. But Sadler was also among the handful of this group who actually rose to positions of power and were able to bring about the fulfilment of England's destined championship of the Jews.[47]

By 1650, a tradition of millenarian support for the Jews, and an appreciation of their place in the long-awaited cosmic drama had already been established. The vague musings of Sir Henry Finch would have been considered quite respectable and even too unambitious in the next generation. As we shall see, direct agitation for readmission began in 1649, and later millenarian pronouncements on the calling of the Jews must be seen parallel to the more practical efforts which were being conducted on their behalf.

John Sadler was not the only millenarian who also played some part in the more mundane struggle for Jewish readmission, and politicians and more sober-minded religious leaders are often to be found rubbing shoulders with extravagant radicals. This is apparent in Mary Cary's work of 1651, which included epistles from Hugh Peter, Henry Jessey, and Christopher Feake. These were all important religious figures, and, as we have seen, Henry Jessey has some claim to being the man

---

this book he thanked God for it. Josselin believed that the Italian Jews who would witness the imminent fall of Rome would then convince their breathren in other places: *Diary*, ed. Macfarlane, p. 268: 15 Jan. 1651–2.

[45] J. Eachard, *Good Newes For All Christian Soldiers* (London, 1645), sig. B2r.
[46] Cary, *Doom*, p. 140.
[47] [J. Sadler], *Rights of the Kingdom* (London, 1649), p. 40; see below, pp. 195, 242.

behind the scenes in the readmission of the Jews. Cary, who became a millenarian at the age of fifteen, was convinced that the Jews would be suddenly and wonderfully converted in a single day, and would be gathered together as a distinct nation and returned to the Holy Land.[48] Hugh Peter and Henry Jessey were both instrumental in achieving effective resettlement for the Jews, and their endorsement of Cary's pamphlet goes some way towards revealing the motives behind their advocacy.

Other millenarians continued Cary's approach to the Jewish question. John Tillinghast, the Cambridge-educated minister of a gathered church in Norfolk, thought that it was 'our special *worke* in this *generation*' to prepare ourselves to receive the conversion of the Jews. Tillinghast remarked that even though he risked seeming 'to tautologize', the imminent conversion of the Jews is so self-evident that he did not need to bother with providing a detailed proof. Tillinghast was especially encouraged by Rabbi Menasseh ben Israel's revelation that the Jews had a 'generall expectation . . . of their Messiahs comming in this *age*'.[49] Nathaniel Homes, one of Menasseh's correspondents, was also an enthusiastic millenarian. The year before the expected Redemption he wrote that 'the Glorious time we speake of, is not far off; but now approacheth, especially in the *introduction* thereunto, *viz*. The Call of the *Jews*.' Homes quoted Menasseh's views at length in this treatise, and applied to the Dutch rabbi in Latin for confirmation of his published opinions; Henry Jessey added a postscript to this letter.[50]

Most of these controversial remarks on the role of the Jews in the Second Coming were made in the context of theoretical, if not academic, discussions. It has been a common pastime to devise calculations about the end of the world, and was especially prevalent in the nineteenth as well as the seventeenth century. The failure of divine history to fulfill the expectations of millenarians left them undiscouraged. The most notorious victim of this system was William Sedgwick, the preacher who made the mistake of prophesying in 1647 that the world would

[48] Cary, *Doom*, pp. 145–6, 161–5, 205–9.

[49] Tillinghast, *Generation Work*, pp. 48–9, 54–5, 57, 59, 64.

[50] Homes, *Resurrection*, sig. A5ʳ, pp. 30, 39, 419–20, 427, 430, 544, 547, 562; N. Homes and H. Jessey to Menasseh ben Israel, 24 Dec. 1649: repr. in P. Felgenhawer, *Bonum Nuncium Israeli* (Amsterdam, 1655), pp. 103–6.

end within a fortnight—he carried the name 'Doomsday Sedgwick' until his death fifteen years later.[51] Zachary Crofton therefore complained that 'many will be ready to look for a *Sedgewicks* Dooms-day.'[52] Hugh Peter spoke of the universal interest in millenarianism when he described 'Some looking to the Prophesies that concern *Gog* and *Magog*: some casting their eye upon the drying up of *Euphrates*, . . . and most men disputing the slaying of the two witnesses; as much conducing to Gods designe in bringing about . . . the fifth Monarchy.'[53]

But millenarians like Nathaniel Homes did not rest content with merely noting the anticipated date of Redemption and then looking forward to that glorious day. Homes's correspondence with Menasseh ben Israel was not simply a scholarly exchange of letters, but also represents one English millenarian's attempt to forge a personal contact with one of the Jews to whom so much had been promised in scripture. This more active side to philo-semitic millenarianism is exemplified by the interest which Homes and others showed in the plight and activities of contemporary Jews. They were particularly entranced by the fragmentary and distorted reports which arrived in England of the sessions of the Council of Four Lands, the parliament of Jewish self-government in Poland and Lithuania. This was provided five years after the fact by a certain Samuel Brett, who claimed to have been the 'chirugeon' of an English ship who was given the command of a Maltese vessel after having cured a prominent citizen of Gallipoli. In the course of his travels in the Levant, Brett came to what he described as a conference of about three hundred rabbis held near Buda 'to examine the Scriptures concerning Christ'. Brett spoke with some of the Jews there in Italian, and one rabbi told him that

he much desired the presence of some Protestant divines, and especially of our English divines, of whom he had a better opinion, than of any other divines in the world; for he did believe that we have a great love to their nation; and this reason he gave me for their good opinion of our divines, because he understood that they did ordinarily pray for the conversion of their nation; which he did acknowledge to be a great token of our love towards them: and especially,

---

[51] *The Clarke Papers*, ed. C. H. Firth (Camden Soc., n.s., xlix, liv, lxi, lxii, 1891–1904), i. 4; Hill, *Antichrist*, p. 104.

[52] Crofton, *Bethshemesh*, p. 36.

[53] H. Peter, *Gods Doings and Mans Duty* (London, 1646), p. 9.

he commended the ministers of London, for excellent preachers, and for their
charity towards their nation

Brett noted that most of the Jews at the conference were unaware that any other form of Christianity existed aside from that
of the Church of Rome, 'by which it appeared that Rome is the
greatest enemy of the Jews' conversion.'[54]

Samuel Brett, the purported author of this pamphlet,
claimed that he had been encouraged to publish his report by
many honest Christians who conceived it to be 'a preparative,
and hopeful sign of the Jews' conversion; and, that it will be
glad tidings to the church of Christ'.[55] It can not have been an
accident that this account was published only a few months
before the meeting of the Whitehall Conference. Somehow the
sessions of the Council of Four Lands had been transformed
into a sort of Jewish Whitehall Conference whose results were
favourable to the adoption of Christianity. Nathaniel Homes
received another report revived at the same time that 'some
antient Rabbies cautioned their Country-men, That if their
expected Messiah did not come in a few years thence following,
they should imbrace the Christian Messiah for the True Messiah.' Homes implied that there might be some connection
between this delegation and the Hungarian conference.[56]

These were but two of the rumours of Jewish activity that
were making their way across Europe during the period
immediately before the convening of the Whitehall Conference.
They are all significant, even the Catzius fantasy, not for the
light they shed on seventeenth-century Jewish history, but
rather as an indication of the interest which millenarians
showed for living Jews rather than theological abstractions. As
one millenarian put it, Christians who doubted the validity of
the promises God made to the Jews had only to 'impartially
consider ye Prophets, & compare them with ye present State of

[54] S. Brett, *A Narrative of the Proceedings* (London, 1655) in *The Harleian Miscellany*, ed.
W. Oldys (London, 1808–13), i. 379–85. On the Council itself, see e.g. H. H. Ben-
Sasson, 'The Middle Ages' in his *A History of the Jewish People* (London, 1976), pp.
677–8.
[55] Brett, *Narrative*, p. 381. Menasseh ben Israel denounced the work as a forgery in his
Vindiciae Judaeorum (n.p., 1656), p. 12.
[56] Homes, 'Chronology', p. 119. Josselin knew of this tale as early as 1651 and noted
it in his diary with a marginal pointing hand for emphasis: *Diary*, ed. Macfarlane, p.
257: 19 Sept. 1651.

ye Nation'.[57] This comparison with modern Jews led some millenarians to take direct action, more forceful than the tentative feelers which Homes and Jessey extended to Rabbi Menasseh ben Israel in Holland. Some men would have agreed emphatically with John Bunyan, who reminded his readers after the Restoration 'that at the day of doom, men shall be judged according to their fruits. It will not be said then, "Did you believe?" but, "Were you *doers*, or *talkers* only?" and accordingly shall they be judged.'[58]

II

Thomas Tany and John Robins would certainly be numbered among the most extravagant philo-semitic millenarian 'doers'. Their notorious and scandalous careers are particularly interesting because they neatly span the period in which the agitation for the readmission of the Jews began, developed and reached its peak with the convening of the Whitehall Conference in December 1655. The different components of the English efforts on behalf of the Jews have been divided and organized conceptually for the purpose of this study, but for both laymen and clergymen preoccupied with the proper understanding of scripture, the Tany–Robins affair formed a backdrop throughout these years, and in many ways served to discredit the more sober millenarianism of the men whose views have already been discussed.

Thomas Tany first surfaced on 25 April 1650 when he published a broadsheet proclaiming the imminent return of the Jews from captivity to the Holy Land. Tany claimed to have been a Jew from the tribe of Reuben who discovered his true origins the previous November after a divine visitation, at which time the Lord changed his Christian name from Thomas to Theaurau John.[59] Tany seems to have been a London goldsmith who circumcised himself in fulfilment of the Mosaic law and in preparation for his great tasks. According to his own account, he first fell foul of law when he refused to pay ship money, and soon found himself in prison, and his horse

---

[57] Bodl., MS Rawl. D 1350, f. 335^r: 'A Discourse . . . Shewing the Restauration of the Jews to their own Country'.

[58] J. Bunyan, *The Pilgrim's Progress* (Penguin edn., Harmondsworth, 1977), p. 115.

[59] T. Tany, *I Proclaime . . . The returne of the Jewes* (London, 1650).

confiscated and sold.[60] Lodowick Muggleton explained that as
the Lord's High Priest, Tany's mission was 'to gather the *Jews*
out of all Nations, and lead them to *Mount Olives* to *Jerusalem*'.
The plan was for Tany to be 'King of seven Nations, and those
People of the *Jews* should live happy under him, only he should
be their King, with many other strange Things'.[61]

Alexander Ross provided a neat summary of Tany's more
strictly theological views, which seem to have been a rather
confused collection of radical religious notions. He denied that
God is the Father, and proclaimed that Christ is Mary and
Mary is Christ. Tany accused the English clergy of being
'thieves, robbers, deceivers, sounding from Antichrist' because
they promoted learning, 'that Whore which hath deceived the
Nations'. He denied that Christ could have ever assumed bod-
ily form, and rejected the authority of Scripture. By 'this and
such like stuffe with which his books are fraughted,' Ross
concluded, 'we may see that he deserveth to have his brains
purged with *Hellebore*, rather than his crazy opinions refuted by
argument, or Scripture.' Ross laid the blame for Tany's scandalous ideas at the door of those who promoted liberty of
conscience.[62]

'Theaurau John' Tany's name was often linked with that of
John Robins. According to Muggleton, who later became one
of the most bitter opponents of both Tany and Robins, whereas
the former claimed to be only a servant of the Lord, the latter
declared himself to be God Almighty and Adam before the Fall
at the same time. Robins was reported to have raised Cain,
Judas, the prophet Jeremiah, and Benjamin the son of Jacob
from the dead. Oddly enough, this most extravagant claim was
supported by Muggleton himself:

I saw all those that was said to be raised by *John Robins*, and they owned
themselves to be the very same Persons that had been Dead for so long time.
. . . Also I saw several others of the Prophets that was said to be raised by him,
and they did own they were the same; for I have had Nine or Tenn of them at
my House at a time, of those that were said to be raised from the Dead.

[60] T. Tany, *The Nations Right in Magna Charta* (n.p., n.d.), p. 8: dated in text (p. 8), 28
Dec. 1650.
[61] L. Muggleton, *The Acts of the Witnesses* (London, 1699), pp. 20–1; idem, *A True
Interpretation of . . . Revelation* (London, 1751), p. 182.
[62] A. Ross, *A View of all Religions* (4th edn., London, 1664), pp. 377–9.

These resurrected men, those who 'spake as an Angel of God', seem to have suffered from wordly want as well, and Muggleton is at pains to record the generosity he showed to them: 'if I had nothing in the House to Eat,' he remembered, 'if I had but Eighteen Pence I would give him one Shilling of it; and if I had but Twelve Pence, I would give him Six Pence of it.' Muggleton may simply have been increasing his opponent's stature in order to enhance the glory of his ultimate victory over Robins, but it is striking that he could declare, even after the fact, that 'I do not speak this from Hearsay from others, but from a perfect Knowledge, which I have seen and heard from themselves.'[63]

This miraculous aspect of Robins's appeal remains difficult to understand. Muggleton, and John Reeve his partner, described the magic which Robins was able to command. Sometimes he would be seen 'riding upon the Wings of the Wind, like unto a Flame of Fire'. Sometimes he would create unnatural light or darkness. One woman was graced with 'his Head only in the Day-time, without a Body' in her chamber, sometimes with the accompaniment of dragons. 'Again, I declare from the Lord,' John Reeve swore, 'that this *John Robins* did present the Form of his Face, looking me in the Face in my Bed, the most Part of a Night'. No wonder that his disciples 'fell flat on their Faces and worshipped him, calling him their Lord and their God'. Robins also commanded them not to have any other gods before him, and allowed some of his followers to exchange wives.[64]

Robins, like Tany, had plans for the Jews. His faithful confided that Robins was to gather out of England and elsewhere 144,000 men and women, apparently Jews, and lead them to the Mount of Olives in Jerusalem where he would 'make them happy'. Robins would feed them on manna, and would divide the Red Sea to speed their passage on to dry land. Presumably in preparation for sustenance by manna, Robins prescribed a special diet for his followers, 'windy things, as Aples, and other Fruit that was windy; and they drank

---

[63] Muggleton, *Acts*, p. 21; J. Reeve and L. Muggleton, *A Transcendent Spiritual Treatise* (n.p., 1756), pp. 7–8: first pub. 1652.
[64] Ibid., p. 8; Muggleton, *Acts*, p. 22.

nothing but Water.' Some were said to have starved to death on this regimen.[65]

The fabulous declarations of Tany and Robins were common knowledge in the streets of London by 1650, according to John Reeve.[66] Thomas Tany was soon in prison, probably for being in breach of the Blasphemy Act of 9 August 1650, which had been aimed especially at his variety of heresy.[67] Tany was arrested along with Captain Robert Norwood, who would be associated with Roger Williams in presenting a plan to Parliament in March 1652 in favour of the toleration of the Jews.[68] Tany answered the charges against him most directly:

Brethren, ye priests ye would be always talking the conversion of the Jews, but you would never have it come to pass as you have pratingly prayed for the conversion of the Jews, and now you begin to persecute Us Jews, all this is because, you are afraid your trade of lyes must down

He frankly admitted his lack of formal education, but said that the 'heavenly light' provided him with some knowledge of Latin, Hebrew, and Greek. Tany was fond of using Hebrew letters in his writings, but it is clear that he knew less than nothing about the language. He even took the opportunity in his answer to allude to his excitable nature: 'I read no books, though I am mad,' he admitted slyly, 'I tell you by madness I am instructed'.[69] Tany had ample time to perfect his knowledge of such holy subjects in prison. 'I am not learned', he continued to insist after his release, 'but in my six months Imprisonment, in *Newgate* and the *Kings-bench*, in them two Land-Colledges I have taken my Degrees'.[70]

Tany carried his campaign forward in spite of these initial setbacks. He seems at one time to have lived in the Strand, afterwards in the City, but by the beginning of 1652 he was living at Eltham. Tany was anxious to make converts, and advertised that he welcomed visitors, who could be directed to

[65] Ibid., pp. 46–7; Reeve and Muggleton, *Treatise*, p. 9.

[66] Muggleton, *Acts*, p. 20.

[67] C. Hill, *The World Turned Upside Down* (New York, 1973), p. 167.

[68] T. Tany, *Theavravjohn His Theousori* (London, 1651), title p. Norwood also provided the epistle and the transcription of Tany's *Theavravjohn His Aurora* (London, 1651?); cf. below, p. 186.

[69] Tany, *Theousori*, pp. 69–78, esp. p. 76. Tany claimed that he learned Hebrew 'all in one day, before night' with the aid of the Holy Spirit (p. 60).

[70] T. Tany, *Theavrauiohn High Priest to the Iewes* (n.p., n.d. = 1652), p. 3.

his lodgings by his publisher, Giles Calvert the radical booksel-ler.[71] Tany felt a sense of urgency to his mission: 'Beloved, do but reade the Bible,' he advised,

and minde how the scope of scripture doth coatresie [sic] one another, to insert the entire certainty of the Jews return from whence the Lord hath scattered them: O *England* thou *Akeldama* to that people! O! thou hast murthered without mercy, know that root shall unroot thee, for thy judgement hastens, and thy sin is brought in remembrance before the Lord.

While no detailed description of Tany's personal religious ritual survives, it appears that despite his fleshly circumcision he was fundamentally a Christian, and did not revere the Mosaic law after the fashion of John Traske and his followers. 'Now know, I am Jew [sic] of the tribe of *Ruben* begotten by the gospel,' Tany explained, 'which is Massah, El, Jah, or Jehovah, Jesus, or Christ, all these are but names of that one merciful thing, that is God.' Although a Jew according to the convenant of Abraham, he still considered himself to be begotten 'by the life of Jesus Christ'.[72] As was usually the case, Tany signed himself with a sword, a sickle, a seal proclaiming his glorious mission, and a collection of his sacred names, such as 'Ruben, Theaurau John, Taniour, Allah, AL, . . . TRU . . . BLU.'[73]

John Robins and his followers, meanwhile, were also having difficulties with the law. In May 1651, six of his followers were arrested on the grounds of unlawful assembly, and were brought before Lawrence Whitaker, JP for Middlesex. On examination they claimed that John Robins was God the Father, that Cain was the third party of the Trinity, and that the unborn child of Joan Robins (John's wife) was the Messiah. They were three men, a widow and her daughter, and another woman, and all were committed to the Gatehouse gaol. Seven more of Robins's group—John and Joan Robins, Joshua Gar-ment and his wife, another man, and two other women—were sent to the New Prison at Clerkenwell within a fortnight. 'They are tearmed', noted John Taylor the anti-sectarian, 'or called by the name of *Ranters*'. Taylor also warned his readers to beware of another similar pamphlet which was circulating,

[71] Ibid., p. 1.
[72] Tany, *Theousori*, p. 42.
[73] Tany, *High Priest*, p. 8.

purporting to recount this case with accuracy, when in fact it
was largely incorrect.[74] This other work was probably the
published version of an impromptu speech to a crowd beneath
his prison window which Robins was said to have delivered
soon after his incarceration there. Certainly the list of Robins's
'Shakers' is entirely different from the one given by Taylor and
in the report of the proceedings: even the name of Robins's wife
is given incorrectly.[75]

The talk which Robins is said to have given contains no
surprises in any case, and is less interesting than the speech
Joshua Garment delivered in his own defence, which was published in one of the news sheets, and further elaborated in a
pamphlet published by Garment himself. Robins's lieutenant
confessed before the court that the glory of the Lord and his
angels appeared to him in 1631, when God's plan for 'the
gathering and deliverance of the twelve scattered Tribes' was
revealed to him. He was told that the opposition of the clergy to
this project would be fierce, so he was commanded to remain
silent until he was contacted once again. The word of the Lord
came to him again in 1647 for several days running. On one of
these occasions, an angel came to him saying, 'Josherbah,
Josherbah, the time draws near that the Jews, even the Hebrews must be gathered and delivered'. Garment was carried
miraculously to 'the South parts of the world' where the angel
showed him 'a poor ragged travelling dispised people, with an
innumerable company, saying, *this is* Levi's *Tribe, and this is the
whole house of* Israel: Then I knew also that the Religious men
should oppose the deliverance of the *Jews*, and that the professors, many of them, should persecute them even unto death,
but the work should go on.' Three years later, he saw John
Robins riding upon the wings of the wind in glory, and was told
that 'this is he that shall in the Name and power of God the
Creator, divide the Seas, and lead the *Hebrews* to their own
Land'. Robins was revealed as the messenger of God, sent 'to
gather and deliver the *Hebrews* without arms offensive or defen-
sive, but only and alone in the power of the Lord God his

---

[74] J. Taylor, *Ranters of both Sexes* (London, 1651), *passim*.
[75] G. H., *The Declaration of John Robins* (London, 1651), *passim*.

Creator'. The following year Garment found himself in the New Prison at Clerkenwell.[76]

The wheels of justice continued to grind in the normal way, despite the pleas of Robins and Garment that Englishmen should prepare for imminent and calamitous change. Garment announced that the deliverance of the Jews would take place twenty days before Michaelmas 1651, only four months away. Garment seems to have recognized some of the chosen people in London, and proclaimed that the 'many Jews that here are in *England* shall go thorow on dry foot towards *Judea*' where they would be reunited with the lost ten tribes. He thought that the Civil War itself, and the 'strange overturnings' in English life during his generation were no less miraculous than the calling and conversion of the Jews, and provided proof sufficient to convince even the most sceptical.[77]

The first group of Robins's followers to be arrested, meanwhile, was still committed to prison without bail, awaiting the next sessions of the peace, which were to be held on 20 June 1651. Although they admitted that they did not know what trade the Messiah was currently practising, nor where he dwelled, nor if his legal name might not be 'Roberts', they were sure that he was 'the God and Father of our Lord and Saviour Jesus Christ'. They also insisted that his wife was carrying the unborn Messiah, that Cain is the third person of the Trinity, and that Robins had the power to raise the dead. Only one man and one woman of the seven were literate enough to sign their names to this declaration; the rest indicated their assent with a mark.[78]

Alexander Ross complained afterwards that for 'such Ranters, a Pillory were more fit than a pulpit', and it does seem that incarceration had some effect towards their religious re-education. Before the next meeting of the sessions, this little group repented of blasphemy and sent a petition to Lawrence Whitaker, the JP who was handling their case. Only Thomas Kearby, the literate man, declined to recant. The petition was

[76] *A Perfect Account*, 21 (28 May–4 June 1651), pp. 166–'166' = 167; J. Garment, *The Hebrews Deliverance at hand* (London, 1651), *passim*.

[77] Ibid., pp. 4–6.

[78] [Anon.], *All The Proceedings At The Sessions . . . 20. the day of Iune, 1651* (London, 1651), pp. 3–4.

obviously drafted for them, and in it they declared themselves to have been led astray by the Devil and 'that wicked Wretch *John Robins*'. For they were only 'poore silly women and others' misled into blasphemy, without 'friends or acquaintance here in the City, but are all in the Country, because our abode was formerly there'. They also asked for release from the payment of fees to the keeper of the prison. This petition was translated into a formal recantation dated 13 June 1651, which was sworn to before Whitaker two days later. The six ex-Ranters were released on bail until the next meeting of the sessions on 20 June, when they were put on probation until the following sessions and were relieved of prison costs. Thomas Kearby, on the other hand, reviled the judges and cursed them, and refused to recant. Kearby was sentenced to six months imprisonment at hard labour according to the provisions of the Blasphemy Act of 1650. The keeper of the prison was directed 'to give him corporall punishment as occasion requireth.'[79] William Birchley, the pro-catholic tolerationist, explained that Kearby was committed to prison not for his opinions, but for his disgraceful behaviour in open court.[80] John Robins himself remained in prison as well.

Despite these inconveniences, Robins, Tany, and their dwindling band of followers continued their divine missions on earth. Tany resumed writing from his lodgings at Eltham, and Robins seems to have communicated with the faithful from his prison window. Unfortunately, their notoriety brought them only severe criticism rather than an increased following. One critic challenged Robins to make a regular tour of the local churches and cemeteries raising the dead. As for his alleged power to divide the sea and to pass over on to dry land, his critic sneered that since 'the Thames is neare, he may do well to try experiments there first.'[81]

More serious dissent within the ranks came from Lodowick Muggleton and John Reeve, those famous sectarians who had once counted themselves among the followers of Tany and Robins. Ironically, their rejection of these pseudo-saviours of world Jewry was not based on disbelief of their supernatural

[79] *Proceedings*, pp. 4–9.
[80] W. Birchley, *The Christian Moderator* (n.p., 1651), p. 21.
[81] *Proceedings*, pp. 12–14.

powers, but rather on a counter-claim of divine intelligence.
Reeve testified that Jesus visited him during the mornings of
3–5 February 1651–2. On the second morning, he was commanded to collect Muggleton and to proceed to the house of one
Thomas Turner, from whence the three were to go to Tany's
lodgings. Reeve was empowered by the Lord to cast either man
into eternal damnation if they declined to follow him, but both
came along willingly, although Turner's wife 'was exceeding
Wrath and Fearful, that her Husband would be brought into
Trouble by it.' She warned Reeve that if he ever came to visit
her husband again 'she would run a Spit in his Guts'. Reeve
had no alternative but to curse her for all eternity, although she
seems not to have been much affected by his spell.[82]

Reeve, Muggleton, and Turner found Tany at home, and
passed on to him the word of the Lord. Reeve rejected Tany's
claim to be the Lord's high priest, on the grounds that he was of
the tribe of Reuben, whereas the priesthood rested with Levi,
which was the tribe that included his colleague Muggleton as a
member. Tany was also disqualified on the grounds that he
stuttered in his speech. Reeve gave Tany a month's time to
mend his ways and renounce his opinions, but Tany carried on
his design by setting up 'Tents for every Tribe, and the Figures
of every Tribe upon the Tent, that every Tribe might know
their own Tent.' When Reeve returned to give Tany the writ of
eternal damnation, he found him locked in his rooms. Reeve left
the document with the landlord.[83]

On the third morning, Reeve was once again commanded to
pay a visit in the company of Muggleton, this time to a certain
woman named Dorcas Boose, who was to bring them to John
Robins, still a prisoner in New Bridewell. The keeper denied
them entrance, but he directed them to a woman disciple of
Robins who was just leaving the gaol, telling her to show the
visitors to the window of his cell. Reeve and Robins had a slight
disagreement on whether the imprisoned messiah ought not to
be addressed with covered head, but eventually the condemnation was delivered. Robins listened patiently, although he later
told a friend that he had felt a burning in the throat as Reeve

[82] Reeve and Muggleton, *Treatise*, pp. 4–5; Muggleton, *Acts*, pp. 42–3.
[83] Ibid., pp. 43–4.

passed judgement upon him. At the end of the speech, Robins replied, 'It is finished, the Lord's Will be done.'[84]

The full import of Robins's concession was apparent within two months, when he wrote a full letter of recantation and so obtained his liberty from prison. When he was out of gaol, according to Reeve and Muggleton,

he gave all his Disciples about *London* the Slip, and with what Silver he had left, that he had cheated from them, *Cain*-like, instead of building of Cities, he went into his own Country, and re-purchased his Land; but it was re-bought with the innocent Blood of many poor innocent Souls, in the highest Nature, that ever any Man gained such a Sum of Silver as he did.[85]

Thus ended the tale of John Robins, although he was still notorious enough in March 1653–4 to merit inclusion in a special list of 'Grand Blasphemers' drawn up for contemplation before an official fast day. His wife Joan, Joshua and Joan Garment, the false Jew of Hexham, and Thomas Tany were included as well.[86] Of this number, Tany perhaps was the one who most deserved this public humiliation, for his career was far from over. He continued publishing even after Reeve pronounced his curse, and went so far as to challenge representatives of Oxford and Cambridge to a disputation in St. Paul's Cathedral on 5 April 1652, although no one seems to have appeared.[87] Tany claimed the crowns of France and Rome on 8 June 1654—he had already demanded that of England nearly four years earlier—in a statement witnessed by Robert Norwood and a certain William Finch.[88] When John Pordage the Ranter preacher in Berkshire appeared before the Ejectors on 19 October 1654, one of the charges against him was that he 'had for some weeks together in his house the same *Everard*, and one *Tawney*, who stiled himself King of the Jews'. This first man may have been William Everard, the famous Digger who also claimed to be of the race of the Jews. Pordage's lame reply was that he was well known for his hospitality and never turned away visitors whatever their doctrines.[89]

[84] Ibid., pp. 45–7.
[85] Reeve and Muggleton, *Treatise*, p. 9.
[86] *A List of some of the Grand Blasphemers* (London, 1654), brdsht.
[87] Tany, *High Priest*, p. 2.
[88] T. Tany, *ThauRam Tanjah his Speech* (n.p., 1654), brdsht.; idem, *Magna Charta*, p. 1. Cf. Tany's *Hear, O Earth* (London, 1654), brdsht.
[89] C. Fowler, *Daemonium Meridianum* (London, 1655), pp. 53–6, 60–1; J. Pordage,

Viewed with hindsight, Tany's career in the early 1650s seems but a prologue to his slapstick raid on Parliament at the end of 1654. 'Theauro John:' Carlyle exclaimed in the nineteenth century,

his labours, life-adventures, financial arrangements, painful biography in general, are all unknown to us; till, on this 'Saturday 30th December 1654,' he very clearly 'knocks loud at the door of the Parliament House,' as much as to say, "What is this *you* are upon?" and 'lays about him with a drawn sword;'—after which all again becomes unknown. Seemingly a kind of Quaker.[90]

As we have already seen, Carlyle was quite wrong about the extent of the evidence which survives concerning Tany and his activities. We also know now that Tany preceded his raid with a remarkable demonstration at Lambeth the previous week. It seems that Tany and his followers were still living in tents in 1654, sometimes at Lambeth and sometimes at Greenwich among other places, proclaiming their mission to gather the Jews and proceed to the Holy Land. In December 1654, according to a number of reports and the testimony of Tany himself, 'with great solemnity he burnt a sword, a great saddle, a pair of pistols, and the Bible together, declaring them the three grand Idols of *England*.' Tany claimed that God himself commanded him to take this action, but those who saw him do it threatened to stone him, so he fired his tent and came to the House of Parliament.[91]

He arrived wearing an 'antique habit' and armed with a rusty sword. Tany asked the door-keeper if he might deliver a petition to Parliament, and was told that he would have to find a member to present it for him. Tany thereupon collared an MP in the entrance-way and explained his case, but was put off with the promise that he 'would assist any civil man in any civil way'. Dissatisfied with this cryptic political language, Tany paced about for an hour and was then joined by another man

---

Innocencie Appearing (London, 1655), pp. 9, 11–13; D. Hirst, 'The Riddle of John Pordage', *Jacob Boehme Qly.*, i (1953–4), no. 6, 5–15. On Everard, see Hill, *World Turned Upside Down*, pp. 228–30 and below, p. 184.

[90] T. Carlyle, *Oliver Cromwell's Letters and Speeches*, ed. S. C. Lomas (London, 1904), ii. 394.

[91] *A Perfect Account*, 209 (3–10 Jan. 1654–5), p. 1666; cf. *The Weekly Intelligencer*, 74 (2–9 Jan. 1654–5), p. 152; T. Burton, *Diary*, ed. J. T. Rutt (London, 1828), i. cxxvi.

also armed with a sword. Fifteen minutes later, after walking about the lobby,

he on a sudden threw off his cloak, and with his sword drawn did run at Mr: *Cooper* the Door-keeper, who did put his thrust by, he afterwards struck at him, and slashed the cloaks of the standers by, and cleered the room of all that were in the Lobby, only Major *Ennis* made up to him, and *Theauro* offering to strike at him, the Major closed with him, and laid him on the ground, but he recovering himself, did run with his sword drawn towards the Parlament door, and bounced at the door with his feet, to have forced his entrance, and just as he had opened the door, the key being in the lock, he was laid hold on[92]

Tany was immediately brought to the bar by order of the House, and when he refused to remove his hat, was relieved of it by the sergeant. He told the members of his bonfire the previous week at Lambeth, and claimed that he drew his sword only because the door-keeper had jostled him. Tany was committed to the Gatehouse not only for drawing his sword at the Parliament door, but also for affirming that the Bible was not the word of the Lord and for burning it. The keeper of the prison was especially charged to take notice of Tany's visitors.[93]

Thomas Tany's case was referred to the same committee of the House which was investigating the offences of John Biddle the Socinian. Their examination reaffirmed that Tany believed himself to have been commissioned to gather the dispersed Jews and to lead them to the Holy Land. As to his raid on Parliament, he revealed that 'he came inspired by the holy spirit, to kill every man that sat in the house, and was resolved thereupon.'[94] One critic said that his direct answers only provided further proof of his madness.[95] Another compared him to Don Quixote and called him a 'great Booby'. Tany's assassination attempt seemed especially ludicrous since it came at the same time as the much more dangerous Royalist insurrections against the Commonwealth. One writer of doggerel made the point explicit:

[92] *Weekly Intelligencer*, 74, pp. 151–2. Cf. *Perfect Account*, 209, pp. 1665–6; *The Weekly Post*, 208 (2–9 Jan. 1654–5), p. 1662; *The Faithful Scout*, 208 (29 Dec.–5 Jan. 1654–5), p. 1660; B. Whitelocke, *Memorials* (Oxford, 1853), p. 592. The latter four sources refer to Tany as a Quaker. Cf. *The Perfect Diurnall*, 265 (1–8 Jan. 1655), pp. 4061–2, 4069.

[93] *Weekly Intelligencer*, 74, p. 152; *Perfect Account*, 209, p. 1666; Burton, *Diary*, i. cxxvi; *Certain Passages*, 74(a) (29 Dec.–5 Jan. 1654–5), pp. 151, 154.

[94] Ibid., p. 158; *Perfect Account*, 209, p. 1666; Burton, *Diary*, i. cxxvi; *The Perfect Diurnall*, 267 (15–22 Jan. 1655), p. 4097.

[95] *Weekly Intelligencer*, 74, p. 152.

> A Plott, a Plott, old *Nick* is dead,
> *John Tawney* did him kill,
> With rusty Sword he hack'd his head,
> but sore against his will.[96]

Tany was reported to have been very moody in prison, where he insisted on having his leg chained 'as a signal of the people of Englands Captivity'. He hoped to wear the chain at his trial, and warned that England would never prosper until Parliament ordered it to be removed. Tany now admitted that although he was still graced with numerous divine revelations, he had not been commanded to attack the Parliament house. He pointed out, however, that the fact that no one was seriously hurt during his frenzy was an additional proof of his divine protection.[97]

Legally, the second offence under the Blasphemy Act was punishable by banishment, but Parliament was dissolved on 22 January 1655, and this seems to have saved Tany from even a lengthy prison sentence.[98] He was released on bail on 10 February, appeared in court again on 2 May, and was finally set at liberty unconditionally on 28 May 1655.[99] The following September he was reported to have pitched a tent in St. George's Fields, the territory of the now-defunct Diggers, and in the neighbourhood of Gerrard Winstanley himself, who lived nearby at Cobham. Tany appears to have had some disciples there, and his connection with the Diggers may have originated as far back as his lodging with Everard in the home of John Pordage.[100]

Whereas John Robins retired gracefully from millenarian advocacy of the Jews to the country after having had a taste of prison life, Tany would not rest content until his mission had been completed. According to Muggleton, 'he made a little Bote to carry him to *Jerusalem*, and going to *Holland*, to call the

---

[96] *Mercurius Fumigosus*, 32 (3–10 Jan. 1655), pp. 249, 252. Cf. *Certain Passages*, 74(b) (5–12 Jan. 1654–5), p. 152 for a satirical connection between Tany and a riot of apprentices.

[97] *The Faithful Scout*, n. no. (5–12 Jan. 1654–5), p. 1668; *The Weekly Post*, 209 (9–16 Jan. 1654–5), p. 1667; *Certain Passages*, 78 (12–19 Jan. 1654–5), p. 156.

[98] Fowler, *Daemonium*, p. 165.

[99] A. Wood, *Athenae Oxonienses*, ed. P. Bliss (London, 1813–20), iii. 598–9. 'He was then, and before,' Wood insists, 'a blasphemous Jew.' (p. 599n.).

[100] *The Weekly Intelligencer* (18–25 Sept. 1655).

Jews there, he and one Captain *James* were cast away and drowned; so all his Power came to nothing.'[101]

The Jewish New Year 5416 began on 22 September 1655, and it is most likely that Rabbi Menasseh ben Israel had come to England by that date. The last report we have of Tany is dated September 1655. Ironically, just as Tany was leaving England with the aim of calling the Jews, the *de facto* Jewish ambassador to the gentiles was arriving in London to begin his great negotiations for Jewish readmission which would lead to the calling of the Whitehall Conference in December. After five years of ceaseless effort on behalf of an imagined Jewish constituency, as Muggleton put it, Tany's 'great matters perished in the Sea.'[102]

III

In view of the outlandish careers of both Robins and Tany, it is hardly surprising to discover that even credulous seventeenth-century Englishmen regarded them as slightly ludicrous. One writer dragged their names into an entirely unrelated story about a maidservant's misadventures. He joked that

the Maide that committed this Piece of Huswifery is next week to be Circumcised . . . and so to be gathered into *Theoreau Johns* flock of *Converted Jews* . . . as they are conducted by *John Robbins* through the *red Sea*, to the Iland in the *Moon*, to recollect their scences, which were lost about a fort-after *Midsummer* come Twelve Moneth.[103]

The importance of Robins and Tany to the readmission of the Jew is that they injected the Jewish question into the news and kept public attention focused on their bizarre plan to gather the Jews personally and lead them back to the Holy Land. The belief that the Jews had an important role to play in bringing about the Second Coming was, as we have seen, a respectable facet of millenarian thinking, which was itself entrenched in English religious thought. Dr B. S. Capp has reckoned with the aid of the catalogue to the Thomason tracts that seventy per cent of the prolific ministers who published their works between 1640 and 1653 can be identified as millenarians.[104] But

[101] Muggleton, *Acts*, p. 44.
[102] Ibid.
[103] *Mercurius Fumigosus*, 32, p. 256.
[104] Capp, *Fifth Monarchy*, p. 38.

this more scholarly brand of millenarian opinion lacked the explosive quality of the antics of men like Robins and Tany, who thrust the Jews before a bemused and curious public, and helped to accustom Englishmen to considering the Jews as a modern living nation as well as the ancient people of God.

Robins and Tany were not the only visionaries who promoted the Jewish cause, although they were certainly the most colourful. Arise Evans, the Welsh tailor–prophet of the interregnum, was another, and Dr Christopher Hill singled him out especially for study in order to demonstrate that it is possible to obtain an idea of what ordinary people were thinking by examining their published remains, instead of relying on the biased evidence of heresy trials and the accounts of those who applauded their suppression. 'So it is worth using every scrap of evidence thrown up in the revolutionary decades,' he explains, 'when discussion suddenly became free and when printing was still a cheap enough process for almost anyone to be able to get his views published.'[105]

Arise Evans is particularly interesting because of his direct personal contact with Menasseh ben Israel, for in some sense he took up the mantle of Tany and Robins after the former had drowned and the latter had retired. This was true even though Evans explicitly rejected Tany, no doubt in order to discourage the obvious comparisons which could be made between them.[106] When Arise Evans published his first work in 1652, he noted that

The Jews look for such an one as ye see in *Manasseh, Ben Israels* book called the hope of *Israel*; and sent to the supreame power of England. An. 1650. one to call and deliver the ten Tribes, and their hope as true, for as . . . *Isaiah* saith . . . the Redeemer shall come to *Sion*? that is, to the Elect Jewes.

Arise Evans was convinced that '*Charles*, the Son of *Charles Stuart* by name, comes to the Elect Jewes, to deliver them from the power of darknesse; and to bring them to Jesus Christ and eternall life.'[107] Evans discussed this theory with Menasseh

---

[105] C. Hill, 'Arise Evans: Welshman in London' in his *Change and Continuity in Seventeenth-Century England* (London, 1974), pp. 58–9. See also C. Hill and M. Shepherd, 'The case of Arise Evans: a historical–psychiatric study', *Psychological Med.*, vi (1976), 351–8.

[106] A. Evans, *To The Most High* (London, 1660), p. 51.

[107] A. Evans, *A Voice from Heaven* (n.p., 1652), p. 11n.

when the famous rabbi came to London in 1655. Menasseh doubted that Charles II was a suitable choice for Messiah; he thought that Oliver Cromwell or the king of Sweden were better candidates. Evans replied, through an interpreter, that 'he that lives five years to an end, shall see King *Charles Steeward* flourish on his Throne to the amazement of all the world, for God will bring him in without blood-shed.' Evans told Menasseh that 'those Jews who would come into *England* without his [Charles's] command, come against God, and their Messiah appointed of God for them; and therefore if they come, they shall in a short time be spoiled and destroyed.' Menasseh was 'the great Jewish Rabby' for Evans despite any differences in views.[108]

Arise Evans was almost a respectable religious radical, a communicant at William Gouge's parish church in Blackfriars, and supported by Gouge when arrested during the middle 1640s. Others who advocated the return of the Jews to Palestine were less stable. Walter Gostelow, one of Arise Evans's demi-Royalist followers, was among this latter group. Gostelow claimed to have had the truth about the calling of the Jews revealed to him while in bed during January 1653. Shortly afterwards he wrote to Cromwell on behalf of Arise Evans, and to Menasseh ben Israel in praise of his *Hope of Israel*. He mentioned to Cromwell in a letter of 22 January 1655–6 that he intended to pass on his book to '*the Jewish Rabbies*' and 'the *See* of *Rome*'. Like Evans, Gostelow believed that Charles II was the Messiah, and insisted as late as 1658 that it would be through him that the Jews would 'know the Lord, receive mercy and go into their own land.'[109]

Both Evans and Gostelow, then, held beliefs quite different from those of John Robins and Thomas Tany in that they centred their millenarian dreams and visions of the calling of the Jews around the person of Charles II. John Sanders, an

---

[108] A. Evans, *Light For the Iews* (London, 1656), pp. 4–5, 20, and *passim*; idem, *A Rule from Heaven* (London, 1659), p. 48; idem, *An Eccho To The Voice from Heaven* (London, 162), sig. Bbb6ʳ, pp. 105–6. He interprets Laud's name with the help of gematria in his *The Bloudy Vision* (n.p., 1653), p. 63.

[109] W. Gostelow, *Charls Stuart And Oliver Cromwel United* (n.p., 1655), pp. 63, 70, 288, 293–304; idem, *The coming of God* (London 1658), sig. E8ʳ; *Thurloe State Papers*, v. 672–5. See also H. Gollancz, 'A Contribution to the History of the Readmission of the Jews', *Trs. Jew. Hist. Soc. Eng.*, vi (1912), 204.

ironmonger of Harborn near Birmingham, also looked forward to the day when God would 'call the *Jewes*, and convert the whole world into one union of Faith', but under Charles II and the restored Rump.[110] Surely this is an English variant of the predominant nationalistic tendency in Continental millenarianism of concentrating chiliastic speculation around particular rulers who thereby acquired messianic attributes. The famous Comenius, one of Alsted's former students, was a well-known exponent of this philosophy, although he shifted his messianic allegiance from George I of Transylvania, to his sons Sigismund and George II, and later flirted with Oliver Cromwell, then Charles X of Sweden, and finally Louis XIV.[111]

This brand of millenarianism often reached England in a rather second-hand fashion, such as through the garbled copy of a work by Paul Grebner, the German theologian and astrologer, in which he was said to have predicted 'a Kingdome to arise of the most ancient Inhabitants in the *Holy Land* . . . All these things shall be effected by a certaine *Northern King*'. William Lilly the astrologer consulted the Grebner manuscript of 1574 and revised this Royalist prophecy to read that

we Christians shall recover the Holy Land, viz. the terrestriall *Jerusalem*, out of the hands of the *Turkes*; then also shall Almighty *God*, by miracle withdraw the people of the *Jews*, from . . . the severall parts of the World, where now they live concealed, and they shall beleeve in the true *Messias*, JESUS CHRIST.[112]

Lilly's pamphlet is listed as one of the most popular books 'Of the Mathematicks' in William London's best-seller catalogue of 1657.[113]

A forgery though it may have been, this notice of a northern king was to prove exceedingly useful to the supporters of the candidature of particular monarchs as the Messiah. Paul Felgenhauer, an exile from Bohemia like Comenius, also believed that the English Civil War heralded 'the Returning of

---

[110] J. Sanders, *An Iron Rod* (London, 1655), f. 2ʳ, p. 36. Cf. Capp, *Fifth Monarchy*, p. 270.

[111] H. R. Trevor-Roper, 'Three Foreigners: The Philosophers of the Puritan Revolution', in his *Religion the Reformation and Social Change* (London, 1967), pp. 237–93; Capp, *Fifth Monarchy*, p. 235.

[112] W. Lilly, *Monarchy or no Monarchy* (London, 1651), pp. 9, 55.

[113] H. Rusche, 'Prophecies and propaganda, 1641 to 1651', *Eng. Hist. Rev.*, lxxxiv (1969), 760; see also his 'Merlini Anglici: Astrology and Propaganda from 1644 to 1651', *Eng. Hist. Rev.*, lxxx (1965), 322–33.

the Tenne Tribes of *Israel*, and the Returning of the *Jewes* to
their Inheritance and Countrey'. Felgenhauer engaged in a
vigorous correspondence with Menasseh ben Israel, and edited
a collection of letters addressed to the Amsterdam rabbi, with a
long introduction.[114] Felgenhauer's friend Peter Serarius also
awaited the imminent return of Christ and the calling of the
Jews, and later became involved with the movement in support
of Sabbatai Ṣevi, the Jewish false Messiah.[115] This is not the
place to make a catalogue of the Continental millenarians who
believed in the calling of the Jews, but suffice it to say that
Evans and Gostelow were much more in their mould when they
cast Charles II in the role of Messiah, in opposition to Tany
and Robins who looked with Menasseh ben Israel towards
Cromwell for the salvation of the Jews.

As we have seen, the extreme views of the millenarians, and
especially of men like John Robins and Thomas Tany, did not
go unchallenged. Thomas Fuller spoke for many when he
objected that it 'is a conceit of the modern *Jews*, that one day
they shall return under the conduct of their *Messias* to the
Countrey of *Canaan*, and City of *Jerusalem*, and be re-estated in
the full possession thereof.' He insisted in any case that 'their
land, now base, and barren, is not worth the regaining'.[116]
Nevertheless, some of these radical ideas were revived during
the revolutionary decades of the late eighteenth century, and
after Napoleon's Egyptian campaign, and several historians
have traced back the British interest in Zionism to the
prophesying of men like Tany, Robins, Evans, and Gostelow.[117]

IV

Various sects of one kind or another proliferated during the
Civil War: Seekers, Ranters, Adamites, Brownists, Grindleto-
nians, Familists, Antinomianists, Mortalists, Muggletonians,

---

[114] P. Flegenhauer, *Postilion, Or a New Almanacke* (London, 1655), pp. 12–13, 34;
idem, *Bonum Nuncium*, pp. 2–91. On Felgenhauer generally, see H. J. Schoeps,
Philosemitismus im Barock (Tübingen, 1952), pp. 18–53.

[115] For Serarius and the entire Sabbatian movement, see G. Scholem, *Sabbatai Ṣevi*
(London, 1973).

[116] Fuller, *Pisgah-Sight*, p. 194.

[117] Especially Vereté, 'Restoration of the Jews'; J. Fraenkel, 'From the English
Hoveve Zion Movement to the Balfour Declaration' (Yiddish), *Yivo Bleter*, xliii (1966),
72; N. Sokolow, *History of Zionism 1600–1918* (London, 1919).

Hermeticists, Anabaptists, Baptists, Pantheists, as well as innumerable astrologers, alchemists, conjurors, witches, faith-healers, magicians, almanac-makers, prophets, and miracle-workers. Believers were faced with a wide market of faiths to chose from, greater than ever before. Many people passed from sect to sect. Milton understood the problem better than most when he wrote that 'As for those many Sects and divisions rumor'd abroad to be amongst us, it is not hard to perceave that they are partly the meere fictions and false alarmes of the Prelates, thereby to cast amazements and panick terrors into the hearts of weaker Christians that they should not venture to change the present deformity of the Church for fear of I know not what worse inconveniencies.'[118]

Yet surely the *combined* effect of these apocalyptic and millenarian speculations was to produce a sense of impending great events. Henry Wilkinson told the House of Commons in 1643 that it was the 'generall talk throughout the household among the domesticks . . . that Christ their king is comming to take possession of his Throne, they doe not onely whisper this, and tell it in the eare, but they speake it publikely'.[119] Christopher Feake, the Fifth Monarchist, complained that many with influence and power were 'much offended, that a company of illiterate men, and silly women, should pretend to any skill in dark prophecies, and to a foresight of future events, which the most learned Rabbies, and the most knowing Politicians have not presumed to hope for.'[120] Nevertheless, millenarian sentiments were expressed not only by common people, but also by men who carried greater individual weight, even by Cromwell himself.

Much of this apocalyptic, millenarian, or general eschatological speculation included mention of the role which the Jews were expected to play. And, as Professor Gershom Scholem writes, 'Speculations of this kind incurred favour in chiliast circles. The copious literature on the subject created an almost pro-Jewish climate of opinion, and some Christian circles in western Europe expected the imminent repentance of Israel

---

[118] *Complete Prose Works of John Milton*, ed. D. M. Wolfe, *et al.* (New Haven, 1953–   ), i. 794 (*Reason of Church-Government*, bk. i, *cap.* vii).

[119] H. Wilkinson, *Babylons Ruine* (London, 1643), p. 21.

[120] C. Feake in Cary, *Doom*, sig. A6.

and their acceptance of Jesus [and] their return to the Holy Land under the rule of a visibly manifest messianic king'.[121] Whichever definition of public opinion we use, the Jews, their contemporary condition and their future tasks, were clearly a topic for conjecture. Yet relatively few of the millenarians arrived at specific proposals for readmission, with precise conditions as to how Jewish immigration could be administered. This in itself is odd in that groups such as the Fifth Monarchists came up with very carefully delineated sketches as to what their ideal world would look like once they accumulated the means to effect it; this is why they were such a potential danger. The manifesto of Thomas Venner's rebels in 1661 even explained that in the millennium there would be a complete ban on the export of unworked leather, of fuller's earth and other raw materials. Brightman, we remember, excluded dogs from his millenarian dream. This is why Thurloe was able to say that the Fifth Monarchists 'speake great words of . . . the beautifull kingdom of holies, which they would erect . . . yet the baits they lay to catch men with are the taking away of taxes, excise, customs, and tithes.'[122]

The importance of the millenarian movement for the readmission of the Jews to England was that it provided a receptive climate for discussion. The millenarians reminded Englishmen of the existence of contemporary Jews, and put them in a favourable light. Those men who gave England a positive role to play in readmission helped to translate this philo-semitic concern into practical action. A millenarian like John Eachard did this when he wrote that 'I am perswaded that the Jewes shall receive their Christs Nativitie day from England . . . I wish if there be any Jewes in England, that are incredulous, in this point, that they might be sent to that place, to prove the truth of it'.[123] Yet as we shall see, most Englishmen were more interested in the calling of the Jews than the readmission of the Jews; they would rather have seen them in Palestine than in London.

[121] Scholem, *Sabbatai Ṣevi*, p. 339.
[122] Capp. *Fifth Monarchy*, pp. 149, 156.
[123] J. Eachard, *Good Newes* (London, 1645), sig. B2.

4

THE DEBATE OVER THE
LOST TEN TRIBES OF ISRAEL

'Because by the strange and admirable Providence of God,' Sir
Matthew Hale said of the Jews, 'even since the Dissolution of
their State and Republick they have been to this day continued
a separated People from the rest of the World'. The reasons for
this unique destiny were obscure: 'Notwithstanding their
remarkable dispersion among all Nations,' he explained, 'they
have yet remained distinct as a signal Monument of the Divine
truth and Justice, and for what other secret ends and purposes,
is best known to the Divine Wisdom.' The survival of the Jews
as a distinct nationality was even more spectacular, Hale
thought, because 'this People hath been in all Ages exercised
with as many Plagues and Slaughters and Devastations of all
sorts, as ever any People under Heaven were.' Paramount
among these catastrophes was when 'the ten Tribes were carried away Captives by *Salmanasser*, . . . and only *Judah* and
Benjamin remained'.[1]

The fate of these lost ten tribes of Israel has been a subject of
debate for millennia, and as we shall see, became one of the
most important considerations in the readmission of the Jews to
England. The lost ten tribes became embroiled in a pressing
controversy during the first half of the seventeenth century
because many of those who predicted that the conversion of the
Jews would take place as a prelude to the Second Coming, or
even coincident with Christ's return, looked beyond the pitiful

---

[1] M. Hale, *The Primitive Origination of Mankind* (London, 1677), pp. 230, 232.

remnant of contemporary Jewry to the entire Hebrew nation,
the descendants of the kingdom of Israel, as well as those of
Judah. '*God before his ancients shall reigne*,' prophesied one English millenarian, 'that is, his ancient people the twelve Tribes.
Israelites and *Jews*, they shall be the subjects of Gods kingdome'.
At that glorious time 'the Cities of the Tribes shall be built
againe, and inhabited by naturall Israelites, especially
Ierusalem, which shall bee the most eminent city then in the
world, or that ever was in the world'.[2] The pronounced Puritan
interest in the lost ten tribes of Israel was thus the logical
product of their belief that a precondition for the Redemption
would be the conversion of all the Hebrews, not just European
Jewry.

We have already seen how other millenarian issues turned
men's minds towards a favourable view of Jews and Judaism.
The belief that the Jews had an important role to play in
England and Palestine after the Second Coming, and that they
held the key to the mysteries of the *lingua humana* undoubtedly
paved the way to the Whitehall Conference. But these philo-
semitic ideas might have remained entirely theoretical if
Menasseh ben Israel had not taken interest in the mystical and
millenarian possibilities of Jewish readmission to England.
And the particular aspect of this pattern of thought which
gripped his attention was the mystery of the lost ten tribes. As
we shall see, it was through the medium of the controversy over
the lost ten tribes that Rabbi Menasseh ben Israel, long famous
on the Continent as the Jewish ambassador to gentile scholars,
was introduced into England, where he would campaign until
his death eight years later for official Jewish readmission.

I

The belief that the lost ten tribes have survived as a secret,
hidden nation in some far-off corner of the globe has a long
history. The basic narrative of the Assyrian conquest in 722 BC
of the ten tribes that comprised the kingdom of Israel is
recounted within the biblical canon itself:

In the ninth year of Hoshea the king of Assyria took Samaria, and carried
Israel away into Assyria, and placed them in Halah and in Habor *by* the river

---

[2] I. Archer, *The Personall Reigne of Christ* (London, 1642), pp. 25–6.

of Gozan, and in the cities of the Medes. . . . So was Israel carried away out of their own land to Assyria unto this day.[3]

The Apocrypha continued the story and revealed that after the conquest the ten tribes

took this counsel among themselves, that they would leave the multitude of the heathen, and go forth into a further country, where never mankind dwelt, That they might there keep their statutes, which they never kept in their own land. . . . Then dwelt they there until the latter time; and now when they shall begin to come, The Highest shall stay the springs of the stream again, that they may go through[4]

These two basic texts provided the foundation for all subsequent speculation about the location and post-biblical history of the vanished Israelites. While Talmudic and Midrashic discussion of this important question was largely closed to gentile inquiry, traditional Jewish views still seeped into the Christian world. Josephus, for instance, assured his readers that at the time of his writing, 'there have been ten tribes beyond the Euphrates—countless myriads whose number cannot be ascertained.'[5] The controversy was soon continued by Christians as well as Jews. A fifth-century Latin poet named Commodianus wrote that when Christ returns he will lead an army of powerful, ravaging descendants of the original Israelites.[6] By the later Middle Ages, this band had evolved into the soldiers of Antichrist, the people of Gog and Magog. This nation, Ezekiel's mythical host, was once thought to be living in the far north, but later became equated with the peoples behind the Caucasus, and the raiding hordes of Central Asia.[7] Matthew Paris posited an Israelite origin for these primitive warriors in 1241, and Sir John Maundeville echoed his ideas a century later.[8] Marco Polo claimed that in 'Georgiana there is a

---

[3] II Kings 17: 6, 23.

[4] II Esdras 13: 41–2, 46–7.

[5] Josephus, *Jewish Antiquities*, xi. 133 (ed. Marcus, pp. 377–9). For the Jewish view of the lost tribes see esp. A. Neubauer, 'Where are the Ten Tribes?', *Jew. Qly. Rev.*, i (1889), 14–28, 95–114, 185–201, 408–23. Also, J. J. Groen, 'Historical and Genetic Studies on the Twelve Tribes of Israel', *Jew. Qly. Rev.*, lviii (1967–8), 1–11; B. Z. Luria, 'The Fate of the Exiles from Samariah' (Hebrew), *Beth Mikra*, lxix (1977), 159–76.

[6] N. Cohn, *The Pursuit of the Millennium* (2nd edn., London, 1970), pp. 28–9.

[7] Ibid. pp. 78–9; Ezek. 38–9; Rev. 20: 8–9; J. Trachtenberg, *The Devil and The Jews* (Philadel., 1961), *cap.* ii; G. K. Anderson, *The Legend of the Wandering Jew* (Providence, 1965), pp. 38–42.

[8] A. H. Hyamson, 'The Lost Tribes, and the Influence of the search for them on the

King called David Melic, which is as much to say [in Hebrew] "David King"; he is subject to the Tartar.[9] According to the fifteenth-century letters of Prester John, the legendary Christian king and priest, his realm was divided from 'the great country of the mighty Daniel, King of the Jews' by a 'river, full of stones, . . . which flows between the sea and the Nine Tribes of Israel. This river runs all the week till the Sabbath day, when it rests; it carries large and small stones to the sea . . . consequently the Nine Tribes of Israel cannot pass the river.'[10] This, of course, was the famous River Sambatyon of Jewish and Christian legend.[11]

But for our purposes, the most important development in the search for the lost ten tribes came with Columbus's discovery, and preoccupation with the ten tribes is evident even in the very first reports of the American Indians. Columbus reported in his journal that when he sent a reconnaissance party into the interior, he included one Luis de Torres, a converted marrano who 'understood Hebrew and Chaldee and even some Arabic.' Torres was meant to be the interpreter of the expedition, in case they encountered any Hebrew-speaking Indians. Luis de Torres returned safely but unsuccessfully from his mission, and was later killed by the Indians in Española when he elected to stay behind.[12]

Historians have come to see that the impact of the new world upon the old was slow and uncertain.[13] The very existence of a hitherto completely unknown race of people threw the traditional ancient and medieval theories about mankind off-balance. For Peter Martyr Anghiera, as for many of his contemporaries, the American Indians seemed 'to lyve in the

Return of the Jews to England', *Jew. Qly. Rev.*, xv (1903), 640–76, repr. in *Trs. Jew. Hist. Soc. Eng.*, v (1908), 115–47; *The Voiage and Travaile of Sir John Maundevile*, ed. J. O. Halliwell (London, 1869), pp. 265ff.; H. Bresslau, 'Juden und Mongolen 1241', *Zts. für die Gesch. Juden Deutsch.*, i (1886–7), 99–102, ii (1887–8), 382–3.

[9] *The Book of Ser Marco Polo*, ed. H. Yule (3rd edn., London, 1921), i. 50.

[10] Neubauer, 'Tribes', pp. 192–3.

[11] See A. Rothkoff, 'Sambatyon', *Ency. Jud.* (Jerusalem, 1971–2), xiv. 762–4.

[12] *The Journal of Christopher Columbus*, ed. C. Jane and L. A. Vigneras (London, 1960), pp. 51, 206. Cf. A. B. Gould y Quincy, 'Nueva Lista Documentada de los Tripulantes de Colon en 1492', *Bol. de la Real Acad. de la Hist.*, lxxv (1924), 34–49.

[13] See esp. *First Images of America*, ed. F. Chiappelli (Berkeley, Cal., 1976); J. H. Elliott, *The Old World and the New* (Cambridge, 1972); M. T. Hodgen, *Early Anthropology in the Sixteenth and Seventeenth Centuries* (Philadelphia, 1964).

goulden worlde of the which owlde wryters speake so much: wherein men lyved simplye and innocentlye without inforcement of lawes, without quarrelling Iudges and libelles, contente onely to satisfie nature, without further vexation for knowlege of thinges to come.'[14] Nevertheless, the most burning theoretical questions regarding the American Indians, in the first half of the sixteenth century, did not concern the origin of this native people, but rather the rights and responsibilities which Europeans had towards them. Scholars, philosophers, and armchair explorers debated the theological merits of conversion, the doctrine of universal papal dominion, and the theory of natural servitude, culminating in the famous face-to-face debate between Las Casas and Sepulveda at Valladolid in 1550.[15]

Even after they recognized that America was a new world and not merely the eastern coast of Asia, the earliest chroniclers were not very curious about the origin of the strange new race they found there. Furthermore, despite the claims of nineteenth-century Anglo-Israelite enthusiasts, even when these first historians did speculate about the Indian ancestors, they usually declined to assign the paternity to the missing Israelites.[16] All of these discussions in any case were conducted within the framework of biblical history. Although a polygenetic solution was later to be put forward by Isaac la Peyrère, virtually all men who wrote about the origin of the Indians agreed that they must in some way be descended from Adam, if not from Noah as well: the chief difficulty was to describe the route of migration, and to fit the chronology with the accepted timetable of Genesis.[17] The ancestry of the Indians could be

---

[14] P. Martyr of Angleria, *The Decades of the newe worlde* (London, 1555) in *The First Three English Books on America*, ed. E. Arber (Birmingham, 1885), p. 71.

[15] See esp. J. H. Parry, *The Spanish Seaborne Empire* (Penguin edn., Harmondsworth, 1973), pp. 174ff.; S. L. Robe, 'Wild Men and Spain's Brave New World' in *The Wild Man Within*, ed. E. Dudley and M. E. Novak (Pittsburgh, 1972), pp. 39–53; J. L. Phelan, *The Millennial Kingdom of the Franciscans in the New World* (2nd edn., Berkeley and LA, 1970).

[16] On the Anglo-Israel movement see J. Wilson, 'The History and Organization of British Israelism' (Oxford Univ. D.Phil. thesis 1966); idem, 'British Israelism' in *Patterns of Sectarianism*, ed. B. R. Wilson (London, 1967), pp. 45–76; idem, 'British Israelism', *Sociological Rev.*, n.s., xvi (1968), 41–57; B. A. Simon, *The Hope of Israel* (London, 1829); idem, *The Ten Tribes of Israel* (London, 1836).

[17] For Isaac la Peyrère, see above, p. 69.

established by comparing their major physical linguistic, religious, and cultural traits with those of more fully documented peoples. Underlying all of these discussions was the conviction that European and Asian culture must be more ancient than that of the Americans.[18] With these qualifications in mind, however, some scattered identification of the American Indians with the lost ten tribes of Israel can be found in the first reports of the new world.

Among the writings of Diego de Landa, bishop of Yucatan, is a good example of the way in which some Spanish chroniclers made reference to the Israelites at the same time that they upheld biblical axioms. In his account, unpublished until the middle of the nineteenth century although written about 1566, he explains that

Some of the old people of Yucatan say that they have heard from their ancestors that this land was occupied by a race of people, who came from the East and whom God had delivered by opening twelve paths through the sea. If this were true, it necessarily follows that all the inhabitants of the Indies are descendants of the Jews; since having once passed the Straits of Magellan, they must have extended over more than two thousand leagues of land which now Spain governs.[19]

Landa's conclusion illustrates some of the fundamental European preconceptions about the new American discovery. The marvels and exotica on the other side of the Atlantic had all to be fitted into the Procrustean bed of scriptural chronology and narrative. Some clues to the origins of the Indians were surely to be found in the Bible, if not in the Apocrypha then in Genesis, or even in Isaiah's promise that the Lord would recover the remnant of his people 'from the islands of the sea.'[20]

Gregorio Garcia, a Spanish Dominican who in 1607 published his theories concerning the origins of the American Indians, employed the method of cultural similarity. Garcia

---

[18] Hodgen, *Anthropology*, p. 313. The more useful secondary sources regarding the origin of the American Indians include T. Bendyshe, 'The History of Anthropology,' *Memoirs . . . Anth. Soc. London*, i (1865), 335–458; A. H. Godbey, *The Lost Tribes A Myth* (Durham, NC, 1930); D. C. Allen, *The Legend of Noah* (Urbana, Ill., 1949); L. E. Huddleston, *Origins of the American Indians* (Austin, Tex. and London, 1967); J. G. Burke, 'The Wild Man's Pedigree', in *Wild Man*, ed. Dudley and Novak, pp. 259–80.

[19] D. de Landa, *Relación de las Cosas de Yucatan*, ed. and trans. A. M. Tozzer (Cambridge, Mass., 1941), pp. 16–17.

[20] Isa. 11: 11.

compared the character traits of Jews and Indians: both were 'medrosos i timidos', and both demonstrated 'la increaulidad' and 'la ingratitud'. He also noted that both Hebrew and the dialect of the Peruvian Indians were guttural languages. Yet Garcia finally concluded that as this entire matter was too recent to have built up a body of learned opinion, the question of the origin of the American Indians was still unsolved.[21]

Other Spanish chroniclers were even more sceptical about a direct link between the American Indians and the Jews. One of the earliest full discussions of the alleged Hebraic antecedents of the Indians appears in the *Apologética Historia* by Bartolomé de Las Casas, the Dominican 'Apostle of the Indies'. Las Casas reported that some Indians, especially in Nicaragua, practised circumcision, which led some people to have imagined or suspected 'que estas gentes indianas descendiesen de la judaica generación'. But, he pointed out, circumcision was also practised by the Egyptians, the Ethiopians, the Syrians, the Phoenicians and others, for religious and hygienic reasons. Las Casas also rejected a connection between Indians and Jews based on philological grounds, since similarities existed not only between Indian languages and Hebrew, but also between American dialects and European languages. This particular work by Las Casas was not published until this century, but his rejection of a link between the ten tribes and the American Indians must surely have become known during his lifetime.[22]

The same scepticism can be found in the writings of other early Spanish chroniclers of the Indies such as Alonso de Zamora and Gerónimo de Mendieta. Zamora's main objection to the hypothesis that America was first peopled by the ten tribes was the unlikelihood that 'desde los tiempos del diluvio, hasta los del Rey Salmanazar estuviera sin poblar esta bellissima, abundante, y riquissima parte del mundo'. Furthermore, God's commandment to Noah and his sons was to 'replenish the earth', which surely must have included the new world as well.[23]

[21] G. Garcia, *Origen De Los Indios* (Madrid, 1729), p. 87; Elliott, *Old World*, pp. 29–30.

[22] B. de Las Casas, *Apologética Historia*, ed. E. O'Gorman (Mexico City, 1967), pp. 531–3.

[23] A. de Zamora, *Historia de la Provincia de San Antonio* (Caracas, 1930), pp. 12–13; G. de Mendieta, *Historia Eclesiástica Indiana* (Mexico City, 1870), pp. 107, 143–5; Gen. 9:1; cf. A. de la Calancha, *Coronica Moralizada* (Barcelona, 1638), pp. 34, 39, 42.

The Spanish writers, naturally enough the first to describe the new race and to point to their similarities with the Jews, were thus indecisive about connections, lineages, and origins. In spite of the proportions that the lost ten tribes controversy would assume in the mid-seventeenth century, the English were similarly undecided about the Indian ancestry as long as they relied on second-hand reports translated from the Spanish. One very early English description of the Indians concluded, 'howe the people furst began In that contrey, or whens they cam, For clerkes it is a questyon.'[24] But the first English book to mention the word 'Armenica' juxtaposed a fantastic account of the new world and its human monstrosities, cannibals, and immorality with an abridgement of the Prester John letter, full of amazement with 'the great kynge of Israhel'.[25] In this way, the lost ten tribes question made a somewhat tentative entrance into England.

The English translation of Peter Martyr's account of the new world was one of the earliest sources available in this country and also points in the direction of the ancient Jewish kingdom, if not to the lost ten tribes themselves. Martyr praised the king of Spain for his efforts in having won a new race of people to Christianity, comparing him to Abraham, who was appointed by God to be the father of a vast nation. For the American Indians were a 'spirituall Israell', so that Ferdinand 'and his posteritie the kynges of Spayne haue nowe planted a newe Israell muche greater then that whiche Moises ledde throughe the red sea.' Martyr believed that the Indians were descended from Adam and Eve, although he provided few specific details about their genealogy. Unlike Las Casas, who wrote forty years later, Peter Martyr was very impressed by the fact that some Indians practised circumcision and spoke a dialect similar to Hebrew.[26]

In spite of these early signs of interest in the fate of the lost ten tribes, it was not until the beginning of the seventeenth century that the missing Israelites became a controversial topic here. The first major English work to challenge the hypothesis that

---

[24] *The Interlude of the Four Elements*, ed. J. O. Halliwell (Percy Soc., xxii, 1848), p. 31.

[25] [Anon.], *Of the newe landes* (Antwerp, 1511?) in *Three English Books*, ed. Arber, pp. xxvii, xxxiii–iv.

[26] Martyr, *Decades*, pp. 51, 99, 169, 186–7.

the Indians were descended from the ten tribes was written between 1609 and 1611 by Giles Fletcher the elder. Fletcher sought to prove that the Tartars, rather than the Indians, were the progeny of the Israelites, although they were no longer divided into biblical tribes. Fletcher produced a number of reasons, including similarities between certain Tartar and Hebrew names, the common practice of circumcision, and the fact that the Tartars have a fort named 'Mount Tabor'. These Israelites were unlike the Jews, who 'are all a poor and servile people to the Towns and Countrys where they dwell.' Fletcher especially mentioned Thomas Brightman as a man 'whom God endued with special gifts, and great brightness after his name, for the full clearing and exposition of that Prophecy, above all that hitherto have written of it.'[27]

Fletcher's attack was in part directed against French thinkers rather than Spanish historians, for by the beginning of the seventeenth century the lost ten tribes controversy had become more international, and was a subject of speculation not only among the explorers themselves, but also among Europeans whose experience of the new world was comparatively limited. The theory that the Israelites had degenerated into warlike Tartars over the centuries had already found acceptance in France by Guillaume Postel, the famous historian, who argued that the peoples of central Asia were in fact the descendants of the lost ten tribes, despite their apparent savage and primitive customs.[28] Postel was not the only Frenchman whose views were noticed in England. Jean de Lery, the French Protestant preacher, put forward the argument that the Israelites, in taking possession of Canaan, forced out the original inhabitants who fled in boats and were carried by the sea currents to Brazil. 'Toutefois par ce qu'on pourroit faire beaucoup d'obiections là dessus,' de Lery admitted, 'i'en laisseray croire à vn chacū ce qu'il luy plaira.'[29] Marc Lescarbot, another French travel writer, particularly singled out de Lery for scorn: the oceans dividing the old and the new worlds were far too great

[27] G. Fletcher, 'The Tartars Or, Ten Tribes' in *Israel Redux*, ed. S. Lee (London, 1677), pp. 1–28. For critical edn. see *The English Works of Giles Fletcher, the Elder*, ed. L. E. Berry (Madison, 1964), pp. 307–31.

[28] G. Postel, *Des Histoires Orientales* (Paris, 1575), pp. 34, 35–7.

[29] I. de Lery, *Histoire D'vn Voyage* (La Rochelle, 1578), pp. 290–2.

for such a journey to have taken place, he objected, 'du moins il n'en est point de mention en tous les livres & memoires qui nous on esté laissez parl'Antiquité.'[30] André Thevet, the French royal cosmographer, recounted the discovery of a Hebrew inscription in the new world. 'Et par cela chacun peut iuger,' he concluded, 'que ce peuple Hebreu a habité non seulement au pays de Iudee, ains par tout ce grand vniuers.'[31] The views of these French thinkers were known in England, and added fuel to the controversy.

Seventeenth-century English travellers to the East often sought information about the Israelites, and thereby helped to provide even more data. Some, like William Lithgow the Scottish travel-writer, had close contact with Jews for the first time when they went abroad. Several Jews accompanied him across the Mediterranean, and others entertained him in the Holy Land: 'we stayed within the Towne', he wrote, 'making merry with our Hebraick friends'.[32] Henry Blount had noted the *Egyptians* to have a touch of the *Merchant*, or *Iew*' about them, so when he made his famous voyage to the Levant, the 'chiefe Sect whereof I desired to be enformed was the Iewes; whose moderne condition is more condemned, then understood by *Christian*-Writers, and therefore by them delivered with such a zealous ignorance, as never gave me satisfaction'. Blount wrote that he discussed a number of questions regarding Jewish rites and beliefs with the rabbi of the Sephardic community at Sofia. The book of Esdras was held 'high in esteeme with them', yet they expressed different views regarding the lost ten tribes. When Blount raised the possibility that the captive Israelites had simply become assimilated after hundreds of years, they 'ashamed of such Apostacy, told me, that those ten Tribes are not found any where, but either swallowed like *Corans* company, or as other *Rabbines* write, blowne away with a whirlewinde.'[33]

---

[30] M. Lescarbot, *Histoire De La Nowelle France* (Paris, 1609), p. 16.

[31] A. Thevet, *La Cosmographie Universelle* (Paris, 1575), f. 1022ʳ.

[32] W. Lithgow, *A . . . peregrination from Scotland* (London, 1614), f. 11ᵛ; idem, *The Totall Discourse of The Rare Adventures* (Glasgow, 1906), p. 257: first pub. 1632. Cf. C. E. Bosworth, 'William Lithgow of Lanark's Travels in Syria and Palestine, 1611–1612', *Jnl. Sem. Stud.*, xx (1975), 219–35. Generally, see B. Penrose, *Urbane Travellers 1591–1635* (Phil. and London, 1942); R. Wittkower, 'Marvels of the East', *Jnl. Warb. Ctld. Inst.*, v (1942), 159–97.

[33] H. B[lount], *A Voyage Into The Levant* (2nd edn., London, 1636), pp. 113–22, esp. p. 121.

Some English travellers to the East helped to strengthen the supporters of the Tartar pedigree. An anonymous traveller reported in 1611 that the Israelites formed only one part of the entire Tartar people, and were those '*Tartars* who are far scitu-ated from the residue, and inhabit that remote *Scithian* promon-tory, . . . wandering vp and downe the country'. He claimed that 'vntil this day, they retaine the names of their tribes, the title of Haebrewes, and circumcision. In al other rites they follow the fashions of the *Tartarians*.'[34] George Sandys came back from his travels to the Levant with a report that the lost ten tribes were 'planted, as some say, beyond the *Caspian* Mountains; from whence they never returned.'[35]

A book that sought to come to some kind of compromise position between the American Indian and Tartar theories was posthumously published in 1614 from the writings of Edward Brerewood, the well-known first professor of astronomy at Gresham College. Brerewood was a member of the Society of Antiquaries, and wrote on logic, linguistics, geography, optics, ancient weights and measures, as well as on astronomy, and his opinions carried great influence.[36] Brerewood admitted that the view that the Tartars were descended from the lost ten tribes had 'not onely found acceptance and entertainement, with sundrie learned and vnderstanding men: but reason and authority are produced, or pretended to establish it for a truth.' Brerewood cited the three main reasons which had been given most often to support this belief: (1) 'that the word *Tatari* . . . signifieth in the *Syriaque* and *Hebrew* tongues, a Residue or Remainder such as these *Tartars* are supposed to bee of the Ten Tribes'; (2) the fact that the Tartars 'haue alwaies embraced (the ancient character of *Iudaisme*) Circumcision'; and (3) the authority of the book of Esdras.[37]

Brerewood rejected all of this evidence, but he retained the Bible as an infallible authority. He reasoned that the presence in America of 'Beares, Lions, Tigers, Wolues, Foxes, &c.

---

[34] [Anon.], *Relations, Of The Most Famous Kingdoms* (London, 1611), p. 336.

[35] G. Sandys, *Sandys Travels* (7th edn., London, 1673), p. 111.

[36] C. Hill, *Intellectual Origins of the English Revolution* (Panther edn., London, 1972), pp. 51–2.

[37] E. Brerewood, *Enqviries Tovching The Diversity of Langvages, and Religions* (London, 1614), pp. 94–7.

(which men as is likely, would neuer to their owne harme transporte out of the one continent to the other)', indicated that these animals must have travelled by land since the time of Noah's landing in Asia after the Flood. Therefore, Asia and America 'are continent one with the other, or at most, disioyned but by some narrow channell of the Ocean'. American Indians, by this logic, must be the descendants of the Tartars of eastern Asia, especially in light of the accepted fact that 'the West side of *America* respecting *Asia*, is exceeding much better peopled then the opposite or East side, that respecteth toward *Europe*.' Brerewood's biblical studies thus led him to a compromise position between the Tartar and the American Indian schools: the Indians were certainly descended from the Tartars, he argued, who in turn may very well be Israelites. According to Brerewood's theory, all the participants in the ten tribes debate were in agreement and were simply calling the same group of people by different names.[38]

Despite first appearances, Brerewood's compromise was not completely absurd. The location of the Tartar homeland was interpreted very broadly in the seventeenth century. Early modern Europeans learned their Mongol and Tartar history from the reports of the thirteenth-century Franciscan friars John de Piano Carpini and William of Rubruck, as well as from Marco Polo and Maundeville. The similarities in language, appearance, culture, and religion led early modern anthropologists to postulate a direct link between the peoples of north-east Asia and the American Indians. In other words, Edward Brerewood had anticipated the modern explanation that the American Indians are the descendants of men who had migrated overland from Asia.

Attention was therefore continually directed back to the American Indians and the genuine possibility that they might be Israelites, although admittedly there were other ideas in the air regarding the origin of the Indians. The Atlantis and Ophir myths are well known,[39] more so than the early modern conjec-

---

[38] Ibid., pp. 96–7.

[39] It was from Ophir that Hiram, king of Tyre, fetched 'gold, four hundred and twenty talents, and brought it to king Solomon' when he built the Temple at Jerusalem. Ophir also provided 'great plenty of almug trees, and precious stones' (I Kings 9: 28 and 10: 11). The exact location of Ophir has puzzled geographers since ancient times. See C. Jack-Hinton, *The Search for the Islands of Solomon* (Oxford, 1969), *cap.* i.

ture that the American Indians were descended from the Welsh. According to legend, Madog ab Owain Gwynedd, a twelfth-century Welsh prince, discovered the new world. An Elizabethan version of the story, which first appeared in a fifteenth-century Welsh poem, explained that therefore 'it is manifest, that that countrie was long before by *Brytaines* discouered, afore either *Columbus* or *Americus Vesputius* lead anie *Spaniardes* thither.' This could be proven by American Indian folk-memories and the English words still remaining in the Indian languages. For example, it was reported, 'they haue a certeine bird with a white head, which they call *Pengwin*' just as in English.[40]

Still, it was the theory of ancestry among the lost ten tribes which was influential in Jewish readmission and, as we shall see, in the growth of English interest in the spiritual future of the inhabitants of the new world. Some of the ethnographic observations must surely have been quite fanciful, but once Englishmen began to go to the new world themselves in greater numbers, they had the opportunity to look at the evidence first-hand instead of relying on Spanish reports or French theories. William Wood, for example, one of the early English travellers, reported that although some 'have thought they might be of the dispersed *Iewes*, because some of their words be neare unto the *Hebrew*', equally by the same method the Indians could be ascribed to many nations 'because they have words which sound after the *Greeke*, *Latine*, *French*, and other tongues'.[41] Thomas Gage the famous traveller agreed with Brerewood's writing. 'And indeed,' he affirmed, 'the *Indians* of *America* in many things seeme to bee of the race and progenie of the *Tartars*'. Gage was too prudent, however, to venture an alternate opinion regarding the lost ten tribes.[42] The ethnographic reports of men like Wood and Gage were amplified after the beginning of the Civil War, when the quantity of literature stressing the role of the Jews in the Second Coming greatly increased. Many men agreed with John Archer, who was con-

---

[40] H. Lhoyd and D. Powel, *The historie of Cambria* (London, 1584), pp. 227–9. Cf. C. Beatty, *The Journal of a Two Months Tour* (London, 1768), pp. 24–7.

[41] W. Wood, *New Englands Prospect* (London, 1634), p. 91. Generally, see C. Steele, *English Interpreters of the Iberian New World* (Oxford, 1975).

[42] T. Gage, *Survey of the West India's* (London, 1648), p. 73.

vinced that the Kingdom of Christ would begin with 'great troubles' for those who would be the subjects of His monarchy, 'both beleeving Gentiles and Jewes with *Israelites* or the *ten Tribes*, who shall be all converted'.[43]

Speculation in this field was not limited to radical Puritans. Church historian Peter Heylyn had published his views on the subject even under James I. Heylyn showed that he was quite familiar with most of the general theories concerning the origin of the American Indians, as well as with the various hypotheses about the lost ten tribes. Heylyn recognized that the Jews 'liue straglingly dispersed in all quarters', but he specifically attacked Brerewood's reasons for identifying the Tartars with the lost ten tribes. Heylyn was also sceptical of the fantastic stories of men with dog's heads and so on which appeared not only in ancient and medieval accounts, but in those of Columbus and early modern writers as well. The American Indians, he thought, 'are without question the progenie of the Tartars'. The fact that some words in their language may be similar to English was unimpressive: even the penguin proof failed to convince him. Heylyn saw the imperialist implications in the theories of the 'more curious then profound Antiquaries'. Some of them, he recalled, 'went about to intitle Q *Elizabeth* to the soueraignty of these Countries: but she wisely did reiect these counsels, & not louing to put her sithe into another mans haruest'.[44]

By the death of Charles I, the debate over the lost ten tribes, with all of its fantastic paternity suits, seemed to have run its course in England. The future master of Magdalene College, Cambridge, John Sadler, wrote in 1649 that 'the World will not admit it of late: Although it was very current a while'. Sadler noted that the Jews, on the other hand, followed

the old prediction in their *Zohar*. which foretels their Redemption should be upon, or about, the yeare last past. To which they add, somewhat they see, or have heard, from their Bretheren of *Iuda*, in *Brasile*: or of *Israel* in other parts of *America*. which they cannot much believe, (till it be better confirmed:) although it be, with many Arguments, asserted by a Grave, Sober Man, of their own Nation, that is lately come from the Western World.[45]

[43] Archer, *Reigne*, p. 15.
[44] P. Heylyn, [*Microcosmos*] (Oxford, 1625), pp. 661–2, 677, 775, 779. Cf. M. Prideaux, *An Easy and Compendious Introduction* (Oxford, 1648), p. 33.
[45] [J. Sadler], *Rights of the Kingdom* (London, 1649), pp. 38–40.

The man Sadler referred to was Aaron ha-Levi, alias Antonio de Montezinos, a marrano recently returned from Quito Province, who testified under oath before Rabbi Menasseh ben Israel of Amsterdam in 1644 that he had met Israelites of the tribe of Reuben, living secretly deep in the interior of the territory. The lost ten tribes debate was suddenly reinvigorated. And the introduction of Menasseh ben Israel to the controversy over the ten tribes changed the entire tenor and direction of the discussion, and gave it a specific, polemical purpose towards Jewish readmission.

II

At the same time when Englishmen were arguing over the fate of the lost ten tribes of Israel, this question was being considered by Jews as well. Although the *Zohar*, the principal kabbalistic text, had promised that the Messiah would come soon after 1300, sixteenth- and seventeenth-century kabbalists reinterpreted the assurance that in 'the year 408 of the sixth millennium [1648] they that lie in the dust will arise'. These kabbalists were experts in gematria—the system of calculating the numerical value of Hebrew words and letters in interpretation—and their research pointed to 1648 as the year of final Redemption.[46]

A renewed interest in the lost ten tribes grew up among Jews in the tense years before 1648. As early as 1517–28, Rabbi Abraham ben Eliezer ha-Levi and his followers in Jerusalem were sending information to supporters in Italy regarding the 'children of Moses'.[47] This was the era of David Reubeni, the self-proclaimed ambassador of the lost Jewish tribes in Arabia. David and his partner Solomon Molko soon met untimely ends—the first in a Spanish prison and the second at the stake—but not before they had presented their request to both Charles V and the Pope for arms to be used against the Turks.

A century later, in 1641, a certain Rabbi Baruch Gad claimed to have met a warrior from the lost tribe of Naphtali on his way from Jerusalem to Persia. Rabbi Baruch brought back a message from the lost ten tribes to Judah and Benjamin,

[46] Zohar I, 139b: G. Scholem, *Sabbatai Ṣevi* (London, 1973), pp. 88–93.

[47] Ibid., pp. 337–8; G. Scholem, 'The Kabbalist R. Abraham ben Eliezer ha-Levi' (Hebrew), *Kiryath Sepher*, ii (1925), 101–41, 269–73; vii (1931), 149–65, 440–56.

recounting the freedom and prosperity of the Israelites. 'And do not ask why we wage no war against the nations [to liberate you],' they explained, 'for you should know that we, the tribe of the children of Moses, cannot cross the river [Sambatyon] until the end be'. Certified copies of this letter were given to at least two emissaries to Europe from the rabbis of Jerusalem during the seventeenth century, and there is no reason to doubt the authenticity of the signatures on the documents.[48] An expansive account of the lost ten tribes also appears in a work by Abraham Jagel, the Italian philosopher and private tutor to moneyed Jewish families in Ferrara and Venice.[49]

The claim by Antonio Montezinos that he had discovered a remnant of Israel in some isolated corner of the globe was thus in line with a well-established Jewish tradition. His story seemed even more plausible to European Jewry after the imagined year of final Redemption, for the infamous Chmielnicki massacres began in 1648, ending eight years later after tens of thousands of Jews had been murdered in Poland, Galicia, Lithuania, White Russia, and the Ukraine. Rabbis throughout Europe believed that the massacres were the first 'birth pangs' of the messianic age.[50] Furthermore, while we have become sensitive to the uncertain impact of the discovery of the new world on European scholars and thinkers, a similar development can be traced among the famous Jewish historiographers of the early modern period. The first detailed description of America appears in the geographical work by Abraham Farissol, the Italian cosmographer, Bible commentator, and anti-Christian polemicist. Farissol juxtaposed an account of David Reubeni's mission with the report of the new world, which may have helped to enhance speculation among Jewish readers about the American Indians and their origins.[51]

Montezinos testified in Amsterdam before Menasseh 'and

[48] Ibid.

[49] A. ben Ḥananiah Jagel, 'Beit Ya'ar Lebanon', Bodl., MS Reggio 8–10, *cap.* xxii: see *Ency. Jud.*, ix. 1268–9.

[50] Scholem, *Sabbatai Ṣevi*, pp. 88–93.

[51] A. Peritsol, *Itinera Mundi*, ed. T. Hyde (Oxford, 1691), pp. 90–6. See also L. Kochan, *The Jew and his History* (London, 1977), pp. 35–58. Nevertheless, according to Dr J. I. Israel, 'There is no evidence that any Mexican Jews agreed with . . . Manasseh ben Israel, and a number of Spanish friars, who thought that the American Indians were the descendants of the ten lost tribes of Israel.': *Race, Class and Politics in Colonial Mexico 1610–1670* (London, 1975), p. 129.

divers other chiefe men of the Portugall Nation'. He said that it was on expedition to Quito Province, in what is now Ecuador, that he confessed to his Indian companion, 'I am an Hebrew of the tribe of *Levi*, my God is *Adonay*, and all the rest are nothing but mistakes and deceites.' This alone was a bold step because Montezinos was a marrano and had just been released from prison in Cartagena, where he had been confined by the Inquisition. The Indian told him that he could find the answer to his problems if he travelled barefoot, rested on Saturday, ate only roasted maize, and followed his instructions. Montezinos eventually arrived at a secret kingdom where the inhabitants repeated the Jewish credo, the *Shema*ᶜ, along with nine vague remarks and prophecies, but refused to allow him to cross the river that bordered their kingdom. Montezinos estimated that he spoke with nearly three hundred Israelite Indians during his three days there, but they would see him only in small groups, and declined to elaborate on their nine cryptic statements.

Montezinos's Indian companion explained afterwards that these were Israelites who had come to the new world and defeated the Indians in the area. The Indians visited them every seventy moons, unless something special occurred, such as Montezinos's visit. They were never allowed to cross the river into the kingdom itself. These secret Israelites believed that the arrival of the Spanish in the new world, the coming of ships to the South Seas, and the visit of Montezinos fulfilled certain prophecies. The Indians explained that

The God of these sonnes of *Israel* is the true God, all that is written in his stories is true, they shall be Lords of all the world in the latter end, a people shall come hither which will bring many things to you, and when the land shall be well provided, these sonnes of *Israel* shall goe out of their habitations, and shall become Lords of all the earth as it was theirs before, if you will be happy joyne your selves to them.

Montezinos returned to the coast and met more 'caciques', Indian representatives to the secret Israelite community.[52]

Menasseh published this account in his book, *The Hope of Israel,* which appeared at Amsterdam in Latin and Spanish in

---

[52] 'The Relation of Master Antonie Monterinos' in *Ievves in America*, ed. T. Thorowgood (London, 1650). Cf. Menasseh ben Israel, *The Hope of Israel* (2nd edn., London, 1652), pp. 1–7.

1650, and at London the same year in an English edition translated by Milton's friend Moses Wall; a second English edition is dated 1652.[53] The first full report which the general English reading public received of Montezinos's discovery came with a French translation of the testimony which Menasseh sent to John Dury in England, where it was rendered into English and published in Thomas Thorowgood's *Ievves in America* in 1650.[54] Thorowgood was completely convinced by Montezinos's report, and cited Peter Martyr, Roger Williams, Elias Levita, Giles Fletcher, Las Casas, Paris, and Brerewood for corroborating evidence. Thorowgood hoped that the discovery that the American Indians were actually Hebrews would 'encourage us who are already desirous, not to civilize onely the Americanes, but even to Gospellize and make them Christian.'[55]

John Dury, the man who introduced Montezinos and Menasseh to the English public, contributed an 'Epistolicall Discourse' to Thorowgood's collection as well. Although 'at first blush,' he confessed, 'the thing which you offer to be believed, will seeme to most men incredible, and extravigent; yet when all things are laid rationally and without prejudice together, there will be nothing of improbability found therein'. Dury was one of the few participants in the debate who utilized Jewish sources and authorities. He had received a third-hand report from a Dutch Jew that the Jewish community 'neere about the Holy Land' had a visit from a messenger of the lost ten tribes, 'to make enquiry concerning the state of the Land; and what was become of the two Tribes and the half which was left in it'. The Israelite said that 'they have increased into a great Nation, and are to come from thence into their owne Land by the direction of God'. Dury also heard of Montezinos and his story, and a query to Menasseh ben Israel produced the report

[53] Second edn. repr. in facsimile in *Menasseh ben Israel's Mission to Oliver Cromwell*, ed. L. Wolf (London, 1901), with critical notes.

[54] See I. Dury, 'An Epistolicall Discourse' in Thorowgood, *Ievves*, sigs. E^v–E2. The first news of Menasseh's interview arrived in England by way of E. Winslow, *The Glorious Progress* (London, 1649), repr. *Coll. Mass. Hist. Soc.*, 3rd ser., iv (1834), 69–98, esp. pp. 73–4.

[55] Thorowgood, *Ievves*, pp. 3, 5, 16, 19, 39, 43, esp. p. 53. Generally, see J. A. de Jong, *As The Waters Cover The Sea* (Kampen, 1970), pp. 57–73.

which Thorowgood printed, a number of months before the rabbi's book was published.[56]

The immediate reaction in England to Montezinos's tale is difficult to determine. Ralph Josselin, a minister in Essex, heard of the discovery as early as March 1650–1, and was fascinated to find that 'Rab: ben. Israel is of opinion that the Jewes are scatterd from the North of Asia and Europe into America.' Josselin drew a pointed hand in the margin for emphasis. By December he had obtained a copy of the book: 'lord my heart questions not the calling home the nation of the Jewes thou wilt hasten in its season, oh my god, oh thou god of the ends of the whole earth: hasten it Amen.' Two days later, working his way through the text, Josselin noted in his diary that 'menasseh Ben Israel conceiveth a great stocke of the Jewes are beyond the mountaines Cordellery about Quiti.'[57]

More academic Englishmen were probably less fascinated and more aware of the obvious resemblance between Montezinos's report and the legend of Prester John. Even more striking is the similarity between Montezinos's story and the accounts of both Eldad Ha-Dani and Benjamin of Tudela. Eldad, the late ninth-century self-styled ambassador from the tribe of Dan, claimed that his clan lived in an independent kingdom in the East, along with the tribes of Naphtali, Gad, and Asher. Eldad also told of the 'children of Moses' imprisoned by the River Sambatyon, and other tribes who lived 'in high mountains' and spoke the Tartar language. A Latin translation of Eldad's account was available to Englishmen by the later sixteenth century.[58] Benjamin of Tudela, travelling in the later twelfth century, also provided some information about the lost tribes. The account of his journey is more significant for our purposes because it was quite well known to seventeenth-century Englishmen. This was no doubt due to the English text which appeared in the monumental collection of travel literature known as *Purchas his Pilgrimes*, published in 1625, probably

---

[56] Dury, 'Discourse', sigs. D–E2: dated 27 Jan. 1649–50; Dury promises to send Thorowgood a copy of Menasseh's book as soon as it it published.

[57] *The Diary of Ralph Josselin*, ed. A. Macfarlane (London, 1976), pp. 238 (13 Mar. 1650–1), 266 (20 and 22 Dec. 1651).

[58] In G. Génébrard, *Chronologia Hebraeorum* (Paris, 1585), pp. 75ff. See also *Eldad Ha-Dani*, ed. A. Epstein (Hebrew) (Pressburg, 1891); *The Ritual of Eldad Ha-Dani*, ed. M. Schloessinger (Leipzig, 1908); A. Shochat, 'Eldad Ha-Dani', *Ency. Jud.*, vi. 576–8.

the largest single work in English which had yet appeared. 'And they say,' Benjamin reported, 'that in those Cities of the Mountaynes Nisbor, foure Tribes of the Israelites inhabit, carried away in the first Captivitie by Salmanasar the King of the Assyrians, to wit, Dan, Zabulon, Asser, and Nephthali'. According to his story, a military expedition under the king of Persia did succeed in reaching the Israelites, who could send messengers from their city in spite of the river which protected them.[59] Menasseh himself recognized the similarity between Montezinos's account and these more ancient narratives, but charitably concluded that they provided corroborating testimony, and that as 'for the other things in the relation of our *Montezinus*, they say nothing which savours of falshood.'[60]

There is little evidence regarding the English assessment of the narratives of Eldad and Benjamin. Mathias Prideaux, fellow of Exeter and son of the bishop of Worcester, wondered whether 'Sir *Iohn Mandevills* Travels, with the strange adventures in them, or *Binjamin Tudelitanus Iewish Iournals* of multitudes of his Countrymen found abroad, deserves the greater credit'.[61] Samuel Purchas appended a marginal remark to Benjamin's account: after the words 'they say', he printed an asterisk, which leads the reader to the warning, 'Marke this, they say, a tale devised by Jewish Fablers.'[62] On the other hand, Edward Pococke, the famous Oxford Hebraist, made numerous notes in his Latin copy of Benjamin's travels, but underlined the editor's very critical judgement concerning Eldad's story.[63] Montezinos's report was somewhat different from the rest, however. This was the first time that the lost ten tribes of Israel had been found in America by a Jewish witness, and the immediacy of his story, and perhaps the underlying familiarity of the genre, seems to have swept away more ancient narratives in its path.

The English and Latin translations of Menasseh's *Hope of Israel* were dedicated to Parliament and the Council of State.

---

[59] S. Purchas, *Purchas His Pilgrimes* (Glasgow, 1905), viii. 523–93, esp. p. 577. Cf. *The Itinerary of Benjamin of Tudela*, ed. M. N. Adler (London, 1907).

[60] Menasseh, *Hope*, p. 46.

[61] Prideaux, *Introduction*, p. 346.

[62] Purchas, *Pilgrimes*, viii. 577.

[63] Benjamin of Tudela, *Itinerarivm D. Beniaminis*, ed. Constantini l'Emperevr (Antwerp, 1633): Bodl., 8° T. 28. Th. BS., p. 211.

'The whole world stands amazed at these things,' Menasseh flattered, 'and the eies of all are turned upon you, that they may see whither all these things do tend'. The rabbi admitted that there 'are as many minds as men, about the originall of the people of *America*'.

Some would have the praise of finding out *America*, to be due to the *Carthaginians*, others to the *Phenicians*, or the *Canaanites*; others to the *Indians*, or people of *China*; others to them of *Norway*, others to the Inhabitants of the *Atlantick Islands*, others to the *Tartarians*, others to the ten Tribes.[64]

Menasseh summarized the main issues in the controversy and printed the testimony of Montezinos which had already been sent to Dury. Montezinos, he affirmed, was 'of honest and known Parents, a man about forty yeares old, honest, and not ambitious.' After six months in Amsterdam, he had returned to Brazil where he died, affirming the veracity of his story on his death bed. Menasseh's array of Christian authorities was particularly impressive, and included Matteo Ricci, Nichola Trigault, Ortelius, John Huarte, Postel, Goropius, Lescarbot, Luther, Grotius, and de Laet.[65]

The Hope of Israel was immediately successful in Jewish and gentile circles alike. Even discounting the unsettled condition of contemporary English politics, Jews had good reason to look towards London for Redemption. The children of Israel had been promised that 'the LORD will scatter thee among all people, from the one end of the earth even unto the other': this prophecy needed to be fulfilled before the End of Days. The classical name for England in medieval Jewish literature is *qeṣeh ha-'ares*, the 'end of the earth', an over-literal translation of 'Angleterre'. Menasseh was able to press subtly for the readmission of the Jews to England by pointing out that the discovery of Jews in America fulfilled another quarter of the prophecy.[66] The change in the English intellectual climate also appeared hopeful:

So at this day we see many desirous to learne the Hebrew tongue of our men. Hence may be seene that God hath not left us; for if one persecute us, another receives us civilly, and courteously; and if this Prince treats us ill, another

[64] Menasseh, *Hope*, sigs. A2ᵛ, A3ᵛ.
[65] Menasseh, *Hope*, sig. Bᵛ; pp. 18, 45.
[66] *Ibid*. p. 31; Deut. 28: 64; Isa. 11:12; C. Roth, 'New Light on the Resettlement', *Trs. Jew. Hist. Soc. Eng.*, xi (1928), 113–4.

treats us well; if one banisheth us out of his country, another invites us by a thousand priviledges[67]

The resettlement of the Jews in England was a necessary precondition for the coming of the Messiah.

Menasseh's little book reinvigorated the issue of the lost ten tribes, and oriented the public mind towards the Jews once again. Sir Edward Spencer, the Recruiter member of Parliament for Middlesex, immediately fired off a reply to Menasseh's theories, but more significantly to his vague suggestions that the ban on Jewish immigration ought to be lifted.[68] Spencer was against millenarian theorizing, and was mainly concerned with devising harsh conditions and safeguards to be applied before the Jews were allowed to return. He wrote that his purpose in putting his views into print was the fact that

the taking off the scandall of our too great desire of entertayning the unbeleeving Nation of the *Jewes*, and yet our earnest wishes of their conversion, hath also another aime, to continue the industry of our learned men in the *Easterne* Tongues, and to encourage some of them to take more paines in endeavoring that Nations Conversion by word and writing

Spencer published a Latin translation of his work, bound together with the English version, so as to give it a broader appeal and a wider audience.[69] We know from Arise Evans, the Royalist millenarian, that it was a best-seller of the day.[70] Menasseh's suggestions had edged the issue of the tribes into a potential political tool, and Spencer was anxious to halt its effectiveness at the outset.

Menasseh seems to have been quite genuine in his endorsement of Montezinos's story; the discovery of a remnant of Israel in the new world was of crucial importance to nearly all theologians who became acquainted with the marrano's testimony, and this was the aspect of *The Hope of Israel* that was

[67] Menasseh, *Hope*, pp. 40–1.

[68] Spencer was elected in 1648 and had sat in several earlier Parliaments; he ceased to attend after Pride's Purge, although he was not expelled. Spencer was born about 1595, graduated from Oxford, and died before the Restoration. For more on him, see D. Brunton and D. H. Pennington, *Members of the Long Parliament* (London, 1954), pp. 28, 216, 242; and D. Underdown, *Pride's Purge* (Oxford, 1971), p. 386.

[69] E. S[pencer], *A Breife Epistle to the Learned Manasseh Ben Israel* (London, 1650), sigs. A2, B10, and *passim*. See also Spencer's 'To the Translator' in Menasseh, *Hope*, pp. 56–7 (5 Oct. 1650) and postscript (25 Oct. 1650), pp. 61–2 (21 Feb. 1650–1).

[70] A. Evans, *An Eccho To the Voice* (London, 1652), p. 106.

given greatest prominence. Thomas Fuller included his own thoughts on the views of Menasseh and Thorowgood ('my worthy friend') in his magnificent, if ludicrously inaccurate, geography of the Holy Land. 'Strange!' he exclaimed,

that the posterity of the two Tribes (*Judah* and *Benjamin*) should be found (almost) *every where*, whilest the offspring of the *ten Tribes* are found *no where*! . . . Not, that he hath utterly extinguished the *being* (an opinion as unreasonable, as uncharitable) but hath hitherto concealed the *known being* of so numerous a nation, whom we may call the *lost-lost sheep of Israel*; both in respect of their spirituall condition, and corporall habitation.

Yet Fuller was not altogether convinced by Montezinos's story, although he admitted that Menasseh's book had made a great impression in England. Fuller wrote that he viewed this new intelligence 'as the *Twilight,* but whether it will prove the *morning twilight,* which will improve it self into full light; or that of the evening, darkening by degrees into silence, and utter obscurity, time will discover.'[71]

III

For the men of the New England Company, the answer to Fuller's question appeared obvious: it was surely a matter of the 'Light appearing more and more towards the perfect Day.'[72] Menasseh's new evidence concerning the origins of the American Indians soon reverberated back to the new world as well. The New England Company was the creation of 'An Act for the promoting and propagating the Gospel of Jesus Christ in New England' which was ordered on 27 July 1649. This Society for Propagation of the Gospel in New England, or the New England Company as it was commonly called, was the oldest English Protestant missionary society, and until 1700 it was the only one in operation. The Company's function was to collect and invest funds, and to spend the interest annually to commissioners in New England, who then paid allowances to the missionaries in the field. The members of the Society were predominantly prosperous London merchants, chosen not for their connections in New England, but rather for their wealth

---

[71] T. Fuller, *A Pisgah-Sight of Palestine* (London, 1650), pp. 191–202, esp. p. 193.
[72] H. Whitfield, *The Light appearing more* (London, 1651): repr. *Coll. Mass. Hist. Soc.*, 3rd ser., iv (1834), 101–47.

and willingness to devote themselves to the cause of the conversion of the Indians. Their job was simply to amass funds, and they did this rather successfully: between 1649 and the Restoration they accumulated nearly £16,000, with much of the support coming from the army, London, and Yorkshire. The Company had bought some property in 1652 from among the sequestered Royalist estates, and this purchase brought in funds, over the objections of the commissioners in America who continually tried to persuade the Society in London to invest in New England itself.[73]

The New England missionaries were thus required to devote much of their time to publicity, and this they accomplished with the publication of a number of tracts about their work in the new world. These pamphlets, disseminated by the Society in London, were among the most influential sources of information about the strange inhabitants of America. And naturally enough, the perceptions these missionaries had of the Indians were affected by the debate over the lost ten tribes which was going on across Atlantic.

Chief among these men was the famous John Eliot, a graduate of Jesus College, Cambridge, born in Hertfordshire one year after the death of Elizabeth. Eliot arrived in Boston in November 1631, and was ordained a Congregationalist minister the following year. Eliot had been interested in Jewish matters even before Montezinos delivered his astonishing testimony: Eliot helped Thomas Weld and Richard Mather in working up a version of Psalms which would eventually become known as the Bay Psalm Book. Although he was firmly convinced that Hebrew would make a very suitable universal language, he argued that the Indians would be converted only if they could be taught the gospel in their own vernacular. The final result of this determination was the Indian Library, a full translation of the Bible into Algonquin, which was not only the first Bible in an Indian language, but also the first edition of Scripture printed in any language on the North American continent.[74]

[73] W. Kellaway, *The New England Company 1649–1776* (London, 1961), pp. 1–4, 11–15, 17, 36, 72.

[74] *Ibid.*, pp. 81–3, *cap.* vi; C. Mather, *Magnalia Christi* (London, 1702), bk. iii, pp. 170–238.

The very first tracts from the New England missionaries expressed some doubt whether the Jews ought not to be converted first before any attempts were made to bring the Indians into the faith. Thomas Lechford wrote from America that 'some say out of *Rev.* 15. last, it is not probable that any nation more can be converted, til the calling of the Jews'.[75] Speaking of the Indians, John Cotton noted that it 'is true, there may be doubt that for a time there will bee no great hope of any Nationall conversion, till Antichrist be ruined, and the Jewes converted'.[76]

These doubts were scattered and forgotten once Menasseh's report reached the missionaries in North America. Edward Winslow, one of the most prominent of these, was most anxious to communicate this new discovery to the English authorities. Writing to Parliament and the Council of State, he requested:

let me acquaint your Honors, that a godly Minister of this City writing to Rabbi-ben-Israel, a great Dr. of the Jews, now living at Amsterdam, to know whether after all their labor, travells, and most diligent enquiry, they did yet know what was become of the ten Tribes of Israel? His answer was to this effect, if not in these words, That they were certainly transported into America, and that they had infallible tokens of their being there.[77]

It was no secret that this 'godly Minister' was the famous John Dury, international crusader for Christian unity and unofficial agent for Cromwell's government in a number of European countries. When Winslow's first report of Menasseh's discovery was completed, this text and a number of John Eliot's letters were collected and edited with a view towards publication. Dury was shown the writings and agreed to contribute an appendix. Dury summed up his general millenarian view as follows:

The palpable and present acts of providence, doe more than hint the approach of Jesus Christ: And the Generall consent of many judicious, and

---

[75] T. Lechford, *Plain Dealing* (London, 1642): repr. *Coll. Mass. Hist. Soc.*, 3rd ser., iii (1833), p. 80.

[76] J. Cotton, *The Way of Congregational Churches* (London, 1648), p. 78. Generally, see R. H. Pearce, 'The "Ruines of Mankind": The Indian and the Puritan Mind', *Jnl. Hist. Ideas*, xiii (1952), 200–17; G. B. Nash, 'The Image of the Indian in the Southern Colonial Mind', *Wm. and M. Qly.*, 3rd ser., xxix (1972), 197–230; N. Salisbury, 'Red Puritans', *Wm. and M. Qly.*, 3rd ser., xxxi (1974), 27–54; J. F. Maclear, 'New England and the Fifth Monarchy', *Wm. and M. Qly.*, 3rd ser., xxxii (1975), 223–60.

[77] Winslow, *Progress*, p. 73.

godly Divines, doth induce *considering minds* to beleeve, that the conversion of the Jewes is at hand. Its the expectation of some of the wisest Jewes now living, that about the year 1650, *Either we Christians shall be Mosaick, or else that themselves Jewes shall be Christians.*

Upon examining the evidence of the New England missionaries, Dury became convinced that there was a strong possibility that the American Indians were descendants of the Jews, 'peradventure some of the 10. Tribes dispersions.' Some of the missionaries' experiences pointed to divine intervention, especially since 'the Jewes of the Netherlands (being intreated thereunto) informe that after much inquiry they found some of the ten Tribes to be in America.' Dury documented these assertions by citing some missionary reports of Indian religion and customs which seemed to agree with biblical accounts of the Jews. Among these proofs was the fact that the 'better and more sober' class of Indians 'delight much to expresse themselves in parables', a known characteristic of Jews. In conclusion, he wrote, these 'and the like considerations prevaile with me to entertain (at least) a *Conjecture*, that these *Indians in America*, may be *Jewes* (especially of the ten Tribes.)'[78]

Whereas the Spanish missionaries were rather more circumspect about ascribing a direct Hebraic ancestry to the Indians despite certain similarities in religion and custom, the English workers were satisfied to make much more radical pronouncements. The testimony of Montezinos, even the very first garbled reports of it, was sufficient to confirm in their minds the lurking suspicion that the lost ten tribes had indeed wandered to the new world. Their ethnographic reports, enshrined in the successful propaganda pamphlets of the New England Company, in turn transmitted these theories to England, where they fed into the existing bulk of literature about the fate of the lost ten tribes.

A letter of John Eliot dated 8 May 1649 shows that although by that date he had still not received text of Montezinos's account, he was already sympathetic to the idea of an Hebraic origin for 'these poor Indians.' Eliot explained that he himself wanted to study the origins of the Indians in order to discover if they were among the benefactors of God's covenant and prom-

---

[78] *Ibid.*, pp. 93–5. For more on the alleged Jewish prognostication for 1650, see above, pp. 105–6.

ise, and were therefore deserving of mercy. If '*Rabbi-Ben-Israel* can make it appear that some of the Israelites were brought into *America*, and scattered here', Eliot thought, it would be 'a great ground of faith for the conversion of the Easterne Nations, and may be of help to our faith for these Indians'. As was often the case, intelligence of the kind Menasseh offered might ultimately be of purely practical advantage to England: at the Resurrection God 'can and will finde out these lost and scattered Israelites, and in finding up them, bring in with them the Nations among whom they were scattered, and so shall *Jacobs* Promise extend to a multitude of Nations indeed'.[79] What the Indians themselves thought of this paternity of dubious respectability is unclear, although John Eliot noted that they became interested in these tribes called Jews, and asked him questions such as 'Why did the *Jewes* give the Watchmen money to tell a lye?' and '*Who killed Christ?*' Unfortunately, Eliot's explanations were not recorded.[80]

Yet even the substantial evidence from New England was insufficient to guarantee unquestioned acceptance in all quarters of Menasseh's radical revision of ethnographic assumptions. One of the most bitter attacks came from Hamon L'Estrange, the Royalist theologian and historian. L'Estrange had received a copy of Thorowgood's pamphlet as a gift from the author, whom he praised despite the intellectual disagreements between them. L'Estrange refuted each of Thorowgood's points in turn. Some appeared completely frivolous, such as Thorowgood's argument that the 'Indians are much given to weeping, especially their women, at burialls, this was in fashion among the Jewes, *Ier.* 19. 17.' Menasseh's recital of 'that waterish fiction' of the sabbatical river was particularly ridiculous: 'he drowns himself in diving for it,' L'Estrange complained. In summary, L'Estrange wrote, 'I confesse I finde him a man of so sharpe an appetite, and strong and easie and Ostrich concoction; as I cannot sit at table any longer with him; and therefore I now rise and offer others every one to feed

[79] Whitfield, *Light*, pp. 119–20.
[80] Winslow, *Progress*, pp. 85, 91. See also J. P. Ronda. '"We Are Well As We Are": An Indian Critique of Seventeenth-Century Christian Missions', *Wm. and M. Qly.*, 3rd ser., xxxiv (1977), 66–82; and J. Bowman, 'Is America the New Jerusalem or Gog and Magog?', *Proc. Leeds Phil. and Lit. Soc.*, vi (1950), 445–52.

according to his own phancie.' Although L'Estrange's quarrel with Menasseh was mainly concerned with his far-fetched comparisons between the American Indians and the Israelites rather than with the efficacy of the comparative method itself, this rebuttal is one of the few that contains at least the elements of such an attack. 'As for *Manassehs* argument a *Simili* (as he calls it)', L'Estrange wrote, the 'Comparison of Americans with Iewish Customes, . . . I may rather call dictates of Nature'. In the final analysis, L'Estrange chose to side with 'that learned and Iudicious *Brerewood*, that the Americans are the race of the Tartars'.[81]

Menasseh's publication simply gave the debate over the lost ten tribes a basic text over which the argument could be centred; the issues continued to be expressed in much the same terms as before. Milton produced nineteen scriptural references referring to 'the calling of the entire nation not only of the Jews but also of the Israelites.'[82] Ralph Josselin sought to strengthen Eliot's view with the aid of gematria:

John Eliot advanceth the worke. Eli is my god. John gracious. the instrument doth speake the gratiousnes of god unto them, in his name is the number of 52. perhaps by that time wee shall see a progresse to purpose.[83]

John Shawe, preacher of the gospel at Kingston, rejoiced in the new discoveries about the Indians, 'especially if they be posterity of the *Iews*, as many affirm that they are!' This very likely was so, Shawe thought, and in that case 'Mr *Brightman* and others may well be owned for Prophets, who above fourty years ago foretold the Calling of the *Jews* to begin about the year 1650.'[84]

Thorowgood finally replied to both critics and admirers the month after the Restoration, in a text edited by Edward Reynolds, Edmund Calamy, Simeon Ashe, and John Dury. John Eliot contributed a short essay to this effort as well, and

[81] H. L'Estrange, *Americans no Iews* (London, 1652), sig. A2ʳ; pp. 11, 75–7 and *passim*.

[82] *Complete Prose Works of John Milton*, ed. D. M. Wolfe, *et al.* (New Haven, 1953–   ), vi. 617 (*Chr. Doc.*, bk. i, *cap.* xxxii).

[83] *Diary*, ed. Macfarlane, p. 238: 13 Mar. 1650–1. '*Eli* means 'my God' and *Yoḥanan* (John), 'God is gracious' in Hebrew. It is unclear how Josselin arrived at the figure of 52; the application of Hebrew gematria to 'Eliot' yields 56, which would have been a more satisfactory answer for him in any case.

[84] J. Shawe, *The Princes Royal* (London, 1650), pp. 6–9, 43: a sermon preached at York, 24 Mar. 1650–1.

used scriptural argument to prove that 'fruitful *India* are *Hebrewes*, that famous civil (though Idolatrous) nation of *China* are *Hebrewes*, so *Japonia*, and these naked *Americans* are *Hebrewes*, in respect of those that planted first these parts of the world'.[85] Eliot thus took the argument as far as it would go, directly to the point of absurdity. When he wrote those words, the New England Company of new world missionaries had actually ceased to exist, for the act which had created it was swept away at the Restoration with the rest of the Cromwellian legislation. But by the beginning of 1662, a new charter was signed, and Menasseh's friend Robert Boyle was named as the first governor.[86] Both the New England Company and the Jewish community in England were by then secure and on solid ground. The association, albeit mainly intellectual, between the Jews and the New England missionaries, had been mutually advantageous during the previous dozen years.

IV

The author of a history of the Caribbean published shortly after the Restoration insisted that 'we conceive it not to be our business to bring upon the Stage that great and difficult Question, to wit, How the race of Men came to spread it self into *America*, and whence they came into that new World'. Those who have attempted to find a solution to this pressing historical problem 'have had so little light to guide themselves by in that obscure piece of Antiquity, that they may be said to have grop'd all their way'.[87] From the point of view of the new-world missionaries, the similarities of custom and religion between the American Indians and the Jews certainly suggested a common descent. The New England Company itself, concerned with raising money rather than with historical inquiry, saw the controversy over the lost ten tribes as a very valuable publicity tool. Thorowgood's first pamphlet on the Jews was not published by them, but it did something to advertise their work, as Thorowgood was a consistently favourable observer. He even collected money for John Eliot in Norfolk. When Thorowgood submitted his second edition to them in 1658, they changed

---

[85] T. Thorowgood, *Jews in America* (London, 1660), p. 17.
[86] Kellaway, *Company*, pp. 41–5.
[87] [C. Rochefort], *The History Of The Caribby-Islands* (London, 1666), pp. 204–6.

their minds several times as to the suitability for publication, and ultimately declined to print the work. Financially this was a wise decision, as Thorowgood brought it out himself, and this certainty of publication may have been behind their rejection rather than any disapproval of its contents.[88]

After 1665, the issue of the lost ten tribes became meshed with the speculations revolving around the activities of Sabbatai Ṣevi (1626–76), the Jewish false Messiah.[89] Meanwhile, the time-worn terms of the debate came under increasing ridicule. Samuel Butler, criticizing the followers of Descartes, complained that

> Horses they affirm to be
> Mere Engines, made by Geometry,
> And were invented first from Engins,
> As *Indian Britans* were from *Penguins*.

A special footnote explained the importance of penguins to the discussion.[90] By the end of the century, an anonymous writer recalled that the 'great Zeal to maintain a *Jewish Tradition*, put many Learned *Christians* upon the rack to make it out. Every corner is search'd to find out a Word, a Rite, or a Custom, in order to derive from thence many Millions of different People.'[91] Menasseh ben Israel's seventeenth-century biographer wrote that the idea of lost tribes living behind the Caspian mountains was an 'odd Fancy they still entertain'.[92]

Despite what the Anglo-Israel enthusiasts wished to believe in the nineteenth century, educated observers were thus quite sceptical by 1700 about the alleged identity between the American Indians and the Jews. On the eve of the Whitehall Conference in 1655, however, the debate over the lost ten tribes was at the peak of its intensity and proved useful to Menasseh's influential supporters. Paramount among these was surely John Dury, whose letter to Menasseh requesting further information about Montezinos started the readmission campaign which would ultimately bring about the convening of the Whitehall Conference on readmission. This service was

[88] Kellaway, *Company*, pp. 41–5.
[89] Scholem, *Sabbatai Ṣevi*, pp. 547–9.
[90] S. Butler, *Hudibras*, ed. J. Wilders (Oxford, 1967), p. 31.
[91] L. P., *Two Essays* London, 1695), pp. 16–17.
[92] Menasseh Ben-Israel, *Of The Term Of Life*, ed. T. Pococke (London, 1699), p. xiii.

accomplished by linking Menasseh's work with that of the New England Company.

When Cotton Mather and the new generation of New England missionaries arrived on the scene, they always paid the greatest respect to Eliot and the other pioneers in the field. But Mather was quite embarrassed by Eliot's supposed discovery of the lost ten tribes. He 'saw some learned Men', Mather explained,

looking for the lost *Israelites* among the *Indians* in *America*, and counting that they had *thorow-good* Reasons for doing so: And a few small *Arguments*, or indeed but *Conjectures*, meeting with a favourable Disposition in the Hearer, will carry some Conviction with them; especially, if a Report of a *Menasseh ben Israel* be to back them.[93]

Nicholas Noyes, another New England preacher, prefaced Mather's collective biography of the early missionaries by lamenting of the Indians that they were '*Conjectur'd* once to be of *Israel's* Seed, But no *Record* appear'd to prove the Deed'.[94] Yet despite the sterile outcome of the controversy, it was the debate over the lost ten tribes that awakened Menasseh's interest in England, and intensified the personal relations which he had maintained with Englishmen for some time, and started the process that would end with effective readmission when vague millenarian speculation was translated into concrete political action.

[93] Mather, *Magnalia Christi*, bk, iii, p. 193.
[94] N. Noyes, 'A Prefatory Poem' in *ibid.*, sig. B^r.

5

RELIGIOUS TOLERATION
AND JEWISH READMISSION

Arise Evans, the Welsh tailor–preacher, was hardly in the
mainstream of religious orthodoxy. Yet even he drew a line
before some varieties of radicalism. 'Beware of Amsterdam', he
warned, 'that damned Rebelious City of Holland, that provoks
God in his face, in which Atheists and Devils have their
abode'.[1] Andrew Marvell expressed his views more poetically:

> Sure when religion did it self embark,
> And from the east would westward steer its ark,
> It struck, and splitting on this unknown ground,
> Each one thence pillaged the first piece he found:
> Hence Amsterdam, Turk-Christian-Pagan-Jew,
> Staple of sects and mint of schism grew;
> That bank of conscience, where not one so strange
> Opinion but finds credit, and exchange.[2]

It was Amsterdam that immediately came to mind when
Englishmen considered open toleration of all religions, Protestant sects as well as Jewish congregations. Interest in the Jews
and their contemporary condition was growing during the first
half of the seventeenth century in England, and by 1653 James
Howell could write to a friend in Amsterdam that 'touching
Judaism, some corners of our City smell as rank of it as yours
doth there.'[3]

Although Jews were not fully emancipated in the Nether-

---

[1] A. Evans, *Light For the Iews* (London, 1656), p. 53.
[2] Lines 67–74 of 'The Character of Holland'.
[3] *Epistolae Ho-Elianae*, ed. J. Jacobs (London, 1890), p. 617.

lands until 1796, it was certainly possible to speak of the 'Dutch Jerusalem' from the end of the sixteenth century. As we have already seen, the chief impulses towards readmission came from Holland: not only was Amsterdam the residence of Menasseh ben Israel, the prime mover of the readmission campaign, but also many English religious sectarians served their radical apprenticeship in Holland and came into contact with Jews for the first time there. When the followers of John Traske wished to embrace Judaism openly, they fled to Holland where they were received with respect. From the English point of view, Amsterdam was the most prominent city that allowed open and public Jewish life and worship and could be examined as a test case of the results of Jewish toleration. The growing contacts between Amsterdam and London, both among Jews and gentiles, provide the backdrop to the entire readmission campaign, especially at the pitch of its excitement in 1655.

The rise in security for Dutch Jewry can be traced from the Union of Utrecht in 1579 which provided the legal basis for Jewish settlement, with its clause that no one was to be persecuted for religious beliefs, and a number of marranos began to trickle in from the south, especially after the fall of Antwerp in 1585. The first group of marranos arriving directly from Iberia to Amsterdam appeared after 1597, and by 1616 a rabbi in Holland reported that

Today, the people [the Jews] are living peacefully in Amsterdam. The population is interested in the growth of the city. They have made laws and rules among which are such as accord freedom of religion to all. Everyone is permitted to live according to his creed. However, he is not to make it publicly apparent that he belongs to a religion different from that of the rest of the city's inhabitants.[4]

These Sephardic Jews were permitted free religious expression and communal life, despite the fact that they were forbidden to engage in retail trade with Christians, and could not hold city or state office, even if they purchased *poortersrecht*, the right of citizenship. Jews could live in any part of the city, and were not required to wear any distinguishing clothing. On

---

[4] H. I. Bloom, *The Economic Activities of the Jews of Amsterdam in the Seventeenth and Eighteenth Centuries* (Port Washington, NY, 1969 [1937]), p. 7.

12 July 1657, the States of Holland, Zeeland, and Westfriesland recognized Jews as subjects of their respective governments, and the States-General followed suit on the next day. Yet this regulation only confirmed what had been accepted in practice for a number of years. In 1642, in an address honouring the visit of Frederick Henry and Queen Henrietta Maria of England to the Sephardic synagogue in Amsterdam, Menasseh ben Israel announced that 'Now, we Portugese [Jews], live safely and make use of liberty like the others. This is a great proof of your virtue and an even greater one of your wisdom.'[5]

As we have already seen, Menasseh's web of contacts extended internationally from Amsterdam. The mushrooming of Hebraic studies, the heated debate concerning the lost ten tribes of Israel, and the personal intervention of John Dury turned his attention towards England. The unsettled condition of English politics after 1640 appeared to provide a unique opportunity for the concentration and mutation of these speculative issues in the service of a campaign to readmit the Jews into England. Menasseh explained his views to an unknown correspondent in London in 1647:

Senhor No puedo enar. That is, Sir, I cannot express the joy that I have when I read your Letters, ful of desires to see your Country prosperous, which is heavily afflicted with Civil wars, without doubt, by the just Judgement of God. And it should not be in vaine to attibute it to the punishment of your Predecessors faults, committed against ours; when ours being deprived of their liberty under deceitfulness, so many men were slaine, only because they kept close unto the Tents of *Moses* their Legislator.[6]

Menasseh no doubt exaggerated even his own eccentric beliefs when he attributed the Civil War to the maltreatment and persecution of Jews in England over the centuries. As we have already seen, throughout the first half of the seventeenth century, almost to the arrival of Menasseh ben Israel in England in September 1655, the most difficult problem for advocates of Jewish readmission was to awaken the public mind to the very existence of contemporary Jewry, as opposed to ancient Israelites. Even when Jews suddenly sprang into the public arena, arguments for the readmission and toleration of them were unlikely to be received with sympathy, initially at

[5] *Ibid.*, pp. 20–2; Menasseh ben Israel, *Gratvlacao . . . Em nome de sua Nacao* (n.p., n.d.).

[6] Repr. [H. Jessey], *A Narrative of the late Proceeds at White-Hall* (London, 1656), p. 13.

least, because of the deep-rooted early modern hostility to religious pluralism, and because of the unique disabilities of the Jewish nation and religion before the bar of public patience.[7]

The first, and almost insurmountable, obstacle to the readmission and toleration of the Jews in England was the religious axiom that disunity must inevitably lead to a plague of disasters in state and society. As Alexander Ross explained, 'Diversity of *Religions* beget envy, malice, seditions, factions, rebellions, contempt of Superiours, treacheries, innovations, disobedience, and many more mischiefs, which pull down the heavy judgements of God upon that State or Kingdom, where contrary *Religions* are allowed'.[8] Religious pluralism was regarded as a Continental phenomenon, imposed on states by necessity rather than upon a principle chosen after careful analysis of alternatives. Roger Williams, famous champion of religious liberty, admitted that 'Some have said that *worldly policie* perswaded, as well as *State-necessity* compelled the States of *Holland* to a prudent permission of different *Consciences*.'[9] Unity in religious expression was conceived of as the natural state of affairs; disunity was the tool of Satan. Those foreign nations which did permit a plurality of religions suffered from particular curses in retribution: France laboured under an arbitrary government while Holland was in the grip of dangerous democracy. Furthermore, in England the head of the Church was identical with the head of state. Religious disloyalty, to some extent, must have involved political disloyalty.

Nevertheless, despite these quite persuasive arguments in favour of religious unity, some sects did win substantial followings, until by the Civil War England played host to an entire menagerie of faiths. The traditional latitudinarian argument, so especially influential after the Restoration, was that the various sects and denominations were bound together by

[7] On religious toleration generally, see W. K. Jordan, *The Development of Religious Toleration in England* (London, 1932–40), esp. vol. ii; S. Ettinger, 'The Beginnings of the Change in the Attitude of European Society Towards the Jews', *Scripta Hierosolymitana*, vii (1961), 193–219; D. M. Wolfe, 'Limits of Miltonic Toleration', *Jnl. Eng. Germ. Philol.*, lx (1961), 834–46; G. K. Hunter, 'The Theology of Marlowe's *The Jew of Malta*', *Jnl. Warb. Ctld. Inst.*, xxvii (1964), 211–40; C. Russell, 'Arguments for Religious Unity in England, 1530–1650', *Jnl. Eccl. Hist.*, xviii (1967), 201–26; H. Butterfield, 'Toleration in Early Modern Times', *Jnl. Hist. Ideas*, xxxviii (1977), 573–84.

[8] A. Ross, [*Pansebeia*]. *Or, A View of all Religions* (4th edn., London, 1664), p. 506.

[9] R. Williams, *The Bloody Tenent Yet More Bloody* (London, 1652), sig. A4[r].

sufficiently significant areas of agreement. Toleration could certainly be extended to a wide variety of groups which differed merely over incidentals, so long as they accepted the validity of the fundamentals. Even during the period of the Civil War, it proved very difficult to extend this sort of liberality to Quakers and Socinians, let alone to Jews.

The revised Agreement of the People in 1649, long enshrined as a corner-stone of religious toleration in England, supported the extension of liberty of conscience only to those 'who profess faith in God by Jesus Christ'. Even this bold statement of liberal intent was deceptive because some of those who based their faith on this axiom were denied freedom of worship in any case, especially the old-style Anglicans who only recently had championed an even more exclusive brand of religious conformity. Roman Catholics were objectionable not so much for their particular interpretation of the Eucharist or the arrangement of sacramental furniture in their churches, but because they were political traitors as well as religious opponents. But even with Catholics, or with the highly objectionable Unitarians, the English authorities were faced with the problem of Englishmen who had undertaken religious professions fundamentally incompatible with the church government in force. Sincere conversion would wash away all sins, religious and political varieties together.

Not so with the Jews. For the Jews were aliens, both from the mercy of God and the English government. Furthermore, it was not even entirely clear whether they were altogether human or whether John was speaking more literally than metaphorically when he reminded the Jews of '*your* father the devil'.[10] The readmission of the Jewish nation and the toleration of Jewish worship was thus a highly complex and perplexing moral problem for theologians and politicians alike. On no account could the Jews be regarded as having the root of the matter in them so as to qualify for latitudinarian generosity. Even their reliance on the Old Testament, so fundamental to Puritan thought, was interpreted as a stiff-necked and perverse cherishing of the ancient law which had been fulfilled and dismissed by the coming of Jesus Christ.

[10] John 8: 44; and on the diabolization of the Jews see especially J. Trachtenberg, *The Devil and the Jews* (Philadelphia, 1961).

Nevertheless, despite ingrained hostility to the notion of religious pluralism in general and, once Englishmen began to consider the plight of contemporary Jewry, to the idea of tolerating a religion which rejected the very first axiom of Christianity, a distinct rise in the number of publications advocating Jewish toleration can be traced. This was especially true after the beginning of the Civil War when religious radicalism burst forth from the constraints of the established Church.

Menasseh understood that the English government was certainly more tolerant than that of Spain or Portugal, although the Netherlands permitted an even greater degree of religious variation. Yet despite the growth of religious toleration which is often seen to blossom in England during the middle years of the seventeenth century, and proved with evidence from the Baptists, the Great Tew circle, the sectaries, and so on, it remained unclear whether or not this liberality was to be extended to the Jews. The argument of William Dell, chaplain to the New Model Army, was that '*unity* is Christian, *uniformity* Antichristian'.[11] The Jews certainly did not fit into the first category; they were often placed in the second.

I

In the early days of the reign of James I, long before the readmission of the Jews was even remotely a serious consideration, contemporary Jewry existed only to be reviled among the most despised religious renegades. As one author phrased it in 1606, the worst form of insult for those who resisted Calvinism was to insist that they 'haue no more religion then *Doggs*, and are worse then Turkes or Jewes: yea or brute beasts'. This became a popular litany in the early seventeenth century, and many religious polemicists made use of an imaginary procession of 'Doggs, Turkes, Jewes, brute beasts, or filthy villaines.'[12]

This brand of intense disdain for Jews is particularly apparent in what was probably the earliest concrete proposal for the readmission of the Jews, which came from the pen of Sir Thomas Sherley, the younger, in a letter to James I. Sherley was an impoverished gentleman, and a member of Parliament, one of the famous *Three English Brothers* whose fictionalized

---

[11] W. Dell, *Several Sermons* (London, 1652), p. 49.
[12] P. Fairlambe, *The Recantation of a Brownist* (London, 1606), sigs. f2^{r-v}.

exploits achieved some sort of notoriety through the subsidized efforts of the playwright Anthony Nixon. Sherley had been employed in the service of the Grand Duke of Tuscany, and spent two years in prison in Constantinople after failing to escape from a disappointing naval expedition. James himself interceded with the Turkish authorities on Sherley's behalf at the end of 1605, but imprisoned him in the Tower in any case two years later for certain flirtations with treason. He was released after two months confinement, and wrote to the earl of Salisbury on 28 December 1607 with a request 'to mediate his restitution to his Majesty's favour.'[13]

Sir Thomas Sherley sent his 'project for Jews' to King James immediately before the indiscretions that caused him to be committed to the Tower. His most recent disgrace was certainly a factor in relegating his plan to an obscure file somewhere in Salisbury's archives, but the proposal itself is somewhat disingenuous. Sherley claimed to have approached representatives of the Sephardic community in the Mediterranean, probably at Leghorn or Venice, with a promise to convince James of the desirability of allowing Jews to settle in Ireland. Sherley was only concerned with the 'profit that may be raised to your Majesty out of the Jews'. This was a means to make

that country very rich, and your Majesty's revenue in Ireland would in short time have risen almost to equal the customs of England. For, first, they were willing to pay your Majesty a yearly tribute of two ducats for every head; and they, being most of them merchants, would have raised great customs where now are none; and they would have brought into the realm great store of bullion of gold and silver by issuing of Irish commodities into Spain, which will be of high esteem there considering their natures, viz. salted salmons, corn, hides, wool and tallow; of all which there will be great abundance if once the people give themselves to the industry, which doubtless they will do as soon as they find that their labours will procure them money.

Sherley offered several plans for James to consider: one included permission for the Jews to build a synagogue, while another prohibited public worship. Sherley was convinced that 'if the Eastern Jews once find that liking of your countries . . . then many of them of Portugal (which call themselves *Morani*

[13] Hist. MSS Comm., ix, *Salisbury MSS*, xix. pp. xxi–ii, 394; A. Nixon, *The three English brothers* (London, 1607); D. W. Davies, *Elizabethans Errant* (Ithaca, NY, 1967), pp. 181–2.

and yet are Jews) will come fleeing hither, and they will bring more wealth than all the rest'. By this means, he argued, 'the most part of the trade of Brazil will be converted hither'.

Sherley's project was completely unscrupulous. Once a number of Jews could be persuaded to come to England, he promised that daily 'occasions will be offered to make greater commodities out of them once you have hold of their persons and goods.' Sherley also offered a warning: 'But at the first they must be tenderly used, for there is great difference in alluring wild birds and handling them when they are caught; and your agent that treats with them must be a man of credit and acquaintance amongst them, who must know how to manage them, because they are a very subtile people.'[14] Perhaps Sherley had himself in mind for the job, although he was hardly a man of credit in any sense of the word. At least he did have some passing acquaintance with Jews, for during this same summer he was negotiating to return three hundred ducats to a group of Jewish creditors in Italy. 'It is no use writing,' advised a colleague in Venice, 'since they will hear of no other terms.'[15]

John Weemse, the Scottish minister, probably never met a Jew in his life, and his agreement with the account of a visitor to Palestine who testified that 'he was much troubled with a loathsome smell and stinke of the Iewes' must be attributed to ignorance rather than to malice. Weemse, like Sherley, devised a plan for the readmission of the Jews to England with a subtle purpose more complex than a pious prayer for universal toleration. Weemse drew a distinction between 'the *Jewes*, now who are *Iewes* by birth, religion, and affection' and those 'who are Iewes both by birth & religion, but not in affection'. The first group included those 'who hate Christ and Christian religion, who raile against him, and blaspheme him, these should not be tollerated . . . These should be put to death'. The second category of Jews were to be tolerated if 'they dwell peaceably amongst us, and abstaine from offences, and some short principles of Christian religion should be taught unto them, as the gentiles who

[14] Hist. MSS Comm., ix, *Salisbury MSS*, xix. 473–4. See also E. R. Samuel, '"Sir Thomas Shirley's Project for Jewes"—the Earliest Known Proposal for the Resettlement', *Trs. Jew. Hist. Soc. Eng.*, xxiv (1974), 195–7. Cf. James Harrington's plan, below, p. 240.

[15] Hist. MSS Comm., ix, *Salisbury MSS*, xix. 225.

were *advenae portae* learned the seven precepts of *Noah*.' Weemse would allow readmitted Jews to circumcise their children and to worship freely and publicly, 'for when there is a permissiō to them granted to worship there must be a place granted also to worship in'. Yet the ultimate aim of readmission was conversion: once the Jews were exposed to the clear, Christian light of the Protestant reformation they were certain to embrace Jesus.[16]

John Weemse represents another strand in the debate over the toleration of the Jews: his goal is conversion, his supporting evidence is biblical, and his theoretical underpinning is logical and anti-millenarian. 'Some of our Writers more subtilely than solidly,' he complained, 'commenting upon the conversion of the Iewes follow them too neare in this conceit of their conversion, and they apply those places of the Prophets more literally than mystically'. The Jews depicted by Weemse ought to be permitted public worship and state toleration 'for the word of God is still the word of God, although they abuse it to a wrong end'. They refuse to acknowledge the true God out of ignorance, but should be allowed to discover the correct path at their own pace within Christian commonwealths. 'It is not the part of religion to compell a man to religion,' he states, 'which should be willingly professed, and not by compulsion.'[17]

The arguments which Sherley and Weemse put forward for the readmission of the Jews and the toleration of their religion provide a useful nucleus for a discussion of the arguments for Jewish readmission. While the classification of these philosemitic religious points is of limited value in determining the background to readmission, they do fall into three fairly distinct patterns which may be useful in isolating the significant issues throughout the controversies of the middle years of the seventeenth century.

Sir Thomas Sherley's 'project for Jews' is a choice example of the opportunistic argument for Jewish readmission. Sherley pressed for readmission on purely economic grounds; he supported his views with reference to his own experience and that

---

[16] I. Weemse, *A Treatise Of The Fovre Degenerate Sonnes* (London, 1636), pp. 330, 337–8. See also J. Bowman, 'A Seventeenth Century Bill of "Rights" for Jews', *Jew. Qly. Rev.*, n. s., xxxix (1949), 379–95.

[17] Weemse, *Sonnes*, pp. 339–40, 375.

of the king of Spain, the duke of Mantua, the duke of Savoy, and
the duke of Florence, who would 'not leave his Jews for all other
merchants whatsoever.'[18] Others would advocate Jewish
readmission for more supernatural reasons. Menasseh ben
Israel, as we have already seen, argued that the English were
afflicted with civil war because of their maltreatment of the
Jews. The Old Testament notion that God went out with the
armies of Israel only when they were faithful to their covenant
was especially powerful. Earthly punishments were sure to
follow on the heels of heavenly transgressions, and other men
after Menasseh would argue that the scourge of civil disturbance was divine retribution for the persecution of the Jews and
the exclusion of God's chosen people from England.

John Weemse, on the other hand, pressed for Jewish immigration rather than for genuine religious toleration. His text was
Romans 10:14: 'how shall they believe in him of whom they
have not heard? and how shall they hear without a preacher?'
For men like Weemse, it was unconscionable to pray for the
conversion of the Jews while denying them the means for their
salvation. These sentiments were made even more familiar by
their presence in the Collect for Good Friday:

Merciful God, who hast made all men, and hatest nothing that thou hast
made, nor wouldest the death of a sinner, but rather that he should be
converted and live; Have mercy upon all Jews, Turks, Infidels, and
Hereticks, and take from them all ignorance, hardness of heart, and contempt
of thy Word; and so fetch them home, blessed Lord, to thy flock, that they
may be saved among the remnant of the true Israelites, and be made one fold
under one shepherd, Jesus Christ our Lord[19]

The Jews were to be readmitted into England as a prelude to
their conversion.

A third alternative was to combine one or both of these views
with a millenarian interpretation of the biblical evidence.
Brightman looked for 'the *calling of the Jewes* to be a Christian
Nation', which would be accompanied by a complete change in
attitude on the part of the Christians. 'The Jewes were alwayes
wont to finde the Gentiles most hatefull and spightfull against
them in former ages', he confessed, 'as who laboured by all

---

[18] Hist. MSS Comm., ix, *Salisbury MSS*, xix. 474.
[19] *Liturgiae Britannicae, or The Several Editions of The Book of Common Prayer*, ed. W.
Keeling (2nd edn., London, 1851), pp. 102–3.

meanes possible to annoy and to mischiefe them; but now the case shall be quite altered, the Jewes shall have no cause to feare any harme or wrong at the hands of the Gentiles'.[20]

Each of these three motives for urging religious toleration of Jews was based on comparatively slight first-hand experience with potential Jewish immigrants or practising Jews living secretly in England. Walter Gostelow, the millenarian Royalist, was thus quite exceptional in being able to announce to Menasseh ben Israel that

About the 18th. year of my age I was in several of your Synagogues, my eldest Brother a Studient and fellow of *Corpus Christi* Colledge in *Oxford*, there with me, to observe, & accomplish himself for the good of others. He, Sir, having conversed with divers of your *Rabbies*, did after tell me what they so believed, as not to be moved from.[21]

The account which Henry Blount gave of the modern Jewish character was derived from the more extended opportunities presented during his 'Voyage into the *Levant*'. Blount reported that Jews 'are generally found the most nimble, and *Mercuriall* wits in the world'. He attributed this, in part, to 'their *Mosaicall* institution of Dyet; a thing of no small effect to refine the bloud, and spirits in so many descents'. On the other hand, Blount also noted that

the *Iewish* complexion is so prodigiously *timide*, as cannot be capable of Armes; for this reason they are no where made Souldiers, nor slaves . . . The other impediment is their extreme corrupt love to private interesse; which is notorious in the continuall cheating, and malice among themselves; so as there would want that justice, and respect to common benefit, without which no civill society can stand.

Nevertheless, Blount's assessment of the Jewish character was not without some degree of even-handedness. 'I yeeld not to those,' he maintained, 'who hold them a peculiar cursed stocke: sloath and nastinesse single them out from other men; so as they are the dregs of the people, rather then of severall descent.' The distinctive Jewish appearance was caused by 'wallowing in the dirt, and Sunne makes them more swarthy then others'. Blount's hostile and damaging impression of modern Jews was much publicized through his famous narrative.[22]

Such accounts could not but impede the efforts for readmission and religious toleration, yet they provided a major source for contemporary opinions regarding the nature of the Jew. Some men, such as Sherley or Gostelow, based their arguments on at least a modicum of first-hand knowledge of Jews and Jewry. Others, such as Weemse or Brightman, relied on the reports of foreign scholars and English travellers abroad. As we shall see, quite a number of learned and influential commentators expressed their views in print, undeterred by the paucity of evidence in maintaining an opinion regarding 'that nation which had given the first noble example of crucifying their King'.[23]

II

By 1640, the increasing instability of English political life was beginning to have effect in the wide variety of radical literature which was available to the English reading public. References to contemporary Jewry, rather than ancient Israelites, multiply during the 1640s and early 1650s, especially after the end of effective censorship, until by Menasseh's arrival in England in 1655 the fate of world Jewry was a topic of intense and immediate concern. By the time of the Whitehall Conference, many men could sympathize with the plea of the preacher Nathaniel Homes to Parliament, the 'Worthies of Israel', to recognize 'how forlorne their condition hath beene, and so unfit to here of greater miserie'.[24]

The opening year of the Civil War also saw the appearance of Sir Thomas Browne's *Religio Medici*, his most famous work. Browne's picture of the Jew remains rather indistinct. His Jews are the 'contemptible and degenerate issue of *Jacob*', immobile in 'such an obstinate and peremptory beliefe . . . without the least hope of conversion'. Nevertheless, Browne is not entirely without sympathy:

---

[22] H. B[lount], *A Voyage Into The Levant* (2nd edn., London, 1636), pp. 114, 123.

[23] *Abraham Cowley: The Essays and Other Prose Writings*, ed. A. B. Gough (Oxford, 1915), p. 87.

[24] N. Homes, *The New World* (London, 1641), sig. A2ʳ, p. 7.

The Jew is obstinate in all fortunes; the persecution of fifteene hundred yeares hath but confirmed them in their errour: they have already endured whatsoever may be inflicted, and have suffered, in a bad cause, even to the condemnation of their enemies. Persecution is a bad and indirect way to plant Religion; It hath beene the unhappy method of angry devotions, not onely to confirme honest Religion, but wicked Heresies, and extravagant opinions.[25]

This is very tolerant talk, and in his own words, 'a conceit fitter for a Rabbin than a Christian'.[26] Yet four years later, Browne devoted an entire chapter of his *Pseudodoxia Epidemica* to an investigation of the popular belief, expressed by John Weemse among others, 'that the Jews stink.' Browne gave little credit to the idea: the Jewish people were an impure race, anyway, due in part to the strong desire that Jewish women felt for Christian men. If the allegation were true, it would be possible to sniff them out of prohibited countries, since 'there are at present many thousand Jews in Spain, France and England'. Furthermore, by this logic converted Jews would be notably offensive as well, while plainly they were not, 'as though Aromatized by their conversion, they lost their scent with their Religion, and smelt no longer then they savoured of the Jew.' Browne cited Blount and Sandys, noting that Christian travellers among the Jews reported that this 'offensive odor is no way discoverable in their Synagogues where many are, and by reason of their number could not be concealed: nor is the same discernable in commerce or conversation with such as are cleanly in Apparel, and decent in their Houses.' Browne finally concluded that it is

a dangerous point to annex a constant property unto any Nation, and much more this unto the Jew; since this quality is not verifiable by observation; since the grounds are feeble that should establish it, and lastly; since if all were true, yet are the reasons alleadged for it, of no sufficiency to maintain it.[27]

Nevertheless, this is precisely the view that Robert Burton expressed in his encyclopaedic examination of melancholy, the sixth edition of which was published in 1641, the year after his death. Burton cited Buxtorf in his assertion of 'goggle eyes' as a

---

[25] T. Browne, *Religio Medici and other works*, ed. L. C. Martin (Oxford, 1967), pp.25–6.
[26] *ibid.*, p. 30.
[27] T. Browne, *Works*, ed. G. Keynes (London, 1928–31), ii. 297–303. For more on the so-called *Foetor Judaicus*, see esp. Trachtenberg, *Devil*, pp. 47–50.

prominent Jewish characteristic. Burton's Jews, 'as a company of vagabonds, are scattered over all parts' where they 'stick together like so many burrs; but as for the rest, whom they call Gentiles, they do hate and abhor'. As for contemporary Jews, he wrote,

I presume no nation under heaven can be more sottish, ignorant, blind, superstitious, wilful, obstinate, and peevish, tiring themselves with vain ceremonies to no purpose; he that shall but read their rabbins' ridiculous comments, their strange interpretation of scriptures, their absurd ceremonies, fables, childish tales, which they steadfastly believe, will think they be scarce rational creatures

Burton was not ignorant of the toleration which the Jews enjoyed on the Continent, but he was not sympathetic to the readmission of the Jews to England, despite their admirable industriousness.[28]

Once press censorship ended with the onset of the Civil War, writers less distinguished than Browne and Burton published their views on the toleration of the Jews, although ultimately their approach to the subject was very similar: the Bible, second-hand accounts of Jewish habits and beliefs, and simple logic were all admitted as evidence. Until the arrival in England in 1654 of Manuel Martinez Dormido, the first professing Jew resident in this country since their expulsion in 1290, the debate over readmission was conducted as a purely theoretical exercise. Occasionally, some men did claim to have had personal contacts with Jews in England, while others reported with confidence about the presence of secret Jews in the country. As we have just seen, even a well-informed observer like Sir Thomas Browne included England with Spain and France as a prominent place of Jewish residence. The Venetian secretary in England reported to the Doge and Senate that English merchants exported goods with the aid of 'Jews from Amsterdam who provide the money and carry away the goods in instalments.'[29] Whether or not the crypto-Jews of seventeenth-century England were known by some contemporaries for what they were, it remains true nevertheless that for the great bulk of writers on the Jewish question, the Hebrews were a Continen-

[28] R. Burton, *The Anatomy of Melancholy*, ed. H. Jackson (Everyman edn., London, 1972), i. 211–12; ii. 70; iii. 322–3, 349, 361–2, 375.
[29] *Cal. S. P. Ven., 1642–3.* p. 252: 13 Mar. 1643.

tal phenomenon, far removed from the English experience. Robert Maton, a Fifth Monarchist, advised that gentiles should not 'contemne or revile the Jewes, a fault too common in the Christian world; and that partly because we are unmindfull as well of that Olive from whence we were taken, as of that into which we are graffed: whose root bears us, & not we the root.'[30] As we shall see, it often proved easier to be merciful to Jews if none were available to receive the gift.

Henry Robinson, the merchant friend of Hartlib and Dury, argued that the Jews had much to teach Christians, and should 'be suddenly recalled, and encouraged to continue by a Liberty of Conscience.' Robinson exclaimed that 'the very Law of *Moses* consisting in a dead letter, which the Divel himselfe could scarce controvert or pick a quarrell with, did not render the Jews so scrupulous and conscionable, as the Gospel doth Christians'. Jews should be permitted to enter into England, but 'how can we thinke they would be willing if they knew might not live amongst us, without being forced to a new Religion, before their reasons and understandings were convinced in the truth thereof?' Despite the principles of universal toleration which were so forcefully proclaimed in this pamphlet, however, Robinson can still state that 'I presume no Protestant will deny, but that we are bound to endeavour the conversion of Papists, Jewes, Turkes, Pagans, Hereticks, with all Infidels & misbe-leevers unto the only true and saving faith in Jesus Christ.'[31]

Similar convictions were expressed in *The Blovdy Tenent, of Persecution* which Roger Williams published anonymously in 1644. 'It is the will and command of *God*,' he announced, that 'a *permission* of the most *Paganish, Jewish, Turkish* or *Antichristian consciences* and *worships,* bee granted to *all* men in all *Nations* and *Countries*: and they are onely to bee *fought* against with . . . the *Word* of *God*.' Individuals from any of these groups could be good citizens, provided that they obeyed the laws of the civil state. Williams had an eye towards conversion as well, and noted that the 'Law of putting to death blasphemers of Christ cuts off al hopes from the Jews of partaking in his bloud.' Williams's pleas for religious toleration were not wholly disin-

---

[30] R. Maton, *Israels Redemption* (London, 1642), p. 69.
[31] [H. Robinson], *Liberty of Conscience* (n.p., 1643), pp. 6–9, 14, 17.

terested: he sailed for what was to become Rhode Island shortly after publication.[32]

During the following two years, the readmission and toleration of the Jews became a more popular subject. Richard Overton the Leveller prayed that 'Turckes, Jewes, Pagans, and Infidels, as wel as Christians' be permitted to live together 'in the *Field* of the *World'*.[33] A short pamphlet written over thirty years earlier by the Baptist Leonard Busher was republished in 1646. Busher cited many of the arguments which had already been introduced by Weemse, Browne, Williams, and others. He noted the experience of the false Christians and secret Jews of Portugal, and argued that Jews, Turks, and Pagans ought to be tolerated 'so long as they are peaceable, and no malefactors'. Busher had hopes for readmission as well, but understood that

if persecution bee not laid downe, and liberty of conscience set up, then cannot the Jews, nor any strangers, nor others contrary minded be ever converted in our Land; for so long as they know aforehand, that they shall be forced to beleeve against their consciences, they will never seek to inhabit there: by which means you keep them from the Apostolique faith, if the apostolique faith be only taught where persecution is.

Busher paid some attention to the economic motive as well, and prayed that the Jews would be able to 'inhabit & dwel under his Majesties Dominion, to the great profit of his Realmes'.[34]

Pleas for Jewish toleration noticeably increased in frequency after about 1646, and Thomas Edwards, the great heresy-hunter, was one of the first to alert the authorities of this disturbing development. 'The sectaries being now hot upon the getting of a Toleration,' he reported,

there were some meetings lately in the City, wherein some persons of the several sects, some Seekers, some Anabaptists, some Antinomians, some Brownists, some Independents met; some Presbyterians also met with them, . . . some professing at one of the meetings, it was the sinne of this Kingdom that the Jewes were not allowed the open profession and exercise of their religion amongst us; only the Presbyterians dissented and opposed it.[35]

One of Edwards's admirers was aghast that the 'monster of

[32] [R. Williams], *The Blovdy Tenant* (n.p., 1644), sig. A2ᵛ, pp. 86, 151, 171.

[33] [R. Overton], *The Araignement of Mr. Persecvtion* (London, 1645), p. 22: repr. *Tracts on Liberty*, ed. W. Haller (New York, 1934), p. 232.

[34] L. Busher, *Religions Peace* (London, 1646), pp. 8, 10, 11, 21–2, 33. See also W. T. Whitley, 'Leonard Busher, Dutchman', *Trs. Bap. Hist. Soc.*, i (1908–9), 107–13.

[35] T. Edwards, *Gangraena* (2nd edn., London, 1646), p. 14.

Toleration' should have emerged from the ruins of the Established Church, and that Christians should have preached an open profession of Judaism. 'Good God!' he cried, 'VVhat times are we faln into?'[36]

Some members of Parliament were also concerned about the support for contemporary Jewry in recent pamphlets, and they expressed their disapproval formally. On the eve of a public humiliation for religious errors of 10 March 1646–7, they issued a catalogue of 'the spreading *Errors, Heresies* and *Blasphemies* of these Times'. One of these was the affirmation that it is 'the will of God, That a permission of the most Paganish, Jewish, Turkish or Antichristian Consciences and worships be granted to all men, in all Nations and Countreys.' The marginal reference was to Williams's 'Bloody Tenent'.[37] Despite this official disapproval of Jewish readmission, Hugh Peter, the Independent army chaplain, hoped that 'Merchants may have all manner of encouragement, the law of Merchants set up, and strangers, even *Jewes* admitted to trade & live with us, that it may not be said we pray for their conversion, with whom we will not converse, we being all but strangers on the Earth.' Peter's idea was that the State would meddle in Church matters no further than 'as a nursing Father, and then all children shall be fed, though they have severall faces and shapes.'[38]

It now seems obvious that many of these fervent pleas for the toleration and readmission of the Jews took on an almost liturgical flavour. The stock catalogue of 'Jews, Turks, Infidels, and Hereticks' from the Book of Common Prayer came to be repeated in complete or abridged form in many of the theoretical discussions of the moral and religious justification for the toleration of Jewish worship. Henry Robinson added Roman Catholics to the list; Roger Williams, Richard Overton, and Leonard Busher modified it somewhat as well. But fundamentally it was recognized that toleration of the Jews was a radical step, of not an extremely dangerous one. Whether or not the proponents of Jewish readmission in these early, confused years of the Civil War actually desired the presence of living Jews on

---

[36] [Anon.], *Anti-Toleration* (London, 1646), sig. A2ʳ·ᵛ, pp. 5, 35, 48.

[37] [Anon.], *Hell broke loose* (London, 1646), title page, p. 3.

[38] H. Peters, *A word for the Armie* (London, 1647), pp. 11, 12.

English soil would become clear during the next decade. For some, the promotion of Jewish readmission and toleration was surely a tactic in a complex strategy aiming at the toleration of more objectionable Christian sects such as the Baptists.

Nevertheless, despite the justified scepticism which must be maintained when examining the debate over the readmission of the Jews in the early days when the actual implementation of this policy seemed very far away indeed, these years were notable for some outstanding indications of a genuine development of English sentiment in favour of the Jews and their culture. Paramount among these is surely the startling purchase by Parliament of a large quantity of Hebrew books at the height of the Civil War itself.

On 24 March 1647–8, the Commons ordered that £2,000 be reserved from the dean and chapter lands towards the library at Cambridge. At the same time, they allocated £500 from the receipts at Goldsmiths' Hall to be paid to George Thomason, the famous bookseller, for the purchase of a 'Collection of Books, in the Eastern Languages, of a very great Value, late brought out of *Italy*, and having been the Library of a learned *Rabbi* there'. Thomason was especially to receive 'the thanks of this House, for his good Affections therein to the Encouragement of Learning in this Kingdom.' The actual administration of the purchase was to be handled by John Selden and John Lightfoot, the Cambridge Hebraist. A further order in the House of Lords four days later specified that the compositions at Goldsmiths' Hall which would be particularly earmarked for the purchase of the books would be 'out of the Arrears of the Two Four Months Assessments that were assessed for the Payment of the *Scottish* Army before *Newarke*'.[39]

The purchase of Hebrew books in the midst of civil war could

---

[39] This sum seems not to have been paid, and at the end of September 1648, when Colonel Humphrey Matthews of Castle Menech, Glamorgan, compounded for delinquency, £500 of his fine was ordered to be set aside for Thomason. Matthews had difficulty in meeting this demand, and the next month the order was issued once again, and in November Thomason was granted interest of 8 per cent on the unpaid balance. Presumably Thomason was satisfied with this arrangement, for the demand seems to have been dropped. In any case, it would appear that Cambridge owes its collection of Hebrew books almost as much to Colonel Matthews as to John Selden: *Commons Jnl.*, v. 512a, 515b, 518a; *Lords Jnl.*, x. 157b, 158a, 161b, 162a; *Cal. S. P. Dom., Comm. for Compounding*, pp. 133, 807, 809, 1855–6; *Catalogue of the pamphlets . . . collected by George Thomason*, ed. G. K. Fortescue (London, 1908), i. vii–iii.

quite easily be regarded as a reckless mistake. The transaction was completed on the eve of the Second Civil War, but the shipment of the books was conducted at the same time that Cromwell's army was fighting the Scots. Certainly this is how the purchase was seen from the other side of the fence, where a Royalist newspaper reported that in the Cambridge library, 'if the Members can spare money, you may chance to find *Rabbi Isaac*, and *Rabbi Moyses*, led in *couples* with Rabbi *Marshall*, and Rabbi *Calamy*, and all the *Rabble* of *Smec*, the first *Founders* of our moderne *Pharisies*, and the *primitive Christians* of this last seven years *Edition*.' The writer claimed that the Hebrew books were procured on the request of John Selden, one so well acquainted with tongues 'as if hee had been one of the *Bricklayers* of old *Babel*'.[40]

Selden was well-known as a 'great Admirer of *Antiquity*' and a champion of Hebrew studies. His interest in Jewish matters was not confined merely to their relevance for his research concerning tithes or the judicial administration of the ancient Jews.[41] Selden's secretary recorded his employer's table talk on a wide variety of issues, including contemporary Jewry. 'Talke what you will of the Jewes,' he reminded his guests, 'that they are curs'd they thrive where ere they come, they are able to oblige the prince of the Country by lending him money. None of them beg, they keep together. And for their hatred, my life for yo[u]rs Christians hate one another as much'. Selden also thought that the Jews were eligible for salvation though they utterly denied Christ, just as the Jews admitted righteous gentiles to the world to come.[42] Selden even purchased used Hebrew books from Menasseh ben Israel. An examination of the list of books Selden bought and the amount he paid for them shows that he was charged very high prices by the standards of the day. A similar study of the books purchased for Cambridge might reveal the same result.[43]

Parliament's purchase of a shipment of Hebrew books for

[40] *Mercurius Pragmaticus*, 1 (28 Mar.–4 Apr. 1648), sig. A2ʳ⁻ᵛ.

[41] See I. Herzog, 'John Selden and Jewish Law', *Pub. Soc. Jew. Juris.*, iii (1931).

[42] *Table Talk of John Selden*, ed. F. Pollock (London, 1927), pp. 54, 123.

[43] Bodl., MS Seld. supra 109, f. 378ʳ: Hebrew book list. See C. Roth, 'A list of books from Manasseh Ben-Israel's stock' (Hebrew), *Aresheth*, ii (1960), 413–4; and generally, I. Abrahams and C. E. Sayle, 'The Purchase of Hebrew Books by the English Parliament in 1647 [*sic*]', *Trs. Jew. Hist. Soc. Eng.*, viii (1918), 63–77.

Cambridge was soon followed by other highly significant official declarations. The Council of War passed a resolution on 25 December 1648, a fortnight after Pride's Purge, recommending the toleration 'of all *Religions* whatsoever, not excepting *Turkes*, nor *Papists*, nor *Iewes*.'[44] The victory of Cromwell's army with its affection for the Jews, their religion and their form of government helped to enhance and intensify the mounting support for readmission. Their formulaic marriage of Turks and Jews softens this military philo-semitism somewhat from our point of view however: Clement Walker the Royalist commentator believed that the decision of the Council of War proved that 'they vote like States-men, as well as their Parliament.'[45] Nevertheless, this endorsement from the military men was sufficient to prompt one of the most remarkable documents of the readmission saga in the period immediately preceeding Menasseh ben Israel's journey to England.

On 5 January 1648–9, Fairfax and the Council of War received a petition from the widow Johanna Cartenright and her son Ebenezer Cartwright, English nationals but resident in Amsterdam. The petitioners, after discussion with the Dutch Jews, noted that 'both they and we find, that the time of hereall draweth nigh'. Towards that end, they prayed 'that the inhumane cruel Statute of banishment made against them, may be repealed, and they under the Christian banner of charity, and brotherly love, may again be received and permitted to trade and dwell amongst you in this Land, as now they do in the Nether-lands.' The readmission of the Jews, they believed, would appease God's wrath towards England. A colophon to the printed petition reported that their request was 'favourably received with a promise to take it into speedy consideration, when the present more publike affaires are dispatched.'[46]

The Cartwrights' petition was the first serious attempt to secure the formal readmission of the Jews to England. The fact that it was acknowledged with a statement of support ratifies

[44] *Mercurius Pragmaticus* (19–26 Dec. 1648).

[45] [C. Walker], *Anarchia Anglicana: . . . The History of Independency. The Second Part* (n.p., 1649), p. 50.

[46] J. Cartenright and E. Cartwright, *The Petition Of The Jewes* (London, 1649), pp. 1–3.

the significance of the document. Elias Ashmole was so moved by the Cartwrights' petition that he included a note about it in his manuscript autobiographical sketch.[47] For previous pleas for toleration had been either liturgical, part of a larger and less outrageous argument, or had been framed in the form of an open letter, as was the case with Hugh Peter's pamphlet addressed to Parliament.

The Cartwrights' petition therefore did not go unnoticed, especially in the Royalist press. One news-sheet was unsurprised by the action of Fairfax and his Council: 'No marvell,' their reporter wrote, 'that those which intend to crucifie their *King*, should shake hands with them that crucified their *Saviour*.'[48] Another Royalist newspaper reminded its readers that the Jews were banished from England 'because they ingrosed Trade and Riches to the prejudice of the natives living in a miserable manner, and yet not before the people had like to have torne them in pieces'.[49] Another news-sheet complained that 'the *Iewes* are too good Companions for such a Heathenish generation, who neither acknowledge *God*, nor *King*, nor *Christ*'. Their reformation would 'introduce the Iewish Religion, and preferre it before *Episcopacy*, or *Presbytery*'.[50] Yet another report featured Jewish Cartwrights asking for help in sending their people to Palestine.[51]

But the most virulent attack on the Cartwrights' petition came from Clement Walker in his history of Independency. Walker thought it was simply a case of the 'Hebrew Jewes' presenting a petition to the 'uncircumcised Jewes of the Councell of Warre'. Walker also printed for posterity a copy of a paper which was published at the time of the Cartwrights'

[47] Bodl., MS Ashm. 1136, f. 147ʳ: E. Ashmole, *Works*, ed. C. H. Jostern (Oxford, 1966), ii. 484. Ashmole studied Hebrew with Solomon Franco, a crypto-Jew of London, from February 1652. Curiously enough, although Franco's name itself is always written in longhand, whenever Ashmole refers to his Hebrew lessons with the Jew it is in cipher (Bodl., MS Ashm. 374, fos. 139ʳ⁻ᵛ, 140: *Works*, ed. Josten, i. 92, ii. 609). Franco became a Christian after the Restoration and published a pamphlet dedicated to Charles II entitled *Truth springing out of the Earth* (London, 1668). Ashmole's copy is in the Bodleian Library: Ashm. 1209 (6).

[48] *Mercurius Pragmaticus*, 40–1 (26 Dec. 1648–9 Jan. 1649). Walker used almost identical words in his criticism of the Council of Officers: *Independency*, p. 83.

[49] *Moderate Intelligencer*, 200 (11–18 Jan. 1649).

[50] *Mercurius Elencticus*, 59 (2–9 Jan. 1648–9), p. 563.

[51] *Perfect Weekly Account*, (10–17 Jan. 1649), p. 351.

petition, revealing the 'last damnable Designe of *Cromwell* and *Ireton*'. The writer claimed that they intended to plunder and disarm the City of London, so as to prevent its citizens from resisting the army. Cromwell and Ireton would then redeem the booty from the army,

and so sell it in bulk to the *Jewes*, whom they have lately admitted to set up their banks, and magazins of Trade amongst us, contrary to an Act of Parliament for their banishment; and these shall be their Merchants to buy off for ready money, (to maintaine such Warres as their violent proceedings will inevitably bring upon them) not onely all Sequestred and Plundred goods, but also the very Bodies of Men, Women, and Children, whole Families taken Prisoners for sale, of whom these Jewish Merchants shall keep a constant traffique with the *Turks*, *Moores*, and other Mahometans[52]

After the sympathy demonstrated in December and January, the readmission of the Jews suddenly became a frightening possibility, and numerous libels regarding the true intentions of the Jews circulated through London. Walker's claim that the Jews intended to sell Englishmen into slavery never really caught the public imagination. Far more influential was the widely believed allegation that, as Walker himself phrased it, 'They offer for their readmission, S. *Pauls* Church, and the Library at *Oxford*, 500000 l. but 700000 l. is demanded: *Hugh Peters* and *Harry Martyn* solicite the businesse.'[53] Hugh Peter and Henry Marten the regicide supported the Cartwrights' petition, and thus apparently were coupled with this particular slander.[54] Even after the Restoration, Peter could be depicted in a print before St. Paul's saying, 'Let it out to ye Jews'.[55]

Although Peter and Marten were often omitted from the story, and the exact price figures varied between reports, the accusation itself was one of the most frequently heard calumnies against the Jews until well after the Restoration. The earl of Monmouth wrote to his daughter at the time of the Whitehall Conference that the Jews 'are to have two sinagogs allowd them in London, wherof St. Paul's to be one. Well, my hart, God's will must bee done and we must submit unto it.'[56] Abraham

---

[52] Walker, *Independency*, pp. 60–2.

[53] *ibid.*, p. 60.

[54] A. Wood, *Athenae Oxenienses*, ed. P. Bliss (London, 1813–20), iii. 1239.

[55] A. Rubens, *A Jewish Iconography* (London, 1954), p. 36.

[56] Printed in the *Times Lit.\Supp.*, 8 Sept. 1921, p. 580, although the letter is obviously dated incorrectly there.

Cowley the poet claimed that Cromwell would have agreed to this transaction if the Jewish 'purses and devotions could have reacht to the purchase.'[57] After Cromwell's death, one observer recalled that this accusation was frequently reported.[58]

It is not surprising that this story soon reached the Continent. The Royalist resident in Venice informed the Doge on 14 February 1650 that the 'church of St. Paul, comparable with St. Peters at Rome, remains desolate and is said to have been sold to the Jews as a synagogue.'[59] A ship's captain recently arrived from England testified before the Inquisition in the Canary Islands in April 1656 that it was the common rumour throughout London that the Jews offered £200,000 for this privilege.[60] In the version that reached France, the Jews were attempting to buy 'the beautiful room in Whitehall' for their synagogue, and they promised not to demolish it.[61] According to another French report, the Cartwrights offered to buy St. Paul's and the Bodleian for £500,000, but the Council of War demanded £300,000 more. Peter and Marten were named as the brokers employed by the Jews.[62] Menasseh ben Israel was astounded at the scope of this libel, especially that 'it hath been rumoured abroad, that our nation had purchased S. *Pauls* Church for to make it their Synagogue, notwithstanding that it was formerly a temple consecrated to the worship of *Diana*.' But during the eventful days of his campaign for readmission, it was only one of 'many other things . . . reported of us that never entred into the thoughts of our nation'.[63]

At the same time these slanders were beginning to disperse in all directions, the more historic deliberations of January 1648–9 were under way. The Cartwrights' petition had been received at the height of the negotiations concerning the form

---

[57] Cowley, *Essays*, p. 87.

[58] *Documents illustrating the history of S. Paul's Cathedral*, ed. W. S. Simpson (Camden Soc., n.s. xxvi, 1880), p. lxiv.

[59] *Cal. S. P. Ven., 1647–52*, p. 138.

[60] H. Beinart, 'The Jews in the Canary Islands: a Re-evaluation', *Trs. Jew. Hist. Soc. Eng.*, xxv (1977), 59.

[61] *Cal. S. P. Dom., 1658–9*, p. 367: dated 6/16 June 1659.

[62] R. Monteth, *The History Of The Troubles Of Great Britain* (London, 1735), p. 473: from the French 2nd edition, 1661.

[63] Menasseh ben Israel, *Vindiciae Judaeorum* (n.p., 1656), p. 12.

which might be assumed by a modified Agreement of the People. Three days later, William Erbery, a millenarian army chaplain, asked Ireton in exasperation during the debates at the Council of War, 'To what purpose will you give that libertie to the Jewes and others to come in unlesse you grant them the exercise of their religion?'[64] Erbery was a proponent of toleration for the Jews, but his efforts here were to be in vain.[65] For on 15 January 1648–9, the Council of Officers approved the modified Agreement of the People, granting toleration only to those who 'profess faith in God by Jesus Christ'.[66] A swift accession to the requests which the Cartwrights sent to Fairfax from Holland was obviously not forthcoming.

This disappointing clause in the Agreement of the People seems to have been the motivating factor behind the appearance the following month of a fifteen-page pamphlet in support of the Jews written by a certain '*Edward Nicholas, Gent.*' Nicholas argued that England's present troubles derived in part from the 'strict and cruel Laws now in force against the most honorable Nation of the world, the Nation of the Jews, a people chosen by God'. Nicholas insisted that only the Jewish elders were guilty of the murder of Christ, and then reported on the issue of the lost ten tribes and on the expulsion of the Jews from Spain. Jews were permitted even in Italy, he wrote, the home of the Pope and his Jesuits, because of the profit which the Italians 'make by the Jews diverse ways'. Nicholas feared that unless the Jews were readmitted to England with all possible rights and privileges, '(God putting their tears into his bottle) God will charge their sufferings upon us, and will avenge them on their persecutors.' Nicholas claimed that he was persuaded to publish his short tract 'not upon any mans motion of the Jews Nation, but a thing that I have long and deeply revolved within my heart'. His efforts were intended 'for the glory of God, the comfort of those his afflicted people, the love of my own sweet

---

[64] *The Clarke Papers*, ed. C. H. Firth (Camden Soc., n.s., xlix, liv, lxi–ii, 1891–1901), ii. 172.

[65] [F. Cheynell], *An Account Given to the Parliament* (London, 1646), p. 35. For more on Erbery, see C. Hill, *The World Turned Upside Down* (New York, 1973), pp. 154–8.

[66] *The Constitutional Documents of the Puritan Revolution*, ed. S. R. Gardiner (Oxford, 1906), p. 370.

native countrey of *England*, and the freeing of my own soul in the day of account.'[67]

This last argument of Edward Nicholas might be more convincing if other biographical information could be used to corroborate it. Unfortunately, this '*Edward Nicholas*, Gent.' is not the same man as Sir Edward Nicholas, Charles II's Secretary of State. The fact that a Spanish translation was published in London the following year might indicate that it was primarily intended for the Sephardic community in London and/or Amsterdam.[68] In spite of the determined efforts by 'Edward Nicholas' to salvage something from the hopes of January, it was clear that formal readmission would have to wait for more settled conditions.

III

'There was also a Petition to repeale the Laws made against the Jews,' a Royalist newspaper reported soon after the Cartwright petition was presented, 'it's true, they may be usefull where the inhabitants, as in *Poland, Spain*, and other parts, live in a way of gallantry, affecting War, to drive a trade, but in a countrey abounding with Merchants, natives, they are as water to the shoos: This is not said as against their having their consciences.'[69] Yet in Holland, the country of merchants *par excellence*, Jews were openly tolerated without any hindrance to 'the industrious inclinations of the Dutch, a concealed mystery unto this day.'[70] Approximately 1,800 Sephardic Jews lived in Amsterdam in 1655; within twenty years over 7,500 Jews were resident there. Amsterdam was the Dutch Jerusalem, and is still known today as '*Mokum*', the Hebrew word for 'a place'.[71] The Netherlands were often used as a model by Englishmen, in political as well as economic discussions. Holland provided a test case with which to illustrate the results of Jewish toleration,

---

[67] E. Nicholas, *An Apology For The Honorable Nation Of The Jews* (London, 1648), pp. 4–5, 6, 8, 11, 14–15.

[68] C. Roth, 'Spanish Printing at Izmir' (Hebrew), *Kiryath Sepher*, xxviii (1952–3), 390–3, concerning Spanish reprint at Smyrna in 1659; M. Munsterberg, 'Notes on Rare Books: *Apologia por la noble nacion de los Iudios*, London 1649', *Boston Pub. Lib. Qly.*, vi (1954), 235–41.

[69] *Moderate Intelligencer* (11–18 Jan. 1649).

[70] *Seventeenth-Century Economic Documents*, ed. J. Thirsk and J. P. Cooper (Oxford, 1972), p. 262: the framework knitters' appeal to Cromwell for incorporation, 1655.

[71] Bloom, *Jews in Amsterdam*, pp. 8, 31.

and was often cited, especially after Rabbi Menasseh ben Israel of Amsterdam was drawn into the English debate by millenarian speculation and his appreciation of the great opportunities presented by England's shifting political climate.

Menasseh first petitioned the English government for readmission late in 1651, the year after his *Hope of Israel* was published, dedicated to Parliament and the Council of State. Two years before his death, soon after the Whitehall Conference had failed to procure the official readmission of the Jews which had been his goal all along, Menasseh recounted the events that led him to his English crusade:

> the communication and correspondence I have held, for some yeares since, with some eminent persons of *England*, was the first originall of my undertaking this design. For I alwayes found by them, a great probability of obtaining what I now request; whilst they affirmed, that at this time the minds of men stood very well affected towards us; and that our entrance into this Island, would be very acceptable, and well-pleasing unto them. And from this beginning sprang up in me a semblable affection, and desire of obtaining this purpose.[72]

This was the period of the mission of Oliver St. John and Walter Strickland to the United Provinces, and it is probable that one or both of them provided Menasseh with advice on the best means to approach Parliament. 'And this the Right Honourable my Lord *St. Iohn* can testifie', Menasseh recalled, that 'when he was Embassadour to the Lords the States of the united Provinces, was pleased to honour our Synagogue at *Amsterdam* with his presence, where our nation entertained him with musick, and all expressions of joy and gladnesse'. On that occasion, the members of the Amsterdam Jewish community also pronounced a blessing, 'not onely upon his honour, then present, but upon the whole Common-wealth of *England*'.[73] In an earlier publication, Menasseh spoke of entertaining the 'Ambassadors of *England*' at the synagogue, so it is likely that Strickland was present as well at that historic service, which must have called to mind the visit of the English queen only nine years before.[74]

---

[72] Menasseh, *Vindiciae*, p. 37.

[73] *Ibid.*, p. 5.

[74] Menasseh ben Israel, *The Humble Addresses* (n.p., n.d. = 1655), sig. A3ʳ. See above, p. 160.

Menasseh seems to have sent a petition for readmission directly to the Council of State, and although this important document is now lost, it is clear that a sub-committee consisting of Bulstrode Whitelocke, Walter Strickland, and Sir Gilbert Pickering was appointed to prepare a suitable reply.[75] The twelve restrictive conditions which Sir Edward Spencer had proposed the previous year in his well-known book indicated that a simple response would not be possible. The Dutch war delayed negotiations with the rabbi from Amsterdam, although Menasseh was issued a passport in November and annually thereafter until the Peace of Westminster in 1654 permitted renewed contacts.[76]

Meanwhile, interest in the Jewish readmission question continued, in spite of the fact that Menasseh was trapped in Holland by 'the checquered, and interwoven vicissitudes, and turns of things here below'.[77] One indication of this was the translation into English of Rabbi Leone da Modena's *Historia de gli riti hebraici* by Edmund Chilmead of Christ Church, Oxford. This work by the famous rabbi of Venice was the most comprehensive handbook of Jewish religion and customs, and was the first such guide written by a Jew in a European language.[78] William Everard the Digger proclaimed that he was 'of the race of the Jews' several months after the presentation of the Cartwright petition. This was surely a metaphorical description rather than a religious confession, but it does indicate that this timely reference had penetrated even to St. George's Hill.[79]

More literary allusions to the Jewish question are also apparent during this period. George Herbert's panegyric of the

---

[75] *Cal. S. P. Dom., 1651*, p. 472.

[76] *Cal. S. P. Dom., 1651–2.* p. 577; *1652–3*, p. 38; *1653–4*, p. 436. The *Cal.* dates first ref. as 22 Nov. 1652, but *Dict. Nat. Biog.*, s.v. 'Manasseh' cites it as 1651, which seems more reasonable.

[77] Menasseh, *Vindiciae*, p. 38.

[78] L. Modena, *The History Of The Rites, Customes, and Manner of Life, of the Present Jews* (London, 1650). See also C. Roth, 'Leone Da Modena and the Christian Hebraists of his Age', *Jewish Studies in memory of Israel, Abrahams,* ed. G. A. Kohut (New York, 1927), pp. 384–401; idem, 'Leone da Modena and England', *Trs. Jew. Hist. Soc. Eng.*, xi (1928), 206–27; idem, 'Léon de Modène, ses *Riti Ebraici* et le Saint-Office à Venise', *Rev. Etud. Juives*, lxxxvii (1929), 83–8; idem, 'Leone da Modena and his English Correspondents', *Trs. Jew. Hist. Soc. Eng.*, xvii (1953), 39–43.

[79] *The Moderate*, 41 (17–24 Apr. 1649); cf. B. Whitelock, *Memorials of the English Affairs* (Oxford, 1853), iii. 18.

country parson was published posthumously in 1652, which included the most detailed exposition of the fate of the Jews that can be found in any of his works. Herbert, the clergyman and metaphysical poet, is often credited with having written 'the first genuinely and deeply sympathetic poem on the Jew', which was published in 1633 as part of the collection of works called *The Temple*.[80] This poem entitled simply 'The Jews', bemoans that 'Poore nation . . . whose streams we got by the Apostles sluce, And use in baptisme, while ye pine and die'. Nevertheless, it is fundamentally a conversionist poem rather than an unambiguous celebration of Hebrew genius and an endorsement of Jewish toleration. Indeed, in the very same volume, Herbert uses the adjective 'Jewish' in a negative and insulting sense, referring to 'Jewish hate', 'a Jewish choice' and 'a Judas-Jew'.[81] This brand of conversionist condescension reached a higher pitch in Herbert's *A Priest To the Temple*, which expressed these sentiments in a less veiled fashion, and at such a time that the arguments he offered were unavoidably amplified. Herbert explained that:

if the Jews live, all the great wonders of old live in them, and then who can deny the stretched out arme of a mighty God? especially since it may be a just doubt, whether, considering the stubbornnesse of the Nation, their living then in their Countrey under so many miracles were a stranger thing, then their present exile, and disability to live in their Countrey. And it is observable, that this very thing was intended by God, that the Jewes should be his proof, and witnesses . . . And their very dispersion in all Lands, was intended not only for a punishment to them; but for an exacting of others by their sight, to the acknowledging of God, and his power, . . . And therefore this kind of Punishment was chosen rather then any other.[82]

By 1652, of course, this account of the Jewish character and destiny could conceivably have a positive effect: the Jews had not yet been dispersed into England. Nevertheless, the net effect of examining all of Herbert's writings that deal with the

---

[80] H. Fisch, *The Dual Image* (London, 1971), p. 40; cf. idem, *Jerusalem and Albion* (London, 1964).

[81] G. Herbert, *The Temple* (Cambridge, 1633) in *Works*, ed. F. E. Hutchinson (Oxford, 1941), pp. 152, 170–1, 530. Cf. H. Vaughan, *Silex Scintillans* (2nd edn., London, 1655), repr. *Works*, ed. L. C. Martin (2nd edn., Oxford 1957), pp. 499–500: 'The Jews', poem not included in 1st edn. of 1650.

[82] G. H[erbert], *A Priest To the Temple* (London, 1652) in *Works*, p. 281. Also on the Jews, cf. idem, *Ovtlandish Proverbs* (London, 1640), in *Works*, pp. 329, 361.

Jews is to diminish somewhat his reputation as an unwavering defender of Jewish religion and culture.

At the same time that George Herbert was posthumously providing an exegesis of the Jewish place in history, others offered more practical plans for realizing their destiny. Among these was Captain Robert Norwood, who pleaded for the readmission and toleration of the Jews in the context of a reply to the charge of blasphemy before the Committee for the Propagation of the Gospel, which had taken notice of his involvement with Thomas Tany the millenarian.[83] Norwood lambasted those who saw the moral and legal justification for their reception and toleration, but declined to execute readmission on the grounds of reason of state. Norwood argued that the Jews should be tolerated in England because, firstly, 'We cannot be perfect without them'. Secondly, 'Our salvation came by their stumbling or falling; and that as their dimishing was the riches of the Gentiles', justice demanded that the Jews receive mercy. 'We daily pray for them', Norwood concluded, 'let it therefore really and truly appear that we be what we seem (or would seem) to be.'[84]

These sentiments were reiterated by Roger Williams, once again in England to seek support for his new Rhode Island settlement. Williams soon became involved in the discussions of the Committee for the Propagation of the Gospel regarding the organization of a modified state church. This Committee was apparently encouraging the public to communicate their views and consciences, and as a matter of course received numerous papers outlining various religious positions. A certain Major Butler had the previous year inquired of Christopher Goad whether he believed that the Jews ought to be readmitted and tolerated in England. Goad replied that he was a great defender of 'those *inward spiritual Iews*, the seed of the blessed, which rejoyce in *Christ Jesus*, and have no confidence in the flesh', but his stand with regard to contemporary practising Jews remained unclear. At any rate, Butler and five others, among whom were Charles Vane and Moses Wall, Menasseh

---

[83] On Norwood, see above, pp. 110, 116.
[84] R. Norwood, *Proposals for propagation of the Gospel* (n.p., n.d. = 1652), pp. 1, 17–18.

ben Israel's translator, presented their paper to the Committee early in 1652.[85]

Their final query was 'Whether it be not the duty of the Magistrate to permit the Jews, whose conversion we look for, to live freely and peaceably amongst us?' Roger Williams provided the commentary to this proposal, and boldly proclaimed that 'I humbly conceive it to be the Duty of the *Civil Magistrate* to break down that superstitious *wall* of *separation* (as to Civil things) between us *Gentiles* and the *Jews*, and freely (without their asking) to make way for their free and peaceable Habitation amongst us.' Williams then summarized the standard religious reasons for readmission: the Jews are the chosen people, and by their fall saved the gentiles, as they themselves will be saved at the End of Days. 'Out of some kind of sense of these things,' Williams noted, Christians pray for the conversion and calling of the Jews. This was a particular obligation of Englishmen, because England 'especially, and the *Kings* thereof, have had just cause to fear, that the *unchristian oppressions, incivilities*, and *inhumanities* of this *Nation* against the *Jews*, have cried to *Heaven* against this *Nation* and the *Kings* and *Princes* of it.' Williams argued that the readmission and toleration of the Jews was necessary to pacify the wrath of God against England.[86]

Roger Williams's defence of the Jews was one of the most comprehensive and powerful statements which had yet appeared in England. He was aware that many of his readers would be scandalized by the very idea of inviting into England the murderers of Christ, a people who rejected the very basic fundamentals of Christianity, and whose crimes in England before the expulsion were notorious. Williams also noted 'their known Industry of inriching themselves in all places where they come.'[87] But in spite of these difficulties, he was confident that the government could make suitable arrangements to protect their own people while still allowing Jews to resettle and to

---

[85] Letter of 8 Mar. 1651–2 in R. W[illiams], *The Fourth Paper, Presented by Maior Butler* (London, 1652), p. 9; cf. title page, p. 3.

[86] Ibid., title p., preface^{r-v}, pp. 3, 11, 18–19. Cf. idem, *The Bloody Tenent Yet More Bloody* (London, 1652), sig. A4^r, pp. 25–6, 40, 284–5.

[87] Idem, *Fourth Paper*, p. 19.

worship freely in England. The precise response to Williams's call for Jewish toleration is difficult to determine, but the Baptist leader Thomas Collier issued a proposal to the Committee for the Propagation of the Gospel which was almost identical to the one which Williams so ardently supported.[88]

The campaign for the readmission of the Jews was thus fairly well under way by 1652. We have already seen how important support from the army was in the initial stages in 1649. By 1652, interest in readmission can be found in the navy as well. Seamen in Leghorn aboard the Phoenix frigate recounted a visit to the synagogue there, where they met with an English-speaking Jew who told them that

They long to hear that *England* would tolerate them; surely the promises of *Jehovah* wil be performed, and he wil give them favour in all Nations. O that ENGLAND may not be slack herein . . . O that the poor Jews might have toleration to COME into *England*

The sailors thought it especially ludicrous that the Jews were tolerated by the Pope, the Turks, and by 'the BARBARIANS', but not by the English. The preacher on board the frigate sent the letter to a friend in London, whence it was published in a news-sheet there.[89]

The second edition of the English translation of Menasseh's *Hope of Israel* also appeared during this period, including a short essay by the editor, Moses Wall. 'Do not think I aime by this Translation, to propagate or commend *Iudaisme*,' he explained. Wall saw eight reasons for tolerating Jews, and chief among them was that 'they have the same Humane nature with us; from this ground we should wish well to all men, whether *Jew* or *Gentile*'. Wall's main interest was still the conversion of the Jews, although he admitted that he had no idea as to how this could be accomplished. It 'will be Gods worke, and not mans', he supposed, 'as much as Pauls conversion was wholly of God; which himselfe makes the type, or patterne of the conversion of his Country-men.' The fame of the most notori-

---

[88] T. Collier, *An Answer To a Book written by one Richard Sanders* (London, 1652), p. 39.

[89] *Severall Proceedings*, 136 (29 Apr. –6 May 1652), repr. [Jessey], *Narrative*, p. 11. The Jews at Leghorn were also said to 'look for Christ to come ten years hence' in *Perfect Passages*, 62 (30 Apr. –7 May 1652), p. [460].

ous Judaizer was still alive: over thirty years the event, Wall still felt it necessary to dissociate himself from 'the wilde opinions of Mr. *Thrask*.'[90]

By the time that Cromwell opened the Barebones Parliament on 4 July 1653, the question of Jewish readmission was thus an issue which had been discussed publicly for quite some time. No doubt the inner motives of the men who advocated the toleration of open Jewish worship were of very varied kinds. Some men, like John Dury or Henry Jessey, recognized the awesome depth of Jewish learning and kabbalah, and the value of the Jewish devotion to the Old Testament. Others harboured more cynical reasons behind their espousal of Jewish toleration. But by the summer of 1653, the Jewish question could not be ignored, not the least because Menasseh ben Israel was now dedicated to achieving their resettlement. The Jews became a constant topic of discussion through the insistent harping on the subject by the millenarian theorists, heartened by the results of the search for the lost ten tribes, and the millenarian activists such as Robins and Tany. And before this Parliament was dismissed for having failed to live up to Cromwell's idealistic plans, for having failed to be Christ's government on earth, millenarianism was still a practical tool for social and political change. The Barebones Parliament was meant to be the instrument of this reform on the eve of the Second Coming. The part of the Jews in this cosmic drama was prominent and, as we shall see, the effective campaign for readmission can be dated from the opening of the Parliament of the saints, when Cromwell charged them 'to usher in the things that God has promised . . . not vainly to look at that prophecy in Daniel'.[91]

---

[90] M. Wall, 'Conversion of the Jewes', in Menasseh Ben Israel, *The Hope of Israel* (2nd edn., London, 1652), sig. B; pp. 48–53, 58.

[91] *The Writings and Speeches of Oliver Cromwell*, ed. W. C. Abbott (Cambridge, Mass., 1937–47), iii. 64.

6

BOTH POLITIQUE AND DIVINE REASONS:

Menasseh ben Israel's Mission to England

'Indeed I do think something is at the door: we are at the threshold', Cromwell reminded the Barebones Parliament as he opened the first session, 'you are at the edge of the promises and prophecies'. This being so, Cromwell pointed out that it was entirely possible that the prophecy, 'He will bring His people again from the depths of the sea', applied not only to the Gospel churches, but also to the Jews. 'And it may be,' he affirmed, 'as some think, God will bring the Jews home to their station from the isles of the sea, and answer their expectations as from the depths of the sea.' Cromwell charged the Parliament of the saints with the task of being the instrument of the divine will: 'Truly you are called by God to rule with Him, and for Him', he admonished.[1]

At long last, it appeared as if Parliament, albeit one of a radically different variety, would execute some of the millenarian proposals that had been put forward in favour of the Jews during the past decade. These hopes were not disappointed.[2] Samuel Herring asked that 'the Jewes should be

[1] *The Writings and Speeches of Oliver Cromwell,* ed. W. C. Abbott (Cambridge, Mass., 1937–47), iii. 61, 64, 65.

[2] But note that the 'humble petition of Robert Rich (Sur named Mordicai) on the behalfe of himselfe and all the seed of the Jewes' was not connected with the Barebones Parliament. The document is mistakenly dated 1653 in the *Cal. S. P. Dom., 1653–4,* p. 331. An examination of the original document (SP. 18/42, f. 237ʳ) reveals that it must have been presented as late as 1657 in connection with the trial and imprisonment of James Nayler. See also *Dict. Nat. Biog., s.v.,* 'Rich, Robert'. Generally, see H. A. Glass, *The Barbone Parliament* (London, 1899); A. Woolrych, 'The Calling of Barebone's

called into this Commonwealth, and have places allotted to them to inhabitt in, and exercise there lyberty, for there tyme is neere at hand.'[3] John Brayne, the Seeker expert on Mosaic law, asked Parliament to arrange to 'teach the Hebrew reading to some' in all towns.[4] According to a letter intercepted by Thurloe's agents, among the motions in the house was one 'that the Jews might bee admitted to trade as well as in Holland'. The writer claimed that by 29 July 1653 there was 'nothing yet done therein, nor in many things had in consultation, that may be very commodious for the commonwealth.'[5] These startling new developments were also reported in the Royalist news letters.[6]

James Howell the Royalist author and translator was appalled and infuriated by these proposals, and appended a special epistle to his edition of Jossipon, the famous chronicle. To this day, he exclaimed, "'tis well known what Runagates and Landlopers they have been up and down the world.' Edward I did not expel the Jews because of their religion, 'but for their notorious Crimes; as, poysoning of wels, counterfeiting of coins, falsifying of seals, and crucifying of Christian children, with other villanies.' Howell sought to explain the perfidy of the Scotch as well. It 'is thought divers families of those banished *Jews* fled then to Scotland,' he revealed, 'where they have propagated since in great numbers; witness the aversion that Nation hath above others to hogs flesh.'[7]

No doubt Howell was justified in fearing an imminent Jewish immigration, for these manifestations of English sympathy were being watched carefully by Jews in the Netherlands. Chanut, the French ambassador to Holland, wrote to his coun-

---

Parliament', *Eng. Hist. Rev.*, lxxx (1965), 492–513; T. Liu, 'The Calling of the Barebones Parliament Reconsidered', *Jnl. Eccl. Hist.*, xxii (1971), 223–36.

[3] *Original Letters and Papers of State Addressed to Oliver Cromwell*, ed. J. Nickolls (London, 1743), p. 100. The Christian name of the Herring in the Barebones Parliament was John: he was one of the two members for Herefordshire and a commissioner for the Propagation of the Gospel in Wales. The identity of Samuel Herring remains obscure. For John Herring, see ibid., p. 92; *Cal. S. P. Dom.*, *1652–3*, p. 412; and T. Liu, 'Barebones', pp. 231, 235.

[4] J. Brayne, *The New Earth* (London, 1653), p. 91

[5] *Thurloe State Papers*, i. 387.

[6] Bodl., MS. Clar. 46, f. 109^r: London, 15 July 1653.

[7] J. Howell, *The VVonderful And most deplorable History of the Latter Times of the Jews* (London, 1653), sigs. A4, B^v–B2. See also L. Wolf, '"Josippon" in England', *Trs. Jew Hist. Soc. Eng.*, vi (1912), 277–88.

terpart in England on 16 October 1654 that 'A Jew in Amsterdam hath informed me for certain, that the three generals of the fleet have presented a petition to his highness the protector, to obtain, that their nation may be received in England, to draw the commerce thither.'[8]

At about the same time, the English authorities received a copy of the Dutch privileges recently granted to Jewish refugees from Pernambuco. The reconquest of that colony by the Portuguese rendered the Jews there liable to persecution by the Inquisition. As a result, the Dutch permitted them to settle in other places along the coast of Guiana under the protection of the Netherlands, and secured their freedom with an eighteen-point list of rights which are reminiscent of the privileges granted to the Jews in the mother country. The document is undated, but its provenance in England is revealed by the name of the addresse: 'S^{nr} Fernando' [Carvajal], the great crypto-Jew of mid-seventeenth century London. Those Jews who chose to emigrate to the 'Wilde Cust' were to be given full liberty of conscience, synagogues, schools, and a cemetery. They were offered numerous financial enticements as well as self-government within the bounds of the law. The 'intension of the s^d Hebrews', the Dutch authorities noted, 'is to Preserue themselfes Peasibly'.[9]

The striking liberality of the Dutch privileges for Jewish refugees from Pernambuco could not but make a powerful impression on the English authorities. The Dutch were acknowledged masters of the economic arts, and plainly they wished to encourage the presence of Jews in their colonial ventures. Far from being a disruptive alien people desiring only to enrich themselves at the expense of the host nation, the Jews were believed to promote the expansion of trade and prosperity. The experience and fortunes of the Dutch were suddenly of immediate and practical importance in any case. For the war with the Netherlands ended with the ratification of the Peace of Westminster on 5 April 1654, just as Pernambuco was finally recovered by the Portuguese. Although some Jews from Per-

---

[8] *Thurloe State Papers*, ii. 651–2.

[9] Brit. Lib., MS Eger. 2395, fos. 46^r–47^r: printed with many mistakes and incorrect identification in *Trs. Jew. Hist. Soc. Eng.*, iii (1899), 82–4. See also M. J. Kohler, 'Some Early American Zionist Projects', *Proc. Am. Jew. Hist. Soc.*, viii (1900), 78.

nambuco accepted the generous Dutch offer to settle in other places under their control, notably New Amsterdam, many others streamed into the Netherlands bewailing their ruined businesses and livelihoods.

Among this number was Manuel Martinez Dormido, alias David Abrabanel. According to his own autobiography, Dormido was born in Andalusia where, although a secret Jew, he acted in the capacity of alderman and royal treasurer along with other government posts. He was eventually prosecuted by the Inquisition, which kept him, his wife, and his sister-in-law in prison for five years 'induring greate penalties miseries and troubles'. Dormido was finally released, and his estate and offices were restored to him, but he was determined to leave Iberia and settle abroad. He transferred his household to Bordeaux, which was reasonably close to the centre of his business in Spain, now managed by his brother. Unfortunately, the early death of his brother eight years later ruined him, so he resolved to emigrate to Holland where he could also live openly as a Jew. Dormido arrived there in April 1640 and was soon made a denizen of Amsterdam and a representative of the city's Jewish community. Being 'much desirous to improoue my sonns in some bussinesses', he sent two of them to Brazil in May 1641, where they prospered until the recent siege and surrender of Pernambuco. The Dormido family was suddenly ruined, notwithstanding the terms of capitulation of the colony which stipulated that private debts were recoverable. His sons were soon home in Amsterdam without their wealth and possessions, with 'onely the hopes lefft vs of Recouring it againe'.[10]

By the time Dormido's sons had returned to Amsterdam, Menasseh ben Israel was free to initiate his mission to England. Illness prevented him from making the trip at that time, so he sent his son Samuel in the company of Dormido, who resolved to implore Cromwell to seek restitution on his behalf from the Portuguese, newly allied with England. They arrived in London on 1 October 1654, where Samuel ben Israel set about studying the prospects for an official resettlement and Dormido

[10] Brit. Lib., MS Eger. 1049, f.6ʳ⁻ᵛ: Dormido to Cromwell, 3 Nov. 1654 (autobiographical account). Printed with many mistakes in *Trs. Jew. Hist. Soc. Eng.*, iii (1899), 90–3.

prepared the materials he would submit for the consideration of the English government.[11]

'Manuel Martines dormido, Alias Dauid Abrabanel, hebrew by nation', presented two separate petitions to Cromwell on 3 November 1654. The first included an autobiographical account and a request that the English government assist him in recovering his property. The second petition was offered in the hope:

that true & vnfalliable states Pollicie bee admited opening the gates to my nation to the ende they may (vnder the Diuine protection & that of y^r. highnese) freely vse theire excersise in the obseruance of y^e. moste holly lawes giuen by god on mounte Sinay, graunting them libertie to come wth. theire famillies and estates to bee dwellers heere wth. the same eaquallnese and conueniences, wch. y^e. inland borne subjects doe injoy[12]

Dormido painted a lurid picture of the Inquisition, which used its 'violent powers to Judge the hidden interiours oneley Reserued to god Creatore', but the prime enticement which he presents for Jewish readmission is the economic advantage which would accrue to the English. Jewish immigration would help in 'origining new traficks and comerses, & increasing those allrady comon & acustumed, wth. greate benefitt to the peoples and increasement to y^e. states Reuenues'. Dormido promised that 'busines will increase and y^e. comerce will become more oppulant' if the Jews are readmitted. The Jews 'haue allwayes binn faithfull and true patricians,' Dormido testified, and he offered 'to lett it know to those of my nation in all places where at prezent they haue theire abidings . . . to the ende without touching at any other place they may come directley'.[13]

Both of these petitions were endorsed by John Sadler, whose sympathy for the Jewish cause had already been shown, and Cromwell recommended them for report to a sub-committee composed of Nathaniel Fiennes, Lisle, Major-General John Lambert, Sir Humphrey Mackworth, and Philip Jones.[14] They reached a decision within a month, and on 5 December 1654

[11] Brit. Lib., MS Eger. 1049, f.6^v.

[12] Ibid.; Brit. Lib., MS Eger. 1049, f.7^{r-v}: Dormido to Cromwell, 3 Nov. 1654 (on behalf of the Jews). Printed with many mistakes in *Trs. Jew. Hist. Soc. Eng.*, iii (1899), 88–90. Cf. SP. 84/161, F. 48^{r-v}: Dormido to Cromwell, 4 Dec. 1655.

[13] Brit. Lib., MS Eger., f.7^{r-v}.

[14] Ibid., f.7^v; *Cal. S. P. Dom., 1654*, p. 393.

the Council of State announced that they 'saw no cause to make any order.'[15]

But Cromwell was not present at the meeting of the Council of State which declined to intercede on Dormido's behalf with the Portuguese authorities. This may have been a deliberate ploy by the other members of the Council, for according to John Sadler, Cromwell was 'pleased in an Especiall manner to recomẽnd these two annexed papers to the speedy consideracon of the Councell; That the Peticon may receive all due Satisfacion, and withall convenient speed.'[16] Certainly there is a formulaic quality to this endorsement, but it is most likely that Cromwell actually did favour Dormido's requests. For on 26 February 1654–5, Cromwell wrote a personal letter in Latin to the king of Portugal, praying for the restitution of Dormido's possessions and the payment of debts due to his sons.[17]

At that date, Dormido was not merely an alien, but in fact lacked any legal justification for his very presence in England. With the rather different exceptions of the two Jewish envoys from the Sublime Porte under Elizabeth, and the Jewish pirate captured during James's reign, Manuel Martinez Dormido was the first practising Jew who voluntarily confessed his faith before the English authorities.[18] Dormido would succeed in London, just as he had done in Holland, but the rather startling fact that an alien Jew should arrive in London and go about his business completely unmolested seems to have passed Englishmen with scarcely a murmur of protest. Not only was he free from legal prosecution and expulsion, but he actually obtained a letter from the Protector in favour of his purely personal business affairs.

The reasons of this highly significant and almost prophetic departure from policy are unfortunately highly obscure. Aside from his manœuvres on behalf of Dormido, and his conduct at the time of the Whitehall Conference, Cromwell has actually left very few traces which might reveal his genuine attitudes

---

[15] Ibid., p. 407.

[16] Brit. Lib., MS Eger, 1049, f.7ᵛ.

[17] Bodl., MS Rawl. A 260, f.57 and A 261, f.37ʳ: Eng. trans. in *Writings and Speeches*, ed. Abbott, iii. 636.

[18] For the Jewish envoys, see L. Wolf, 'Jews in Elizabethan England', *Trs. Jew. Hist. Soc. Eng.*, xi (1928), 1–91. For Samuel Palache the Jewish pirate, see above p. 39.

towards the Jews. We know that Cromwell used Jewish spies in gathering intelligence even before the Whitehall Conference and seems to have continued with this practice more openly afterwards. Bishop Burnet claimed that Cromwell 'more upon that account than in compliance with the principle of toleration, brought a company of them into England, and gave them leave to build a synagogue.' As Burnet noted, it was manifest 'what dealers the Jews were every where in the trade that depends on news'.[19] Scholars who have sought to rescue Cromwell from the taint of association with millenarianism have alleged that his interest in Jewish readmission was solely the product of his appreciation of Jewish wealth and economic power. But his actions throughout the debate over the Jewish question can be explained without recourse to the *deus ex machina* of economic self-interest. Certainly it seems as if he held fast to the principle he proclaimed as early as 1648 in an anonymous letter from the siege of Pontefract to Colonel Robert Hammond:

I profess to thee I desire from my heart, I have prayed for it, I have waited for the day to see union and right understanding between the godly people (Scots, English, Jews, Gentiles, Presbyterians, Independents, Anabaptists, and all).[20]

It may well be true that Cromwell abandoned many of his more outlandish millenarian hopes after the dismissal of the Barebones Parliament, but he was consistent in his quiet support for Jewish readmission and toleration throughout his years of power.

Although the culmination of the English philo-semitic movement, the Whitehall Conference, would take place at the end of the year, until the fall of 1655 events seemed to move almost more slowly than before. Some of the government manœuvres on behalf of the Jews must have leaked out to the interested public. At the beginning of 1655, Ralph Josselin, the

---

[19] G. Burnet, *History of My Own Time,* ed. O. Airy (Oxford, 1897–1900), i. 127. On Cromwell's Jewish spies, see: T. Burton, *Diary,* ed. J. T. Rutt (London, 1828), ii. 471 and note in *Trs. Jew. Hist. Soc. Eng.,* x (1924), 38; L. Wolf, 'Cromwell's Jewish Intelligencers', in his *Essays,* ed. C. Roth (London, 1934), pp. 93–114.

[20] *Writings and Speeches,* ed. Abbott, i. 676–8.

Essex minister, who learned about current affairs from the news sheets and political gossip,

> at night dreamed one came to mee and told me that Thurloe was turned Jew; I answered perhaps it was a mistake, he might declare he was a Jew born, the Jewes having lived here, and he pretend by old writings his pedigree from them, to ingratiate with the Jewes, or some compliance with them.

Josselin was so concerned by this night visitation that he drew a pointing hand in the margin directed at this notation in his diary.[21]

London's secret Jews were stirring as well, although only a few traces of activity survive in the written records. On 27 April 1655 Abraham de Mercado and his son David Raphael were permitted to emigrate to Barbados, where the father was given leave to practise medicine by order of Cromwell himself. The pass clearly stated that Mercado was a 'Hebrew'.[22] About this time one of the servants of Antonio Ferdinando Carvajal, the great crypto-Jew of London, was given leave to go to Flanders, where he no doubt reported on the growing strength of the pressure towards readmission, and the results of Dormido's petitions.[23]

Most interesting for our purposes is the forged doctoral diploma in philosophy and medicine from the University of Oxford which appeared to have been issued to Samuel ben Israel, Menasseh's son, on 6 May 1655. Unfortunately, the University registers make no mention of Menasseh's son, and a line-by-line examination of the form and phraseology of the document by the keeper of the University archives in 1876 revealed it to be a brazen forgery. In fact, it seems to be an adaptation of the form then in use by the University of Padua with, as the then keeper wrote, 'alterations wilfully and insufficiently made.'[24] The true character of the diploma was certainly unknown in the seventeenth century: Samuel ben Israel's tombstone in the Jewish cemetery at Middelburg in the

[21] *The Diary of Ralph Josselin*, ed. A. Macfarlane (London, 1976), p. 337: 4 Jan. 1654–5.

[22] *Cal. S. P. Dom., 1655*, p. 583.

[23] Ibid., p. 580.

[24] First printed and accepted as genuine by H. J. Koenen, *Geschiedenis der Joden in Nederland* (Utrecht, 1843), pp. 440–4. Proved false by J. Griffith, repr. *Trs. Jew. Hist. Soc. Eng.*, i. (1895), 49–54.

Netherlands is inscribed with the name 'Doctor Semvel'.[25] The forged Oxford diploma appears to have been Samuel's symbol of success to show his father on his return to Holland, for only ten days after the imaginary date of award, Samuel ben Israel was issued a pass to the Netherlands.[26] Events in England had moved sufficiently far along the road to readmission that the most sensible course seemed to be to fetch Menasseh from abroad and bring him to London where he could conduct negotiations personally.

The historic significance of this visit was not lost on the great rabbi of Amsterdam. Shortly before he left for London, he circulated a letter to world Jewry explaining the motivation behind his journey. He recounted the messages of support for readmission he had received from England, and noted that illness and political reasons had prevented him from making a personal appeal earlier. England would provide a convenient place of refuge for the oppressed Jews of Europe, especially those of Spain and France who were compelled to practise their faith in secrecy. Furthermore, he wrote,

I have been informed by letters, and by faithful correspondents, that to-day this English nation is no longer our ancient enemy, but has changed the Papistical religion and become excellently affected to our nation, as an oppressed people whereof it has good hope.

Menasseh closed his epistle, addressed particularly to the Jews of Italy and Holstein, with the hope that his readers would pray to God for sympathy for 'the most benign and valorous Prince, his Highness, the Lord PROTECTOR, and in those of his most prudent council'. The copy of the letter in the archives of Venice is graced with the autograph signature of Menasseh himself.[27]

Menasseh's encyclical letter is dated 2 September 5415 [1655]; the Jewish new year 5416 began on 22 September O.S., and it is possible that the rabbi arrived in London before that date and officiated at the religious ceremonies of the secret Jewish community in the City. In any case, we know that he

[25] Inscriptions on tombstones of Middelburg cemetery printed in *Trs. Jew. Hist. Soc. Eng.*, vii (1915), 123–46: see p. 127.

[26] *Cal. S. P. Dom., 1655*, p. 585.

[27] Printed Portuguese original with autograph signature in Venetian State Archives: photograph and Eng. trans. in *Trs. Jew. Hist. Soc. Eng.*, xi (1928), 116 and opp., 136.

lodged in the house of a certain Anthony Dolliver, who was probably not a Jew, 'in the *Strand* over against the *New-Exchange* in *London*.'[28] On the last day of October, Menasseh went in person to the meeting of the Council of State armed with copies of his *Humble Addresses*, which were formally received and noted in the Order Book.[29] This was the first official action of Menasseh ben Israel's mission to England. Menasseh stayed in London over two years, 'being very courteously received, and treated with much respect', until the public movement for Jewish readmission had run its course, and the rabbi was forced to appeal to Cromwell against the circumstances which had 'layd me prostrat at your feet, crying, Help, most noble prince for Gods sake'.[30]

II

The swift improvement of Jewish fortunes in England rapidly became a subject of international discussion, and as such soon came to the attention of exiled Royalists as well as ruling Parliamentarians. Sir Marmaduke Langdale informed Charles II as early as 29 June 1655 that 'the Jews, who are numerous and rich, . . . offer great matters for their privileges in England.'[31] By September, Charles's Secretary of State Sir Edward Nicholas was writing to a correspondent that 'Cromwell has agreed with the Jews, and some of their Rabbis are learning English, and will go from several parts to settle Judaism in England; they have already meetings in London.'[32] The source for this startling if exaggerated piece of intelligence was probably Richard Overton the Leveller, now flirting with the Royal-

---

[28] Menasseh ben Israel, *The Humble Addresses* (n.p., n.d.), p. 23. Thomason dated this tract as 5 Nov. 1655, and noted that it was printed in London. Another edn., with 26 pp. instead of 23 pp., was probably printed in Amsterdam, since it lacks Menasseh's address. See also L. Wolf, 'Menasseh ben Israel's Study in London', *Trs. Jew. Hist. Soc. Eng.*, iii (1899), 144–50.

[29] *Cal. S. P. Dom., 1655*, p. 402.

[30] Menasseh ben Israel, *Vindiciae Judaeorum* (n.p., 1656), p. 38; SP. 18/156, f. 173[r]: Menasseh to Cromwell, 17 Sept. 1657.

[31] *Calendar of the Clarendon State Papers*, iii, ed. W. D. Macray (Oxford, 1876), p. 42. On the Royalists generally, see M. Wilensky, 'The Royalist Position Concerning The Readmission of Jews to England', *Jew. Qly. Rev.*, n.s., xli (1950–1), 397–409 = trans. of *cap.* ix of his *Polemics Concerning the Return of the Jews to England* (Jerusalem, 1941 and 1943), which is in Hebrew. See also W. S. Samuel, 'Sir William Davidson, Royalist, (1616–1689) and the Jews', *Trs. Jew. Hist. Soc. Eng.*, xiv (1940), 39–79.

[32] *Cal. S. P. Dom., 1655*, p. 336: Nicholas to Jane, 14/24 Sept. 1655.

ists on the Continent. Overton reported to Langdale on 13 September 1655 that

I made inquiry into the condition of the Jewes, soe farr as was necessary. I find they are in conjunction with Cromwell; some of their Rabbies are learning English on purpose to live in England and must go speedily over. They have their meetings at London, and those Rabbies are to be sent thither for y^t purpose, soe y^t I am very glad I dealt with them by proxe; not one of them knowes any thing of me or what my intentions were. Had they, Cromwell should have known it.[33]

Sir Marmaduke Langdale immediately communicated this important information to Nicholas. Langdale wrote that he had discussed the Jewish question with Edward Sexby the Leveller 'who seamed much to favour them as necessary for a kingdome'. Langdale believed that the Jews and the Levellers agreed on many theological points in any case. Overton was assigned to report on the plans of the Dutch Jews in regard to England, through the assistance of his comrades in Holland.

The intelligence that Overton supplied could not but be greeted with alarm. 'I am very sorry they agre with Cromwell', Langdale confessed,

The Jewes are considerable all the world ouer, and the great masters of money. If his Ma^{ty} could either haue them or diuert them from Cromwell, it were a uery good seruice. I heard of this 3 yeares agone, but hoped the Jewes, that understand the interest of all the princes in the world, had bene to wise to aduenture themselues and estates under Cromwell, where they may by his death or other alteracion in that kingdome runn the hazard of an absolute ruine

Langdale thought that the chief reason for this lapse in traditional Jewish political acumen was that they hated monarchy in general, and particularly the English kings, in revenge for the re-expulsion of the tiny crypto-Jewish settlement during the reign of James I.[34]

Nicholas was initially inclined to discount Overton's information, and explained to Langdale that

[33] *The Nicholas Papers*, ed. G. F. Warner (Camden Soc., n.s., xl, l, lvii; 3rd ser., xxxi; 1886–1920), iii. 44. For Overton's views on Jewish toleration, see above, p. 173.

[34] Ibid., iii. 51: 20 Sept. 1655. For the re-expulsion, see E. R. Samuel, 'Portuguese Jews in Jacobean London', *Trs. Jew. Hist. Soc. Eng.*, xviii (1958), 182–5; *Cal. S. P. Ven.*, *1607—10*, p. 320; C. Roth, *A History of the Jews in England* (3rd edn., Oxford, 1964), p. 284.

It seemes to me somewhat incredible, for the reasons yourself gives, that there should be any cummunication betweene Cromwell and the Jewes, who are a very crafty and worldely-wise generation, and I am perswaded will not easily be drowne to settle where there . . . is so much uncerteynty of duration as there is in the present Gouvernment in England.

Nicholas promised to pass on the letter to Charles in any case.[35] Overton's intelligence about the Jews was confimed several days later, when Nicholas received a letter from Joseph Jane at The Hague, reporting that Menasseh, 'a learned Rabbi among them att Amsterdam' had gone to London, although 'he pretended only a short stay.' Jane wrote that he knew nothing of the purpose of Menasseh's visit.[36] The next month, Overton himself sealed the accuracy of his earlier letter. 'I have heard further in confirmation of y^t business of the Jewes out of England', he reported, 'they are confederates with the Monster'.[37]

The frantic letters passing among exiled Royalists, the secretive correspondence between Brussels, Delft, Cologne, and The Hague, highlight the effects of Menasseh ben Israel's historic voyage to England. It seemed especially paradoxical to the Royalists that Menasseh should come in the name of world Jewry, and as the apparent ambassador of the Jews in Amsterdam, when the Jewish merchants and traders of their acquaintance were ordinarily quite sober-minded, unwilling to hazard the precarious freedom they had won in a number of mercantile cities in northern Europe. As early as March 1648–9, Sir Edward Nicholas received a report from an informer at Rouen, who had asked an English-speaking Jew there for his opinion regarding Parliament and the English army 'now they had revoked the Laws that were made against the Jews'. He replied that 'he thought that there were no such villains in the world as they are, and believed that none of his religion would ever adventure themselves among such bloody traitors as had murdered their own King.'[38] Recent events seemed to have given the lie to this early Jewish reaction to the Cartwright petition. Nicholas and his group seem to have been unaware of the division within the Jewish community at Amsterdam, and of

[35] Hist. MSS Comm., lv, *Var. Coll.*, ii. 351–2: 18/28 Sept. 1655.
[36] *Nicholas Papers*, ed. Warner, iii. 62: 28 Sept. 1655.
[37] Ibid., iii. 95: 22 Oct. 1655.
[38] T. Carte, *A Collection Of Original Letters* (London, 1739), i. 233.

the reluctance of many Jews there to sanction the mission of their eccentric rabbi.[39]

Overton's information was substantially accurate despite the fact that Menasseh's list of requests had not yet been presented to Cromwell and the Council of State. These were not submitted until 13 November 1655, and give an indication of his objectives in the readmission campaign. The original text of the petition is in French, and includes seven points for the consideration of the Council. Menasseh's first request was for the general readmission of the Jews as ordinary citizens. He also pleaded for a public synagogue and religious toleration, and the right to consecrate a cemetery. Economic rights were not neglected: Menasseh asked for the privilege of trading freely in all varieties of merchandise. He also suggested that the Jews be permitted to try their own cases according to Mosaic law, with right of appeal to English civil law. The entire apparatus of readmission could be supervised by a person of quality who would receive the passports of the immigrant Jews and swear them to fidelity to England. Finally, Menasseh requested that if any anti-Jewish legislation remained in force, this might be annulled so as to leave the Jewish community in greater security. 'Lesquelles choses nous concedant', Menasseh pledged, 'nous demeurerons tousiours les tres affectionnes et obligez a prier dieu pour la prosperité de uostre altesse, & de uostre illustre et tres sage conseil.' The rabbi also hoped that God would give 'heureux succez a toutes les entreprises de uostre Serenissime Altesse Amen'.[40]

The Council of State received Menasseh's requests, and appointed a sub-committee to investigate the possibility of acceding to them. The committee consisted of seven of the eleven members of the Council present at the meeting of 13 November 1655, that is, President Henry Lawrence, Sir Gilbert Pickering, Sir Charles Wolseley, Lisle, Francis Rous, Major-General John Lambert, and Colonel William Sydenham.[41] The events of the next few days, however, are tainted with uncer-

[39] See C. Roth, 'The Mystery of the Resettlement', in his *Essays and Portraits* (Philadelphia, 1962), pp. 86–107.

[40] SP. 18/101, fos. 275^r–276^r. Eng. trans., SP. 18/101, f. 277^{r-v}; also in Bodl., MS Rawl. C 206, f. 107^{r-v}.

[41] *Cal. S. P. Dom., 1655–6*, p. 15.

tainty. We know that the next day, on 14 November, Lisle, Wolseley, and Pickering met with Lawrence to select the men who would be invited to attend the Whitehall Conference called to advise them on the suitability of Jewish readmission.[42] By that date, it was clear that whatever decision was reached, it would require the recommendation and endorsement of a broadly based body of community leaders.

There is a document preserved among the state papers which is clearly the report of the sub-committee itself, but as it is undated there is no way to determine if the seven men offered their advice to the Council before or after the Whitehall Conference which was summoned to advise it on the Jewish readmission question.[43] It seems likely, however, that the date tentatively given in the Calendar of State Papers, 13 November 1655, is correct since after the failure of the Whitehall Conference to produce the verdict that Cromwell desired, he could hardly have allowed the Council sub-committee to reach that conclusion in defiance of the advisory body which it had agreed to consult. The substance of Menasseh's petition was already known long before it was entered among the Council records, and the surviving documentation probably illustrates merely the outlines of the negotiations about the Jews during this month. Cromwell hoped for a swift conclusion of the preliminaries to Jewish readmission, which were probably arranged during the first fortnight in November, between Menasseh's initial overtures to the Council and the meeting at which the delegates to the Whitehall Conference were selected.

In any case, at some point, probably on 13 November 1655, the Council of State acknowledged the receipt of the sub-committee's report on the thesis 'That, the Jewes deservinge it, may be admitted into this nation to trade, and trafficke, and dwel amongst vs as providence shall giue occasion'. Their most significant concession was the decision that 'as to poynt of Conscience we judge lawfull for the Magistrate to admit', but only on the condition that an appended list of seven restrictions

---

[42] Ibid., p. 20.
[43] SP. 18/101, fos. 281ʳ–283ʳ. For two views on the dating of this document, see *Menasseh Ben Israel's Mission to Oliver Cromwell*, ed. L. Wolf (London, 1901), pp. xlv, liv–v, lxxxiv; and Roth, *History, cap.* vii.

were enforced. According to the report, there were a number of weighty reasons which militated against unrestricted Jewish immigration. The motives and grounds discussed in Menasseh's book, they thought, were 'such as we conceaue to be very sinfull for this or any Christian State to receaue them vpon.' Public Jewish worship might influence sober Christians from their devotions, and would certainly be scandalous in any case, 'evill in it selfe'. Jewish marriage and divorce customs were contrary to English law, and Jews could not be trusted to keep their oaths, nor should Englishmen forget the injuries against them 'in life, chastity, goods or good name' before the expulsion. The final objection foreshadowed the debate in the Whitehall Conference the next month: the authors of the report pointed out that 'great prejudice is like to arise to the natiues of this Coṁonwealth in matter of trade, which besides other dangers here mentioned we find very coṁonly suggested by the inhabitants of the City of London.'[44] The merchants would elaborate on this point at the Conference.

Nevertheless, despite these very vociferous objections to the resettlement of the Jews in England, the members of the subcommittee did not entirely rule out the possibility of readmission. Instead, they offered a list of seven conditions which, if satisfied, might protect Englishmen against the economic and religious rapacity of the Jews. The first of these was that the Jews permitted to come into England should be prohibited from maintaining 'any publicke Judicatoryes, whether Civill or Ecclesiasticall', because these would give the Jews somewhat more than the status of aliens. Jews should be prohibited from defaming Christianity, from working on Sunday, and from employing Christian servants. They should be excluded from public office, and should be restrained from taking revenge on any of their number who converted to Christianity. Jews should also be prohibited from printing anything 'which in the least opposeth the christian religion in our language'.[45] This last proviso was even more generous than it might appear at first glance, for by removing Hebrew books from the purview of the censor, Anglo-Jewry would have been spared the dangerous

---

[44] SP. 18/101, fos. 281^r–283^r.
[45] Ibid.

and degrading investigation of the Talmud so common on the Continent.

On 14 November 1655, Lisle, Wolseley, and Pickering met with Lawrence to select the delegates to the Whitehall Conference which was to advise the Council sub-committee and the Council itself as to whether these restrictions and safeguards would be sufficient to protect the nation against the likely disadvantages of Jewish immigration.[46] The list of delegates was presented and approved by the Council of State on the following day, and on 16 November 1655, each of the twenty-eight advisers was sent a letter signed by Lawrence summoning them

> to meete with a Comittee of the Councell on Tuesday the foureth of December next in yᵉ afternoone neare the Councell Chamber in Whitehall To the intent some proposalls made to his Highness in referrence to the nation of the Jewes may bee considered[47]

Over half of those who received this letter were primarily clergymen, including such well-known figures as Thomas Goodwin, John Owen, Matthew Newcomen, Anthony Tuckney, and Henry Jessey. Walter Strickland, one of the diplomats who took part in the abortive Dutch negotiations in 1651, was called, as was his partner on that occasion, Oliver St. John, although the latter declined to attend. Two other lawyers did appear, John Glynne, lord chief justice of the upper bench, and William Steel, chief baron of the Exchequer. The merchants were represented by Lord Mayor Dethick, Sir Christopher Packe the former lord mayor, Aldermen Riccard and Cressett, and Sheriff Thompson. William Kiffin the merchant–parson also attended, as did Benjamin Whichcote the provost of King's College, Cambridge, and Ralph Cudworth, the Regius professor of Hebrew. The function of this august gathering was 'to meet with the Committee', which took part in the discussion as well.[48] Menasseh ben Israel noted the care with which this Whitehall Conference was planned: perceiving England to be 'very tender hearted, and well-wishing to our sore-afflicted Nation', he pinned his hopes on the 'Assembly at *Whitehall*, of

---

[46] *Cal. S. P. Dom.*, *1655–6*, p. 20.
[47] SP. 25/76, pp. 383/378–384/379: Council of State Order Book, entry for 15 Nov. 1655.
[48] *Cal. S. P. Dom.*, *1655–6*, p. 23.

Divines, Lawyers, and Merchants, of different perswasions, and opinions.'[49]

III

The coming of Jews to England after an interval of over three centuries was a phenomenon which was bound to take on certain improbable, even bizarre characteristics. The period of the Whitehall Conference must therefore be seen through a haze of fantasy. For example, Joseph Spence, an eighteenth-century parson, heard a tale through Dr Francis Lockier, the dean of Peterborough born thirteen years after the Whitehall Conference, who had it from Lord Molesworth, who was supposedly in the room when the Jews offered Lord Godolphin £500,000 for purchase of the town of Brentford along with the right to settle there with full privileges of trade. It was said that they would have paid as much as one million pounds. According to Spence, the 'agent from the Jews said, that the affair was already concerted with the chiefs of their brethren abroad; that it would bring the richest of their merchants hither, and of course an addition of above twenty millions of money to circulate in the nation.' Molesworth pressed Godolphin to accept such a generous offer, but the latter wisely pointed out that the clergy and the merchants were sure to oppose: 'he gave other reasons too against it, and in fine it was dropped.'[50]

Other more contemporary accounts were not nearly so shop-worn, but were no less fantastic. Henry Townshend recorded in his diary a few weeks after the Conference had ended that Menasseh and the Jews were willing to pay handsomely for the privilege of resettlement, They offered '£100,000 fine and £50,000 per annum, and also securing all persons from any Jewish Merchant breaking out of the public stock, and to bring in a Bank of £300,000 at 4 per cent.'[51] Henry Fletcher Cromwell's seventeenth century biographer, claimed that the Jews would have paid £200,000 for readmission and toleration.[52] Giovanni Sagredo, the Venetian ambassador to Eng-

---

[49] Menasseh, *Vindiciae*, p. 38.

[50] J. Spence, *Anecdotes, Observations, and Characters* (2nd edn., London, 1858), p. 58.

[51] H. Townshend, *Diary*, ed. J. W. Willis (Worcestershire Hist. Soc., xxxi, 1915–20), p. 30.

[52] [H. Fletcher], *The Perfect Politician* (London, 1660), p. 291.

land, reported to the Doge three days after the Conference ended that

A Jew came from Antwerp and cleverly introduced himself to the Protector, having known him in that city when he was privately travelling in Flanders before he reached his present elevation. When introduced to his Highness he began not only to kiss but to press his hands and touching his whole body with the most exact care. When asked why he behaved so he replied that he had come from Antwerp solely to see if his Highness was of flesh and blood since his superhuman deeds indicated that he was more than a man and some divine composition issued from heaven.[53]

Forty years after the events themselves, the author of another Continental account would claim that it was the Jews of Asia who sent Jacob ben Azabel and David ben Eleazar of Prague, and Menasseh ben Israel to Cromwell to negotiate for the return of the Jews. While waiting to see Cromwell, they were said to have made a detour to the Bodleian and Cambridge University libraries, and then to have persuaded the Protector to sell them the most valuable books and manuscripts deposited there. Cromwell agreed to the purchase in order to take revenge against the Royalists in these centres of learning. On one of their cataloguing trips to Cambridge, the Jewish delegation found time to pay a visit to Huntingdon to establish from the parish registers whether Cromwell was of Jewish stock and if so, if he was of the Davidic line and therefore might be the Messiah. The writer maintained that it was the ridicule heaped on Cromwell by the news of this genealogical expedition, and a short pamphlet published about this time entitled 'Cromwell, Lion of the Tribe of Judah', that drove him to reject Jewish resettlement before his standing with the English people was damaged further.[54]

Fortunately, much more reliable accounts of the Whitehall Conference exist, even aside from the summaries printed in the news-sheets. Two complete narratives were both published anonymously, one by Henry Jessey the Baptist Saturday-

[53] *Cal. S. P. Ven., 1655–6*, pp. 160–1.

[54] Raguenet, *Histoire d'Olivier Cromwel* (Utrecht, 1692), ii. 83–6. Similarly, G. Leti, *La Vie D'Olivier Cromwel* (Amsterdam. 1746), iv. 371–6: ded. dated 10 Jan. 1694; and De Larrey, *Histoire D'Angleterre* (Amsterdam, 1707–13), p. 341. The Jews of Prague may not have been entirely mythical if Jacob ben Azabel is the same man as 'Jacob Aszik, Hebreo d'Praga' who sent a petition to Charles II after the Restoration for permission to farm taxes among the Jews: Hist. MSS Comm., xxii, *Leeds MSS*, p. 38.

Sabbatarian, and the other by Nathaniel Crouch, who wrote numerous works under the name of Robert or Richard Burton until his death in about 1725.[55] Jessey especially emphasized the interest which the Whitehall Conference had aroused throughout England, and acknowledged that he was moved to publish an accurate account of the meeting by demand from friends in the Provinces.[56]

The Whitehall Conference was opened by Cromwell himself on 4 December 1655 near the chambers of the Council of State. Menasseh's seven-point petition was read aloud, and Cromwell directed the Conference to consider whether the Jews were presenting unreasonable requests, and if not, whether it would be lawful to readmit them, and under what conditions. The terms of the debate having been set, Cromwell thereupon dismissed the Conference until 7 December, to enable the members to consider Menasseh's petition.[57] They reconvened on that day in the afternoon in a session which was, like the previous meeting, closed to outsiders. Some information inevitably leaked out, and the intelligence which appeared in the newspapers loyal to Cromwell could very well have been planted there by government officials. But whatever the source of these reports, it is clear that the broad outlines of the proceedings at Whitehall were communicated to the public, and that they usually square with the more reliable accounts which emerged long after the members had been dismissed and sent home. It is therefore instructive initially to examine the reflections of the Whitehall Conference in the most contemporaneous reports before supplementing them with the later complete chronicles of Jessey and Crouch.

References to the Conference while it was in session appear in a wide variety of locations, not only in newpapers, but also in private letters and the reports of foreign ambassadors. The first account of the meeting of 7 December 1655, in which the issue

---

[55] *Dict. Nat. Biog.*, *s.v.*, 'Burton, Robert or Richard'.

[56] [H. Jessey], *A Narrative Of the late Proceeds at White-Hall* (London, 1656); [N. Crouch], 'The Proceedings of the *Jews* in *England* in the year 1655', in *Two Journeys to Jerusalem*, ed. R. B[urton=Crouch] (London, 1719), pp. 167–74. This book was published in several forms under different titles, including *Memorable Remarks* and *Judaeorum Memorabilia*.

[57] [Crouch], 'Proceedings', pp. 167–8; *The Publick Intelligencer*, 10 (3–10 Dec. 1655), p. 159.

of Jewish readmission was debated initially, appeared in the news sheets: 'nothing was concluded, but there is another conference appointed to be on Wednesday next.'[58] The envoy of the Grand Duke of Tuscany in London, Francesco Salvetti, also reported that as yet opinion ran counter to Jewish readmission.[59] Among the most interesting of the private letters during these crucial days were those written by Captain Francis Willoughby, the navy commissioner at Portsmouth, to Robert Blackborne, the secretary to the Admiralty commissioners. Two days after the close of the second meeting of the Whitehall Conference, Blackborne provided Willoughby with a summary of the main events there, as far as he knew them. Willoughby was very concerned by these developments, and commented that if Jews were permitted to live in England, he hoped the next issue would be 'whether a nation shall be suffered to liue amongst vs to blaspheme Christ by a law'.[60]

Cromwell was worried as well, for the Conference seemed reluctant to expedite the readmission of the Jews. After the second meeting, the Council of State agreed to pack the Conference with supporters of Jewish toleration, and the names of Hugh Peter, Peter Sterry, and John Boncle (Bunkley) were added to the list of members.[61] Boncle's role at the Conference remains hidden,[62] and no record survives of Sterry's activities there.[63] Peter, as we have already seen, supported the Jewish case in print.[64] Arise Evans, the Royalist millenarian, told the

---

[58] Ibid., p. 160; *Mercurius Politicus*, 287 (5–13 Dec. 1655), pp. 5815–16.

[59] Salvetti's letters are preserved in the State Archives of Florence, but copies exist in Brit. Lib., Addit. MS 27962. A transcript from the Florence MSS with a partial trans. from the Italian was repr. by C. Roth, 'New Light on the Resettlement', *Trs. Jew. Hist. Soc. Eng.*, xi (1928), 112–42. For this reference, Francesco Salvetti to Senator Bali Gondi, 7/17 Dec. 1655, see ibid., pp. 128, 137–8.

[60] SP. 18/102, f. 5ʳ: Willoughby to Blackborne, 10 Dec. 1655.

[61] *Cal. S. P. Dom., 1655–6*, p. 52.

[62] All of the records of the Whitehall Conference refer to Boncle as 'Bulkeley' or 'Bulkley', always of Eton College, but surely this is the same man. Boncle was headmaster at Eton from 22 Aug. 1654 to 18 Sept. 1655, and a fellow there until the Restoration. He was a Cambridge man who was admitted MA of Oxford on 22 Dec. 1652 on special letters from Cromwell, and was appointed master of Charterhouse in 1653: A. Wood, *Fasti Oxonienses*, ed. P. Bliss (3rd edn., London, 1815–20), ii. 174; *The Eton College Register 1441–1698*, ed. W. Sterry (Eton, 1943), p. xxi; Vict. Cty. Hist., *Bucks*, ii. 197.

[63] V. de Sola Pinto, *Peter Sterry* (Cambridge, 1934), p. 31.

[64] See above, p. 174.

story that when he visited Peter in July 1652 with a copy of Sir Edward Spencer's answer to Menasseh ben Israel, Peter became very offended and threw Evans out of his chambers, ordering him to take the book with him.[65] In any case, even the attendance of Cromwell and the three philo-semites at the third meeting on 12 December 1655 proved ineffective: 'not comming to any conclusion, the conference is put off till Friday.'[66]

The obstacles in the path of Jewish readmission were becoming apparent, even to those who received only second- or third-hand reports of the Whitehall Conference and the deliberations there. Major-General Edward Whalley wrote to Thurloe from Nottingham on 12 December that

I am glad so godly and prudent a course is taken concerning the Jewes; yet cannot conceive the reason, why so great varietye of opinion should bee amongst such men, as I heare are called to consult about them. It seemes to me that there are both politique and divine reasons; which strongly make for theyre admission into a cohabitation and civill commerce with us.

Whalley did not neglect the economic factors of Jewish readmission. 'Doubtlesse to say no more,' he reminded Thurloe, 'they will bring in much wealth into this commonwealth'. But his grounds for Jewish readmission were not entirely self-serving: Whalley pointed out that it was unreasonable to pray for the conversion of the Jews while at the same time denying the means. 'Besides,' he recalled, 'when wee were aliens from the covenant of promise, they prayed for us.'[67]

Whalley could not have known the details of the meeting of 12 December, but by the time Willoughby sent his next letter to Blackborne, he already thanked him for his 'full relation' of that session. 'I know not but y^t m^r peeters came as neere as some others in his aduice', Willoughby mused,

itt is a busines of noe smaule consernm^t the lord in mercy direct in itt, they are indeed a people to whome many glorious promises are made: but they are a people as full of blasphemy as any vnder ye sun. a selfe seeking generation, & those psons in pticular who are ye greatest sticklers I feare minding little but there own accomodacōn: And whether they be able to proue them selues Jews is a question to mee[68]

[65] A. Evans, *An Eccho To The Voice from Heaven* (London, 1652), pp. 105–6.
[66] *Mercurius Politicus*, 287 (5–13 Dec. 1655), p. 5820.
[67] *Thurloe State Paper*, iv. 308.
[68] SP. 18/102, f. 74^r: Willoughby to Blackborne, 15 Dec. 1655.

Willoughby's obscure reference at the end of the letter was amplified in his next epistle, which he wrote two days later in response to Blackborne's report written on 15 December, the day after the fourth and penultimate session of the Whitehall Conference. Willoughby confessed that he found himself agreeing with Hugh Peter once again, especially in the light of the fact that 'there may be iust ground to question whether they be Jewes.' For it seemed to him that 'some of them may haue bin obserued to haue made but litle contience of there owne prinsiples'.[69] Willoughby, and many of his contemporaries, were only now coming to realize that thousands of Jews were forced to become marranos, and to practise their faith in total secrecy under the guise of Roman Catholicism.

While Francis Willoughby and Robert Blackborne were exchanging letters, the Tuscan envoy was reporting on the Conference to Italy. On 14 December 1655, the day of the penultimate meeting, Salvetti noted that 'very few of this nation are agreed to let them make their nest in these lands'.[70] This pessimistic assessment was reiterated by Thurloe himself, in a letter to Henry Cromwell, with the army in Ireland:

The point of conscience hath beene only controverted yet, viz. wheither it be lawefull to admitt the Jewes . . . The divines doe very much differ in their judgements about it, some beinge for their admittance upon fittinge cautions, others are in expresse termes against it upon any termes whatsoever. The like difference I finde in the counsell, and soe amongst all Christians abroad.

Thurloe noted that readmission was being 'debated with much candor and ingenuitye, and without any heat.' Nevertheless, although the Jews had made 'an earnest desire' to Cromwell for readmission, Thurloe was 'apt to thinke, that nothinge will be done therein.'[71]

Thurloe's assessment of the first four sessions of the Whitehall Conference was probably the most well-informed of the contemporaneous reflections of these meetings. Although not a member of the Conference itself, Thurloe may be assumed to have been privy to the closed sessions between 4–14 December 1655. It was only in the spring of 1656, when Henry

---

[69] SP. 18/102, f. 76ʳ: W. to B., 17 Dec. 1655.
[70] Salvetti to Senator Bali Gondi, 14/24 Dec. 1655: repr. Roth, 'New Light', pp. 128–9, 138.
[71] *Thurloe State Papers*, iv. 321.

Jessey published his eye-witness account, that full details of these private meetings were revealed to all. Crouch's narrative seems to have been copied directly from Jessey's, but with the important addition of the names of the speakers so that we can isolate the philo-semites at the Whitehall Conference. Jessey neatly divided the range of opinion there into three parts. 'The most' feared that if the Jews were readmitted they would seduce and cheat the English. 'The Major part' thought that the Jews might be tolerated if suitable precautions could be devised. 'Some' argued that once these safeguards were invented the English positively had a duty to readmit the Jews, not merely the opportunity to allow their immigration.[72]

The delegates in the first group, those who believed that England would suffer from Jewish readmission, were primarily merchants, although there were some divines who argued that 'though never such cautions to prevent those evils were prescribed, yet they would not be observed; and therefore they could not consent to their coming.'[73] Matthew Newcomen even argued that if the Jews were readmitted they might begin offering children to Moloch. He reminded scoffers that although such practices might seem abhorrent to sober Christians, the opinions of the Quakers and the Ranters also seemed unreasonable, yet there were many who subscribed to them.[74] Nevertheless, it was London merchants who dominated this faction at the Whitehall Conference: their argument was that Jewish readmission would enrich foreigners at the expense of Englishmen. Even some divines worried about showing mercy to the Jews at the expense of the merchants. The philo-semites pointed out that since the Jews were primarily international traders, and did not deal in 'Husbandry, nor buying houses, nor in Manufactures', therefore:

the Jews coming and so trading might tend to the bringing lower the prizes of all sorts of commodities imported; and to the furtherance of all that have commodities vendible to be exported; and to the benefit of most of our Manufactures (where they shal live) by their buying of them. And thus, though the Merchants gains were somewhat abated, it might tend to the benefit of very many in our Nation, even in outward things, besides the hopes of their conversion; which time (it's hoped) is now at hand, even at the door.

[72] [Jessey], *Narrative*, pp. 2–3.
[73] Ibid., p. 2.
[74] Ibid., p.8; [Crouch], 'Proceedings', pp. 168–9.

This last somewhat incongruous point, Jessey noted parenthetically, 'was spoken of at a more private meeting.'[75]

The second faction, a majority of the delegates according to Jessey, believed that the Jews might be readmitted under suitable precautions. This argument enjoyed the weighty backing of Justices Glynne and Steel, who revealed to the Conference that 'there is no Law against their coming'. This judgement was quite correct, in fact, since the Jews had been expelled by royal order of Edward I, rather than by Parliament, and presumably a protectoral decree could countermand the expulsion. Glynne and Steel recommended that Jews be permitted in England for a trial period, under 'tearms, and agreements'. If the Jews failed to live up to expectations, they could be expelled once again with 'no just cause of exceptions.'[76] This simple declaration by two of the leading lawyers in the land was very influential in the Conference, and Jessey alluded to it several times in his narrative. The precise date on which this crucial piece of information was revealed is not known, but on 14 December 1655, the day of the penultimate session, John Evelyn recorded in his diary that 'Now were the *Jewes* admitted'.[77] The statement by Glynne and Steel is the only one which might have prompted such a conclusion.

Here again, the arguments put forward by delegates in this second faction were divine as well as politique. Jessey himself elaborated on the hope that the Jews might be converted if exposed to the pure light of the English Reformation. He argued that the English were especially likely to promote their conversion because gentiles must provoke the Jews to jealousy and then emulation, and examples of holy life were prevalent in England.[78] Some divines had explained that although they earnestly wished for the conversion of the Jews, they worried lest their readmission serve to provide yet another sect to mislead Christians. Lawrence and Lambert therefore replied that sectarians, who 'are carried away under notion of further light, or of new discoveries of Christ, or the Gospel' were unlikely to become converts to Judaism, which denies the most

---

[75] [Jessey], *Narrative*, pp. 8–9.
[76] Ibid., pp. 5, 8, 9; [Crouch], 'Proceedings', pp. 169–72.
[77] *Diary of John Evelyn*, ed. E. S. de Beer (Oxford, 1955), iii. 163.
[78] [Jessey], *Narrative*, p. 4.

fundamental points of all Christian faiths. In any case, they noted, there was so much in Judaism which was 'very ridiculous' that it was unlikely Jews could win many proselytes in England.[79] Another delegate pointed out that it was unfair to permit Turks to trade and enter England if this privilege were denied to the Jews.[80] In short, this second group would have permitted Jewish immigration, with the understanding that certain safeguards— such as prohibitions against proselytizing, cheating, blaspheming Christ and Christianity— would have to be instituted to protect native Englishmen.

The third faction at the Whitehall Conference argued that not only did the Jews deserve to be readmitted, but England had a positive duty to readmit them, and if they failed to grasp this opportunity, the vengeance of God would be upon their heads. Justice Steel provided the Conference with a long summary of the history of the Jews in England before the expulsion in 1290. As one of the participants commented, the only conclusion that could be drawn from this sorry tale was that the Jews under English rule had '*suffered very great injuries,* and cruelties, and murders . . . as our own Chronicles shew'. This injustice was especially reprehensible because even after the Jews rejected Jesus Christ, and God rejected them, they still remained His chosen people, 'beloved for their Fathers sakes'. If God plagued Israel after Saul's death until justice had been done to the mistreated Gibeonites, how much more so would England be afflicted if some kind of restitution were not made to the Jews? Readmission to England was particularly important to the Jews at this time, it was pointed out by Jessey and others at the Conference, because they were suffering in eastern Europe in the Swedish wars, which had the additional effect of interrupting the flow of alms to the Jews of Jerusalem, who in turn were being persecuted by the Turks. 'Other Jews in several Nations persecuted by Papists,' Jessey reminded the members, 'unless they will turn Papists: many of these desiring by their Letters to *R. Manasses Ben Israel (as he said he had shewed to the Lord Protector)* that he would intreat favour of our State'. Although the Lord may be displeased with the Jews, he 'hath a

[79] Ibid., p. 8; [Crouch], 'Proceedings', p. 168.
[80] [Jessey], *Narrative*, p. 8.

special eye to them; observing all the unkinde carriage of others towards them'. In any case, Englishmen knew the burdens of exile and persecution under Mary, and 'should the more pity and harbour persecuted strangers, especially the persecuted Jews'.[81]

The millenarian aspect of Jewish readmission was especially pertinent for this most philo-semitic faction at the Whitehall Conference. 'In our Nation', noted Joseph Caryl, 'the good people generally have more beleeved the promises touching the calling of the Jews, and the great riches and glory that shall follow to Jews, and us Gentiles'. These heavenly goals still lay before them, and in England the faithful 'have (and do stil) more often, and earnestly pray for it, then any other Nation that we have heard of.'[82] Philip Nye and Thomas Goodwin joined Caryl in putting forward this third position most vociferously before the Conference. All of the philo-semites at the meeting agreed that once the Jews were readmitted to England, the way would be clear for them to convert to Christianity. The only technical question still unresolved was whether they would suddenly be converted together after the personal appearance of Christ on earth, or as individuals 'as of French, &c.'[83]

The published narratives, personal letters, and official accounts make it abundantly clear that Menasseh understated the point when he remarked that the members of the Whitehall Conference were 'of different perswasions, and opinions. Whereby mens judgements, and sentences were different.'[84] This assessment was written in April 1656, long after the final, and public, meeting of the Conference on 18 December 1655. Unfortunately for the advocates of Jewish readmission, by the time the Conference reconvened for what was to be the last time, a number of events had already turned the tide against any formal resettlement.

IV

Menasseh's presentation of a seven-point petition to the Council of State on 31 October 1655 for open toleration of the Jews

---

[81] Ibid., pp. 3–7, 9; [Crouch], 'Proceedings', pp. 169–73.
[82] Ibid., p. 173; [Jessey], *Narrative*, pp. 6–8.
[83] Ibid., pp. 3–4, 5–6; [Crouch], 'Proceedings', pp. 172–3.
[84] Menasseh, *Vindiciae*, p. 38.

was, as we have seen, the culmination of a process which had begun years before, at least from 1649 when John Dury sent his query to the Dutch rabbi. Yet the accounts of the Whitehall Conference that have survived neglect to mention Dury or Samuel Hartlib, two of the men who forged a powerful tool for readmission out of the useful but inert material of abstract philo-semitism.

During the critical period of the Whitehall Conference, however, John Dury was on the Continent, acting as Cromwell's unofficial agent in the Netherlands, Switzerland, and Germany. Hartlib's own general views on the subject are clear, although he seems to have wanted to keep the details to himself once the Conference was under way. This is the impression he gives in a letter to Dr John Worthington, one of his most faithful correspondents. 'I suppose our friends that are members of it will write freely & impartially of that business', Hartlib explained, but he revealed his hope 'that the Caraites might be invited hither and encouraged, being such as begin to look towards their engraffing again.'[85]

Dury's absence from England obliged Hartlib to write to him at Cassel for his view on readmission, now that toleration of the Jews had become more of a practical proposition.[86] Dury did not complete his reply until 8 January 1656, despite his claim that it had been written 'in haste', and by then the Conference had already been over for three weeks. Nevertheless, the document is important because it illustrates the development in the attitude of one committed and well-informed philo-semite, who began to waver when faced with the prospect of living Jews rather than theological abstractions. Others at the Conference shared his fears, and his views were expressed there in any case, as we shall see, through Thomas Barlow.

Dury argued that the admission of the Jews into a commonwealth was not only lawful, but 'expedient'. His outline of the conditions under which Jews could be tolerated demonstrate his conviction that the prime purpose of Jewish immigration

---

[85] *The Diary and Correspondence of Dr. John Worthington*, ed. J. Crossley (Chetham Soc., xiii, xxxvi, cxiv, 1847–86), i. 78: 12 Dec. 1655. The Karaites are a Jewish sect that rejects the rabbinic tradition, including the Talmud, and relies instead on Scripture alone.

[86] Ibid., i. 83: Hartlib to Worthington, 10 Mar. 1655–6.

was conversion. Jews were to be compelled to listen to pro-selytizing sermons without debate, and were to be forbidden to discuss their religion with Christians. Dury discounted any economic factors, and sought to readmit the Jews on purely religious and conversionist grounds. The English government, in turn, was to safeguard the rights of Jews in every country, by including special clauses in contracts with nations that regu-larly oppressed their Jewish populations. Dury listed a number of other restrictive conditions, and minimized his earlier mil-lenarian ideals: 'the times and seasons of their deliverance,' he explained, 'are in God's hand alone, and that we are very much inclined to mistake in conjectures of that nature'.[87]

Dury's cautious reply is almost surprising in light of his powerful philo-semitic ideals. Dury and Samuel Hartlib, the two Baconian bulwarks of their Comenian 'Invisible College', had begun to concern themselves with the Jews by the early 1640s. It was one of these men who published the anonymous *Englands Thankfulnesse*, which proposed a 'care to make Christ-ianity lesse offensive, and more knowne unto the Jewes, then now it is, and the Jewish State and Religion as now it standeth more knowne unto Christians.' This knowledge was especially desirable because the 'Jewish Nation is neither the smallest Nation of the world in number, nor in respect of God's Councell revealed concerning them, the smallest of esteeme, although hitherto very little regarded.'[88] When Hartlib received a £50 grant from Parliament to carry him through a difficult financial period in January 1645, he promised to direct his efforts to have 'the most remotest Parts from Christendome and our Elder Brethren (I meane the Jews) taken into serious considerations and overtures'. Dury was working on plans to convert the Jews as early as 1646, and thought of using men like Adam Boreel,

---

[87] J. Dury, *A Case of Conscience, Whether it be lawful to admit Jews into a Christian Common-wealth?* (London, 1656): repr. *The Harleian Miscellany*, ed. W. Oldys (London, 1808–13), vii. 251–6, esp. p. 255. The original MS of Dury's reply is now Brit. Lib., Addit. MS 4459, fos. 164ʳ–165ᵛ, although it is not so entered in the catalogue. Fos. 166ʳ–167ʳ are Dury's note concerning the Jews in Hesse, which he promised to send to Hartlib.

[88] [Anon.], *Englands Thankfulnesse* (London, 1642), repr. *Samuel Hartlib and The Advancement of Learning*, ed. C. Webster (Cambridge, 1970), pp. 90–7, esp. p. 95. For the philo-semitism of this group generally, see H. R. Trevor-Roper, 'Three Foreigners: The Philosophers of the Puritan Revolution', in his *Religion the Reformation and Social Change* (London, 1967), pp. 237–93.

Christian Ravius, and Menasseh ben Israel for that purpose. He believed that a Latin translation of the Talmud might help the 'common sort of Jews' to improve their understanding of the rudiments of their own religion. Dury was thinking of the Jews again in 1649, and wrote that he thought God would convert them soon. A translation of the kabbalistic books might be useful, he felt, and could be completed by either Johann Stephan Rittangel, professor of oriental languages at Königsberg University, or Boreel from Holland, who was already editing the Mishna in Latin.[89] By the end of 1649 he was corresponding with Menasseh concerning the lost ten tribes, and would soon introduce the narrative of Montezinos to the English public.[90]

Dury and Hartlib became more interested in the practical aspects of the Jewish question after Menasseh's *Hope of Israel* was published in 1650. Hartlib's university scheme included a college 'For Conversions or correspondency of Jews and advancement of Oriental Language and Learning'.[91] We have already seen Dury and Hartlib at work in the search for a universal language which might restore Hebraic clarity. Dury's plan for a Reformed School took note of the fact that the language 'which in an extraordinary way will in due time by useful hereunto, is Hebrew, and the Oriental Tongues which are a kinne unto it.'[92]

Once the Whitehall Conference was in session, however, these Hebraic sentiments had to be defined with more precision. Even before his complete reply reached Hartlib, Dury wrote to England on 18 December 1655, the day of the last session of the Whitehall Conference, explaining that although Jews might be of some use in the war against Spain, restraints must be placed on their activities nonetheless. Dury sent the

---

[89] G. H. Turnbull, *Hartlib, Dury and Comenius* (London, 1947), pp. 26, 257, 261. Hartlib still believed in 1660 that the 'world may not expect any great happiness before the conversion of the Jews be first accomplished' (Worthington, *Diary*, ed. Crossley, i. 249–50: H. to W., 17 Dec. 1660).

[90] See above, pp. 143–4, 151–2, 154.

[91] C. Webster, *The Great Instauration* (London, 1975), p. 223; *Hartlib*, ed. Webster, p. 60.

[92] J. Dury, *The Reformed School* (London, n.d.): repr. *Hartlib*, ed. Webster, p. 155, tentatively dated 1650. Cf. J. M. Batten, *John Dury Advocate of Christian Reunion* (Chicago, 1944), p. 138.

fair copy of his proposals to Thurloe, who had also requested Dury's opinion of Menasseh's controversial plan.[93] Soon after he dispatched his reply, however, Dury received a copy of Menasseh's specific petition to the Council of State, and became so concerned that he amended even his moderate report in a letter to Hartlib dated 22 January 1656. England would do best 'to go warily, and by degrees' concerning the Jews, he thought, and Menasseh's request was excessive in any case. Dury noted that the Jews 'have ways beyond all other men, to undermine a state, and to insinuate into those that are in offices, and prejudicate the trade of others; and therefore, if they be not wisely restrained, they will, in short time, be oppressive; if they be such as are here in Germany.' This final judgement appeared as a postscript when the pamphlet was published in June 1656.[94]

John Dury was hardly an opponent of the Jews: even the year after his pamphlet appeared, Dury was involved with Henry Jessey in providing charity for the Jews of Jerusalem who were reduced to poverty when the Swedish navy's blockade of eastern Europe halted the flow of Jewish alms.[95] Dury's aim was to convert the Jews to Protestant belief, and he wished to maintain adequate safeguards to prevent them from infecting others with Judaizing heresies. Dury's pamphlet reached London far too late to have any effect on the Conference proceedings, but this viewpoint was expressed in a work by Thomas Barlow which seems to have been completed before the meetings at the request of one of the delegates. Barlow, librarian of the Bodleian during the Civil War and Commonwealth and later the bishop of Lincoln, similarly expressed a belief in the principle of Jewish toleration, but limited their freedom with a list of seventeen conditions. Barlow's Jews were forbidden to employ Christian servants, or to leave their homes on Good Friday. They were required to wear distinguishing dress and to submit themselves to religious persuasion by Christians.[96] Both Dury

---

[93] Turnbull, *Hartlib, Dury and Comenius*, p. 282.

[94] Dury, *Conscience*, p. 256.

[95] [Anon.], *The Life and Death of Mr. Henry Jessey* (n.p., 1671), pp. 69, 75; see also [H. Jessey?], *An Information, Concerning The Present State of the Jewish Nation in Europe and Judea* (London, 1658), p.13.

[96] T. Barlow, 'The Case of the Jews', repr. in his *Several Miscellaneous and Weighty Cases of Conscience* (London, 1692), pp. 67–73.

and Barlow were primarily concerned with the effect that Jewish readmission would have on the state as a whole, over and above any benefits which might accrue to individual Jews by embracing Christ. A 'Publique good is nothing else but the universall private good of every one in the life of God,' Dury explained, 'for that which serveth the turne of some only, although they may be many, and even the greater part, is not to be counted truly Publique'.[97] Dury and Barlow therefore helped to support the advocates of Jewish readmission at Whitehall, although arguably had the Jews been readmitted according to their abridgements of the medieval codes, the legal position of Anglo-Jewry might have become even more precarious than it was already.

The most influential opponent of readmission was William Prynne, the great polemicist, who followed the proceedings of the first four meetings of the Whitehall Conference with a less sympathetic eye. According to his own account, Prynne was accosted at Whitehall by Philip Nye, hurrying past on his way to the Conference, who informed him of the lawyers' judgement that there was no legal bar to Jewish readmission, and wondered if Prynne would agree with this view. Prynne replied that the Jews had been expelled by both king and Parliament, and could not be readmitted without the consent of the Commons. Prynne pointed out that the principal causes of the expulsion included the facts that the Jews 'had been formerly great Clippers and Forgers of Mony, and had crucified three or four Children in *England* at least'. Nye, who by this time was most anxious to arrive at the Council chambers before the session began, declined to accept Prynne's reading of the histories.[98]

Whether or not it was Philip Nye who provoked Prynne into writing his famous attack on the readmission of the Jews is relatively unimportant. But Prynne's testimony is rendered slightly suspect, not only because he was such a strong critic of readmission, but also because his account of Nye's views does

---

[97] J. Dury, *A Motion Tending to the Publick Good* (London, 1642): repr. *Hartlib*, ed. Webster, p.99. See M. L. Wilensky, 'Thomas Barlow's and John Dury's Attitude Towards the Readmission of the Jews to England', *Jew. Qly. Rev.*, n.s., 1 (1959–60), 167–75, 256–68, basically trans. of his *Return*, pp. 124–31, 164–74. Also, see S. Levy, 'John Dury and the English Jewry', *Trs. Jew. Hist. Soc. Eng.*, iv (1903), 76–82.

[98] W. Prynne, *A Short Demurrer To the Jewes* (2nd edn., London, 1656), i. sig. A3^{r-v}.

not entirely square with the reports of Jessey and Crouch. In the *Demurrer*, Prynne has Nye agreeing with the author's belief

That it was now a very ill time to bring in the Jews, when the people were so dangerously and generally bent to Apostacy, and all sorts of Novelties and Errors in Religion; and would sooner turn Jews, than the Jews Christians.[99]

Nye seems to have expressed exactly the opposite point of view at the Whitehall Conference, arguing that it was incumbent upon England to readmit the Jews precisely because they were in great straits on the Continent. In any case, Prynne mentions throughout his text that the *Demurrer* was in some sense a reply to Nye's doubts of the veracity of the traditional accusations against the Jews before the expulsion, and in this aim he succeeds admirably.[100]

Prynne explained that once the Whitehall Conference was already in session he began to collect materials hurriedly so that his book 'might come into the world in *due season,* before any *final Resolves* upon the late *Whitehall Debates*'. The first part of his *Demurrer* was already in the hands of interested delegates before the final meeting on 18 December 1655, and therefore was probably one of the most important factors in the ultimate failure of the Conference to come to any formal conclusion about the desirability of readmission. Prynne wrote afterwards that he hoped both parts of his work together would provide 'a perpetual Barr to the Antichristian Iews re-admission into England, both in this new-fangled age, & all future Generations; maugre all printed pleas, and Endeavors for their present Introduction'.[101]

The success of Prynne's work was no doubt due to the fact that it is not by any means an hysterical denunciation of the Jews and their alleged crimes. Instead, it is, as Prynne himself described the work, an 'exact *Chronological Relation*' which he had 'collected out of the best Historians and Records'.[102] His report of foreign practice with regard to the Jews made a neat summary of many of the diffuse observations scattered throughout the travel literature. This basic narrative was supplemented with description of the obstacles to readmission to

[99] Ibid., i. sig. A3ᵛ.
[100] [Crouch], 'Proceedings', pp. 172–3; [Jessey], *Narrative*, pp. 3–6.
[101] Prynne, *Demurrer*, ii. sig. A2.
[102] Ibid., i. title page.

be found both in English law and in Scripture. Prynne even refused to accept that the Jews might be called at the End of Days. Yet in spite of his declared hostility to the Jews, Prynne's history remains a faithful compilation of the materials available in his day for a history of the Jews in England. His horrific account of the almost-forgotten ritual murder calumnies regarding William of Norwich in 1144 and Little St. Hugh of Lincoln in 1255, added to the condemnation of imagined economic crimes before the expulsion, could not help but influence the delegates at the final meeting of the Whitehall Conference.[103]

For our purposes here, the most interesting aspect of the *Demurrer* is Prynne's account of contemporary public opinion regarding the Jews, and the way in which his attack helped to feed the sense of panic among opponents of readmission at the end of 1655. He claimed that en route from Whitehall to his rooms at Lincoln's Inn, he encountered seven or eight maimed soldiers on crutches who begged money from him. 'We must now all turn Jews,' one of them told his companion, 'and there will be nothing left for the poor.' By the back gate of Lincoln's Inn he met another group of poor people, who cried to each other, 'They are all turned Devils already, and now we must all turn Jews.' Ralph Josselin, the Essex preacher, also recorded the 'great rumours of the Jewes being admitted into England, hopes thereby to convert them' which abounded before the last session. Even Josselin, who was a student of Hebrew, an admirer of Menasseh ben Israel and deeply concerned about the fate of the Jews, prayed that the Lord would 'hasten their conversion, and keepe us from turning aside from Christ to Moses of which I am very heartily afraid'. Prynne noted that it was 'unexpected concurrent Providences and Speeches' such as these which prompted him to summarize, with proper footnotes, the record of the Jews in England before 1290.[104]

Prynne's reasoned if critical summary of Anglo-Jewish history was rendered more polemical with the recent publication

---

[103] Cf. M. Wilensky, 'The Literary Controversy in 1656 Concerning the Return of the Jews to England', *Proc. Am. Acad. Jew. Res.*, xx (1951), 357–93, basically trans. of his *Return*, pp. 132–64.

[104] Prynne, *Demurrer*, i. sig. A3ᵛ–4ʳ; *The Diary of Ralph Josselin*, ed. A. Macfarlane (London, 1976), p. 358: 16 Dec. 1655.

of a translation of a century-old work by Sebastian Münster,
the German cosmographer. The translator was a professional
convert from Judaism named Paul Isaiah alias Eleazar Bargishai, who included an anti-Jewish commentary of his own.
Isaiah also claimed that

though perhaps there may not be now in *England*, any great numbers of
professed Iewes (some to my owne knowledge there are, who have their
synagogues, and there exercise Iudaisme) Yet, they who live here, as often as
they are bound to use their office of Prayer (which is twice a day) so often are
they bound to blaspheme Christ, and to curse him, and all true Christians
which beleeve in him.[105]

Prynne's scholarly but hostile compendium, reinforced by
Isaiah's denunciation, weakened the position of the English
philo-semites, so that by what was to be the final meeting of the
Whitehall Conference on 18 December 1655, the proponents of
Jewish readmission must have lost all hope of a formal reset-
tlement.

V

Although it appears that Cromwell intended the meeting of 14
December to conclude the issue, another session was scheduled
for 18 December 1655, and unlike the others, this one was open
to the public. One of those who pressed in among the crowd was
the young Paul Rycaut, later to become well-known for his
activities in the East, and among the Jews for his efforts to have
them expelled after the Restoration. Rycaut was very impressed by Cromwell's address to the assembled delegates, and
remembered years later that he had never heard a man speak so
well in his life. According to Rycaut, Cromwell first allowed the
Jews to present their case, although there is no record that
Menasseh ben Israel attended any of the sessions of the
Whitehall Conference.[106] More likely, someone read the rabbi's
proposals to the Conference members and the crowd of
interested observers, since Menasseh's seven-point petition
was printed in the news-sheets as part of the report of the

---

[105] P. Isaiah, *The Messias of the Christians* (London, 1655), sig. A7. Isaiah's previous
anti-Jewish works were: 'E. Bargishai', *A Brief Compendium of the vain Hopes* (London,
1652); P. Isaiah, *A Vindication of the Christians Messiah* (London, 1654). For more on him,
see above, p. 33.

[106] Spence, *Anecdotes*, pp. 58–9.

meeting.[107] Rycaut recounted that Cromwell then asked the clergy to summarize their position, which they did in most negative terms. The Protector reminded them that the Jews would one day be called into the Church, and pointed out that it was the duty of all good Christians to work towards that end. Furthermore, given the exalted and purified state of religion in England, it would be particularly desirable to readmit the Jews so as to prevent them from falling into the hands of the idolators on the Continent. The merchants then spoke against the Jews and argued that they would take trade from Englishmen and behave dishonestly. Cromwell seemed to agree with them and began to speak of the Jews as the most contemptible and despicable people on earth. After this diatribe he is quoted asking the merchants, 'Can you really be afraid . . . that this mean despised people should be able to prevail in trade and credit over the merchants of England, the noblest and most esteemed merchants of the whole world!'[108]

Unfortunately, despite the attractive qualities of Rycaut's narrative, it retains a somewhat fairy-tale flavour, especially in light of his inaccurate conclusion that, having silenced the critics of readmission, Cromwell 'was at liberty to grant what he desired to the Jews.'[109] In any case, although Rycaut's memory may have been faulty after decades, we may accept his account of the agenda of the final meeting, if not his conclusions.

The more reliable reports of Jessey and Crouch continue the narrative to the very end of the session, and provide the text of Cromwell's closing address. In dismissing the Whitehall Conference. Cromwell reminded the delegates that he had no interest in Jewish readmission which was not congruent with scripture, 'and that since there was a Promise of their Conversion, means must be used to that end, which was the preaching of the Gospel, and that could not be had unless they were permitted to reside where the Gospel was preached.' He had hoped that the Conference would have come to a definite conclusion at least in regard to the theoretical virtue of Jewish toleration, if not to the

---

[107] *The Publick Intelligencer*, 12 (17–24 Dec. 1655), pp. 191–2; *Mercurius Politicus*, 289 (20–7 Dec. 1655), pp. 5842–3.

[108] Spence, *Anecdotes*, pp. 58–9.

[109] Ibid., p. 59.

legality of readmission, but unfortunately this was not to be. The entire question now seemed even more insoluble, Cromwell noted, but he hoped the Lord would direct him and the Council of State to the good of the nation. 'And thus,' Jessey concludes, 'was the dismission of that Assembly.'[110]

The immediate reaction to the failure of the Whitehall Conference to perform according to expectation is difficult to determine. Jessey noted that throughout the Conference, Cromwell 'shewed a favourable inclination towards our harbouring the afflicted Jews'.[111] Thurloe wrote to Henry Cromwell in Ireland the week after the last meeting, informing him that he had no more news about the Whitehall Conference. 'I doe assure you', he noted sardonically,

that his highnes is put to exercise every day with the peevishnes and wrath of some persons heere. But the Lord enables hym with comfort to beare the hard speeches and reproaches, which he is loaded with from day to day; and helps hym to returne good for evill, and good will for their hatred, which certeinelye is the way to heape coales of fire upon their head, to melt them, and bringe them into a better frame and temper[112]

Some members of the Council of State, Jessey claimed, supported Jewish readmission while others declined to allow it, no doubt putting Cromwell in this bad humour.[113]

The only other hint of official reaction to the unfruitful results of the Conference at Whitehall can be gleaned from the pages of the two semi-official news-sheets of the Commonwealth. Significantly, it was not until the final meeting of the Whitehall Conference was over that the newspapers printed Menasseh's seven-point petition. Earlier editions referred rather vaguely to 'the Proposals of *Manasseh Ben Israel* on the behalf of the Jewish Nation'. As to the outcome of the Conference, the editors merely noted that it 'ended without any further adjournment' after Cromwell had expressed himself 'thereupon with indifferency and moderation'. At the end of the day, it was reported, 'nothing at all hath been concluded as to

---

[110] [Crouch], 'Proceedings', pp. 173–4; [Jessey], *Narrative*, p. 9.
[111] Ibid., p. 10.
[112] *Thurloe State Papers*, iv. 343.
[113] [Jessey], *Narrative*, p. 10.

their admission; his Highness proceeding in this, as in all other Affairs, with good advice, and mature deliberation.'[114]

Nevertheless, one is left with the impression that the news was reported with careful regard for the effect it would have on the readers, and even on the delegates themselves. The numbers in which the third meeting was reported, that is to say the first meeting in which Peter, Sterry, and Boncle were included to support the proponents of Jewish readmission, also contained accounts of the unhappy plight of the Jews in eastern Europe. In one number it was reported that the Jews of Poland had presented a petition to the Emperor for protection, as they had 'been soundly pillaged, and many massacred in *Poland*.'[115] A later issue mentioned that many Jews had come to Hamburg, having been 'ruinated and plundred of all their Goods in Poland.'[116] At the same time, a news-sheet reported the impending visit to Vienna of the 'Patriarch or Generall of the Jewes' from Jerusalem connected with the appearance of an 'unknown starr very bright going from the East towards the North.'[117] When examined alongside of the chronology of the debates at Whitehall, it appears that Menasseh's supporters were engaging in a rather crude attempt to manage the news.

The Italian envoys, of course, had their own sources of information, even if their accounts were not entirely accurate. Nevertheless, the letters they sent back to Venice and Tuscany provide virtually the only record which has survived of the after-effects of the Whitehall Conference during January and early February, when the public prosecution of Jewish readmission ground to a halt. Salvetti, the Tuscan envoy, wrote on 21/31 December 1655 that although the Conference had come to no conclusion, it was merely postponed rather than dismissed.[118] Sagredo, the Venetian ambassador to England, agreed that after 'long disputes and late at night the meeting dissolved without any conclusion, the discussion being postponed to

---

[114] *Mercurius Politicus*, 289 (20–7 Dec. 1655), pp. 5842–3; *The Publick Intelligencer*, 12 (17–24 Dec. 1655), pp. 191–2.

[115] *The Publick Intelligencer*, 11 (10–17 Dec. 1655), p. 169.

[116] *Mercurius Politicus*, 289, p. [5841].

[117] *Mercurius Politicus*, 228 (13–20 Dec. 1655), p. 5831.

[118] Salvetti to Senator Bali Gondi; and to the Grand Duke, 21/31 Dec. 1655: repr. Roth, 'New Light', pp. 129–30, 138–9.

another more convenient day.' More significantly, Sagredo believed that

Meanwhile the Jews, having powers to spend a great deal of money, are getting a hold and it is believed that they will make no mistake in winning over the divines and the ministers, and that they will be able to break down every obstacle by the power of gold.[119]

On that date Salvetti thought that although there was still much opposition to readmission, Cromwell would soon make a final decision.[120] The following week, Salvetti informed the Grand Duke that the 'greatest business that the Lord Protector has on his hands today is that of the Jews, which depends entirely on his will.' According to Salvetti,

His decision is awaited with impatience by the people, who fear that it will be more favourable for these fellows than is generally desired. This is founded on the opinion that, had His Highness not been inclined to concede them at least part of what they wish, he would not have received their petition and proposals in the first instance. Nevertheless, the wiser sort believe that His Highness will proceed very cautiously, and will declare his decision with prudence rather than precipitancy.[121]

The views of Salvetti and Sagredo were corroborated a few days later in an intercepted Royalist letter of intelligence which noted that the 'Jewes though the generality . . . oppose . . . will be admitted by way of connivancy'.[122]

Cromwell seems to have intended to allow the entire matter to cool off somewhat rather than to attempt an immediate resolution of the Jewish question in the face of strong opposition in the Whitehall Conference and among the public outside. By the end of December nothing had yet been resolved, despite the impatience and anxiety of Menasseh and other interested parties. On 31 December 1655, Menasseh paid a visit to the Dutch ambassador to inform him that he did not intend to bankrupt Holland of its Jewish merchants and traders, only to find a refuge for the crypto-Jews suffering at the hands of the Inquisi-

[119] *Cal. S. P. Ven., 1655–6*, pp. 160–1.

[120] Salvetti to Senator Bali Gondi; and to the Grand Duke, 21/31 Dec. 1655: repr. Roth, 'New Light', pp. 129–30, 138–9.

[121] Salvetti to the Grand Duke, 28 Dec./7 Jan. 1655–6: repr. Roth, 'New Light', pp. 131, 139–40.

[122] SP. 18/102, f. 171: H. Robinson to G. Williamson, 31 Dec. 1655.

tion.[123] Cromwell had still declined to act by 11/21 January 1655–6, and Salvetti wrote that therefore 'it is not believed that he will declare it so soon as they desire, since it is a matter of great consequence, and such as to cause general disgust in this nation.'[124] The following week brought no further revelations, but Salvetti now thought that Cromwell would 'postpone action while conniving in the meantime at religious exercise in their private houses, as they do at present' in lieu of granting the Jews permission to maintain a public synagogue.[125] This expedient solution to the request for Jewish toleration seems to have been carried out by Cromwell's government, and Salvetti confirmed this 'connivance' at private religious assemblies in two other letters in the second half of the month.[126] Salvetti's report of 8/18 February 1655–6 makes no mention of the Jews for the first time in over two months, and on 15/25 February he concluded with the note that Jewish readmission was no longer a subject of popular debate.[127]

VI

The failure of the Whitehall Conference to come to any definite conclusions about the readmission of the Jews was a bitter disappointment to the English supporters of Menasseh ben Israel's mission to London. The public phase of the campaign for readmission was over: opposition from merchants and clergymen proved too strong to permit any formal invitation to the exiled Jews to return to England. Cromwell appears to have toyed with the idea of making some kind of official statement, but instead chose to let the matter rest in obscurity. The sub-committee of the Council of State declined even to submit a report of their findings. As early as the middle of January 1655–6, the fears of the Royalists had been somewhat allayed, and the unpleasant prospect of rich and influential, Continental

---

[123] *Thurloe State Papers*, iv. 333.

[124] Salvetti to the Grand Duke, 11/21 Jan. 1655–6: repr. Roth, 'New Light', pp. 131, 140–1.

[125] S. to the Grand Duke, 18/28 Jan. 1655–6: repr. Roth, 'New Light', pp. 131–2, 141.

[126] S. to Senator Bali Gondi, 25 Jan./4 Feb. 1655–6; S. to the same, 1/11 Feb. 1655–6: repr. Roth, 'New Light', pp. 132–3, 141.

[127] S. to Senator Bali Gondi, 8/18 Feb. 1655–6; S. to the same, 15/25 Feb. 1655–6: see Roth, 'New Light', p. 132.

Jews in the service of the Commonwealth no longer seemed likely. 'I had almost forgot', Colonel Robert Whitley mentioned casually to Sir Edward Nicholas in a letter from Calais, 'y^t Cromwell sayes it is an vngodly thing to introduce ye Jewes; but, if he refuse y^m, it is because they refuse to purchase it at ye summe desired unlesse they may haue ye authority of a parlement for theire being there with safety.'[128] Whitley was mistaken in believing that any monetary transaction was involved, for Menasseh was virtually alone at this time in trying to procure a formal readmission. The crypto-Jews of the Commonwealth were content to worship in secrecy as long as their trade was left undisturbed. In any case, the lawyers at the Conference had determined that no additional legislation was needed to readmit the Jews, and even Prynne's research did not altogether establish that the expulsion under Edward I had been ratified by Parliament.

Cromwell certainly did not believe that it would be ungodly to readmit the Jews, merely that it was untimely to do so publicly. As with Dormido, his actions spoke louder than his words. Antonio Ferdinando Carvajal, the greatest figure in the Jewish community under Cromwell, had submitted a very audacious request to the Protector on 9 November 1655, only four days before Menasseh sent his seven-point petition to Cromwell in the name of the Jewish nation. Carvajal explained that he had most of his estate in the Canary Islands, and was therefore forced to devise some means of rescuing what he could to protect himself against the new embargo and seizure of the property of English subjects. Carvajal pointed out that the Spanish ambassador had already taken notice of his endenization in England, which rendered him liable to prosection in Spanish territory. As Carvajal explained it to the Protector, his plan was to fit out a ship with a Dutch crew and a false bill of lading to take away his goods from the Canaries. Carvajal hoped that Cromwell would 'give order to the men of warre of this commonwealth to bee ayding and assisting to the shipp in her voyadge homewards' so that he could smuggle his goods into London. Cromwell recommended this petition to the consideration of the Council on 9 November 1655, but it was

---

[128] *Nicholas Papers*, ed. Warner, iii. 255: 14/24 Jan. 1655–6.

formally recorded only on 18 December 1655, the very day of the last meeting of the Whitehall Conference. The entire affair was cleared up the following June.[129]

Carvajal's scheme, and Cromwell's favourable response to it, is emblematic of the attitude of the Anglo-Jewish community to the Whitehall Conference, and of the Protector's dealings with them. It is remarkable that the leading member of the secret Jewish congregation in London should promote a purely private affair before Cromwell within a matter of days after Menasseh ben Israel arrived in London to seek the annulment of the expulsion order against the Jews. And it is no less surprising that this private petition should have been considered by the Council of State on the very day that the hopes of official readmission were dashed for ever.

Menasseh had not come to England merely in order to ratify the *de facto* toleration of the Jews which already existed, but in order to secure Cromwell's endorsement of his plan to make England a refuge for victims of the Inquisition. Menasseh was not the only one who suffered from the rejection by the delegates of Whitehall. Henry Jessey recorded that

Many Jewish Merchants had come from beyond seas to *London*, and hoped they might have enjoyed as much priviledge here, in respect of Trading, and of their Worshipping . . . here, in Synagogues, publickly, as they enjoy in *Holland* . . . But after the conference and Debate at *White-Hall* was ended, they heard by some, that the greater part of the Ministers were against this: therefore they removed hence again to beyond the Seas, with much grief of heart, that they were thus disappointed of their hopes.[130]

Menasseh himself failed to realize that his mission had ended in utter failure, and had merely secured the judgement that in theory there was no legal bar to Jewish resettlement. As late as April 1656 he was still awaiting a final determination from Cromwell.[131] The secret Jews of London would soon mount a campaign for toleration on their own for entirely different reasons, but Menasseh's role would be minimal. Within three

[129] SP. 18/102, fos. 83ʳ–84ᵛ. On Carvajal generally, see L. Wolf, 'The First English Jew', *Trs. Jew. Hist. Soc. Eng.*, ii (1896), 14–46.

[130] [Jessey], *Narrative*, p. 10. One of these Jews was Raphael Supino of Leghorn: see Roth, 'New Light', pp. 118–26, 137.

[131] [Jessey], *Narrative*, p. 10; Menasseh, *Vindiciae*, pp. 38–9.

years, John Sadler could lament that 'He had stayed heere so long, that he was allmost ashamed to returne to those that sent him; or to exact theyr maintenance Heere where they found so little success, after so many Hopes'.[132]

[132] SP. 18/200, f. 23: John Sadler to Richard Cromwell, 4 Jan. 1658–9.

CONCLUSION

'Twere strange if this Prophetick
year wch brought (1656)

Such Expectation, should have
nothing wrought[1]

This cry of despair was no doubt shared by many millenarians after the imagined year of Redemption ended without any cosmic sign. Menasseh ben Israel himself was lost in disappointment by the end of 1656, for the dismissal of the Whitehall Conference without having agreed on an official invitation to the exiled Jews to return to England represented a complete failure of his mission.

But the very decision to call a special meeting of England's leading divines, merchants and lawyers to discuss the fate of the Jews was itself of momentous importance, and was the result of a half-century of growing English philo-semitism much more complex than the simple bibliolatry of Puritanism. For England was one of the Protestant countries that had not harboured a Jewish population for a number of centuries. The Jews were not a constant presence to be explained and reviled: interest in contemporary Jewry was a by-product of other concerns. As we have already seen, John Traske and his band of Judaizers came to the radical conclusion from their biblical studies that the Mosaic law had not been abrogated by the coming of Christ, and their scandalous if not ostentatious practice of Jewish law brought down upon them a hail of publicity which in turn forced them upon the attention of everyone between ordinary Englishmen and the king himself. More scholarly researchers,

---

[1] J. Waite in C. Beck, *The Universal Character* (London, 1657), sig. A6^r.

obsessed with the imagined mystical and magical properties of Hebrew, joined the movement in search of a universal language for mankind, which would eliminate the distance between words and things. Their attention was soon directed to contemporary Jews as the repositories of kabbalistic knowledge, who could unlock the secret doors with their Hebrew language. Other Englishmen were working on millenarian interpretations of history, anxiously awaiting the End of Days. Their calculations incontrovertibly demonstrated that the Jews had a key role to play in this final cosmic drama. Like the Traskites, some of these dreamers were driven to put their abstract ideas into practice: Thomas Tany, John Robins, and their followers made preparations to lead the Jews back to Palestine and found themselves at the centre of a storm of controversy. These were speculative issues which focused attention on Jews and Judaism, but as yet did little towards effecting readmission.

The search for the lost ten tribes provided the trigger for practical action on behalf of resettlement, for it was this debate that brought Menasseh ben Israel to England through the good offices of John Dury, who was already interested in eschatology and the mystical elements of Hebrew. A consistent demand for religious toleration of the Jews (albeit towards their ultimate conversion) helped to keep contemporary Jewry before the public eye. After 1649, when a formal petition for readmission was presented by the Cartwrights, the pressure for Jewish resettlement grew until Cromwell and his Council felt it expedient to call the Whitehall Conference. By the time Menasseh arrived in England in September 1655, he was merely reaping the fruits of a movement which had been gaining in strength and publicity at least since the reign of James I.

Menasseh's mission to England brought together a number of disparate intellectual movements. The radical, but not wholly unreasonable interpretation of biblical law by John Traske had recently been revived by Theophilus Brabourne and Henry Jessey. The illogical aspects of the search for a universal language and of the Hebraic element in this quest had not yet been revealed by 1655, and in fact the operation was at its height just then. The antics of Tany and Robins had made the Jews a highly topical subject at that particular moment. Montezinos's fantastic discovery of a tribe of Israelite Indians in South America seemed to have brought that debate to a desirable conclusion, and even compelled Englishmen to allow the Jews to disperse to another corner of the earth. The more marginal religious sectarians who promoted toleration of the Jews, such as the Baptists, were still sufficiently insecure to present the Jewish argument in order to strengthen their own position. None of these groups which effectively promoted readmission could yet be disregarded, as would happen after 1655. The stage had been set for the Whitehall Conference, and Menasseh seized the opportunity eagerly.

Once the sessions began in December 1655, however, more serious and rational considerations came to be discussed, such as the effect Jewish immigration might have on the English economy and religion. The lawyers soberly ruled in favour of the Jews' return, but opposition was too strong to allow for any official declaration. Menasseh had already played his hand, but nevertheless he continued to wander about London in a vain attempt to use his influence to procure some sort of official statement from Cromwell's government. He received Ralph Cudworth, the Regius professor of Hebrew, and gave him a manuscript which summarized the Jewish objections to Christianity.[2] He consulted with Henry Thorndike about the plans already in motion to produce the famous Polyglot Bible of Brian Walton.[3] But unfortunately there was very little he could

---

[2] The MS was 'Porta Veritatis' by 'Jacob Aben Amram Judaeo', dated 5394 (1634), now Balliol Coll., MS 251. The author may have been Duarte Pinheiro/Pinhel/Pinelli, an Italian marrano, although it was widely believed to be the work of Menasseh ben Israel himself. Cudworth's copy was eventually sold to Richard Kidder, bishop of Bath and Wells, who left it to Balliol. Kidder claims Menasseh as the modest author of this 'Master-piece' in his *Demonstration Of The Messias* (London, 1684–1700), ii. sig. A4ʳ⁻ᵛ, but his note dated 1700 on f. 2ᵛ of the MS itself is less certain: 'But I can affirm that I take it to be the greatest effort against Christianity that I ever saw in any language whatsoever', Kidder wrote. 'And for that reason I do declare that it is my will that it be not sold to any private person, for any price how great soever. Lest by that means it should be printed, without an answer, to the prejudice of Christianity. I rather will that it should be burnt, or given to some public library upon sufficient Caution that it be never lent out of the said library, not transcribed, but locked up by itself and consulted, upon occasion, in the library, by such onely as shall be allowed by the owners of the said Library.' Another copy of 'Porta Veritatis' is now Brit. Lib., MS Harl. 3427–8, and others are said to be deposited in Hamburg and Amsterdam. See *Catalogue of the Manuscripts of Balliol College*, ed. R.A.B. Mynors (Oxford, 1963), pp. 274–5; C. Roth, *A Life of Menasseh ben Israel* (Philadelphia, 1945), pp. 321–2.

[3] *Cal. S. P. Dom., 1655–6*, pp. 366–7. Walton's *Biblia Sacra Polyglotta* was published in 1657.

do, and the prospect of returning home empty-handed to Amsterdam could not have been attractive.

As we have seen, the efforts for Jewish readmission and toleration between 1649 and 1655, and indeed throughout the first half of the seventeenth century, were conducted in isolation from the intended beneficiaries of this movement. The mission of Menasseh ben Israel to England cast an unwelcome spotlight on the little Jewish colony in the City, led by Antonio Ferdinando Carvajal and Antonio Rodrigues Robles, and revealed their identities publicly, even though some well-travelled Englishmen may have already suspected their true faith. But attention was not called to them unduly even after the Whitehall Conference, and they continued to receive Jewish visitors from abroad without molestation.[4] One of their number, Simon de Caceres, was even referred to casually as a Jew in an official document of 22 January 1655–6, as if his presence in London was not even slightly irregular.[5] Most probably they would have continued in this fashion for much longer, had not international affairs forced them to climb on the bandwagon which Menasseh had already provided, and which lay unwanted and unused.

This personal crisis for Anglo-Jewry was sparked by the war with Spain, which rendered the goods and property of enemy Spaniards liable for confiscation. Robles was soon denounced by a scrivener named Francis Knevett on 13 March 1655–6, who apparently was thereby betraying the confidence of the marrano community in London with which he had business connections. Robles at first tried to bluff his way through by claiming to be a Portuguese, but eventually he and his co-religionists were driven to confess the truth before the authorities. The Robles case forced England's secret Jews to reveal themselves formally to the English government and public, and compelled them to acquiesce in the movement on their behalf.[6]

---

[4] Brit. Lib., Addit. MSS 34015, fos. 25, 43, 46, 73: alien arrivals in London, 1656–7. These fos. include notices of individuals who were obviously Jews who had arrived in London between 14 Aug. 1656 and 13 June 1657. Repr. *Trs. Jew. Hist. Soc. Eng.*, x (1924), 127–8.

[5] *Cal. S. P. Dom., 1655–6*, p. 128.

[6] SP. 18/125, f. 118: Spanish paper of discovery; SP. 18/126, f. 280^{r-v}: testimony of

The famous petition of England's secret Jewish community was received by Cromwell on 24 March 1655–6.[7] Little choice had been left to them but to throw themselves on the mercies of the Protector, whose sympathetic views had already been amply revealed. The list of signatories included all of the great figures of that community, except Robles himself, who submitted his own petition separately.[8] Simon (Jacob) de Caceres signed, as did Carvajal and Dormido, who apparently had decided to settle in England. Three other London Jews appended their signatures, but the most famous name was that at the head of the list: Menasseh ben Israel. For in March 1656 the two strands of the Jewish reaction to English philosemitism intertwined briefly, only to unravel again within a few short months.

'The Humble Petition of The Hebrews at Present Residing in this citty of London' included rather more modest requests than those which Menasseh had presented to the Protector four months previously. The Jewish community began by thanking Cromwell for having been pleased to graunt them favours and protection 'in order that wee may with security meete priuatley in owr particular houses to owr Deuosions'. But the vicissitudes of Robles during the past fortnight had demonstrated to them that toleration on a more secure foundation was required. Now they requested that 'such Protection may be graunted vs in Writting as that wee may therew[th] meete at owr said priuate deuosions in owr Particular houses without feere of Molestation either to owr persons famillys or estates'. All they desired was to live peaceably under the authority of the English government. They also requested permission to establish a Jewish cemetery outside the city limits. The seven signatories closed praying for Cromwell's long life and prosperity. The Protector referred the document to the consideration of the Council of State, along with the separate petition of Antonio Robles.[9]

The Robles case, meanwhile, dragged on for almost two

Philipp de la Loyhoy, 26 Mar. 1656. Many of the documents from the Robles case are repr., with many mistakes, in *Trs. Jew. Hist. Soc. Eng.*, i (1895), 77–86.

[7] SP. 18/125, f. 169: large photograph in *Bevis Marks Records*, i, ed. L. D. Barnett (Oxford, 1940), opp. title page.

[8] SP. 18/126, fos. 275–276: Robles to Cromwell, 24 Mar. 1655–6.

[9] SP. 18/125, f. 169.

months. Menasseh's precise role in this investigation is unclear; his main concern presumably lay with the progress of the general petition of the Jewish community which was before the Council of State. The deliberations of the Whitehall Conference had been conducted in isolation from the realities of the Jewish presence in London, and the advantages and drawbacks of Jewish readmission had been discussed in abstraction. The failure of Robles's petition might have caused a formal re-*expulsion* of the Jews from England, for it revealed the extent of the Jewish population in London. Menasseh therefore worked feverishly to influence the outcome of the case. He may have had a hand in the writing of Henry Jessey's narrative of the Whitehall Conference, which was finished on 1 April 1656, just as Robles was confessing his Judaism before Colonel Philip Jones, one of the members of the Council sub-committee which had dealt with Dormido's petition.[10] As of that day, Jessey noted, 'no absolute *Answer* is yet returned' from Cromwell.[11] Nine days later Menasseh reiterated this statement at the conclusion of his *Vindiciae Judaeorum*, his powerful refutation of common slanders against the Jews.[12] This, his greatest work, is one of the most cogent defences of the Jewish people, and has been translated and reprinted many times during the past three centuries.

By 14 May 1656, the Admiralty commissioners had taken notice of the examinations and depositions of numerous witnesses.[13] The fact that Robles attended Mass until the outbreak of hostilities with Spain, and was not circumcised in any case, they explained, 'induceth vs to conceave he is either noe Jew or one that walkes under loose principles, and very different from others of that profession'. The commissioners therefore concluded that they 'upon examinacon doe not finde any convicting evidence to cleare vp either the Nation or Religion of the peticoñer.'[14] The ships, goods, and other property which had

---

[10] SP. 18/126, f. 288: testimony of Robles, 1 Apr. 1656.

[11] [H. Jessey], *A Narrative Of the late Proceeds at Whitehall* (London, 1656), p. 10.

[12] Menasseh ben Israel, *Vindiciae Judaeorum* (n.p., 1656), pp. 38–9.

[13] SP. 18/126, fos. 277–88; SP. 18/127, f. 46ʳ⁻ᵛ.

[14] SP. 18/127, f. 83: report of Admiralty commissioners, 14 May 1656. The report was signed by Robert Blackborne, who reported on the Whitehall Conference to Willoughby: see above, pp. 209, 210–11.

been seized from Robles were restored to him two days later.[15] The Council of State, on the other hand, chose to ignore the petition from the seven Jewish leaders.

An open Anglo-Jewish community was thus a new reality after the end of the Robles case. Curiously enough, however, the debate over the desirability of Jewish readmission continued to be expressed in much the same terms as before. The volume of pamphlet literature dealing with the Jewish question continued unabated, and even increased. William Tomlinson issued a broadsheet in favour of Jewish readmission the month following the Whitehall Conference, and noted that 'there are many in this Nation whose bowels are as well enlarged to receive them, as they have been to pray for them.'[16] Worried by Prynne's bitter attack against the Jews, Thomas Collier published a short rebuttal, sympathizing with 'those poor rejected people (at this time) desiring to have a being amongst us'.[17] Two anonymous writers set down their views on readmission in print, one positive and the other negative. The opponent of resettlement seems to have been particularly shocked by the sudden revelation of secret Jews in London. 'Since the time they have been bolder to return hither,' he warned:

its more then to be feared, they have made many Proselytes; and that if they might with impunity shew themselves, and had toleration of their Religion, and an open way of their Worship granted, hundreds . if not thousands, would then appear, who now are veiled under the name of Christians.[18]

Margaret Fell, later wife of George Fox the Quaker, published an epistle to Menasseh ben Israel, 'who art come into this English Nation *with all the rest of thy Brethren* . . . which is a Land of gathering, where the Lord God is fullfilling his promise'.[19] Fell and Fox both wrote a number of works directed towards the Jewish people during this period.[20]

---

[15] *Cal. S. P. Dom., 1655–6*, p. 325.

[16] W. Tomlinson, *A Bosome opened To The Jews* (n.p., 1656), brdsht.

[17] T. Collier, *A Brief Answer* (London, 1656), p. 2.

[18] H. W., *Anglo-Judaeus* (London, 1656), p. 49. See also [Anon.], *The Case of the Jewes Stated* (London, 1656); J. Copley, *The Case of the Jews is altered* (London, 1656).

[19] M. Fell, *For Manasseth Ben Israel* (London, 1656), p. 3.

[20] Esp. idem, *A Loving Salutation To The . . . Jewes* (London, 1656); idem, *A Call Unto . . . Israel* (London, n.d.); G. Fox, *A Declaration to the Iews* (London, 1661); idem, *An Answer To the . . . Iewes* (London, 1661); idem. *An Epistle . . . Also to the Jews* (n.p., 1673); idem, *A Looking-Glass For The Jews* (Philadelphia, 1784). See also H. Barbour, *The*

Charles and his exiled Royalists, unlike the philo-semitic pamphleteers, were quick to recognize the new situation, and seem to have tried to reap some advantage from the newly forged Anglo-Jewish identification with the Protectorate: their plan was to appeal to the Royalist sympathies among the leaders of the parent community in Amsterdam who might be more willing in consequence to curry favour with them as a form of insurance. Lieutenant-General Middleton appears to have been informed of this intention by 'some principle persons' of the Jewish congregation there, who also assured him that they had had nothing to do with Menasseh's mission, and in fact disavowed it entirely. The Dutch Jews also wished Charles a speedy Restoration. The exiled monarch therefore commissioned Middleton to promise them that if they provided him with money, arms, or ammunition, after his return to power Charles would

abate that rigour of the Lawes which is against them in our severall dominions, and . . . they shall lay a signal obligacion upon us, it will not only dispose us to be gratious to them, and to be willinge to protecte them, but be a morall assurance to them that wee shall be able to do whatsoever wee shall be willinge when we can iustly publish and declare to all men how much wee have bene beholdinge to them, and how farr they have contributed towards our restoration[21]

There is no evidence that the Jews of Amsterdam provided Charles with anything more substantial than good wishes, although some sort of secret support might help to explain his protection of the Jews after 1660. In England however, Fernando Mendes da Costa, 'a Jewish merchant, that hath a fine house near London, well known to his highness [Cromwell]', was denounced for receiving £4,000 to be used in helping to finance Royalist plots. The officer charged with investigating the case, brought forward by a woman of demonstrably disre-

---

Quakers in Puritan England (New Haven and London, 1964), p. 188; A. Coudert, 'A Quaker-Kabbalist Controversy', *Jnl. Warb. Ctld. Inst.*, xxxix (1976), 171–89.

[21] Brit. Lib., MS Eger. 2542, f. 240ᵛ: Charles to Middleton, 24 Sept. 1656, repr. C. H. Firth, *Scotland and the Protectorate* (Scot. Hist. Soc., xxxi, 1899), p. 343. Middleton was warned in a separate letter of the same date that 'if you finde ther professyons to be only generall . . . you shall requite them only with as generall expressions' (Brit. Lib., MS Eger. 2542, f. 239ᵛ: repr. ibid., p. 342). Similarly, see Brit. Lib. Addit. MSS 4106, f. 253: memo of first letter; and Hist. MSS Comm., lxxii, *Laing MSS*, i. 301: copy of second letter.

putable character, dismissed the accusations along with 'many other stories too tedious to relate'.[22]

The great crisis of Anglo-Jewry had passed, and the secret community in London had revealed itself; everyone concerned was forced to adapt himself to the altered circumstances. James Harrington addressed the issue directly in *Oceana*, his famous utopian work. In a barely disguised reference to Ireland, Harrington argued that her economic position might best be improved:

> by planting it with Jewes, allowing them their own Rites and Lawes, for that would have brought them suddainly from all parts of the World, and in sufficient numbers; and though the Jews be now altogether for Merchandize, yet in the Land of *Canaan* (since their exile from whence they have not been Landlords) they were altogether for agriculture; and there is no cause why a man should doubt, but having a fruitfull Country and good Ports too, they would be good at both.

Harrington's plan was to grant the Jews a perpetual lease to Ireland, initially for the cost of the maintenance of a provincial army during the first seven years, and afterwards for an annual revenue of £2,000,000. This might solve England's new Jewish problem, for to 'receive the Jewes after any other manner into a Commonwealth, were to maim it', because they never assimilate, and instead become parasites on the state.[23]

Yet Menasseh ben Israel, like the philo-semitic pamphleteers, seems to have failed to recognize that a new era had begun for Jews in England. His single-minded dedication to obtaining a formal declaration of Jewish toleration and freedom of worship blinded him to the substantial benefits which had been achieved informally, and to the practical determination of the English government to allow the Jews to continue living in England unmolested. Menasseh thus alienated the leaders of Anglo-Jewry, who were anxious to effect a smooth transition to toleration, and they turned their backs on him. Sometime during 1656 they agreed to bring over Rabbi Moses Athias from Hamburg to lead their congregation.[24] Menasseh

---

[22] *Thurloe State Papers*, v. 572, 578.

[23] J. Harrington, *The Common-Wealth Of Oceana* (London, 1656), sig. B2: repr. *The Political Works of James Harrington*, ed. J. G. A. Pocock (Cambridge, 1977), p. 159. See also S. B. Liljegren, *Harrington and the Jews* (Lund, 1932).

[24] J. Cassuto, 'Aus dem ältesten Protokollbuch der Portugiesisch-Jüdischen Gemeinde in Hamburg', *Jrb. Jüd.–Lit. Gft.*, vi (1909), 184.

may have been considered for the post, but there is no evidence that his name was put forward at all. He seems to have been ill for some time in any case, and was forced to turn to Cromwell for assistance: 'I make my moan to your Highnesse,' he pleaded, 'as the alone succourer of my life, in this land of strangers'.[25] Cromwell, however, recognized Menasseh's services even if the Jews turned a deaf ear to him, and granted the rabbi a state pension of £100 per annum, payable quarterly, and commencing from 20 February 1656–7.[26] At least two payments of £25 each were made to Menasseh between Michaelmas 1656 and Michaelmas 1658.[27] The Jews of London, meanwhile, were at work acquiring a burial ground in the manor of Stepney, for which they paid approximately twenty times the fair rent of the tiny plot, suggesting that their formal request for a cemetery had not yet been granted at least by February 1657.[28]

By the middle of September 1657, Menasseh's hopes and patience were finally exhausted. His son Samuel having recently died, Menasseh turned to Cromwell once again for financial help to enable him to carry the body back to Holland. Menasseh offered to surrender his pension seal for £300, and to cease troubling Cromwell with his millennial dreams and pleas for aid.[29] Menasseh apparently was willing to renounce his pension for even two hundred pounds because of the intense pressure of his debts and his need to return to Holland immediately. This sum seems not to have been paid, and Menasseh was forced to return empty-handed, but he never reached Amsterdam, and died *en route* in Middelburg.[30] Samuel ben Israel was buried there, but Menasseh's body was carried

---

[25] SP. 18/153, f. 253: Menasseh to Cromwell, undated=prob. end of 1656. Repr. *Menasseh ben Israel's Mission to Oliver Cromwell*, ed. L. Wolf (London, 1901), pp. lxxxvi–vii.

[26] Dep. Keeper Pub. Rec., *5th Report*, App. II, p. 263.

[27] Hist. MSS Comm., vii, *App. to 8th Rep.*, Pt I, pp. 94b–95a.

[28] A. S. Diamond, 'The Cemetery of the Resettlement', *Trs. Jew. Hist. Soc. Eng.*, xix (1960), 163–90; H. S. Q. Henriques, *The Jews and the English Law* (London, [1908]), pp. 109–12.

[29] SP. 18/156, f. 173: Menasseh to Cromwell, 17 Sept. 1657. Repr. *Menasseh*, ed. Wolf, p. lxxxvii.

[30] SP. 18/200, f. 23: John Sadler to Richard Cromwell, 4 Jan. 1658–9. Repr. *Menasseh*, ed. Wolf, pp. lxxxvii–viii.

to the Jewish cemetery at Ouderkerk near Amsterdam, where he was laid to rest.[31]

Menasseh's widow was left destitute and was forced to rely on charity. She sent several begging letters to Cromwell before his death in September 1658, which were entrusted to Thurloe and John Sadler, long a friend of the Jews. By the beginning of January 1658–9, she had persuaded Sadler to plead her case before Richard Cromwell. Sadler asked the new Protector to pay the two hundred pounds 'to the said Widow, & Relations of a Man so Eminent & ffamous in his owne & many other Nations; & for the honour of Christian Religiō with many other Reasons'.[32] It is unknown whether Richard honoured his father's debt.

Thus, by Cromwell's death, the Jews were firmly established in England. Some disagreement did ensue even in the last years of the interregnum over the right of Jews to remain in England, and their value to the state, but by and large their position was secure.[33] Carvajal died and was honoured by a special knell of the bells of St. Katherine Creechurch,[34] and Samuel Pepys paid his first visit to the synagogue.[35] Jews were moving openly in London now, and one in a case before the Admiralty commissioners 'produced great testimonies under the hand of the late Lord Protector'.[36]

The Jews were therefore understandably nervous when Charles was restored to his throne in 1660. Events soon proved that their fears were unwarranted: they weathered a concerted attempt from City circles to have the Jews expelled, and a long and fascinating description of a visit to their synagogue in 1662 by John Greenhalgh depicts them as comfortable and secure.[37]

---

[31] Middelburg burial register in *Trs. Jew. Hist. Soc. Eng.*, vii (1915), 123–46: see p. 127; photograph of Menasseh's tombstone in L. A. Vega, *The Beth Haim of Ouderkerk* (Assen/Amsterdam, 1975), p. 33.

[32] SP. 18/200, f. 23: Sadler to Richard Cromwell, 4 Jan. 1658–9.

[33] L. Wolf, 'The Jewry of the Restoration', *Trs. Jew. Hist. Soc. Eng.*, v (1908), 13–18; idem, 'The First Stage of Anglo-Jewish Emancipation', in *Essays*, ed. C. Roth (London, 1934), pp. 115–43.

[34] Extract from churchwarden's account book repr. *Misc. Jew. Hist. Soc. Eng.*, ii (1935), 26 n.

[35] Bodl., MS Carte 73, f. 325: Pepys to Edward Montagu, 3 Dec. 1659. Cf. W. S. Samuel, 'Caravajal and Pepys', *Misc. Jew. Hist. Soc. Eng.*, ii (1935), 24–9.

[36] *Cal. S. P. Dom., 1659–60*, p. 291.

[37] *Original Letters Illustrative of English History*, ed. H. Ellis (2nd ser., iv, 1827), pp.

This impression is sustained by another account from Pepys written the following year.[38]

Confirmation of the status of the Jews in writing, which they had requested in their petition at the height of the Robles case, was finally achieved after a further petition of 22 August 1664 signed by Dormido and two others. Henry Hennett replied on behalf of the king that the Jews might 'promise themselves y[e] effects of y[e] same favour as formerly they have had so long as they demeane themselves peaceably and quietly with due obedience to his Ma[ties] Laws & without scandal to his Government'.[39] Further orders to this effect were issued in 1674 and 1685.[40]

Thus, less than a decade after Menasseh arrived in London, the Jews were granted a formal statement of toleration. By the end of the century, on 23 June 1700, Solomon de Medina received a knighthood, and thereby became the first Jew to be so honoured.[41] Although Jews in England would not become fully emancipated until the middle of the nineteenth century, their residence here rested on a secure foundation with the admission at the Whitehall Conference that 'there is no Law that forbids the Jews return into *England*'.[42]

II

'The long, heavy, and sad punishment inflicted on this dejected, despised, and dispersed people,' one anonymous author wrote in defence of the Jews after Prynne's attack, 'hath various and strong impressions upon mens spirits; some scorning any society with them, others hating their very name, and persons, and some compassionating their despicable condition'. It was true that God had scattered the Jews among all nations, he pointed out, 'and if so, why not some into *England*, as well as other Countries? why we less charitable then all, or most of other Nations?'[43] By the time these words were written,

---

3–21: repr. with notes in *Trs. Jew. Hist. Soc. Eng.*, x (1924), 49–57. On the proposed re-expulsion, see Wolf, 'Restoration', pp. 13–18.

[38] S. Pepys, *Diary*, ed. R. Latham and W. Matthews (London, 1970), iv. 334–5: 14 Oct. 1663.

[39] *Cal. S. P. Dom., 1663–4*, p. 672: photograph in *Bevis Marks*, ed. Barnett, plate iii: cf. pp. 8–9.

[40] Ibid., plate iv and p. 11; plates v, vi, and p. 15.

[41] O. K. Rabinowicz, *Sir Solomon de Medina* (London, 1974), p. 20.

[42] [Jessey], *Narrative*, p. 9.

[43] D.L., *Israels Condition and Cause pleaded* (London, 1656), pp. 1–2, 4.

the Jewish readmission question had passed from millenarian speculation into the realm of state policy. Menasseh wandered about London for some time, and returned to Holland, a dying and disappointed man. The newly emerged Anglo-Jewish community grew and developed according to its own momentum, driven by forces wholly removed from the bizarre elements connected with the calling of the Whitehall Conference and Menasseh ben Israel's mission to England.

For after 1655 the conjuncture of Judaizers, Hebraists, millenarians, and tolerationists broke up and dispersed as each aspect was regarded as either ridiculous or irrelevant. Some tolerationists, notably Henry Jessey, John Dury, and John Sadler, continued to work on behalf of the Jews, but the quest for a universal language already seemed chimerical and the search for the lost ten tribes was beginning to look absurd. Brabourne, Tany, and Robins died or faded away. The service which these peripheral movements performed was to bring the Jewish question to public attention and to present contemporary Jews in a sympathetic light. This may not have been their prime purpose, but this was the effect of their activity, and their importance for the readmission of the Jews to England. Once Menasseh ben Israel's attention was turned to England, the campaign for readmission gained a life of its own which carried it to the Whitehall Conference.

Englishmen who became curious about the Jews and their religion in the first half of the seventeenth century turned to the Judaizers, the Hebraists, the millenarians, and the tolerationists, groups whose activities often had ignited that concern in the first place. The ultimate product of this interest was the Whitehall Conference, and its failure demonstrated that the readmission of the Jews to England was meant to be the means to an end for each of these groups, whether the end of Papistical ceremony, the end of the world, or the end of sectarian persecution. These English philo-semites wanted Hebrew without tears, philo-semitism without Jews. This proved to be impossible, and once Cromwell and Charles II realized that the Jews as a nation could never be admitted through the front door, they were anxious to go around the back themselves and let them in through the entrance reserved for tradesmen.

BIBLIOGRAPHY

1. *Manuscript Sources*

OXFORD

Balliol College Library
    251: 'Porta Veritatis' by 'Jacob Aben Amram Judaeo', 5394 [1634].

Bodleian Library
  Ashmole MSS:
      374, fos. 139–40: Ashmole's note on Hebrew lessons with Franco.
      1136, f. 147^v: Ashmole's note on Cartwright petition.
  Carte MSS:
      73, f. 325: S. Pepys to E. Montagu, 3 Dec. 1659.
  Clarendon MSS:
      46, f. 109: Royalist news-letter, 15 July 1653.
  Rawlinson MSS:
      A 260, f. 57: Cromwell to king of Portugal, 26 Feb. 1654–5.
      A 261, f. 37^v: the same.
      C 206, f. 107^{r-v}: English translation of Menasseh's proposals.
      D 828, records of the Baptist Church at Lothbury Square, London, 1652–4.
      D 1350, f. 335: 'A Discourse . . . Shewing the Restauration of the Jews'.
  Reggio MSS:
      8–10: A. ben Ḥananiah Jagel, 'Beit Ya'ar Lebanon', *cap.* xxii.
  Selden MSS:
      supra 109, fos. 349, 392: Pococke to Selden on Hebrew type, 1652.
      f. 378: Hebrew book-list from Menasseh ben Israel.
  Tanner MSS:
      160, f. 71: P. Chamberlen to Sancroft, 21 July 1680.
  Addit. MSS:
      C 303, fos. 38^v–45: Traske's punishment, 1618.
  MS notes:
      8^0 T. 28. Th. BS., p. 211: Pococke's copy of *Itinerarivm D. Beniaminis.*

Regent's Park College
[Stinton, B.], 'A Repository of Divers Historical Matters relating to the English Antipedobaptists': *c.* 1712.

LONDON

British Library
Egerton MSS:
1049, f. 6^{r-v}: Dormido to Cromwell, 3 Nov. 1654 (autobiographical account).
f. 7^{r-v}: Dormido to Cromwell, 3 Nov. 1654 (on behalf of the Jews).
2395, fos. 46–7: privileges to Jewish refugees from Pernambuco.
2542, fos. 238^r–239^v: Charles II to Middleton, 24 Sept. 1656.
fos. 240^v–241^r: Charles II to Middleton, 24 Sept. 1656 (particularly on the Jews).
Harl. MSS:
3427–8: 'Porta Veritas', by 'Jacob Aben Amram Judaeo', 5394 [1634].
Addit. MSS:
4106, f. 253: memorandum of Brit. Lib., MS Eger. 2542, fos. 240^v–241^r.
4459, fos. 164^r–165^v: original MS of Dury's *Case of Conscience*.
fos. 166^r–167^v: Dury's note on the Jews of Hesse.
29868, fos. 15–16: da Costa lists of secret Jews in London, *c.* 1660.
34015, fos. 25, 43, 46, 73: Jewish aliens arriving in London, 1656–7.

Guildhall Library
10091/6, f. 26^v: John Traske marries Dorothy Coome, 12 Feb. 1616–17.

Public Record Office
SP. 18/*passim*: State Papers, Domestic, Interregnum.
SP. 25/*passim*: Council of State Order Book.

Dr Williams's Library
3008 D 22: Henry Jessey's copy of *Spes Israelis* (Amsterdam, 1650) with Jessey's MS notes and Menasseh's signature on title page.

THESES

McIntosh, M. M. C., 'The Phonetic and Linguistic Theory of The Royal Society School', Oxford B. Litt. thesis 1956.
Wilson, J., 'The History and Organization of British Israelism: Some Aspects

of the Religious and Political Correlates of Changing Social Status', Oxford
D. Phil. thesis 1966.

2. *Select Printed Sources*

A. PRIMARY WORKS

The place of publication, when known, is London except when stated otherwise.

Abbot, George, *Vindiciae Sabbathi* (1641).

Allegations for Marriage Licences issued by the Bishop of London 1611 to 1828, ed. G. J.
    Armytage (Pubs. Harleian Soc., xxvi, 1887).

Alsted, J. H., *The Beloved City* (1643).

Andrewes, Lancelot, *A Speech Delivered in the Starr-Chamber Against The Two
    Ivdaicall Opinions of Mr. Traske* (1629) in *Miscellaneous Works of Lancelot
    Andrewes*, ed. J. Bliss (Library of Anglo-Catholic Theology, xii, 1854).

*Anti-Toleration, Or a Modest Defence of the Letter of the London Ministers to the
    Reverend Assembly of Divines* (1646).

Arber, Edward (ed.), *The First Three English Books on America* (Birmingham,
    1885).

Archer, John, *The Personall Reigne of Christ Vpon Earth* (1642).

The Arraignment and Tryall With A Declaration of the Ranters (1650).

Ashmole, Elias, *Fasciculus Chemicus* (1650).

—— *Theatrum Chemicum Britannicum* (1652).

—— *Works*, ed. C. H. Josten (1966).

Bacon, Francis, *Works*, ed. J. Spedding, *et al.* (1857–9).

Barlow, Thomas, 'The Case of the Jews' in his *Several Miscellaneous and Weighty
    Cases of Conscience* (1692).

Baxter, Richard, *Reliquiae Baxterianae*, ed. M. Sylvester (1696).

Beatty, Charles, *The Journal of a Two Months Tour* (1768).

Beck, Cave, *The Universal Character* (1657).

Benjamin of Tudela, *Itinerary*, ed. Marcus Nathan Adler (1907).

Bevis Marks Records, i. ed. Lionel D. Barnett (Oxford, 1940).

Birchley, William, *The Christian Moderator* (1651). Second edn., 1652.

B(lount), H(enry), *A Voyage into the Levant* (2nd edn., 1636).

Bodley, Sir Thomas, *Letters*, ed. G. W. Wheeler (Oxford, 1926).

(Botero, Giovanni), *Relations, Of The Most Famovs Kingdoms And Common-
    Weales Thorovgh The World* (1611).

Boyle, Robert, *Works*, ed. T. Birch (1772).

Brabourne, Theophilus, *A Defence Of that most Ancient and Sacred ordinance of
    Gods, the Sabbath Day* (2nd edn., 1632).

—— *A Discourse upon the Sabbath Day* (1628).

—— *A Reply to Mr. Collings Provocator Provocatus* (1654).

—— *The Second Vindication of my First Book . . . Being A Reply to Mr Collings his
    second Answer to it* (1654).

Brayne, John, *The New Earth, or, The True Magna Charta . . . Called The Jews
    Commonweal* (1653).

Brerewood, Edw(ard), *Enqviries Tovching The Diversity of Langvages, and Relig-
    ions through the chiefe parts of the world* (1614).

Brett, Samuel, *A Narrative Of the Proceedings Of a great Councel of Jews, . . . on the 12th of October 1650* (1655). Repr. in *The Harleian Miscellany*, ed. W. Oldys (London, 1808–13), i. 379–85.

Bright, Timothe, *Characterie An Arte of shorte, swifte, and secrete writing by Character* (1588).

Brightman, Thomas, *The Revelation of St. Iohn Illustrated* (4th edn., 1644). Includes *Commentary On The Canticles* and *Exposition . . . Of Daniel.*

Broughton, H(ugh), *Ovr Lordes Famile . . . opened against a Iew, Rabbi David Farar* (Amsterdam, 1608).

Browne, Sir Thomas, *Religio Medici and other works*, ed. L. C. Martin (2nd edn., Oxford, 1967).

—— *The Works of Sir Thomas Browne*, ed. Geoffrey Keynes (2nd edn., 1964).

Burnet, Gilbert, *History of My Own Time*, ed. O. Airy (Oxford, 1897–1900).

—— *The Life of William Bedell* (1692).

Burton, Robert, *The Anatomy of Melancholy* (1948). Everyman edn.

Burton, Thomas, *Diary*, ed. John Towill Rutt (1828).

Busher, Leonard, *Religions Peace: Or, A Plea for Liberty of Conscience* (1646).

Butler, Samuel, *Hudibras*, ed. J. Wilders (Oxford, 1967).

Calancha, Antonio de la, *Coronica Moralizada* (Barcelona, 1638).

Calendar of State Papers, Domestic, Elizabeth, James I, Charles I, Interregnum.

Calendar of State Papers, Venetian, 1607–10, 1642–3, 1647–52, 1655–6.

Calendar of the Committee for Compounding.

Calvert, Tho., *The blessed Jew of Marocco . . . by Rabbi Samuel a Iew, turned Christian* (York, 1648).

Cartenwright, Johann and Ebenezer Cartwright, *The Petition of the Jewes* (1649).

Cary, M(ary), *The Little Horns Doom & Downfall* (1651). Alias Mary Rande.

Chamberlain, John, *Letters*, ed. Norman Egbert McClure (Philadelphia, 1939).

(Cheynell, F.), *An Account Given to the Parliament* (1647).

Clare, Iohn, *The Converted Iew* (1630).

Clarendon, Edward Hyde, earl of, *Calendar of the Clarendon State Papers*, vols. 2–3, ed. W. D. Macray (Oxford, 1869, 1876), vol. 4 ed. F. J. Routledge (Oxford, 1932), vol. 5 ed. Routledge (1963).

Collier, Thomas, *An Answer To a Book written by one Richard Sanders* (1652).

—— *A Brief Answer to some of the Objections and Demurs Made against the coming in and inhabiting of the Jews in this Common-wealth* (1656).

Collings, John, *Indoctus Doctor Edoctus: Or a Short Answer To a little tract of Theophilus Brabourn's* (1654).

—— *A New Lesson For The Indoctus Doctor: Or Rather, A Fescue, and a pair of Spectacles to help him to read the former, better* (1654).

—— *Responsoria ad Erratica Piscatoris. Or, A Caveat for Old and New Prophanenesse.* (1653).

—— *Responsoria Bipartita . . . The second part in answer to Theophilus Brabourn* (1654).

Columbus, Christopher, *Journal*, ed. and trans. Cecil Jane *et al.* (1960).

Comenius, J. A., *The Way of Light*, trans. E. T. Campagnac (Liverpool, 1938).

Copley, Joseph, *The Case of the Jews is altered* (1656).

Corbett, Richard, *The Poems* . . ., ed. H. R. Trevor-Roper and J. A. W. Bennett (Oxford, 1955).

Coryat, Thomas, *Coryat's Crudities* (Glasgow, 1905).

Cotton, John, *The Way of Congregational Churches Cleared* (1648).

Cowley, Abraham, *Essays and Other Prose Writings*, ed. Alfred B. Gough (Oxford, 1915).

—— *Poems* (1656).

Cromwell, Oliver, *The Letters and Speeches*, . . . *with Elucidations by Thomas Carlyle*, ed. S. C. Lomas (1904).

—— *The Writings and Speeches*, ed. Wilbur Cortez Abbot (Cambridge, Mass., 1937–47).

(Crouch, Nathaniel), 'The Proceedings of the *Jews* in *England*' in *Two Journeys to Jerusalem*, ed. R. B(urton=Crouch) (1719), pp. 167–74. This book was published in several forms under different titles, including *Memorable Remarks* and *Judaeorum Memorabilia*.

Dalgarno, George, *Didascalocophus Or The Deaf and Dumb mans Tutor* (Oxford, 1680).

—— *Works* (Edinburgh, 1834).

Davis, John, *A Short Introduction to the Hebrew Tongue* (1656).

The Day-Breaking, if not The Sun-Rising of the Gospell With the Indians in New-England. (1647).

De Larrey, *Histoire D'Angleterre* (Rotterdam, 1707–13).

Dell, William, *Several Sermons* (1652).

Digby, Kenelm and Thomas White, *Peripateticall Institutions* (1656).

Dissenters and Schismaticks Expos'd (1715).

Dod, J. and R. Cleaver, *A Plaine and Familiar Exposition of the Ten Commandements* (6th edn., 1615).

Donne, John, *Essays in Divinity*, ed. Evelyn M. Simpson (Oxford, 1952).

—— *Sermons*, ed. Evelyn M. Simpson & George R. Potter (Berkeley and Los Angeles, 1953–62).

Doomes-Day or The great Day of the Lords Iudgement . . . *With The gathering together of the Jews in great Bodies under Josias Catzius* . . . *for the conquering of the Holy Land* (1647).

Dow, Christopher, *A Discourse of The Sabbath and The Lords Day* (2nd edn., 1636).

Dowel, John, *The Leviathan Heretical* (Oxford, 1683).

Draxe, Thomas, *The Worldes Resvrrection, or The generall calling of the Iewes* (1608).

Dury, John, 'An Appendix', in E. Winslow, *The Glorious Progress*, pp. 93–8.

—— *A Case Of Conscience, Whether it be lawful to admit Jews into a Christian Common-wealth?* (1656). Repr. *Harl. Misc.*, ed. Oldys, vii. 251–6.

—— 'An Epistolicall Discourse' in T. Thorowgood, *Iewes in America*, sigs. D–E4ᵛ.

—— 'An Epistolical Discours' in S. Hartlib, *Clavis Apocalyptica* (1651), pp. 1–79 (1st ser.).

—— *Israels Call To March Ovt Of Babylon Unto Jerusalem* (1646).

E., I., *The Land of Promise* . . . *To those that teach a deliverance of the Iewes out of all Countries to the Land of Canann* (1641).

Eachard, John, *Good Newes For All Christian Soldiers* (1645).

Eden, Richard, *The History of Trauayle* (1577).

Edmundson, Henry, *Lingua Linguarum The Naturall Language of Languages* (1655).

Edwards, Thomas, *Gangraena* (2nd edn., 1646).

Eldad Ha-Dani, *The Ritual of Eldad Ha-Dani,* ed. Max Schloessinger (Leipzig and New York, 1908).

Eliot, John, 'The learned Conjectures of Reverend Mr. *John Eliot*' in T. Thorowgood, *Jews in America*, pp. 1–22 (2nd ser.).

—— *Tears of Repentance* (1653). Repr. in *Coll. Mass. Hist. Soc.*, 3rd ser., iv. 197–260.

Ellis, Henry, *Original Letters Illustrative of English History* (2nd ser., 1827).

An Endevovr After The reconcilement . . . In a discourse touching the Iews Synagogues (1648).

Erra Pater, *A Prognostication for ever, made by Erra Pater, a Iew, borne in Iury* (n.d., but not before Feb. 1649).

Evans, Arise, *The Bloudy Vision* (1653).

—— *An Eccho To The Voice from Heaven* (1652).

—— *The great & bloody Visions* (1654).

—— *King Charls his Starre* (1654).

—— *Light For the Iews: Or, the Means to convert them, in Answer to a Book of theirs, called The Hope of Israel, Written and Printed by Manasseth Ben-Israel, Chief Agent for the Jews here* (1656).

—— *A Rule from Heaven* (1659).

—— *To The Most High and Mighty Prince, Charles the II* (1660).

—— *A Voice From Heaven* (1652).

Evelyn, John, *Diary*, ed. E. S. de Beer (Oxford, 1955).

F., E. de CV, *Englands Deplorable Condition . . . Also, a Petition for the Jews* (1659).

Fairlambe, Peter, *The Recantation of a Brownist* (1606).

D., B. (Falconer, John), *A Briefe Refvtation of Iohn Traskes Ivdaical and Novel Fancyes* (1618).

(Farisol, Abraham), *Itinera Mundi*, trans. Thomas Hyde (Oxford, 1691).

Fawcet, Samuel, *A Seasonable Sermon for these Trovblesome Times* (1641).

Felgenhauer, Paul, *Bonum Nuncium Israeli* (Amsterdam, 1655).

—— *Postilion, Or a New Almanacke* (1655).

F(ell), M(argaret), *A Call Unto The Seed of Israel* (n.d.).

(——) *A Loving Salutation To The . . . Jewes* (1656).

—— *For Manasseth Ben Israel. The Call Of The Jewes out of Babylon* (1656).

(Finch, Henry), *The Worlds Great Restavration. Or The Calling Of The Ievves* (1621).

Fisher, Edward, *A Christian Caveat To the Old and New Sabbatarians* (4th edn., 1651).

Flecknoe, Richard, *Miscellania* (1653).

—— *A Relation Of ten Years Travells* (1656).

Fletcher, Giles, the elder, *The English Works*, ed. Lloyd E. Berry (Madison, 1964).

—— 'The Tartars Or, Ten Tribes' in S. L(ee), *Israel Redux*, pp. 1–28.

(Fletcher, Henry), *The Perfect Politician: Or, A Full View . . . of O. Cromwel* (1660).

Fowler, Christopher, *Daemonium Meridianum Satan at Noon* (1655).

F(ox), G(eorge), *An Answer To the Arguments of the Iewes* (1661).

(——) *An Answer To Thomas Tillams Book Called, The seventh-day-Sabbath* (1659).

—— *A Declaration to the Iews For them to Read Over* (1661).

—— *An Epistle To all Professors . . . Also To the Jews and Turks* (1673).

—— *A Looking-Glass for the Jews* (Philadelphia, 1784).

Foxe, John, *A Sermon preached at the Christening of a certaine Iew* (1578).

Fuller, Thomas, *The Church-History of Britain* (1656).

—— *A Pisgah-Sight of Palestine* (1650).

Gage, Thomas, *A New Survey of the West-India's: Or, The English American* (2nd edn., 1655). Another edn. 1648.

Gale, Theophilus, *The Covrt of the Gentiles* (Oxford, 1669–77).

Garcia, Gregorio, *Origen De Los Indios De El Nuevo Mundo* (Madrid, 1729). First published in 1607.

Gardiner, S. R., ed., *The Constitutional Documents of the Puritan Revolution* (Oxford, 1906).

Garment, Joshuah, *The Hebrews Deliverance at hand* (1651).

Gell, R(obert), *Noah's Flood Returning* (1655).

Gibbens, Nicholas, *Qvestions And Dispvtations Concerning the Holy Scriptvre* (1602).

Godwyn, Thomas, *Moses & Aaron. Civil And Ecclesiastical Rites, Used by The ancient Hebrewes* (7th edn., 1655).

Gonzalez de Mendoza, Juan, *The Historie of the great and mightie kingdome of China* (1588).

Goropius Becanus, Johannes, *Origines Antwerpianae* (Antwerp, 1569), pp. 539–51.

Gostelow, Walter, *Charls Stuart and Oliver Cromwel United* (1655).

—— *The coming of God in Mercy, in Vengeance* (1658).

Gouge, William, *A Learned and very useful Commentary on . . . Hebrewes* (1655).

—— *The Progresse of Divine Providence* (1645).

Gower, Stanley, *Things Now-a-doing* (1644).

The Great Day at the Dore . . . against all those Cabbilisticall Millenaries, and Jew restorers for a thousand yeares (1648).

Grotius, Hugo, *On the Origin of the Native Races of America*, ed. Edmund Goldsmid (Edinburgh, 1884).

Guibelet, Jourdain, *Examen de L'Examen des Esprits* (Paris, 1631).

H., G., *The Declaration of John Robins, the false Prophet, otherwise called the Shakers God* (1651).

H., W., *Anglo-Judaeus, or the History of the Jews, Whilst here in England* (1656).

Hale, Matthew, *The Primitive Origination of Mankind* (1677).

Hale, William, *A Series of Precedents . . . extracted from Act-Books of Ecclesiastical Courts in the Diocese of London* (1847).

The Harleian Miscellany, ed. W. Oldys (1808–13).

Harrington, James, *The Common-Wealth Of Oceana* (1656).

—— *The Political Works of James Harrington*, ed. J. G. A. Pocock (Cambridge, 1977).

Harris, Alexander, *The Œconomy of the Fleete,* ed. A. Jessopp (Camden Soc., n.s., xxv, 1879).

Harris, John, *The Pvritanes Impvritie* (1641).

Harrison, Iohn, *The Messiah Already Come . . . to convince the Iewes . . . Written in Barbarie, in the yeare 1610, and for that cause directed to the dispersed Iewes of that Countrie* (Amsterdam, 1619).

Havers, G. & J. Davies, *Another Collection of Philosophical Conferences of the French Virtuosi* (1665).

Hebdon, Returne, *A Guide To the Godly . . . Left to Mris. Traske* (1648).

Hell broke loose: Or, A Catalogue Of many of the spreading Errors, Heresies and Blasphemies of these Times (1646).

(Helwys, Thomas), *Persecution for Religion Judg'd and Condemn'd* (1662). Repr. in E. B. Underhill, *Tracts,* pp. 83–180.

—— *A Short Declaration of the mistery of iniquity* (1612).

Herbert, George, *Works,* ed. F. E. Hutchinson (Oxford, 1941).

Heylyn, Peter, *The History of the Reformation of the Church of England* (3rd edn., 1674).

—— *The History of the Sabbath* (1636).

—— [*Microcosmos*] *A Little Description of the Great World* (2nd edn., 1625).

Historical Manuscripts Commission, vii, *App. to 8th Report.*

—— viii, *App. to 9th Report.*

—— ix, *Salisbury MSS.*

—— xxii, *Leeds MSS.*

—— lv, *Various Coll., II.*

—— lviii, *Bath MSS.*

—— lxxi, *Finch MSS.*

—— lxxii, *Laing MSS.*

—— lxxiii, *Exeter MSS.*

The History of King=Killers (1719).

Hobbes, Thomas, *Behemoth,* ed. F. Tönnies (1889).

—— *Leviathan,* ed. C. B. Macpherson (1968). Pelican edn.

Homes, Nathaniel, 'A brief Chronology concerning the Jews', in *Two Journeys to Jerusalem,* ed. R. B(urton=Nathaniel Crouch), pp. 118–23. Dated 1665.

—— *The New World, or The New Reformed Chvrch* (1641).

—— *The Resurrection Revealed . . . the raising of the Jewes* (1654).

Howell, James, *Epistolae Ho-Elianae,* ed. Joseph Jacobs (1890).

—— *The VVonderful and most deplorable History of the Latter Times of the Jews* (1653).

Huarte, John, *Examen de Jngenios. The Examination of mens Wits* (1594).

Hudson, William, *A Treatise of the Court of Star Chamber* (n.d., but before 1635). Repr. in *Collectanea Juridica,* ii. 1–240.

The Humble Petition and Representation of the . . . Anabaptists (1660). Repr. in E. B. Underhill, *Tracts,* pp. 287–308.

The Interlude of The Four Elements, ed. James Orchard Halliwell (Percy Soc., xxii, 1848).

Isaiah, Paul, alias Eleazar Bargishai, *A Brief Compendium of the vain Hopes of the Jews Messias* (1652).

—— *The Messias Of The Christians, and the Jewes* (1655).

—— *A Vindication Of the Christians Messiah* (1654).

James I, *A Fruitefull Meditation* (1603).

—— *A Mediatation vpon The Lords Prayer* (1619).

(Jessey, Henry?), *An Information, Concerning The Present State of the Jewish Nation in Europe and Judea . . . a way for their Conversion to Christ* (1658).

(——) *A Narrative Of the late Proceeds at White-Hall, Concerning The Jews* (1656).

Jones, Thomas Wharton, ed., *A True Relation of the Life and Death of . . . William Bedell* (Camden Soc., n.s., iv, 1872).

Ben Jonson, ed. C. H. Herford and E. and P. Simpson (Oxford, 1925–52).

Josselin, Ralph, *Diary*, ed. Alan Macfarlane (1976).

Josselyn, John, *An Account of Two Voyages to New-England* (1674).

Journals of the House of Commons, v.

Journals of the House of Lords, x.

Kenyon, J. P., ed., *The Stuart Constitution* (1969).

Kidder, Richard, *A Demonstration of the Messias . . . proved especially against The Jews* (1684–1700).

L., D., *Israels Condition and Cause pleaded; Or some Arguments for the Jews Admission into England* (1656).

Landa, Diego de, *Relación de las Cosas de Yucatan*, trans. Alfred M. Tozzer (Cambridge, Mass., 1941). Written about 1566.

Laud, William, *A Sermon Preached Before His Maiesty, . . . the nineteenth of Iune, at Wansted. Anno Dom. 1621.* (1621).

Lechford, Thomas, *Plain Dealing: or, Newes from New-England* (1642).

L(ee), S(amuel), *Israel Redux: Or The Restauration of Israel* (1677).

Leibniz, G. W., *Opuscules et fragments inédits*, ed. Louis Couturat (Paris, 1903).

Leigh, Edward, *Critica Sacra . . . Observations on all the Radices or Primitive Hebrew Words* (3rd edn., 1662). First edn., 1641.

Lery, Iean de, *Histoire D'vn Voyage Fait en la Terre dv Bresil* (La Rochelle, 1578).

Lescarbot, Marc, *Histoire de la Nowelle France* (Paris, 1609).

—— *Nova Francia: Or the Description of . . . New France* (1609).

L'Estrange, Hamon, *Americans no Iewes* (1652).

—— *The Reign of King Charles* (1655).

Leti, Gregoire, *La Vie D'Olivier Cromwel* (Amsterdam, 1746).

Ley, John, *Sunday a Sabbath* (1641).

Lhoyd, H. and Dauid Powel, *The historie of Cambria, now called Wales* (1584).

El Libro de los Acuerdos: Being The Records and Accompts of the Spanish and Portuguese Synagogue of London from 1663 to 1681, trans. Lionel D. Barnett (Oxford, 1931).

The Life and Death of Mr. Henry Jessey (1671).

Lilly, William, *Monarchy Or No Monarchy in England* (1651).

A List of some of the Grand Blasphemers and Blasphemies, Which was given in to The Committee for Religion (1654).

Lithgow, William, *A . . . peregrination from Scotland, to the most famous King-domes in Europe, Asia and Affricke* (1614).

—— *The Totall Discourse of The Rare Adventures & Painefull Peregrinations* (Glasgow, 1906). First pub. 1632, enlarged edn. of 1614.

Liturgiae Britannicae, or The Several Editions of The Book of Common Prayer (2nd edn., 1851).

Livro De Bet Haim Do Kahal Kados De Bet Yahacob, ed. Wilhelmina C. Pieterse (Assen, 1970).

(Lodowyck, Francis), *A Common Writing* (1646).

—— *The Ground-Work* . . . *For the Framing of a New Perfect Langvuage: And an Vniversall or Common Writing* (1652).

—— *Works*, ed. Vivian Salmon (1972).

Lynche, Richard, *An Historical Treatise of the Travels of Noah into Europe* (1601).

The Book of Ser Marco Polo, ed. Henry Yule (3rd edn., 1921).

Mather, Cotton, *Magnalia Christi Americana: Or The Ecclesiastical History of New-England* (1702).

Maton, Robert, *Christs Personall Reigne on Earth* . . . *the Jewes Conversion to the Faith and Restoration into a visible Kingdom in Judea* (1652).

—— *Israels Redemption* (1642).

The Voiage and Travaile of Sir John Maundevile, ed. J. O. Halliwell (1869).

Mede, Joseph, *Daniels Weekes* (1643).

—— *Remaines On some Passages in The Revelation* (1650).

—— *Works* (1677).

Menasseh ben Israel, *Esperança De Israel* (Amsterdam, 1650).

—— *Gratvlaçao de Menasseh Ben Israel* . . . *Ao Celsissimo Principe De Orange Frederique Henrique* . . . *Em compahnia da Serenissima Raynha Henrica Maria* (1642?).

—— *The Hope of Israel*, ed. Moses Wall (2nd edn., 1652).

—— *Of The Term Of Life*, ed. T. Pococke (1699).

—— 'The Relation of Master Antonie Monterinos', in T. Thorowgood, *Ievves in America*, pp. 129–38.

—— *Spes Israelis* (Amsterdam, 1650).

—— *To His Highnesse The Lord Protector* . . . *The Humble Addresses of Menasseh Ben Israel* (n.d.=1655). Some copies printed in Amsterdam?

—— *Vindiciae Judaeorum* (1656).

Mendieta, Gerónimo de, *Historia Eclesiástica Indiana* (Mexico City, 1870).

Mersenne, Marin, *Correspondance*, ed. P. Tannery *et al.* (Paris, 1945–   ).

(Mexia, Pedro), *The Foreste or Collection of Histories* (1571).

—— *Times Store-Hovse* (1619).

Middlesex County Records, iii, ed. J. C. Jeaffreson (Middlesex County Rec. Soc., 1888).

County of Middlesex, Calendar to the Sessions Records, ed. William Le Hardy (1935–7).

Milton, John, *Complete Poems and Major Prose*, ed. M. Y. Hughes (New York, 1957).

—— *Complete Prose Works*, ed. D. M. Wolfe, *et al.* (New Haven, 1953–   ).

—— *Works*, ed. F. A. Patterson, *et al.* (New York, 1931–40).

Modena, Leone da, *The History of the Rites, Customes, and Manner of Life, of the Present Jews, throughout the world*, trans. Edmund Chilmead (1650).

Monteth, Robert, *The History of the Troubles of Great Britain* (1735). Trans. from 2nd French edn., 1661.

More, Henry, *Conjectura Cabbalistica* (1653).

Muggleton, Lodowick, *The Acts of the Witnesses of the Spirit* (1699).

—— *A True Interpretation of* . . . *Revelation* (1665).

—— *A True Interpretation of the Eleventh Chapter of the Revelation* (1751).

The Nicholas Papers, ed. G. F. Warner (Camden Soc., n.s., xl, l, lvii; 3rd ser., xxxi; 1886–1920).

Nicholas, Edward, *An Apology For The Honorable Nation of the Jews* (1648), Pseud.

Nickolls, John, ed., *Original Letters and Papers of State* (1743).

Norice, Edw(ard), *The New Gospel, not the True Gospel. Or, A discovery of the Life and Death, Doctrin, and Doings of Mr. Iohn Traske* (1638).

—— *A Treatise Maintaining that Temporall Blessings are to bee sought . . . also a Discovery of the late dangerous errours of Mr. Iohn Traske* (1636).

Norton, John, *Abel being Dead yet speaketh; Or, The Life & Death Of . . . John Cotton* (1658).

Norwood, Robert, *Proposals for propagation of the Gospel, Offered to the Parliament* (n.d.=1651–2).

(Overton, Richard), *The Araignement of Mr. Persecvtion* (1645). Repr. in *Tracts on Liberty*, ed. W. Haller (New York, 1934).

Owen, John, *Of the Divine Originall . . . of the Scriptvres* (Oxford, 1659).

P., L., *Two Essays sent in a Letter from Oxford* (1695).

A Pack of Hell-hounds (n.d.).

Pagitt, E., *Heresiography* (6th edn., 1661).

A Paper, shewing that the great Conversion and Restauration of all Israel and Judah will be fulfilled at Christs second coming . . . (1 May 1674).

Pepys, Samuel, *Diary*, ed. Robert Latham and William Matthews (1970–   ).

Peter, Hugh, *Gods Doings, And Mans Duty* (1646).

—— *A word for the Armie. And two words to the Kingdome* (1647).

Philo-Judaeus, J.J., *Resurrections of Dead Bones, or the Conversion of the Jews* (1655).

Plot, Robert, *The Natural History of Oxford-Shire* (Oxford, 1677).

Plymouth Municipal Records, Calendar, ed. R. N. Worth (Plymouth, 1893).

Pordage, John, *Innocencie Appearing* (1655).

Postel, Guillaume, *Des Histoires Orientales* (Paris, 1575).

The Pourtraiture of his Royal Highness, Oliver (1659).

Powell, Vavasor, *Concordance . . . Also a Collection of those Scripture-Prophesies which relate to the Call of the Jews* (1671).

Prideaux, Mathias, *An Easy and Compendious Introduction For Reading all sorts of Histories* (Oxford, 1648).

Privy Council, Acts, 1613–14, 1615–16.

All the Proceedings at the Sessions of the Peace holden at Westminster, on the 20. day of Iune, 1651 (1651). Concerning Robins.

Prynne, William, *A Short Demurrer To the Jewes Long discontinued barred Remitter into England* (2nd edn., 1656).

—— *The Second Part* (1656).

The Whole Book of Psalmes (n.p.=Cambridge, Mass., 1640), Bay Psalm Book.

Deputy Keeper, Public Records, *App. to 5th Rep.*

Purchas, Samuel, *Pvrchas his Pilgrimage* (2nd edn., 1614).

—— *Purchas His Pilgrimes* (Glasgow, 1905). First pub. 1625.

Raguenet, *Histoire D'Olivier Cromwel* (Utrecht, 1692).

Reeve, John and Lodowick Muggleton, *A Transcedent Spiritual Treatise* (1756).

Richardson, Samuel, *The Necessity of Toleration in Matters of Religion* (1647). Repr. E. B. Underhill, *Tracts*, pp. 233–85.

Robertson, William, *The First Gate . . . The Second Gate . . . to the Holy Tongue* (1654–5).

(Robinson, Henry), *Liberty of Conscience* (1643).

(Rochefort, Charles), *The History of the Caribby-Islands* (1666).

Rogers, John, *Ohel or Beth-Shemesh A Tabernacle for the Sun* (1653).

R(oss), A(lexander), *A View of the Jewish Religion* (1656).

—— *[Pansebeia]. Or, A View of all Religions in the World* (4th edn., 1664).

S., I., *An Invitation of a Seeker* (1670).

(Sadler, John), *Rights of the Kingdom* (1649).

Sanders, John, *An Iron Rod Put Into The Lord Protectors Hand* (1655).

Sandys, George, *Sandys Travels* (7th edn., 1673).

The Second Part of Saint George for England [1659].

Selden, John, *Table Talk*, ed. Sir Frederick Pollock (1927).

Shawe, John, *The Princes Royal* (1650).

Shepard, Thomas, *Theses Sabbaticae. Or, The Doctrine Of The Sabbath* (1649).

Simpson, W. Sparrow, ed., *Documents Illustrating the History of S. Paul's Cathedral* (Camden Soc., n.s., xxvi, 1880).

South, Robert, *A Sermon Preached At the Cathedral Church of St. Paul, Novemb. 9. 1662* (1663).

Spence, Joseph, *Anecdotes, Observations, and Characters, of Books and Men.* (2nd edn., 1858).

S(pencer), E(dward, Sir), *A Breife Epistle to the Learned Manasseh Ben Israel* (1650).

—— *'To the Translator of Menasseh; Ben Israels spes Israelis'*, in Menasseh ben Israel, *Hope*, pp. 56–7, 61–2.

Sylvester, Josuah, *Du Bartas His Diuine Weekes* (1641).

—— *Works*, ed. Alexander B. Grosart (Edinburgh, 1880).

Tany, Thomas, *Hear, O Earth, ye earthen men and women* (1654).

—— *I Proclaime From the Lord of Hosts The returne of the Jewes From their Captivity* (1650).

—— *The Nations Right in Magna Charta* (n.d.=1651).

—— *ThauRam Tanjah his Speech* (1654).

—— *Theavra UIO Hn High Priest to the Iewes, his Disputive challenge to the Universities of Oxford and Cambridge* (n.d.=1651).

—— *Theavravjohn His Aurora in Tranlagorum* (1651).

—— *Theavravjohn His Theousori Apokolipikal* (1651).

Taylor, John, *Ranters of both Sexes* (1651).

—— *A Swarme of Sectaries* (1641).

Thevet, André, *La Cosmographie Vniverselle* (Paris, 1575).

Thorowgood, Tho(mas), *Iewes in America, Or, Probabilities That the Americans are of that Race. With . . . earnest desires . . . to make them Christian* (1650).

—— *Jews in America* (1660).

A Collection of the State Papers of John Thurloe, Esq., ed. T. Birch (1742).

Tillinghast, John, *Generation Work* (1653).

Tomlinson, W., *A Bosome opened To The Jewes* (1655–6).

Townshend, Henry, *Diary*, ed. J. W. Willis Bund (Worcestershire Hist. Soc., xxxi, 1915–20).

Traske, John, *A Pearle For a Prince* (1615).

—— *The Power of Preaching* (1623).

—— *A Treatise of Libertie From Iudaisme* (1620).

Tyndale, W., *An Answer to Sir Thomas More's Dialogue, The Supper of the Lord*, ed. H. Walter (Parker Soc., xxxviii, 1850).

Udall, John, *The Key Of The Holy Tongve* (Leiden, 1593). Repr. in 1650.

(Urquhart, Thomas), *The Discovery of A most exquisite Jewel* (1652).

—— *Logopandecteision, Or An Introdvction To The Vniversal Langvage* (1653).

—— *Works* (Edinburgh, 1834).

Ussher, James, *Works*, ed. C. R. Elrington and J. M. Todd (Dublin, 1847–64), vol. xvi.

Valentine, Thomas, *A Charge Against the Jews . . . for not coming to Christ* (1647).

Vaughan, Henry, *Works*, ed. L. C. Martin (Oxford, 2nd edn., 1957).

Verstegan, Richard *alias* Richard Rowlands, *A Restitvtion of Decayed Intelligence* (Antwerp, 1605). 2nd edn., London, 1655.

Verus Pater, Or, A bundell of Truths . . . And dedicated to the ancient memory of old Erra-Pater (1622).

Wakefield, Robert, *oratio de laudibus & vtilitate triū linguar/* (n.d.=1524).

(Walker, Clement), *Anarchia Anglicana: Or, The History Of Independency. The Second Part* (1649).

Wall, Moses, 'Considerations Upon the Point of the Conversion Of the Jews', in Menasseh ben Israel, *Hope*, pp. 47–62.

The Wandering-Jew, Telling Fortvnes to English-men (1640).

(Warner, John), *The Devilish Conspiracy . . . Executed by the Jewes, against . . . Christ* (1648).

Webb, John, *An Historical Essay Endeavoring a Probability That the Language Of the Empire of China is the Primitive Language* (1669).

Webster, Jo(hn), *Academiarum Examen, Or The Examination of Academies* (1654).

Weemse, Iohn, *The Christian Synagogue* (1623).

—— *An Explanation Of The Ceremoniall Lavves Of Moses* (1632).

—— *An Exposition Of The Morall Law, Or Ten Commandments* (1632).

—— *A Treatise Of The Fovre Degenerate Sonnes* (1636).

Whately, William, *Prototypes, Or, The Primarie Precedent Presidents Ovt Of The Booke Of Genesis* (1640).

White, Fr(ancis), *An Examination and Confutation of a Lawlesse Pamphlet* (1637).

—— *A Treatise Of The Sabbath-Day* (3rd edn., 1636).

Whitelocke, Bulstrode, *Memoirs, Biographical and Historical*, ed. R. H. Whitelocke (1860).

—— *Memorials of the English Affairs . . . To The End of the Reign of James the first* (1709).

—— *Memorials of the English Affairs from the beginning of the reign of Charles the First to the Happy Restoration* (Oxford, 1853).

Whitelocke, James, *Liber Famelicus of Sir James Whitelocke*, ed. John Bruce (Camden Soc., lxx, 1858).

Whitfield, Henry, *The Light appearing more and more towards the perfect Day* (1651). Also repr. *Coll. Mass. Hist. Soc.*, 3rd ser., iv. (1834), 101–47.

Whitgift, John, *Works*, ed. John Ayre (Parker Soc., 1851–3).

Wilkins, John, *An Essay Towards a Real Character, And a Philosophical Language* (1668). Printed for the Royal Society.

—— *Mercvry, Or The Secret and Swift Messenger: Shewing, How a Man may with Privacy and Speed communicate his Thoughts to a Friend at any distance* (1641). Another edn. pub. at London in 1694.

(—— and Seth Ward), *Vindicae Academiarum Containing, Some briefe Animadversions upon Mr Websters Book, stiled, The Examination of Academies* (Oxford, 1654).

Williams, R. F., ed., *The Court and Times of James the First* (1849).

(Williams, Roger), *The Blovdy Tenent, of Persecution* (1644).

—— *The Bloody Tenent Yet More Bloody* (1652).

—— *The Fourth Paper, Presented by Maior Butler, To the Honourable Committee of Parliament, for the Propagating the Gospel* (1652).

Winslow, Edward, *A further Account of the progress of the Gospel Amongst the Indians In New England* (1660).

—— *The Glorious Progress of the Gospel* (1649). Repr. *Coll. Mass. Hist. Soc.*, 3rd ser., iv (1834), 69–98.

Wood, Anthony, *Athenae Oxonienses*, ed. Philip Bliss (1813–20).

—— *Fasti Oxonienses*, ed. Philip Bliss (1815–20).

—— *The History and Antiquities of the University of Oxford*, ed. John Gutch, (Oxford, 1792–6).

—— *Life and Times*, ed. Andrew Clark (Oxford Hist. Soc., 1891–1900).

Wood, William, *New Englands Prospect* (1634).

Worthington, John, *Diary and Correspondence*, ed. James Crossley and R. C. Christie (Chetham Soc., xiii, xxxvi, cxiv, 1847–86).

Yonge, Walter, *Diary*, ed. George Roberts (Camden Soc., xli, 1848).

Zamora, Alonso de, *Historia de la Provincia de San Antonio del Nuevo Reino de Granada* (Caracas, 1930).

The Zohar, ed. Harry Sperling & Maurice Simon (1931–4).

B. NEWSPAPERS

Certain Passages (1654–5).

The Faithfull Scout (1654–5).

Mercurius Fumigosus (1655).

Mercurius Politicus (1655–6)

Mercurius Pragmaticus (1648–9).

The Moderate (1649).

The Moderate Intelligencer (1649).

A Perfect Account (1651–5).

The Perfect Diurnall (1655).

Perfect Passages (1652).

Perfect Proceedings (1655).

The Publick Intelligencer (1655–6).

The Weekly Intelligencer (1654–5).

The Weekly Post (1655).

C. SELECT SECONDARY WORKS

Abercrombie, D., 'Forgotten Phoneticians', *Trans. Philol. Soc. 1948*, 1–34.

Abrahams, B. Lionel, 'The Expulsion of the Jews from England in 1290', *Jew. Qly. Rev.*, vii (1895), 75–100, 236–58, 428–58.

Abrahams, I. and C. E. Sayle, 'The Purchase of Hebrew Books by the English Parliament in 1647', *Trs. Jew. Hist. Soc. Eng.*, viii (1918), 63–77.

Abulafia Corcos, D., 'Samuel Pallache and his London Trial' (Hebrew), *Zion*, xxv (1960), 122–33.

Adler, E. N., 'A Letter of Menasseh Ben Israel', *Trs. Jew. Hist. Soc. Eng.*, v (1908), 174–83.

Adler, M., 'History of the "Domus Conversorum" from 1290 to 1891', *Trs. Jew. Hist. Soc. Eng.*, iv (1903), 16–75.

—— *Jews of Medieval England* (1939).

Allen, D. C., *The Legend of Noah* (Urbana, 1949).

—— 'Some Theories of the Growth and Origin of Language in Milton's Age', *Phil. Qly.*, xxviii (1949), 5–16.

Allen, W. S., 'Ancient Ideas on the Origin and Development of Language', *Trans. Philol. Soc. 1948*, 35–60.

Anderson, G. K., *The Legend of the Wandering Jew* (Providence, 1965).

Appleton, W. W., *A Cycle of Cathay: The Chinese Vogue in England during the Seventeenth and Eighteenth Centuries* (New York, 1951).

Arkin, M., 'West European Jewry in the Age of Mercantilism: An Economic Interpretation', *Hist. Jud.*, xxii (1960), 85–104.

Armytage, W. H. G., *Heavens Below: Utopian Experiments in England 1560–1960* (1961).

Avis, P. D. L., 'Moses and the Magistrate: a Study in the rise of Protestant Legalism', *Jnl. Eccl. Hist.*, xxvi (1975), 149–72.

Bailey, M. L., *Milton and Jakob Boehme* (New York, 1914).

Ball, B. W., *A Great Expectation: Eschatological Thought in English Protestantism to 1660* (Leiden, 1975).

Balliol College, *Catalogue of the Manuscripts*, ed. R. A. B. Mynors (Oxford, 1963).

Barbour, H., *The Quakers in Puritan England* (New Haven and London, 1964).

Bardach, E., 'Philosemitism and the Resettlement of the Jews in England', *King's Crown Essays*, viii (1960), 44–63.

Barnett, R. D., 'The Burial Register of the Spanish and Portuguese Jews, London 1657–1735', *Misc. Jew. Hist. Soc. Eng.*, vi (1962), 1–72.

Baroway, I., 'Toward Understanding Tudor-Jacobean Hebrew Studies', *Jew. Soc. Stud.*, xviii (1956), 3–24.

Batten, J. M., *John Dury: Advocate of Christian Reunion* (Chicago, 1944).

Beinart, H., 'The Jews in the Canary Islands: a Re-evaluation', *Trs. Jew. Hist. Soc. Eng.*, xxv (1977), 48–86.

Bendyshe, T., 'The History of Anthropology', *Men. Antho. Soc. Lond.*, i (1865), 335–458.

Ben-Sasson, H. H., *A History of the Jewish People* (1976).

Black, G. F., 'The Beginnings of the Study of Hebrew in Scotland', in *Studies in Jewish Bibliography*, ed. L. Ginzberg, et al. (New York, 1929), pp. 463–80.

Blau, J. L., *The Christian Interpretation of the Cabala in the Renaissance* (New York, 1944).

Bloom, H. I., *The Economic Activities of the Jews of Amsterdam in the Seventeenth and Eighteenth Centuries* (Port Washington, NY, 1969 [1937]).

Blunt, J. E., *A History of the Establishment and Residence of the Jews in England* (1830).

Blunt, J. H., *Dictionary of Sects, Heresies, Ecclesiastical Parties, and Schools of Religious Thought* (London, Oxford, and Cambridge, 1874).

Bonfante, G., 'Ideas on the Kinship of the European Languages from 1200 to 1800', *Jnl. Wrld. Hist.*, i (1953–4), 679–99.

Borst, A., *Der Turmbau von Babel* (Stuttgart, 1957–63), III/1.

Bossy, J., *The English Catholic Community 1570–1850* (1975).

Bosworth, C. E., 'William Lithgow of Lanark's Travels in Syria and Palestine, 1611–1612', *Jnl. Sem. Stud.*, xx (1975), 219–35.

Bowman, J., 'Is America the New Jerusalem or Gog and Magog? A Seventeenth Century Theological Discussion', *Proc. Leeds Phil. and Lit. Soc.*, vi (1950), 445–52.

—— 'A Seventeenth Century Bill of "Rights" for Jews', *Jew. Qly. Rev.*, n.s., xxxix (1949), 379–95.

Bresslau, H., 'Juden und Mongolen 1241', *Zft. Ges. Jud. Deutsch.*, i (1886–7), 99–102.

Brugmans, Hk. and A. Frank, *Geschiedenis Der Joden In Nederland* (Amsterdam, 1940).

Brunton, D. and D. H. Pennington, *Members of the Long Parliament* (1954).

Bueno De Mesquita, D., 'The Historical Associations of the Ancient Burial-Ground of the Sephardi Jews', *Trs. Jew. Hist. Soc. Eng.*, x (1924), 225–54.

Burke, J. G., 'The Wild Man's Pedigree: Scientific Method and Racial Anthropology', in Dudley and Novak, *Wild Man*, pp. 259–80.

Burrage, C., *The Early English Dissenters* (Cambridge, 1912).

Butterfield, H., 'Toleration in Early Modern Times', *Jnl. Hist. Ideas*, xxxviii (1977), 573–84.

Capp, B. S., *The Fifth Monarchy Men* (1972).

—— '*Godly Rule* and English Millenarianism', *Past and Present*, lii (1971), 106–17.

—— 'The Millennium and Eschatology in England', *Past and Present*, lvii (1972), 156–62.

Carlton, W. J., *Timothe Bright* (1911).

Carte, T., *A Collection of Original Letters and Papers* (1739).

Carter, A. C., *The English Reformed Church in Amsterdam in the Seventeenth Century* (Amsterdam, 1964).

C(assuto), J., 'Aus dem ältesten Protokollbuch der Portugiesisch–Jüdischen Gemeinde in Hamburg', *Jbh. Jüd. Lit. Gft.*, vi–ii (1909), vi. 1–54; vii. 159–210.

Ch'en, Shou-yi, 'John Webb: A Forgotten Page in the Early History of Sinology in Europe', *Chinese Soc. and Pol. Sci. Rev.*, xix (1935), 295–330.

Chiappelli, F. (ed.), *First Images of America: The Impact of the New World on the Old* (Berkeley, 1976).

Chomsky, Noam, *Cartesian Linguistics* (New York and London, 1966).

Christianson, P., *Reformers and Babylon: English Apocalyptic Visions from the Reformation to the Eve of the Civil War* (Toronto, 1978).

Cohen, A., *An Anglo-Jewish Scrapbook 1600–1840 The Jew through English Eyes* (1943).

Cohen, J., 'On The Project of a Universal Character', *Mind*, lxiii (1954), 49–63.

Cohn, N., *Europe's Inner Demons* (1975).

—— *The Pursuit of the Millennium* (2nd edn., 1970).

Collinson, P., 'The Beginnings of English Sabbatarianism', *Stud. Ch. Hist.*, i (1964), 207–21.

Cornelius, P., *Languages in Seventeenth- and Early Eighteenth-Century Imaginary Voyages* (Geneva, 1965).

Coudert, A., 'A Quaker-Kabbalist Controversy: George Fox's Reaction to Francis Mercury van Helmont', *Jnl. Warb. Ctld. Inst.*, xxxix (1976), 171–89.

Couturat, L., *La Logique de Leibniz* (Paris, 1901).

—— and L. Leau, *Histoire de la langue universelle* (Paris, 1903).

Cox, R., *The Literature of The Sabbath Question* (Edinburgh, 1865).

Crosby, T., *The History of the English Baptists* (1738–40).

Curtis, M. H., *Oxford and Cambridge in Transition 1558–1642* (Oxford, 1959).

Daiches, D., *The King James Version* (Chicago, 1941).

David, M. V.–, *Le Débat sur les écritures et l'hiéroglyphe aux XVIIe et XVIIIe siècles* (Paris, 1965).

Davies, D. W., *Elizabethans Errant: The Strange Fortunes of Sir Thomas Sherley and His Three Sons* (Ithaca, NY, 1967).

Davies, H. N., 'Bishop Godwin's "Lunatique Language"', *Jnl. Warb. Ctld. Inst.*, xxx (1967), 296–316.

De Bethencourt, C., 'Lettres de Menasseh ben Israel à Isaac Vossius (1651–1655)', *Rev. Etud. Jvs.*, xlix (1904), 98–109.

Debus, A. G., *Science and Education in the Seventeenth Century: The Webster—Ward Debate* (London and New York, 1970).

De Jong, J. A., *As The Waters Cover The Sea: Millennial Expectations in the Rise of Anglo-American Missions 1640–1810* (Kampen, 1970).

DeMott, B., 'Comenius and the Real Character in England', *Proc. Mod. Lang. Assoc.*, lxx (1955), 1068–81.

—— 'Science versus Mnemonics: Notes on John Ray and on John Wilkins' *Essay toward a Real Character*', *Isis*, xlviii (1957), 3–12.

—— 'The Sources and Development of John Wilkins' Philosophical Language', *Jnl. Eng. Germ. Philol.*, lvii (1958), 1–13.

Diamond, A. S., 'The Cemetery of the Resettlement', *Trs. Jew. Hist. Soc. Eng.*, xix (1960), 163–90.

—— 'The Community of the Resettlement, 1656–1684: A Social Survey', *Trs. Jew. Hist. Soc. Eng.*, xxiv (1975), 134–50.

Dictionary of National Biography.

Dottin, G., *La Langue Gauloise* (Paris, 1920).

Dudley, E. and M. E. Novak, eds., *The Wild Man Within* (Pittsburgh, 1972).

Elliott, J. H., *The Old World and the New 1492–1650* (Cambridge, 1972).

Elliott, R. W. V., 'Isaac Newton as Phonetician', *Mod. Lang. Rev.*, xlix (1954), 5–12.

—— 'Isaac Newton's "Of An Universall Language"', *Mod. Lang. Rev.*, lii (1957), 1–18.

Elman, P., 'The Economic Causes of the Expulsion of the Jews in 1290', *Econ. Hist. Rev.*, vii (1937), 145–54.

Emery, C., 'John Wilkins and Noah's Ark', *Mod. Lang. Qly.*, ix (1948), 286–91.

—— 'John Wilkins' Universal Language', *Isis*, xxxviii (1947–8), 174–85.

Encyclopaedia Judaica (Jerusalem, 1971–2).

Ettinger, S., 'The Beginnings of the Change in the Attitude of European Society Towards the Jews', *Scripta Hierosolymitana*, vii (1961), 193–219.

Fines, J., '"Judaising" in the Period of the English Reformation—The Case of Richard Bruern', *Trs. Jew. Hist. Soc. Eng.*, xxi (1968), 323–6.

Firth, C. H., ed., *Scotland and the Protectorate* (Scot. Hist. Soc., xxxi, 1899).

Firth, J. R., *The Tongues of Men* (1937).

In Memory of J. R. Firth, ed. C. E. Bazell, *et al.* (1966).

Firth, K. R., *The Apocalyptic Tradition in Reformation Britain 1530–1645* (Oxford, 1979).

Fisch, H., *The Dual Image* (1971).

—— *Jerusalem and Albion* (1964).

Fish, S. E., *Surprised By Sin* (Berkeley and London, 1971).

Fletcher, H. F., *Milton's Rabbinical Readings* (Urbana, 1930).

—— *Milton's Semitic Studies* (Chicago, 1926).

—— *The Use of the Bible in Milton's Prose* (Urbana, 1929).

Formigari, L., *Linguistica ed empirismo nel Seicento inglese* (Bari, 1970).

Fraenkel, J., 'From the English Hoveve Zion Movement to the Balfour Declaration' (Yiddish), *Yivo Bleter*, xliii (1966), 72–147.

Frank, J., *The Beginnings of the English Newspaper 1620–1660* (Cambridge, Mass., 1961).

Friedman, J., 'Michael Servetus: the Case for a Jewish Christianity', *Sixteenth Cent. Jnl.*, iv (1973), 87–110.

Friedman, L. M., 'A Petition for the Readmission of the Jews', *Trs. Jew. Hist. Soc. Eng.*, xvi (1952), 222–3.

Friedrich, P., *Timothe Brights Characterie entwicklungsgeschichtlich und kritisch betrachtet* (Leipzig, 1914).

Fuks, L., 'Het Hebreeuwse Brievenboek van Johannes Drusius Jr.', *Stud. Rosenthaliana*, iii (1969), 1–52.

—— and R., 'The Hebrew Production of the Plantin–Raphelengius Presses in Leyden, 1585–1615', *Stud. Rosenthaliana*, iv (1970), 1–24.

Funke, O., 'On the Sources of John Wilkins' Philosophical Language (1668)', *Eng. Stud.*, xl (1959), 208–14.

—— *Zum Weltsprachenproblem in England im 17. Jahrhundert* (Heidelberg, 1929).

Gamble, J. L. and C. H. Greene, 'The Sabbath in the British Isles' in *Seventh Day Baptists in Europe and America* (Plainfield, NJ, 1910), pp. 21–115.

Gans, M., *Memorboek* (Baarn, 1971).

Gaster, M., *History of the Ancient Synagogue of the Spanish and Portuguese Jews* (1901).

Glass, H. A., *The Barbone Parliament* (1899).

Glassman, B., *Anti-Semitic Stereotypes Without Jews* (Detroit, 1976).

Godbey, A. H., *The Lost Tribes A Myth* (Durham, NC, 1930).

Gollancz, H., 'A Contribution to the History of the Readmission of the Jews', *Trs. Jew. Hist. Soc. Eng.*, vi (1912), 189–204.

Gould y Quincy, A. B., 'Nueva Lista Documentada de los Tripulantes de Colón en 1492', *Bol. Real. Acad. Hist.*, lxxv (1924), 34–49.

Graetz, H., *History of the Jews*, iv and v (1891–8).

Greene, C. H., 'Trask in the Star-Chamber, 1619', *Trs. Bap. Hist. Soc.*, v (1916–17), 8–14.

Greenslade, S. L., ed., *The Cambridge History of the Bible . . . From The Reformation* (Cambridge, 1963).

Groen, J. J., 'Historical and Genetic Studies on the Twelve Tribes of Israel and Their Relation to the Present Ethnic Composition of the Jewish People', *Jew. Qly. Rev.*, lviii (1967–8), 1–11.

Gunnell, W. A., *Sketches of Hull Celebrities* (Hull, 1876). Note that the MSS printed here are of doubtful authenticity.

Hall, D. D., *The Faithful Shepherd: A History of the New England Ministry in the Seventeenth Century* (Chapel Hill, NC, 1972).

Halpern, I., 'On the Threatened Expulsion of Polish and Lithuanian Jewry in the Latter Half of the Seventeenth Century' (Hebrew), *Zion*, xvii (1952), 65–74. Concerning the charity work of Dury and Jessey.

Harris, I., 'A Dutch Burial-Ground and its English Connections', *Trs. Jew. Hist. Soc. Eng.*, vii (1915), 113–46. The cemetery at Middelburg.

Henriques, H. S. Q., *The Jews and the English Law* (1908).

—— *The Return of the Jews to England* (1905).

Henriques de Castro, D., *Keur Van Grafsteenen op de Nederl.-Portug.-Israël. Begraafplaats te Ouderkerk aan den Amstel* (Leiden, 1883).

—— *1675–1875. De Synagoge der Portugeesch–Israelitische Gemeente Te Amsterdam* (The Hague, 1875).

Herzog, I., 'John Selden and Jewish Law', *Pub. Soc. Jew. Juris.*, iii (1931).

Hill, C., *Antichrist in Seventeenth-Century England* (1971).

—— *Change and Continuity in Seventeenth-Century England* (1974), esp. for the essay, 'Arise Evans: Welshman in London', pp. 48–77.

—— *Intellectual Origins of the English Revolution* (Panther edn., 1972).

—— *Puritanism and Revolution* (2nd edn., New York, 1964).

—— *Society and Puritanism* (2nd edn., New York, 1967).

—— *The World Turned Upside Down* (New York, 1972).

Hill, C. and M. Shepherd, 'The case of Arise Evans: a historical-psychiatric study', *Psychological Med.*, vi (1976), 351–8.

Hirst, D., *Hidden Riches* (1964).

—— 'The Riddle of John Pordage', *Jacb Boehme Soc. Qly.*, i. n°. 6 (1953–1954), 5–15.

Hodgen, M. T., *Early Anthropology in the Sixteenth and Seventeenth Centuries* (Philadelphia, 1964).

Howell, R., *Newcastle Upon Tyne and the Puritan Revolution* (Oxford, 1967).

Huddleston, L. E., *Origins of the American Indians* (Austin, Tex., and London, 1967).

Hunter, G. K., 'The Theology of Marlowe's *The Jew of Malta*', *Jnl. Warb. Ctld. Inst.*, xxvii (1964), 211–40.

Hutin, S., *Les Disciples Anglais de Jacob Boehme aux XVIIe et XVIIIe siècles* (Paris, 1960).

Hyamson, A. M., *A History of the Jews in England* (1908).

—— 'The lost tribes, and the influence of the search for them on the return of the Jews to England', *Jew. Qly. Rev.*, xv (1903), 640–76. Similarly in *Trs. Jew. Hist. Soc. Eng.*, v (1908), 115–47.

—— *The Sephardim of England* (1951).

Israel, J., *Race, Class and Politics in Colonial Mexico 1610–1670* (1975).

Jack-Hinton, C., *The Search for the Islands of Solomon 1567–1838* (Oxford, 1969).

Jacobs, J. & L. Wolf, *Bibliotheca Anglo-Judaica* (1888).

James, M., *Social Problems and Policy During the Puritan Revolution 1640–1660* (1930).

Jordan, W. K., *The Development of Religious Toleration in England* (1932–40).

Kayserling, M., *The Life and Labours of Manasseh Ben Israel* (1877). Pub. as *Misc. Heb. Lit.*, 2nd ser., ii. 1–96, from German orig. edn., Berlin, 1861.

Kellaway, W., *The New England Company 1649–1776* (1961).

Kellenbenz, H., *Sephardim an der Unteren Elbe* (Wiesbaden, 1958).

Knappen, M. M., *Tudor Puritanism* (2nd edn., Chicago, 1970).

Knowlson, J. R., 'The Idea of Gesture as a Universal Language in the XVIIth and XVIIIth Centuries', *Jnl. Hist. Ideas*, xxvi (1965), 495–508.

—— *Universal language schemes in England and France 1600–1800* (Toronto and Buffalo, 1975).

Kobler, F., 'Sir Henry Finch (1558–1625) and the first English advocates of the Restoration of the Jews to Palestine', *Trs. Jew. Hist. Soc. Eng.*, xvi (1952), 101–20.

Kochan, L., *The Jew and his History* (1977).

Koenen, H. J., *Geschiedenis der Joden in Nederland* (Utrecht, 1843).

Kohler, M. J., 'Some Early American Zionist Projects', *Pub. Am. Jew. Hist. Soc.*, viii (1900), 75–118.

Koyré, A., *La Philosophie de Jacob Boehme* (Paris, 1929).

Kuhn, A. K., 'Hugh Grotius and The Emancipation of the Jews in Holland', *Pub. Am. Jew. Hist. Soc.*, xxxi (1928), 173–80.

Lach, D., 'The Chinese Studies of Andreas Müller', *Jnl. Or. Soc.*, lx (1940), 564–75.

—— 'Leibniz and China', *Jnl. Hist. Ideas*, vi (1945), 436–55.

Lamont, W. M., *Godly Rule: Politics and Religion, 1603–60* (1969).

Lehmann, R. P., *Anglo-Jewish Bibliography 1937–1970* (1973).

Leonard, G. H., 'The Expulsion of the Jews by Edward I', *Trs. Roy. Hist. Soc.*, 2nd ser., v (1891), 103–46.

Levy, A., 'The Origins of Scottish Jewry', *Trs. Jew. Hist. Soc. Eng.*, xix (1960), 129–62.

Levy, S., 'John Dury and The English Jewry', *Trs. Jew. Hist. Soc. Eng.*, iv (1903), 76–82.

Liljegren, S. B., *Harrington and the Jews* (Lund, 1932).

Lillywhite, B., *London Coffee Houses* (1963).

Lipman, V. D., ed., *Three Centuries of Anglo-Jewish History* (1961).

Liu, T., 'The Calling of the Barebones Parliament Reconsidered', *Jnl. Eccl. Hist.*, xxii (1971), 223–36.

Loewe, R., 'Jewish Scholarship in England', in Lipman, *Three Centuries*, pp. 125–48.

Luria, B. Z., 'The Fate of the Exiles from Samariah' (Hebrew), *Beth Mikra*, lxix (1977), 159–76.

McLachlan, H. J., *Socinianism in Seventeenth-Century England* (Oxford, 1951).

Maclear, J. F., 'New England and the Fifth Monarchy: The Quest for the Millennium in Early American Puritanism', *Wm. and M. Qly.*, 3rd ser., xxxii (1975), 223–60.

Martin, C. T., 'The Domus Conversorum', *Trs. Jew. Hist. Soc. Eng.*, i (1895), 15–24.

Metcalf, G. J., 'Abraham Mylius on Historical Linguistics', *Proc. Mod. Lang. Assoc.*, lxviii (1953), 535–54.

Modder, M. F., *The Jew in the Literature of England* (Philadelphia, 1960=1939).

Morton, A. L., *The English Utopia* (1952).

—— *The World of the Ranters* (1970).

Munsterberg, M., 'Notes on Rare Books: *Apologia por la noble nacion de los Iudios*, London 1649', *Boston Pub. Lib. Qly.*, vi (1954), 235–41.

Nash, G. B., 'The Image of the Indian in the Southern Colonial Mind', *Wm. and M. Qly.*, 3rd ser., xxix (1972), 197–230.

Neubauer, A., 'Where Are the Ten Tribes?', *Jew. Qly. Rev.*, i (1888–9), 14–28, 95–114, 185–201, 408–23.

Nuttall, G. F., *Visible Saints: The Congregational Way 1640–1660* (Oxford, 1957).

Osterman, N., 'The Controversy over the Proposed Readmission of The Jews to England (1655)', *Jew. Soc. Stud.*, iii (1941), 301–28.

Padley, G. A., *Grammatical Theory in Western Europe 1500–1700 The Latin Tradition* (Cambridge, 1976).

Parkes, J., 'Jewish-Christian Relations in England', in Lipman, *Three Centuries*, pp. 149–68.

Partridge, A. C., *English Biblical Translation* (1973).

Patinkin, D., 'Mercantilism and the Readmission of the Jews to England', *Jew. Soc. Stud.*, viii (1946), 161–78.

Payne, E. A., 'More about the Sabbatarian Baptists', *Bap. Qly.*, xiv (1951–2), 161–6.

—— 'Thomas Tillam', *Bap. Qly.*, xvii (1957–8), 61–6.

Pearce, R. H., 'The "Ruines of Mankind": The Indian and the Puritan Mind', *Jnl. Hist. Ideas*, xiii (1952), 200–17.

Penrose, B., *Urbane Travellers 1591–1635* (Philadelphia and London, 1942).

Phelan, J. L., *The Millennial Kingdom of the Franciscans in the New World* (Berkeley and Los Angeles, 1956; 2nd edn., 1970).

Phillips, H. E. I., 'An Early Stuart Judaising Sect', *Trs. Jew. Hist. Soc. Eng.*, xv (1946), 63–72.

Picciotto, J., *Sketches of Anglo-Jewish History* (1875).

Pinto, V. de S., *Peter Sterry* (Cambridge, 1934).

Platts, L. A., 'Seventh-Day Baptists in America Previous to 1802', in *Seventh Day Baptists*, pp. 119–46.

Pollard, A. W., and G. R. Redgrave, *Short Title Catalogue . . . 1475–1640* (1950).

Popkin, R. H., 'Menasseh ben Israel and Isaac La Peyrère', *Stud. Rosenthaliana*, viii (1974), 59–63.

Prest, W. R., 'The Art of Law and the Law of God: Sir Henry Finch (1558–1625)' in *Puritans and Revolutionaries*, ed. D. Pennington and K. Thomas (Oxford, 1978), pp. 94–117.

Rabinowicz, O. K., *Sir Solomon de Medina* (1974).

Ralph, P. L., *Sir Humphrey Mildmay: Royalist Gentleman* (New Brunswick, 1947).

Randolph, C. F., *A History of Seventh Day Baptists in West Virginia* (Plainfield, NJ, 1905).

Richardson, H. G., *The English Jewry under Angevin Kings* (1960).

Robe, S. L., 'Wild Men and Spain's Brave New World', in Dudley and Novak, *Wild Man*, pp. 39–53.

Roberts, M., *Gustavus Adolphus: A History of Sweden 1611–1632* (1953).

Robinson, I., 'Isaac de la Peyrère and the Recall of the Jews', *Jew. Soc. Stud.*, xl (1978), 117–30.

Ronda, J. P., '"We Are Well As We Are": An Indian Critique of Seventeenth-Century Christian Missions', *Wm. and M. Qly.*, 3rd ser., xxxiv (1977), 66–82.

Rosenberg, E., *From Shylock to Svengali: Jewish Stereotypes in English Fiction* (1961).

Rosenthal, E. I. J., 'Edward Lively: Cambridge Hebraist', in *Essays and Studies Presented to S. A. Cook*, ed. D. W. Thomas (1950), pp. 95–112.

—— 'Rashi and the English Bible', *Bull. J. Ryl. Lib.*, xxiv (1940), 138–67.

Ross, J. M., 'Naturalisation of Jews in England', *Trs. Jew. Hist. Soc. Eng.*, xxiv (1974), 59–70.

Rossi, P., *Clavis Universalis: Arti Mnemoniche e Logica Combinatoria da Lullo a Leibniz* (Milano–Napoli, 1960).

Roth, C., 'An Attempt to Recall the Jews to England, 1648', *The Jewish Monthly*, i, no. 12, 11–17.

—— 'Edward Pococke and the First Hebrew Printing in Oxford', *Bodl. Lib. Rec.*, ii (1948), 215–20.

—— *Essays and Portraits in Anglo-Jewish History* (Philadelphia, 1962).

—— 'The Hebrew Press in London; a bibliographical experiment' (Hebrew), *Kiryat Sepher*, xiv (1937), 97–104, 379–88.

—— *A History of the Jews in England* (3rd edn., Oxford, 1964).

—— *A History of the Marranos* (Philadelphia, 1941).

—— 'Jews in Oxford after 1290', *Oxoniensia*, xv (1950), 63–80.

—— *The Jews in the Renaissance* (New York, 1959).

—— 'The Jews of Jerusalem in the Seventeenth Century: An English Account', *Misc. Jew. Hist. Soc. Eng.*, ii (1935), 99–104.

—— 'Leone Da Modena and the Christian Hebraists of his Age', in *Jewish Studies in memory of Israel Abrahams*, ed. G. A. Kohut (New York, 1927), pp. 384–401.

—— 'Leone da Modena and England', *Trs. Jew. Hist. Soc. Eng.*, xi (1928), 206–27.

—— 'Leone da Modena and his English Correspondents', *Trs. Jew. Hist. Soc. Eng.*, xvii (1953), 39–43.

—— 'Léon de Modène, ses *Riti Ebraici* et le Saint-Office à Venise', *Rev. Etud. Jvs.*, lxxxvii (1929), 83–8.

—— *A Life of Menasseh Ben Israel: Rabbi, Printer, and Diplomat* (Philadelphia, 1934).

—— 'A list of books from Manasseh Ben-Israel's stock' (Hebrew), *Aresheth*, ii (1960), 413–14.

—— *Magna Bibliotheca Anglo-Judaica* (2nd edn., 1937).

—— 'The Marrano Typography in England', *Trans. Biblio. Soc. 1960*, 118–28.

—— 'The Middle Period of Anglo-Jewish History (1290–1655) Reconsidered', *Trs. Jew. Hist. Soc. Eng.*, xix (1960), 1–12.

—— 'New Light on the Resettlement', *Trs. Jew. Hist. Soc. Eng.*, xi (1928), 112–42.

—— 'The Origins of Hebrew Typography in England', *Jnl. Jew. Biblio.*, i (1938), 1–8.

—— 'The Resettlement of the Jews in England in 1656', in Lipman, *Three Centuries*, pp. 1–25.

—— *The Rise of Provincial Jewry* (1950).

—— 'Sir Thomas Bodley—Hebraist', *Bodl. Lib. Rec.*, vii (1966), 242–51.

—— '1656: English Jewry's annus mirabilis: was there a formal readmission?' *Commentary*, xxi (1956), 509–15.

—— 'Spanish Printing at Izmir' (Hebrew), *Kiryat Sepher*, xxviii (1952–3), 390–3.

—— *Studies in Books and Booklore* (Westmead, Farnborough, Hants, 1972).

Rubens, A., *Anglo-Jewish Portraits* (1935).

—— *A Jewish Iconography* (1954).

Rupp, G., 'Andrew Karlstadt and Reformation Puritanism', *Jnl. Theo. Stud.*, n.s., x (1959), 308–26.

Rusche, H., 'Merlini Anglici: Astrology and Propaganda from 1644 to 1651', *Eng. Hist. Rev.*, lxxx (1965), 322–33.

—— 'Prophecies and propaganda, 1641 to 1651', *Eng. Hist. Rev.*, lxxxiv (1969), 752–70.

Russell, C., 'Arguments for Religious Unity in England, 1530–1650', *Jnl. Ecc. Hist.*, xviii (1967), 201–26.

Salisbury, N., 'Red Puritans: The "Praying Indians" of Massachusetts Bay and John Eliot', *Wm. and M. Qly.*, 3rd ser., xxxi (1974), 27–54.

Salmon, V., 'Language-Planning in Seventeenth-Century England; Its Context and Aims', *In Memory of J. R. Firth*, pp. 370–97.

Saltman, A., 'Prynne, the Sabbath and the Jews', *The Jewish Academy*, n.s., iv (1947), 35–9.

Samuel, E. R., 'The First Fifty Years', in Lipman, *Three Centuries*, pp. 27–44.

—— 'Portuguese Jews in Jacobean London', *Trs. Jew. Hist. Soc. Eng.*, xviii (1958), 171–230.

—— '"Sir Thomas Shirley's Project for Jewes"–The Earliest Known Proposal for the Resettlement', *Trs. Jew. Hist. Soc. Eng.*, xxiv (1974), 195–7.

Samuel, W. S., 'Carvajal and Pepys', *Misc. Jew. Hist. Soc. Eng.*, ii (1935), 24–9.

—— 'The First London Synagogue of the Resettlement', *Trs. Jew. Hist. Soc. Eng.*, x (1924), 1–147.

—— 'A Jewish Naval Officer under the Stuarts?', *Misc. Jew. Hist. Soc. Eng.*, iii (1937), 105–7.

—— 'The Jewish Oratories of Cromwellian London', *Misc. Jew. Hist. Soc. Eng.*, iii (1937), 46–56.

—— *et al.*, 'A List of Jewish Persons Endenizened and Naturalised 1609–1799', *Misc. Jew. Hist. Soc. Eng.*, vii (1970), 111–44.

—— 'Sir William Davidson, Royalist (1616–1689) and the Jews', *Trs. Jew. Hist. Soc. Eng.*, xiv (1940), 39–79.

—— 'The Strayings of Paul Isaiah in England, 1651–1656', *Trs. Jew. Hist. Soc. Eng.*, xvi (1952), 77–87.

Saraiva, A. J., 'Antonio Vieira, Menasseh ben Israel et Le Cinquième Empire', *Stud. Rosenthaliana*, vi (1972), 25–57.

Schischa, A., 'Spanish Jews in London in 1494', *Trs. Jew. Hist. Soc. Eng.*, xxiv (1975), 214–15.

Schoeps, H. J., *Barocke Juden Christen Judenchristen* (Bern and München, 1965).

—— 'Philosemitism in the Baroque Period', *Jew. Qly. Rev.*, n.s., xlvii (1956–7), 139–44.

—— *Philosemitismus im Barock* (Tübingen, 1952).

Scholem, G., *Kabbalah* (Jerusalem, 1974).

—— 'The Kabbalist R. Abraham ben Eliezer ha-Levi' (Hebrew), *Kiryat Sepher*, ii (1925), 101–41, 269–73; vii (1931), 149–65, 440–56.

—— *Major Trends in Jewish Mysticism* (Jerusalem, 1941) 3rd edn., 1955.

—— *The Messianic Idea in Judaism* (1971).

—— *On The Kabbalah and Its Symbolism* (1965).

—— *Sabbatai Ṣevi The Mystical Messiah 1626–1676* (1973).

Secret, F., *Les Kabbalistes Chrétiens de la Renaissance* (Paris, 1964).

—— *Le Zôhar chez les Kabbalistes Chrétiens de la Renaissance* (Paris and The Hague, 2nd edn., 1964).

Seventh Day Baptists in Europe and America (Plainfield, NJ, 1910).

Shaftesley, J. M., ed., *Remember the Days: Essays on Anglo-Jewish History presented to Cecil Roth* (1966).

Shane, A. L., 'Rabbi Jacob Judah Leon (Templo) of Amsterdam (1603–1675) and his connections with England', *Trs. Jew. Hist. Soc. Eng.*, xxv (1977), 120–36.

Shapiro, B. J., *John Wilkins 1614–1672* (Berkeley and Los Angeles, 1969).

Simon, B. A., *The Hope of Israel* (1829).

—— *The Ten Tribes of Israel* (1836).

Sisson, C. J., 'A Colony of Jews in Shakespeare's London', *Essays and Stud. by Mem. Eng. Assoc.*, xxiii (1938), 38–51.

Sokolow, N., *History of Zionism 1600–1918* (1919).

Sparrow, J., '*The Hope of Israel, A Breif Epistle*, and *Silex Scintillans*', *Trs. Jew. Hist. Soc. Eng.*, xx (1964), 232–8.

Steele, C., *English Interpreters of the Iberian New World from Purchas to Stevens* (Oxford, 1975).

Stein, S., 'Phillipus Ferdinandus Polonus: A Sixteenth-Century Hebraist in England', *Essays In honour of . . . J. H. Hertz*, ed. I. Epstein, *et al.* (1944), pp. 397–412.

Steiner, G., *After Babel* (1975).

Stern, A., 'Menasseh Ben Israel et Cromwell', *Rev. Etud. Jvs.*, v (1882), 96–111.

Stokes, H. P., *A Short History of the Jews in England* (1921).

Stoughton, J., *Ecclesiastical History of England* (1867–74).

Strype, J., *Annals of the Reformation* (Oxford, 1824).

—— *Works* (Oxford, 1821–8).

Tait, J., 'The Declaration of Sports for Lancashire (1617)', *Eng. Hist. Rev.*, xxxii (1917), 561–8.

Thirsk, J. and J. P. Cooper, eds., *Seventeenth-Century Economic Documents* (Oxford, 1972).

Thirtle, J. W., 'Dr. Peter Chamberlen. Pastor, Propagandist, and Patentee', *Trs. Bap. Hist. Soc.*, iii (1912–3), 176–89.

—— 'A Sabbatarian Pioneer—Dr. Peter Chamberlen', *Trs. Bap. Hist. Soc.*, ii (1910–1), 9–30, 110–17.

Thomas, K., *Religion and the Decline of Magic* (Penguin edn., Harmondsworth, 1973).

Thomason, George, *Catalogue of the Pamphlets . . . collected by*, ed. G. K. Fortescue (1908).

Tolmie, M., *The Triumph of the Saints: The Separate Churches of London 1616–1649* (Cambridge, 1977).

Toon, P., ed., *Puritans, the Milennium and the Future of Israel* (Cambridge & London, 1970), esp. his essay on Jewish immigration, pp. 115–25.

Torbet, R. G., *A History of the Baptists* (2nd edn., 1966).

Tourneur, V., *Esquisse d'une histoire des études celtiques* (Liège, 1905).

Tovey, D'Blossiers, *Anglia Judaica: or the History and Antiquities of the Jews in England* (Oxford, 1738).

Trachtenberg, J., *The Devil and the Jews* (Philadelphia, 1961), 1st pub. 1943.

Trask, W. B., *Capt. William Traske and Some of his Descendants* (Boston, 1904).

—— *The Traske Family in England* (Boston, 1900).

Trevor-Roper, H. R., *The European Witch-Craze of the 16th and 17th Centuries* (Pelican edn., Harmondsworth, 1969).

—— *Historical Essays* (New York, 1966). Two essays on the Jews.

—— *Religion the Reformation and Social Change* (1967). Esp. 'Three Foreigners: The Philosophers of the Puritan Revolution', pp. 237–93.

Turnbull, G. H., *Hartlib, Dury and Comenius* (1947).

Tuveson, E. L., *Millennium and Utopia* (2nd edn., New York, 1964).

Underdown, D., *Pride's Purge* (Oxford, 1971).

Underhill, E. B., ed., *Tracts on Liberty of Conscience* (1846).

Underwood, A. C., *A History of the English Baptists* (1947).

Van Den Berg, J., 'Eschatological Expectations Concerning the Conversion of the Jews in the Netherlands during the Seventeenth Century', in Toon, *Puritans*, pp. 137–53.

Vega, L. A., *The Beth Haim of Ouderkerk aan de Amstel* (Assen/Amsterdam, 1975).

Vereté, M., 'The Restoration of the Jews in English Protestant Thought, 1790–1840', *Mid. Eastern Stud.*, viii (1972), 3–50. An earlier version was published in Hebrew in *Zion*, xxxiii (1968), 145–79.

Walker, D. P., *The Ancient Theology* (1972).

—— 'Leibniz and Language'. *Jnl. Warb. Ctld. Inst.*, xxxv (1972), 294–307.

Webster, C., *The Great Instauration* (1975).

——, ed., *Samuel Hartlib and The Advancement of Learning* (Cambridge, 1970).

Welsby, P. A., *Lancelot Andrewes 1555–1626* (1958).

Werblowsky, R. J. Z., 'Milton and the *Conjectura Cabbalistica*', *Jnl. Warb. Ctld. Inst.*, xviii (1955), 90–113.

White, B. R., 'Samuel Eaton (d. 1639) Particular Baptist Pioneer', *Bap. Qly*, n.s., xxiv (1971–2), 10–21.

—— 'Henry Jessey A Pastor in Politics', *Bap. Qly.*, n.s., xxv (1973–4), 98–110.

—— 'Henry Jessey in the Great Rebellion', in *Reformation Conformity and Dissent*, ed. R. B. Knox (1977), pp. 132–53.

—— 'John Pendarves, the Calvinistic Baptists and the Fifth Monarchy', *Bap. Qly.*, n.s., xxv (1973–4), 251–71.

—— 'John Traske (1585–1636) and London Puritanism', *Trs. Cong. Hist. Soc.*, xx (1968), 223–33.

Whiting, C. E., *Studies in English Puritanism From The Restoration to the Revolution, 1660–1688* (1931).

Whitley, W. T., *The Baptists of London 1612–1928* (n.d. = 1928).

—— 'Leonard Busher, Dutchman', *Trs. Bap. Hist. Soc.*, i (1908–9), 107–13.

—— *A History of British Baptists* (1923).

—— 'The Jacob-Jessey Church, 1616–1678', *Trs. Bap. Hist. Soc.*, i (1908–9), 246–56.

—— 'Militant Baptists 1660–1672', *Trs. Bap. Hist. Soc.*, i (1908–9), 148–55.

—— 'Records of the Jacob-Lathrop-Jessey Church 1616–1641', *Trs. Bap. Hist. Soc.*, i (1908–9), 203–25.

—— 'Rise of the Particular Baptists in London, 1633–1644', *Trs. Bap. Hist. Soc.*, i (1908–9), 226–36.

—— 'Seventh Day Baptists in England', *Bap. Qly.*, xii (1946–8), 252–8.

Wilensky, M., 'Thomas Barlow's and John Dury's Attitude Towards the Readmission of The Jews to England', *Jew. Qly. Rev.*, 1 (1959–60), 167–75, 256–68. Basically trans. of his *Return*, pp. 124–31, 164–74.

—— 'The Literary Controversy in 1656 Concerning the Return of the Jews to England', *Proc. Am. Acad. Jew. Res.*, xx (1951), 357–93. Basically trans. of his *Return*, pp. 132–64.

—— *Polemics Concerning the Return of the Jews to England* (Hebrew) (Jerusalem, 1941 & 1943).

—— 'The Royalist Position Concerning The Readmission of Jews to England', *Jew. Qly. Rev.*, xli (1950–1), 397–409. Basically trans. of his *Return*, *cap.* ix.

Williams, A., *The Common Expositor: An Account of the Commentaries on Genesis 1527–1633* (Chapel Hill, NC, 1948).

Willson, D. H., *King James VI and I* (1956).

Wilson, J. F., *Pulpit in Parliament* (Princeton, 1969).

Wing, D., *Short-Title Catalogue . . . 1641–1700* (New York, 1951).

Wittkower, R., 'Marvels of the East: A Study in the History of Monsters', *Jnl. Warb. Ctld. Inst.*, v (1942), 159–97.

Wolf, L., 'American Elements in the Re-Settlement', *Trs. Jew. Hist. Soc. Eng.*, iii (1899), 76–100.

—— 'Maria Fernandez de Carvajal', *Misc. Jew. Hist. Soc. Eng.*, i (1925), xviii–xx.

—— 'Cromwell's Jewish Intelligencers', in his *Essays*, pp. 93–114.

—— 'Crypto-Jews Under the Commonwealth', *Trs. Jew. Hist. Soc. Eng.*, i (1895), 55–88.

—— *Essays in Jewish History*, ed. C. Roth (1934).

—— 'The First English Jew', *Trs. Jew. Hist. Soc. Eng.*, ii (1896), 14–46. Concerning Carvajal.

—— 'The First Stage of Anglo-Jewish Emancipation', in his *Essays*, pp. 115–43.

—— 'The Jewry of the Restoration. 1660–1664', *Trs. Jew. Hist. Soc. Eng.*, v (1908), 5–33.

—— 'Jews in Elizabethan England', *Trs. Jew. Hist. Soc. Eng.*, xi (1928), 1–91.

—— 'Jews in Tudor England', in his *Essays*, pp. 73–90.

—— '"Josippon" in England', *Trs. Jew. Hist. Soc. Eng.*, vi (1912), 277–88.

—— , ed., *Menasseh Ben Israel's Mission to Oliver Cromwell* (1901).

—— 'Menasseh ben Israel's Study in London', *Trs. Jew. Hist. Soc. Eng.*, iii (1899), 144–50.

—— 'Status of the Jews in England After the Re-Settlement', *Trs. Jew. Hist. Soc. Eng.*, iv (1903), 177–93.

Wolfe, D. M., 'Limits of Miltonic Toleration', *Jnl. Eng. Germ. Philol.*, lx (1961), 834–46.

Woolf, M., 'Foreign Trade of London Jews in the Seventeenth Century', *Trs. Jew. Hist. Soc. Eng.*, xxiv (1974), 38–58.

Woolrych, A., 'The Calling of Barebone's Parliament', *Eng. Hist. Rev.*, lxxx (1965), 492–513.

Yaari, A., *Studies in Hebrew Booklore* (Hebrew) (Jerusalem, 1958).

Yates, F. A., *The Art of Memory* (1966).

—— *Giordano Bruno and the Hermetic Tradition* (1964).

—— *The Rosicrucian Enlightenment* (1972).

—— 'Science, Salvation, and the Cabala', *N.Y. Rev. Books*, 27 May 1976, 27–9.

INDEX